Contents

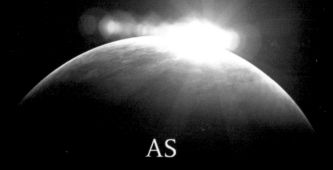

AS

AS

Introduction:
What is philosophy of religion?

Philosophy of religion is different from religion itself, and from theology. Religion involves holding a range of beliefs about ultimate questions, and putting these beliefs into practice, often as part of a community of people who share the same beliefs. Religion is notoriously difficult to define; many attempts to distil in words the essence of religion end up including belief systems that are not normally considered to be religions, or else they exclude belief systems that are usually defined as religious. To talk of religion in terms of belief in God, for example, rules out much of Buddhism; and to define religion as including belief in life after death puts Judaism into a 'grey area'. However, very broad definitions about 'communities with shared goals' or 'focus on matters of ultimate importance' can pin the label 'religion' onto membership of Greenpeace or fanatical football supporting.

Does committed membership of a pressure group count as 'religion'?

In spite of the difficulty of finding an adequate definition for it, religion is nevertheless clearly an important aspect of many people's lives and has a profound impact on culture and world politics.

To think about

How would you define 'religion'?

Theology involves clarifying religious beliefs and expanding on them, seeing how they relate to each other and spelling out their implications for believers in the context of religious life. Within Christianity, theological debate might include questions of whether those who live on after death in a spiritual form can see what is going on in the physical world they have left behind; questions of how Jesus could be both God and human at the same time; questions of the true meaning of scriptural terms, and discussions of how they might be applied in a culture different from the one in which they were written. Sometimes, theological study involves or overlaps with the philosophy of religion, but often the two are distinct.

Philosophy of religion concerns itself with exploring religious beliefs and concepts to see whether they can stand up to rational argument. Different beliefs about religious ideas (including beliefs in atheist ideas as well as theistic belief) are examined, using logic and reasoned criticism, in an attempt to deepen understanding, to separate the true from the false where possible, and to clarify the implications of committing to particular choices of faith. The philosophy of religion involves raising many different questions, for example:

• Does the concept of 'God' make rational sense?
• Are the various attributes traditionally ascribed to God compatible with each other?
• Are there good reasons to believe that God exists?
• Are there good reasons for believing that there is no God?
• Is it reasonable to have a religious faith?
• Is it possible to talk of God in a meaningful way?
• Is religious belief compatible with other kinds of belief, such as belief in the claims of science?
• Does it make sense to suggest that God acts in the world through miracles?
• Does it make sense to talk of life after death?

Some religious believers object to the idea of subjecting their beliefs to philosophical scrutiny. They argue that the truths of religion are given by God and can therefore be trusted completely with faith; questioning them suggests that we know better than God and might be able to prove God wrong. They suggest that if we have difficulty understanding religious truths, then the fault lies with our own intellectual limitations. Others, however, argue that it is impossible to have faith in something without understanding it, and that beliefs which do not stand up to philosophical investigation are not worth holding.

To think about

Does it matter if what we believe is actually true? Does it do any harm to hold a false belief, if it provides us with comfort and helps us to enjoy life?

Before the Middle Ages, Jewish and Christian scholars tended to concern themselves with theology, rather than with philosophy of religion. The early church addressed issues of Christology (the nature of Jesus as both human and divine), the meaning of sin and salvation, leadership of the church and the status of scripture. There was always some interest in the philosophy of religion, but theology held people's interest more. Many Christian beliefs had been shaped by Greek ideas and were expressed using Greek conceptual terms, because the first Christians lived in a Greek-influenced culture; but even though these Greek ideas had influenced the formation of beliefs, the actual philosophy of such thinkers as Socrates, Plato and Aristotle was largely ignored.

However, in the Middle Ages, the Crusades brought Christians into contact with the Muslim world. Christians began to discover the work of Arab academics who had preserved the writings of the ancient Greek philosophers, and suddenly Greek philosophy seemed exciting and new.

It was perhaps inevitable that some people began to look at their own Christian beliefs with more philosophical eyes, asking themselves whether the claims made by the church and in the Bible were really as rational as they had always been told, and whether they could stand up to scrutiny and criticism. Perhaps religious belief was unnecessary; perhaps the world could be understood in other ways, without reference to God. Leading Christian thinkers felt the need to explain their faith and to support and defend it with philosophical reasoning in the face of such challenges. It began to become clear, too, that Greek influences on Christian belief had sometimes given rise to confusion, where Greek responses to ultimate questions were at odds with the teachings of the Bible.

Ancient Greek influences on Christian philosophy of religion

How did Greek ideas become entwined with biblical beliefs?

Much of the philosophy of religion as we know it today has come from Western traditions, and because of the culture in which it grew, it has usually concentrated on the beliefs of Christianity. Ideas from Greek philosophy greatly influenced the writers of the New Testament, because the writers were raised in the context of Greek culture even though they came from Palestine (modern Israel).

For a long time before the birth of Jesus, Palestine had been a Jewish nation, worshipping only one God and following (or disobeying) the commandments given to the people by Moses at the time of the Exodus. However, Palestine was (and Israel still is) located at a key point for trade routes, forming a land bridge between continents, and throughout its history it has very rarely been at peace. Whenever a nation in the Near East rose to power, its rulers wanted Palestine.

Alexander the Great of Greece (356–323 BCE) was no exception. Alexander was one of the most successful military leaders in the whole of history, and although he probably never visited Jerusalem, the leaders of the city were quick to pay tribute to him when he established his empire. Alexander had been tutored by the great Greek philosopher Aristotle, and raised in Greek culture, so when his armies moved into Palestine, Greek culture became predominant. The Jews were allowed to continue practising their own religion and customs as long as they caused no trouble, and many of them still preferred to speak in their own language, though Greek became the language of the educated classes. Coins bore bilingual mottos in both Hebrew and Greek; Greek manners, Greek traditions and Greek ways of thinking spread through the whole of society. Although some Jews held fast to their ancient laws without making many concessions to a different way of life, there were others who managed to combine Greek culture with biblical religion, and of course others who abandoned the Jewish faith altogether in favour of the Greek gods.

Alexander the Great brought Greek culture to the lands of the Bible, and Greek ideas became interwoven with biblical beliefs.

The earliest Christians, therefore, were people whose whole way of understanding the world had been shaped by Greek thinking. It was natural that when they embraced the Christian faith and began to establish the first churches, they tried to clarify their understanding of belief in the philosophical terms they had learned from the Greeks. They adopted concepts from Plato and Aristotle when they expressed and explained ideas about the nature of God, the soul, life after death and morality; but sometimes, these concepts did not quite fit with the ideas and imagery of the Old Testament, raising questions for philosophers of religion: Can God change his mind, responding to prayers and to events, or does he always remain exactly the same? Does God know the future in a timeless way, or does he have to wait and see what people will do before he decides how to act? Is there life after death, and if so, in what form might we continue to live once the body has died? Is God perfectly loving, and if so, why do we suffer?

Socrates

Socrates (470–399 BCE) is often considered to be the founder of the kind of philosophy that we have today, because his teaching was the first to encourage a critical questioning of commonly-held assumptions. Before Socrates, there were many interesting ideas circulating that offered different ways of understanding the world, but there seemed to be no way of knowing which, if any, was right. What was needed, Socrates felt, was a critical method of uncovering the truth. People needed to be trained to look beneath superficial appearances and learn how to ask questions, how to recognise the difference between knowledge and opinion, and how to form judgements.

If Socrates made written records of his ideas, as far as we know none of them has survived. However, Plato, who was a pupil of Socrates, admired his teacher enormously and included Socrates' views in his own writings, so through reading Plato we can gain some idea of the kind of person Socrates was and the ways he practised his philosophy. Xenophon and Aristophanes also referred to Socrates in their writings, which helps us to piece together a picture of the way Socrates thought.

One of the key features of Socrates' teaching was his habit of using questions to help find the answer to a problem. He would take a concept such as 'justice' and try to work out what we actually mean by it, rather than assuming that everyone has a common understanding of what justice is about. Having questioned and clarified it, he would then be more able to consider problems such as how a country should be run. Socrates did not assume that he knew all the answers, but thought it was important that people should recognise the limitations of their own knowledge and be prepared to accept that there might not be any final, definitive solutions. He used questions not only to clarify, but also to challenge, and sometimes as a way of exposing ignorance. His questioning sometimes forced people to admit that they did not really know what they were talking about or that their views did not make sense.

To think about

Today, the practice of asking questions in order to clarify ideas is still used, and is called 'the Socratic method'. For example, in counselling, if someone has a problem the counsellor is often trained not to tell them what to do, but to encourage them to come to their own conclusions by asking questions such as 'What do you think triggered these feelings?' 'Have you considered talking to her about it?' 'What do you think will happen if you do that?' Why do counsellors adopt this approach, rather than simply telling the person how to deal with the problem? Do you think it would be better if they just said 'Do this'?

Socrates began a great many debates, and made people realise that there might be more than one way of understanding an issue and that their view might not be as right as they thought. But since Socrates exposed the ignorance of people in authority, he was seen as subversive. He made himself unpopular, although he had an enthusiastic following among the young people of the city of Athens. Plato referred to him as a 'gadfly' – an insect that irritates horses and can cause them to bolt. The insect's size is minute in comparison with the horse, just as Socrates was small in comparison with the whole population of Athens, but his ability to irritate was great.

Eventually, Socrates was arrested. He was charged with not believing in the Greek gods and with corrupting the young. These were serious offences, which potentially carried the death penalty. Socrates' friends and pupils were horrified when he was found guilty. According to Xenophon and Plato, Socrates was offered a way out, but he was determined to stay true to his principles and to accept the sentence of death rather than back down; he made it clear that in his view, it was better to die with integrity than to be false, even if it meant sacrificing his life. Socrates drank the poisonous hemlock he was given by his executioners, and died.

To think about

Is it better to die than to sacrifice your principles? Or is survival more important?

Plato was present throughout the trial and execution of his beloved teacher. He was appalled at Socrates' death, and was determined to preserve the thoughts and methods of his teacher in his own writings. Plato liked to write his philosophy in the form of dialogues, where concepts are discussed between different characters. He often gave the name 'Socrates' to the character with the clearest insight, who showed up his opponents' arrogance and ignorance.

It can be difficult to distinguish Socrates' thoughts from Plato's original thinking. Plato clearly admired Socrates immensely, and he was likely to have attributed an idea to Socrates even if he had thought of it himself. Many scholars believe that Plato's earlier writings reflect the words of Socrates, where Plato recorded genuine conversations that he remembered, but they think that as Plato got older, he found much more to say on all sorts of subjects, including some that he might never have discussed with Socrates. Sometimes, Plato may have put words into Socrates' mouth that were actually his own ideas.

Socrates' method of asking questions and holding concepts up to rational scrutiny is a method still used by philosophers today.

Plato

Plato is regarded by many as the greatest philosopher who ever lived, and it has been said that all other philosophy is simply 'footnotes to Plato'. Of course, Plato did not cover every topic of philosophical investigation, nor did he give definitive answers to all questions about the meaning of life, but the issues that he raised still divide thinkers today. His writing is clear, interesting and accessible; many people think that Plato's work is the finest of all surviving Greek literature.

Plato came from an aristocratic Athenian family whose members were closely involved in politics and who had some quite decided views. Plato was still a relatively young man, probably in his early thirties, when Socrates died, and the death had a profound effect on him. Perhaps Plato thought that Socrates would not really go through with the execution and would admit that he had been wrong in order to avoid punishment, or perhaps Plato thought that the city leaders would back down, recognise Socrates' wisdom and let him go. But to Plato's shock, nothing happened to save Socrates.

Key term

forms – a name Plato gave to ideal concepts.

After Socrates' death, Plato began to write as a way of keeping Socrates' memory alive and defending him against those who spread rumours to discredit his memory. Plato also left Athens for a while on a series of not altogether successful visits to other countries. When he returned to Greece, he used the money he had acquired to found a school called the Academy, where he taught both male and female students until he died at the age of 81.

Plato's writings have had a lasting and profound influence on Christian thought.

Plato and the Theory of Forms

One of Plato's best-known ideas is his Theory of Forms. Plato noticed (along with other philosophers both before and since) that the physical world is always changing, and nothing ever stays the same. Even apparently static, solid objects are changing in ways that might not be immediately visible to our senses. They are growing or decaying, becoming scratched or stained, fading in the sunlight or darkening with age, getting warmer or cooling down… For Plato, this presented a problem. How could people attain true and certain knowledge, if the objects they wanted to know about were never the same from one moment to the next? As soon as people thought they had understood something, it was different again. Could we never get beyond guesswork and opinion?

To think about

The philosopher Heraclitus, who lived before Plato, was known for his wise sayings. He claimed that 'you can never step into the same river twice'. What do you think he meant? Was he right?

Plato came to the conclusion that the things we see around us in the physical world are always in a state of change, and therefore they can never be the objects of completely true knowledge. However, he argued that there are other realities of which we can have certain knowledge, in a different 'world', which are eternal and always stay the same. These realities are concepts, which Plato called 'Forms' or 'Ideas'. We gain true knowledge, according to Plato, through our reason.

In Plato's view, the different things that we see in the physical world around us, and that we learn about through experience using our five senses, are imitations and examples of their ideal Form. When we see someone doing an act of justice, we recognise it as justice because we know what 'true justice' really is, as a concept. We realise that the human example of justice that we are witnessing is not perfect justice, because in this changing world nothing ever is perfect; but for Plato, the very fact that we realise it is not perfect demonstrates that we have an inner understanding of what 'ideal justice' or 'the Form of Justice' might be.

To think about

What might 'perfect generosity' involve?

In the same way, we might see examples of circles in mathematics and in the physical world around us. We see things that are circular, such as plates and clocks and wheels, and recognise their circularity. We might be required to draw circles in maths lessons. However, any circle we see in the physical world is never going to be a perfect circle. There will always be some little irregularity that makes it very nearly a circle, but not quite. Our mental concept of the 'Form of a Circle' will be a perfect circle, but whenever it is translated into the physical world, it loses some of that perfection – because, mathematically, the infinite series of points that make up the circumference of a circle do not take up any physical space, but as soon as we draw a circle, the line enclosing the circle is spatial.

Plato believed that the physical world in which we live is full of these imperfect imitations. We recognise all sorts of things for what they are, only because of our knowledge of their Forms. So, for example, if we see a tree, we know what it is even when we have not seen that particular tree before, because we understand the concept 'tree'. We recognise it as an example of something that reflects the 'Form of Tree'. Here we see something which imitates it – although always less than perfectly.

Plato was not simply showing how we apply language to objects. In his view, the physical tree that is available to the senses is inferior to the concept or Form of Tree, because the physical tree is undergoing a process of change. The leaves might be coming into bud, or turning yellow for the autumn, or dropping; the tree might be a little taller than it was last year. Eventually, the tree will die and rot away. However, the Form of Tree is eternal. The idea or Form of the tree, unlike the physical tree, never changes. It does not depend on physical circumstances for its existence. For this reason, the Form of Tree can be the object of true knowledge even though the physical tree cannot.

The trees we see in everyday life are in a constant process of change. However, our mental concept of 'tree' always stays the same, in Plato's view.

Plato believed that the unchanging nature of the Forms made them in many ways 'more real' than the ordinary physical objects we can perceive with our senses. Physical, material things are given their reality by the Forms, according to Plato; they 'participate in' the Forms. Plato also thought that we have an understanding of the Forms from birth, even if we do not realise it. We just know, by intuition, what the Form of Beauty is or the Form of Symmetry (or even the Form of Frog), and we make judgements about different qualities of things in the physical world by comparing them with our concepts. Plato decided that, as we seem to have this intuition about the Forms, it must be because at some point, before we were born, we experienced them. This led him to the conclusion that people must have immortal souls and must have lived in the realm of Forms before being born into the material world as human beings.

The Forms, then, are perfect exemplars of different aspects of the world. Material, physical 'stuff' is by nature changing and chaotic, but the Forms exist changelessly. They do not exist within time or space, because they are concepts rather than 'things'.

Sometimes, Plato writes as though there are Forms only of qualities, such as Beauty or Mercy. However, at other times he seemed to think that there is a Form for each different thing in the world: a Form of Spade, a Form of Earwig, a Form of Rose and so on. Taken to extremes, this can make Plato's theory seem rather ridiculous – are we really supposed to believe that there is an Ideal Form of Computer Mouse or an Ideal

Form of Pyjamas? However, this might be seen as missing the point of what Plato was trying to say. For Plato, by far the most important Forms were those of noble qualities, and in particular, the Form of the Good.

The Form of the Good

According to Plato, the different Forms were related to each other, and were arranged in a hierarchy. The most important of all of the Forms was the Form of the Good, which illuminates all of the other Forms and gives them their value. For example, Justice, Wisdom, Courage and even Beauty are all aspects of goodness. As with the other Forms, goodness is something we have never seen perfectly exemplified in this physical world, but nevertheless we have all seen actions and role models that we recognise to be 'good'. We recognise their goodness because we understand how they correspond to our intuitive knowledge of the Form of the Good, and we can identify what it is about the actions or the people that is good – we can also recognise the respects in which they fall short of perfection.

True knowledge, for Plato, is a knowledge of goodness. A 'philosopher' is someone who loves *(philos)* wisdom *(sophia)*, and who recognises the nature of true goodness. A lover of wisdom is not going to be someone who simply knows the truth. Love involves action, not passivity. The genuine lover of wisdom, the real 'philosopher', will want to put that wisdom into practice by teaching others and by setting an example, and this, for Plato, was the reason why countries should be ruled by philosopher kings.

Part of Plato's argument was that if someone knows what is good and what is bad, he or she will choose the good. It is only ignorance which causes immorality. People steal or tell lies because they are ignorant of the Form of Honesty. If they became more philosophical and looked for the Form of the Good, they would make better moral decisions.

Plato's Demiurge

Plato believed that the world was created by a god he called the Demiurge. The Demiurge made the world by fashioning it out of material that was already there, but which was a shapeless mess before the Demiurge got to work. The name 'Demiurge' itself comes from the Greek word for a craftsman or workman.

Plato called the creator of the universe 'Demiurge', which means craftsman. The Demiurge fashioned the universe out of material that already existed.

In Plato's work *Timaeus,* he describes how the Demiurge is good and desires the best for humanity. The Demiurge tries to make the universe as well as he can, but he is limited by his materials, and so the final result is as good as he can manage; it was never going to be perfect anyway, because it is physical and therefore changeable. When Plato applies the word 'good' to the Demiurge, he means that the Demiurge can be judged in comparison with the Form of the Good. The Demiurge is not in any sense 'Goodness-Itself' or 'the source of all goodness', but is a being which can be measured against the external standards of the Forms.

The Analogy of the Cave

One of Plato's best-known works is *Republic,* which he wrote when he was about 40. It is undoubtedly one of the finest pieces of philosophical literature ever written. Plato was living in Athens at a time when it was a centre of culture, learning and activity, yet it was also a time when the city was in decline. He was deeply concerned about his fellow citizens and felt that it was his mission to present to people a better, more ethical and more considered way of living.

In *Republic,* Plato illustrates aspects of his philosophy by giving an analogy that has become famous. He asks us to imagine a strange scenario of people being held prisoner in a cave, and then plays out a series of events to clarify and emphasise his points.

When he gives the cave analogy, Plato wants us to understand:
- The relation between the physical, material world and the higher world of the Forms.
- The ways in which material, physical concerns can blind people to what is really important.
- The ignorance of humanity when people do not engage in philosophy.

- The potential for true knowledge that philosophy brings.
- That there is another world which we cannot see from the position that we are in, yet which we can reach and which will give us enlightenment.
- The initial difficulties of grappling with philosophy.
- The hostility that people often feel when faced with philosophical ideas that challenge their previously-held beliefs.
- The injustice of the death of Socrates.
- That education is a 'leading-out'. It is not stuffing people's minds with information, but a drawing-out of things they already know and an encouragement for them to become new kinds of people.

Plato asks us to imagine prisoners in a cave who live in a world of shadows and echoes.

In this passage from Book VII of Plato's *Republic* (translated by Benjamin Jowett), Plato presents us with a dialogue between Socrates and a man named Glaucon. Socrates asks Glaucon to imagine a scene in an underground cave. In the cave there are prisoners, who have been there since childhood; Plato wants us to understand that they have no memory of ever having lived in any other way. The prisoners are chained in such a way that they can only face in one direction, and are unable to move their heads. They all sit facing the back wall of the cave. The only light available to them comes from a fire, which is behind them so that they cannot see it. All they can see is the light that the fire produces, reflected off the cave wall. Between the fire and the prisoners, still behind them, is a low wall. Plato asks us to think of it as being rather like the lower edge of a puppet theatre.

And now, I said, let me show in a figure how far our nature is enlightened or unenlightened: – Behold! human beings living in a underground den, which has a mouth open towards the light and reaching all along the den; here they have been from their childhood, and have their legs and necks chained so that they cannot move, and can only see before them, being prevented by the chains from turning round their heads. Above and behind them a fire is blazing at a distance, and between the fire and the prisoners there is a raised way; and you will see, if you look, a low wall built along the way, like the screen which marionette players have in front of them, over which they show the puppets.

I see.

People move along the low wall, carrying a variety of different objects, and as they pass the fire, shadows of the objects are thrown onto the cave wall where the prisoners can see them.

And do you see, I said, men passing along the wall carrying all sorts of vessels, and statues and figures of animals made of wood and stone and various materials, which appear over the wall? Some of them are talking, others silent.

You have shown me a strange image, and they are strange prisoners.

Like ourselves, I replied; and they see only their own shadows, or the shadows of one another, which the fire throws on the opposite wall of the cave?

True, he said; how could they see anything but the shadows if they were never allowed to move their heads?

And of the objects which are being carried in like manner they would only see the shadows?

Yes, he said.

All the prisoners are able to see, then, is shadows of these different objects, and shadows of each other. They cannot see what they or the objects are made of, and they have no reason to suppose that some objects are made of one thing and others are made of another. There is no way that they can begin to question the 'essence' of different aspects of their world, because as far as they are concerned, they already know the answers. They see only a two-dimensional shadow and not solid objects.

And if they were able to converse with one another, would they not suppose that they were naming what was actually before them?

Very true.

And suppose further that the prison had an echo which came from the other side, would they not be sure to fancy when one of the passers-by spoke that the voice which they heard came from the passing shadow?

No question, he replied.

To them, I said, the truth would be literally nothing but the shadows of the images.

That is certain.

Likewise, the only sounds the prisoners are able to hear are voices and echoes. Because of their situation, they are unable to distinguish real voices from the echoes of voices, so they are unable to distinguish between reality and appearance and do not even know that there is any difference. When they name the shadows they see in front of them, they think they are naming real objects.

Plato has set up a scene where people are as far removed from reality as possible. Nothing they perceive with their senses gives them true information. They see and hear only shadowy, flickering images of the way things really are, and they are completely unaware of their own ignorance. As far as they realise, this is the truth. We, Plato's readers and listeners, of course are in the privileged position of knowing exactly what the prisoners are missing. We know that there is a whole world out there, beyond the cave, that they could be enjoying and which would greatly increase their knowledge: just as Socrates knew that there is a whole world of Forms 'out there' that people ignorant of philosophy are missing.

Then Plato asks us to imagine what will happen if the prisoners are released from their chains, and can turn around and see what has been happening. Initially, each prisoner will be completely puzzled and at a loss to understand what it is that he is being shown. If he is shown the actual objects that were making the shadows, he will not at first be able to recognise them, and he will think that the shadows were 'more real' than the solid objects. He will find the whole experience painful because his muscles have been unused for so long, and the glare from the fire will hurt his eyes. However, as he gets used to the light, he will gradually become accustomed to it, and his vision will begin to improve. Plato wants us to understand that when we begin to question the world around us, when we start to wonder what is real and what is illusory, and when we begin to ask ourselves whether we could have been wrong until now, it is a painful experience. Most people only undertake philosophy reluctantly – but it is, nevertheless, a profoundly worthwhile thing to do.

And now look again, and see what will naturally follow if the prisoners are released and disabused of their error. At first, when any of them is liberated and compelled suddenly to stand up and turn his neck round and walk and look towards the light, he will suffer sharp pains; the glare will distress him, and he will be unable to see the realities of which in his former state he had seen the shadows; and then conceive some one saying to him, that what he saw before was an illusion, but that now, when he is approaching nearer to being and his eye is

When the prisoners are able to look directly at the fire rather than just at the shadows, they find the experience painful at first.

turned towards more real existence, he has a clearer vision, – what will be his reply? And you may further imagine that his instructor is pointing to the objects as they pass and requiring him to name them, – will he not be perplexed? Will he not fancy that the shadows which he formerly saw are truer than the objects which are now shown to him?

Far truer.

And if he is compelled to look straight at the light, will he not have a pain in his eyes which will make him turn away to take and take in the objects of vision which he can see, and which he will conceive to be in reality clearer than the things which are now being shown to him?

True, he said.

Once the former prisoner has become more comfortable with looking at the fire, it is time for him to leave the cave and make his way outside. He does not want to go. He has been comfortable with his life of ignorance, and experience already tells him that changing his ideas is a painful challenge. However, he is led up through the mouth of the cave, which is 'steep' and 'rugged' as a metaphor for his struggles. At last, he is out in the light, where the sun rather than the fire gives the real world a sharp clarity.

And suppose once more, that he is reluctantly dragged up a steep and rugged ascent, and held fast until he is forced into the presence of the sun himself, is he not likely to be pained and irritated? When he approaches the light his eyes will be dazzled, and he will not be able to see anything at all of what are now called realities.

Not all in a moment, he said.

He will require to grow accustomed to the sight of the upper world. And first he will see the shadows best, next the reflections of men and other objects in the water, and then the objects themselves; then he will gaze upon the light of the moon and the stars and the spangled heaven; and he will see the sky and the stars by night better than the sun or the light of the sun by day?

Certainly.

Again, the prisoner's initial reaction is one of pain and irritation. His eyes are so dazzled at first that he cannot see anything clearly, but gradually he adjusts. First he understands shadows, and then reflections; he is more comfortable at night than during the day. But later on, as his abilities develop, he is able to see in daylight.

Last of all he will be able to see the sun, and not mere reflections of him in the water, but he will see him in his own proper place, and not in another; and he will contemplate him as he is.

Certainly.

He will then proceed to argue that this is he who gives the season and the years, and is the guardian of all that is in the visible world, and in a certain way the cause of all things which he and his fellows have been accustomed to behold?

Clearly, he said, he would first see the sun and then reason about him.

As the former prisoner adjusts to his new life, his wisdom grows. He begins to recognise the importance of the sun in illuminating all of his other knowledge. He realises that the sun gives structure to his life, and that it enables him to see other things as they really are.

Plato gave the metaphor of the sun to clarify his understanding of the Form of the Good.

With this metaphor, Plato wants us to understand the sun as the Form of the Good. The shadowland is something we experience when we are ignorant of the Form of the Good. When we never ask ourselves about the nature of goodness, we live in a world of illusions, where none of our 'knowledge' is really knowledge at all. It is only when we have an understanding of the Good that everything else falls into place. Knowing what Goodness is allows us to know what Justice is, or Truth, or Patience.

The former prisoner has reached a state of knowledge at last. However, because he has this newly-acquired wisdom, he realises that he has an obligation to help others who are still in ignorance.

And when he remembered his old habitation, and the wisdom of the den and his fellow-prisoners, do you not suppose that he would felicitate himself on the change, and pity them?

Certainly, he would.

And if they were in the habit of conferring honours among themselves on those who were quickest to observe the passing shadows and to remark which of them went before, and which followed after, and which were together; and who were therefore best able to draw conclusions as to the future, do you think that he would care for such honours and glories, or envy the possessors of them? Would he not say with Homer,

> *Better to be the poor servant of a poor master, and to endure anything, rather than think as they do and live after their manner?*

Yes, he said, I think that he would rather suffer anything than entertain these false notions and live in this miserable manner.

Imagine once more, I said, such an one coming suddenly out of the sun to be replaced in his old situation; would he not be certain to have his eyes full of darkness?

To be sure, he said.

And if there were a contest, and he had to compete in measuring the shadows with the prisoners who had never moved out of the den, while his sight was still weak, and before his eyes had become steady (and the time which would be needed to acquire this new habit of sight might be very considerable) would he not be ridiculous? Men would say of him that up he went and down he came without his eyes; and that it was better not even to think of ascending; and if any one tried to loose another and lead him up to the light, let them only catch the offender, and they would put him to death.

No question, he said.

Plato asks us to imagine that the prisoners in the cave have made up a simple game to pass the time. As they sit in their chains watching the shadows go past them on the wall opposite, they try to guess what might be coming next. Those who get it right the most often are the winners, and they are prized amongst the community of prisoners for this special skill – even though it is only guesswork and therefore they are getting it right through pure chance rather than genuine ability.

When the former prisoner goes back into the cave to help his friends to their release, the prisoners are not impressed. The enlightened man finds the darkness a struggle now. He cannot see in the cave as well as he used to. Those who are still prisoners look at him and decide that they certainly have no desire to go wherever he has been, because they are better off where they are. In fact, they feel so hostile towards the suggestion that they would be prepared to kill him if he tried to lead them out of the cave.

Plato wants to show, then, that Socrates was well aware of the dangers he faced in trying to bring philosophy to others. He knew that people did not like to have their assumptions, prejudices and superstitions called into question. He knew that, when people start to ask themselves questions about what justice really is, or where the true nature of goodness might be found, they could end up with more questions than answers, and perhaps feel themselves to be less knowledgeable than before. But, in Plato's view, Socrates was willing to take this risk, because for him the human search for the truth was more important than life itself.

At the end of the story, Socrates explains its meaning to Glaucon:

This entire allegory, I said, you may now append, dear Glaucon, to the previous argument; the prison-house is the world of sight, the light of the fire is the sun, and you will not misapprehend me if you interpret the journey upwards to be the ascent of the soul into the intellectual world according to my poor belief, which, at your desire, I have expressed whether rightly or wrongly God knows. But, whether true or false, my opinion is that in the world of knowledge the idea of good appears last of all, and is seen only with an effort; and, when seen, is also inferred to be the universal author of all things beautiful and right, parent of light and of the lord of light in this visible world, and the immediate source of reason and truth in the intellectual; and that this is the power upon which he who would act rationally, either in public or private life must have his eye fixed.

I agree, he said, as far as I am able to understand you.

Moreover, I said, you must not wonder that those who attain to this beatific vision are unwilling to descend to human affairs; for their souls are ever hastening into the upper world where they desire to dwell; which desire of theirs is very natural, if our allegory may be trusted.

Yes, very natural.

And is there anything surprising in one who passes from divine contemplations to the evil state of man, misbehaving himself in a ridiculous manner; if, while his eyes are blinking and before he has become accustomed to the surrounding darkness, he is compelled to fight in courts of law, or in other places, about the images or the shadows of images of justice, and is endeavouring to meet the conceptions of those who have never yet seen absolute justice?

Anything but surprising, he replied.

Plato's story works on several different levels. His audience would have realised that the prisoner who escaped was meant to be Socrates himself, and that those who had tried and executed Socrates were those ignorant prisoners who had stayed behind and who preferred the comfort of their chains to the challenges of freedom. However, the released prisoner also represents all those who undertake philosophy. Those in the cave are representative of all those who prefer to live an 'unexamined life', and who are content to be impressed with appearances. The ones who are willing to climb the steep slope out of the cave, and to persevere with the journey, are those who recognise their inborn ability to perceive the truth behind the illusions presented to our five senses. They recognise that this is not the real world, but that reality is invisible.

An evaluation of Plato's thought

Of course, not everyone has accepted Plato's understanding of the world and of reality. Plato was convinced that there were two realms, one of ideas (Forms) and one of matter (the physical world). However, some people argue that he never gives us any compelling reasons for accepting that this is so – he simply asserts it.

Plato argues that the physical world is not as 'real' as the world of Forms, but this does not convince everyone. Many people argue that the physical world has a very definite reality, saying that if you hit your head on a bookcase, then you have a pretty good indication that the physical world is real. Scientists argue that the physical world is worth studying in its own right and can give us true insights into the nature of reality – and many scientists claim that this physical world is the only reality there is. For some, such as Richard Dawkins, it is nonsense to talk of a transcendent 'other world' beyond the physical. This world might be changeable, but we can still study it with all its changes and processes, and gain true and valuable knowledge which benefits us all in our daily lives.

To think about

If I take my daughter shopping, she has in her mind the 'perfect Form' of the pair of shoes she wants to buy (or, more often, that she wants me to buy for her). She has the concept of these ideal shoes, down to the last detail; but it is very rarely possible to find an actual example of such a pair of shoes in a shop. Which pair of shoes has the greater reality – her idea of Perfect Shoes, or the physically-existent but inferior shoes on the shelves of the actual shop? Is it possible for things to be 'real' in different ways?

As we have seen, some people, including Aristotle, criticised Plato's Theory of Forms on the grounds that it becomes ridiculous when pushed to its logical extremes. We might be happy to accept that there are 'ideal concepts' in mathematics, such as the concept of infinity, or the concept of a square root or a prime number. We might even be happy to accept that we have 'ideal concepts' of qualities such as Truth, Justice, Generosity or Goodness. However, it is harder to accept that there might be ideal forms of negative qualities such as Jealousy or Spite, and harder still to accept that every physical thing in the world has an ideal form.

To think about

You offer your friends a cup of tea. One asks for very weak and milky tea with no sugar; another likes a saturated sugar solution of strong tea; another asks for black Earl Grey; and another prefers not to have any tea at all unless it's Fair Trade.
So, what is the Ideal Form of a Cup of Tea?

What is the Ideal Form of a Cup of Tea?

27

A problem with the Theory of Forms can be seen if we use the example of plants. Is there an Ideal Form of Plant, in general – in which case, what would it be like? Would it have large or small leaves, coloured flowers, soft fruit, nuts, a scent, thorns, branches, catkins? Or is there perhaps one Form of Rose, and another Form of Pineapple, and a separate Form of Potato and another Form of Cactus and so on, for each species? However, if each species has a different Form, the problem still exists, because of the variation within that species. What is the Ideal Form of Rose – a Gertrude Jekyll, maybe, or a Blush Noisette? Is it a climber, a standard, a rambler, a bush? Suppose we decide that the Ideal Form of Rose is a good red Dublin Bay, and that other roses are inferior imitations of this ideal Form; we are still left with the problem of whether it is a tall or short specimen, whether it is in flower or not … and if we end up deciding that there must be one Form for those Dublin Bays with 100 leaves, and another for those with 101, then we might as well have a separate Form for each individual rose plant. Our Forms have stopped being universal at all.

It could be argued, however, that this criticism is a misunderstanding of Plato. Plato's thinking concentrated on the Forms of qualities, and plenty of philosophers would agree that we all have an intuitive knowledge of what goodness is, or of what justice is. Plato's theory might fail if pushed to logical extremes, but there is nothing to compel us to push it so far. Plato himself was ambiguous about whether there is a Form for literally everything in the world.

Plato could be criticised for not being entirely clear about the relation between the Forms and the objects of this world – in other words, the relation between concepts and phenomena. He talks about the phenomena 'participating in' their ideal Forms, but is not clear about how this works.

Some have disliked Plato's ideas because his dualism has been taken to extremes by those who came after him. Plato believed, as we know, that the changing physical world inhabited by the body is inferior to the transcendent, spiritual world of the Forms available to the soul through reason. This has led later thinkers to the idea that bodily pleasures are bad, and that people should punish their bodies if they want to make spiritual progress. They should, perhaps, shun all but the simplest food, wear plain clothes, be celibate and avoid pleasure for its own sake. However, this asceticism was not Plato's own position. Rather than condemning physical pleasures completely, he saw them as unimportant in comparison to philosophy.

Plato believed that knowledge of the Form of the Good was the highest possible kind of knowledge, underpinning everything else. However, this raises difficulties. Some people have argued that it is nonsense to talk as though we all share a concept of goodness and can know what it is. Thinkers such as A.J. Ayer have argued that when we talk of something as being 'good' or 'bad', we are simply expressing our own emotional reaction to it, and not referring to any real knowledge. Some people, such as Aristotle, have argued that there cannot be a single Form of the Good, because goodness always relates to specific actions, situations and people. There cannot be just Goodness-Itself, on its own, unrelated to anything. Morality, Aristotle thought, cannot be eternal and changeless with a single 'right answer', because no two situations are the same.

Plato's view of goodness is also challenged because of the way in which he relates it to philosophy. It appears that only those of a certain intellectual calibre are capable of being or doing good; those with learning difficulties, then, could never be good people because they would not understand philosophical issues. This can seem to be an unnecessarily unfair and elitist approach; and not everyone would agree that better philosophers are always more moral people than the less intellectually gifted.

Many would disagree with Plato's view that people only do wrong when they are ignorant of what is right; they argue that people often know perfectly well that something is morally wrong, but they go ahead and do it anyway. Perhaps Plato is over-optimistic in his view of human nature.

To think about

Do you think that people who commit crimes or who are violent only do these things because they are ignorant of what is right? Or do they know their deeds are wrong, but not care?

Practice exam questions

(a) Explain Plato's teaching about reality in his analogy of the cave.

In this part of the question, your knowledge and understanding will be assessed. Examiners will be looking to see whether you have an accurate understanding of the key ideas of Plato as expressed in the analogy of the cave, and whether you can explain these ideas clearly, using the correct vocabulary where appropriate. (It would be good to use the terms 'dualist' and 'Forms'.) You do not need to give your opinions about Plato's views here, because you have been asked to 'Explain'. Your own opinions can wait until part (b).

In this part (a), you need to focus on Plato's understanding of reality, rather than simply retelling the analogy of the cave. You should try to explain Plato's ideas about the Forms being 'more real' than the physical world, and his ideas about the limitations of a changing physical world as a place where we can gain true knowledge. Make reference to the cave analogy throughout your answer, picking out specific examples to illustrate your points (such as the shadows, or the sun).

(b) 'There is nothing wrong with being ignorant, as long as you are contented.' Discuss.

When a question asks you to 'discuss', it means that you should demonstrate skill in evaluation. You need to show why some people might agree with the statement, and why others might disagree. As well as presenting these different opinions, you also need to assess them by saying whether you think they are right or wrong. For high marks, support your opinions with reasons.

Part (b) usually gives you an opportunity to develop and assess the material you have presented in part (a). For this question, although the statement does not explicitly mention Plato, it would be good to refer to Plato's thinking as part of your answer. Clearly, Plato would disagree with this statement, as he thought ignorance bound people to a 'land of shadows'. Even though the people in the cave were quite content with their lifestyle, they were ignorant, and Plato thought this was not a good way to be, because he felt that knowledge was more important than contentment. However, you might be able to contrast Plato's views with a different way of thinking. Perhaps you could think of examples where living in happy ignorance would be better than knowing the truth.

Aristotle

In the view of many scholars, Aristotle was an even greater philosopher than Plato. Plato may have asked some vital philosophical questions and suggested some startlingly original approaches to them, but his theories are not readily acceptable by everyone, and some believe that Plato's arguments in support of his theories are not particularly successful.

Aristotle would have agreed. He was a great admirer of Plato, but found it difficult to agree with Plato's views. In particular, he did not accept that there is another world, more real than this one, which can be the object of true knowledge. In Aristotle's view, the physical world around us is the key to knowledge, and we can learn about it using our senses.

The painter Raphael illustrated the differences between Platonic and Aristotelian approaches to philosophy in his famous 'The School of Athens', painted at the beginning of the sixteenth century (this rather misleading name was given to the painting at a later date). Raphael places Plato and Aristotle at the centre of the picture, directly in front of the main source of light, showing them to be the most enlightened and perhaps the most illuminating of all the sixty figures in the painting. Plato, on the left, holds a copy of his book *Timaeus*, while Aristotle holds a copy of his own *Ethics*. Plato's body language expresses his idealism. His hand, and his book, are vertical, pointing upwards to show Plato's belief in another, superior world 'above' this one. Aristotle, in contrast, holds his hand and his book flat to represent the Earth, on which both his feet are squarely planted. This world, he seems to be saying, is where the truth can be found – the physical world under our feet, the world of sense experience and of science.

Detail from Raphael's painting School of Athens. *Here, Raphael captured the stark differences of approach between Plato and Aristotle.*

In spite of their differences, Plato and Aristotle greatly admired one another. Aristotle was the brightest of Plato's students at the Academy. He came from a well-off Macedonian family, and arrived in Athens at the age of 17 to study as a pupil of Plato. Following in the traditions of Plato and Socrates, Aristotle began to question the beliefs and assumptions he had always held – and also to question Plato's beliefs and assumptions. In the course of this, he decided against many of Plato's ideas and provided his own ways of looking at the world.

Aristotle rejected the idea that there is a 'world of Forms', separate from this world. He thought that there was nothing to be gained from the dualist approach. Ideas, he thought, can have no real existence on their own: they have to relate to something here in the physical world of our own experience. Our journey to knowledge has to start here, where we are, and must be gained through observation of the world around us.

For Aristotle, observation of the natural world was crucial. Aristotle was the founder of many of the sciences we recognise today: physics, biology, psychology, meteorology and astronomy. He had an insatiable desire to understand the world as it makes itself available to our five senses, and to see if there were universal rules which governed natural processes and which we could understand.

To think about

Do you think that science is the best way to discover truths about the world? What (if any) are some of the other possible ways of acquiring knowledge, apart from science?

Aristotle on cause and purpose

One question that fascinated Aristotle was the question of cause. Why are things the way that they are – what caused them? What is the 'essence' of this thing or that thing? Why does it exist in the world at all?

In exploring this question, Aristotle recognised that something can have several different explanations for its existence, on different levels. If I ask, for example, what is the 'cause' of my desk, I can answer in a variety of different ways. I could say that it is 'caused' by wood, because it is a wooden desk, so without the wood and the glue and the nails, I would not have a desk. Or, I could say that the desk is caused by the person who made it. Someone has taken this wood and the nails and the glue, and worked to make them into a desk shape – if this person had not bothered, then I would have no desk (or at least, not this one). A third answer I could give is that the desk is 'caused' by having a large and stable flat surface to work on, and sturdy legs that will hold the weight of my computer. If it lacked these characteristics, it would not be my desk. Finally, I could say that the desk exists in order to fulfill a purpose. People need desks so that they don't have to squat on the floor to do their writing; they need desks so that they have something to cover with heaps of miscellaneous paper. The desk has a function, an ultimate purpose to perform, which is why anyone bothered making one at all.

Aristotle, then, thought that 'cause' could be understood in four different ways, to which he gave different names.

1. He called the first the **material cause.** This explains what something is made from. This is a question scientists often try to answer when they are learning about something. They take the thing apart and look at the various kinds of matter of which the object is composed, sometimes through a microscope. So the material cause of a rat would be the blood, the muscles, the fur, the liver, the bones and all the other bits biologists find when they dissect rats. However, the material cause does not explain everything. A heap of bits of rat does not, alone, provide an explanation of the rat itself, although investigating an object's material will help us to understand important aspects of it, and should not be ignored.

2. The second is known as the **efficient cause.** This is the name Aristotle gave to the activity that makes something happen. The rat's efficient cause is the activity of Mummy Rat and Daddy Rat; the efficient cause of my desk is the activity of the carpenter who made it. Aristotle expressed this in terms of the actualising of potential. Wood has the potential to be made into furniture, but it needs the efficient cause of the carpenter to realise this potential. Efficient cause brings about change in something.

3. The third is known as the **formal cause.** This is how Aristotle termed the form, or shape, that something has. The formal cause gives something its shape and allows it to be identified as whatever it is. There are lots of things made by the activity of carpenters, using wood and glue and nails, that are not desks, but my desk is a desk because it is desk-shaped. Within limits, there are other shapes it could be while still being a desk, but there are certain characteristics of form that a desk has to have in order to be recognised as such.

4. The fourth, and for Aristotle most important, cause is the **final cause.** The final cause of something is its purpose, its reason for existing at all. This can be understood as its 'telos', which means 'end' (as in 'means to an end'). The final cause, or purpose, or telos, of a desk is that it can be put to use for writing. The final cause of a mug is for holding drinks; the final cause of fur is to keep the rat warm enough. This idea of final cause was to be of great significance to Thomas Aquinas when he made use of Aristotelian philosophy in his own theology and ethics.

Aristotle used his concept of final cause when he discussed the nature of goodness and the right way for people to behave. He thought that something was 'good' when it fulfilled its 'telos'. An axe is a good axe if it cuts well; boots are good boots if they

The formal cause of a canoe is its shape, which enables us to identify it as a canoe and not just a lot of fibreglass or wood. If it were a different shape entirely, it would not be a canoe.

keep your feet warm and dry; a person is a good person if … he or she does whatever it is that people are meant to do.

Aristotle's Prime Mover

Looking at cause and effect made Aristotle wonder about the existence of the universe as a whole. He had found a way of understanding, at different levels, the causes of individual objects within the universe, but what about the universe itself, in its entirety? The two 'causes' that bothered him the most when applied to the universe were the efficient cause and the final cause. What causes the different objects in the universe to actualise their potential? What is the purpose of the universe as a whole?

Aristotle, like many other philosophers before him, realised that the universe was in a constant state of change and motion. Therefore, he thought, there must be some kind of efficient cause, someone or something performing some kind of action, to make all this change and motion happen. He considered the idea that there might be an endless chain of cause and effect, with each movement being caused by a moving thing, which was being caused by another moving thing and so on for ever, but he rejected this idea. He did not think that endless cause and effect provided a satisfactory solution.

The cause of the universe, Aristotle thought, must be God. God must be the Prime Mover (sometimes called the Unmoved Mover), a cause which actualises the potential in everything else. However, the Prime Mover must be something that causes without being affected (otherwise it would simply be another link in the endless chain). The Prime Mover must be a being with no potential; something which already is everything that it could be, 'pure actuality' with no potential to change or to be acted upon.

In Aristotle's view, the Prime Mover was the first of all substances. It causes movement and change in all other things, but it does not do this in a physical way by giving them some kind of push, since if it did, the act of 'pushing' would affect the Prime Mover. Instead, the Prime Mover causes change and motion by attracting other things towards itself. It does nothing; but it is the object of everything. The final cause of movement is a desire for God. Everything in the universe is drawn towards God's perfection and wants to imitate it, and so by this great attraction, the Prime Mover causes movement in everything else.

Aristotle worked out the implications of his ideas about the Prime Mover, and came to several conclusions about the nature of God.

1. He believed that God does not depend on anything else for his existence. If he did, then he would have to be capable of change – if, for example, God relied on sunlight for his existence, then God would change and die if the sun fizzled out. But as God has no potential, which means he has no capacity for change, then he must exist independently, or 'necessarily'.

2. He must also be eternal, because of this lack of potential. If God cannot change, then he cannot cease to be; and if he exists, then he must have always existed.

3. God must be perfectly good, because badness is related to some kind of lack, an absence of something that ought to be there – and if God is pure actuality, then he must contain everything that ought to be there, so he must be perfect.

4. God must be immaterial, and beyond time and space. All matter is capable of being acted upon, and so God cannot be made of matter. But if God is immaterial, Aristotle thought, then God cannot perform any kind of physical activity – he cannot actually do anything. God must be purely spiritual, pure thought, and not thinking about anything that could cause him to change; which led Aristotle to conclude that God must think only of himself and his own perfect nature.

In Aristotle's thought there is the picture of God as 'wholly simple'. This is an idea which has had an enormous effect on the shaping of ideas about the nature of God. From Aristotle, we inherit the idea that God is unchanging. God cannot suffer. He cannot change his mind, and so he cannot be persuaded. God is unrestricted by time and space, so that the future and the past are the same for God. When these ideas are woven into the fabric of Christianity, they create knots that can be difficult to untie.

Although Aristotle was a genius, he did not inherit Plato's Academy; Plato left it to a nephew instead. Perhaps this was because of family loyalties on the part of Plato; perhaps it was because of Aristotle's Macedonian ancestry, which might have led to friction. But probably, it was because Plato knew that his own beliefs and the beliefs of Aristotle were just too different.

Aristotle thought that the 'telos' or the final cause of anything was its most significant explanation.

An evaluation of Aristotle's thought

Aristotle's work is difficult to evaluate because it often lacks clarity. While Plato wrote in clear and elegant prose, with plenty of examples to make sure that others would understand him, Aristotle's work is very difficult to follow. Many scholars believe that the surviving writings of Aristotle were never meant for publication, but are lecture notes. Maybe the notes were made by his students, who jotted down in an abbreviated way the main gist of what they understood. They could have added their own comments and ideas as they went along, giving the impression that Aristotle was contradicting himself or going off at tangents. Whatever the reasons, it remains the case that Aristotle is unclear. Some people find this almost impossibly frustrating, while others find it an exciting challenge.

Some, however, criticise Aristotle for his rejection of Plato's belief in another world, more real than this one. Perhaps Aristotle should have been more willing to accept the possibility that we can gain knowledge through other means, as well as through the physical world. Perhaps it also makes sense to talk of 'spiritual knowledge' or 'intuitive knowledge', rather than simply confining ourselves to the scientifically demonstrable.

Aristotle's belief that the universe must have a 'telos' has been criticised by many thinkers, including Russell, Sartre and Dawkins. They claim that it makes no sense to talk of a 'purpose' for the universe. It just exists, without any kind of reason or goal. There is nothing that a universe is 'supposed to do'. It is simply the result of chance.

Those who do not believe that the universe requires some kind of explanation are likely to question Aristotle's conclusions about the existence of an Unmoved Mover. Perhaps cause and effect is eternal, in an infinite chain, or perhaps it all began as a result of blind chance. The idea of a Prime Mover to start it all off could seem an unnecessary complication.

Theists often object to the concept of God as presented by Aristotle. They argue that Aristotle's God is almost irrelevant to the universe, because he has no interaction with it and is unaffected by it. Theists might claim that the God of their own experience is very different from the one Aristotle arrived at through logic, and that perhaps philosophical logic has its limitations. Perhaps there are other ways in which God can be known, which reveal God's personality as an active being.

Practice exam questions

(a) Explain Aristotle's understanding of causality.

For this part of the question, you need to show that you understand Aristotle's concept of the four causes. This would be a good choice of question in an examination (as long as you have revised) because it is easy to structure your answer into four different sections, where you say something about each one of the four causes. In order to gain high marks, you should make sure that you have named each one accurately, that you have given as detailed and clear an explanation as you can, and that you have given some examples to demonstrate your understanding. Try to use some specialist vocabulary with confidence – you will already be using the names of the causes, but you could also introduce terms such as 'potential' and 'telos'.

(b) 'Aristotle was wrong to believe that everything has an ultimate purpose.' Discuss.

In this part of the question, you are being asked to evaluate Aristotle's concept of the Final Cause. You will have already explained what this is in part (a), so there is no need to repeat your explanation here. Instead, you need to decide whether you agree with Aristotle that everything has a 'telos', and you need to be able to support your opinions with reasoning. Show that you understand why some people might have a different point of view, and say why you disagree with them and prefer your own position. You could make reference to different thinkers who have agreed or disagreed with Aristotle on this point, such as Aquinas or Bertrand Russell.

Judaeo-Christian influences on philosophy of religion

Although the ancient Greeks had a significant influence on the shaping of Christian beliefs and ideas, there was also an even more important influence: the Jewish scriptures, known to Christians as the Old Testament.

As we have seen, most philosophy of religion as we know it comes from within the Christian tradition. Because Christianity began and grew within the context of the Roman world, Christian understandings of the nature of God developed from the interweaving of biblical ideas and concepts from the ancient Greek philosophers. Christians inherited the language, symbolism and poetry of the Old Testament, in which God is anthropomorphised, involved with the world and unpredictable; but the early Christian fathers also came from a culture in which classical ideas of a timeless and spaceless First Cause were very attractive. In particular, ideas from Plato and Aristotle were adopted and woven into Christian interpretations of the nature of God – sometimes successfully, and sometimes in a way that produces at least apparent contradictions. Philosophers of religion have to try to untangle these ideas and work out which, if any, make more sense.

The Jewish scriptures present a way of understanding the world which is in sharp contrast to the world-view offered by Plato and Aristotle. The philosophical tradition of questioning and of supporting ideas with reasoned argument is at odds with the Bible, which assumes from the outset that God exists and that there are self-evident truths about him. The Bible is not written in an argumentative style but as a series of stories. Poetry and myth are used to convey truth, interspersed with historical accounts, genealogies, letters, prophecy and accounts of visions.

In the Bible, God is at the centre. God is not an explanatory factor with a secondary place, but is the focus. The God of the Bible is very much an active force in the world, taking an interest in the personal lives and morality of individuals. He is concerned for all kinds of people, whether they are intellectually able or not. God speaks to them personally; God intervenes in nature to perform miracles; God made all people, and the rest of the universe, according to his own plan. The biblical God sets the standard for goodness and then demands that people follow it, rewarding them when they are faithful to his commands and punishing them when they fall short or deliberately disobey.

The Jewish scriptures, or Old Testament, gave Christians a framework for understanding the nature of God.

The concept of God as creator

According to the Bible, God is responsible for bringing the universe into existence. Everything that exists owes its existence to God's creative activity, and nothing is made except that which is made by God – so if there are evil forces in the universe, they had no part to play in creation.

The universe is seen in the Bible as set apart from God. God is not 'Nature-Itself', and the different elements of the universe are not considered to be in some way component parts of God; God is transcendent over his creation and exists separately from it.

There are many passages in the Bible which portray the creative activity of God, for example in Job and in the Psalms, but of course the major creation stories of the Bible are found in the opening chapters of Genesis.

Genesis itself is not an independent book, written by a single author, that can be interpreted alone as a simple text. It forms part of a much longer narrative, called the Hexateuch (the first six books of the Bible), taking the story of the Jewish nation from Creation to the entrance of the tribes into Canaan in the book of Joshua. Gerhard von Rad, in *Genesis: A Commentary* (SCM Press, 1961), writes:

The basic theme of the Hexateuch may be stated as follows: God, the Creator of the world, called the patriarchs and promised them the Land of Canaan. When Israel became numerous in Egypt, God led the people through the wilderness with wonderful demonstrations of grace; then after their lengthy wandering he gave them under Joshua the Promised Land.

This theme is often known amongst biblical scholars by the German term *Heilsgeschichte*, or salvation-history. The Bible tells the story of how God has saved his creation, and the early parts of Genesis should be seen as fitting in to this larger picture. They set the scene, to make sense of the times when God made a covenant with Abraham; when the people were in slavery in Egypt; when they were rescued by God with the aid of Moses, and given the Ten Commandments when the Sinai covenant was made; and finally (in the Hexateuch) when they were led into the Promised Land. One of the purposes of the writers of the creation stories in Genesis, then, was to introduce this theme of salvation history. It is important for the interpretation of any text, whether biblical or not, to consider the purposes of the writer or writers in order to gain an understanding of its meaning, and so an understanding of the creation stories in Genesis is aided by a consideration of the purposes of its writers.

When reading the creation accounts in Genesis, although there is the message of faith in God as creator, it needs to be seen as secondary to the purpose of showing God's saving role through history. God can save the people from slavery, can make binding covenants with Noah, and with Abraham and Moses, because he is the creator of the universe.

Another purpose of the Genesis stories is to display God's power. God is understood as omnipotent, or 'all-powerful' – the whole of the universe is created by God and is subject to God. God is so powerful that he can create whatever he likes, just by saying the word, and there is nothing in the universe to compare with him.

What, then, were the main purposes of the writer or writers of the Genesis creation stories? It is sometimes suggested that part of their purpose was to counter the views put forward in other creation stories from other cultures. Genesis rejects the idea that God is just a local national deity; he is not just the God of the Jews, one of a number of gods of equal power. Genesis makes a firm claim that this saving God of history is the only, omnipotent, creator God. God is not one of the forces of nature or Nature-itself; God does not pervade the universe but stands apart from his creation as transcendent.

God as creator in Genesis

In the beginning God created the heavens and the earth. Now the earth was formless and empty, darkness was over the surface of the deep, and the Spirit of God was hovering over the waters. And God said, 'Let there be light', and there was light. God saw that the light was good, and He separated the light from the darkness. God called the light 'day', and the darkness he called 'night'. And there was evening, and there was morning – the first day. (Genesis 1:1–5)

The general picture of the beginning of the world here is rather like the creation

In the traditions of Christianity, Judaism and Islam, God is not part of creation but transcends it.

myth of Babylon, where, before the heavens and earth were created, there existed dark and swirling waters. Some scholars argue that the writers of Genesis used the Babylonian story when they were writing their own – although, of course, other people would argue that Genesis is a book from God and any similarities with other stories are just coincidence. The 'Spirit of God' hovering over the waters is translated in some versions of the Bible as a 'wind'. God's Spirit is also symbolised elsewhere in the Bible in terms of a mighty or rushing wind, for example in the story of Pentecost in Acts 2:2, where the Holy Spirit is given to the first Christians.

God is seen as imposing order, through effortless creativity, over the chaos of the waters. Was the description of water existing before God began his work meant to be a symbolic way of representing chaos before the origins of the universe? Or did the writers think that they were recording fact, writing down 'science' as they knew it? Certainly this second verse seems to speak of some sort of reality existing which might have always existed, rather than God making the world out of complete nothingness. The opening verses show God giving order and form, creating out of chaos – is this the same as creation out of nothing?

Traditionally, Christians and Jews have held the belief that God created every-thing out of nothing. Where there was no matter, God created matter: nothing

Did God create 'out of nothing' or did he create out of material which eternally existed?

pre-existed the universe, except for God himself. This doctrine is known as *creatio ex nihilo* – creation out of nothing. Perhaps the wording in Genesis is ambiguous about this. Some scientists believe that matter must have existed in some form for eternity, because in their view it is impossible for matter to appear out of nowhere; and it is possible to interpret the Genesis account in this way, where God uses formless but already existent 'stuff' and fashions it in his own way to make the universe. However, this view is less popular among religious believers, because it seems to give a view of God that is not as impressive as a God who creates out of nothing. If God does not create out of nothing, then it means there is something (matter) which is also eternal, like God; so God is not unique. It also seems to undermine the cosmological argument for the existence of God (see pages 84-99), which claims that the universe cannot have caused itself but must have been caused by God. If matter is eternal, then maybe the universe did cause itself after all, reducing God to some kind of designer rather than the creator of all.

To think about

Do you agree that a God who creates out of nothing is more impressive than a God who creates out of matter which already exists?

God's first creation is light – it is not seen as part of God himself, but as a separate creation. It is not light from the sun or moon, which are created later, but an object in itself, made to negate the darkness of chaos and to make the rest of creation possible. Creation is not some kind of emanation of God's being in Genesis; he remains all the time separate and distinct from it.

Each of the six days of creation is presented in a pattern: 'God said, Let … And so it was'. The emphasis is on God's word, finding immediate fulfilment. This displays belief in God's absolute rule over creation, and also that creation reflects God's purposes – an idea that is given great significance in teleological (design) arguments for God's existence.

Most of the acts of creation are given the verdict 'good', and the whole picture when completed is also given the same judgement: 'God saw all that he had made, and it was very good.' The Old Testament writers were not blind to the fact that the world contains evil and suffering, but at the same time neither did they consider the physical world to be bad, or an opposite to the spiritual world – this was a Greek idea, particularly favoured by Plato, but for the writers of the Bible, the physical world is good.

God separates the elements of light and darkness, as day and night. The word 'day' is used in two senses: 'day' as in daytime as opposed to night-time, and also 'day' meaning the whole 24-hour cycle. But, as Robert Davidson writes in his commentary *Genesis 1–11* (Cambridge University Press, 1979):

> *Attempts to make it still more flexible, to mean different aeons or stages in the known evolution of the world, and thus reconcile Genesis 1 with modern scientific theory, are misguided. The appeal of Genesis 1 is to the imagination; it is poetic, a hymn written for faith by faith. It is not a scientific hypothesis, nor does it need to be reconciled with any such hypothesis.*

> *And God said, 'Let there be an expanse between the waters to separate water from water'. So God made the expanse and separated the water under the expanse from the water above it. And it was so. God called the expanse 'sky'. And there was evening, and there was morning – the second day.* (Genesis 1:6–8)

The waters are divided by the vault of heaven, which seems to have been understood in terms of a solid, dome-like structure arching over the earth. The 'waters', which are the source of rain, are placed above the vault, and the waters below are to form seas and rivers. The verb used to describe the making of this vault is the word for 'hammered', suggesting God fixing this giant hemisphere into place just as a builder would hammer a roof-beam. The book of Job uses the same idea: 'Can you beat out the vault of the skies, as he does, hard as a mirror of cast metal?' (Job 37:18). Sometimes God's creativity is seen in terms of his making something, like a craftsman, gradually fashioning it and shaping it to take the form he intends it to have; and sometimes it is described in terms of the spoken word, where things appear immediately and fully formed simply because God has commanded them to exist.

> *And God said, 'Let the water under the sky be gathered to one place, and let dry ground appear'. And it was so. God called the dry ground 'land', and the gathered waters he called 'seas'. And God saw that it was good.* (Genesis 1:9–10)

The work of the second day is completed on the third, where the water under the dome is organised into oceans, leaving some drained dry land. It is clear from other places in the Old Testament that the earth is regarded as a solid disc set upon the waters beneath and surrounded by water. The security of the earth depends upon God keeping the waters in check, so in the story of Noah, the flood comes because God decides to stop maintaining this order.

God distinguishes things according to their nature, and gives them names; this is echoed later in Genesis when Adam names the animals. In Old Testament times, giving something or someone a name had great importance, showing the command that the namer had over the named.

Then God said, 'Let the land produce vegetation: seed-bearing plants and trees on the land that bear fruit with seed in it, according to their various kinds'. And it was so. The land produced vegetation: plants bearing seed according to their kinds and trees bearing fruit with seed in it according to their kinds. And God saw that it was good. And there was evening, and there was morning – the third day. (Genesis 1:11–13)

In the Genesis story, plants grow and bear different kinds of fruit because God commands it.

The first signs of organic growth appear, in the form of plants such as cereals, and also fruit trees, such as citrus and olive trees. Here, God commands the earth to be creative, and then the earth brings forth the plants, in a kind of combination of the ideas of God as creator and 'Mother Nature' continuing the same creativity.

And God said, 'Let there be lights in the expanse of the sky to separate the day from the night, and let them serve as signs to mark seasons and days and years, and let them be lights in the expanse of the sky to give light on the earth'. And it was so. God made two great lights – the greater light to govern the day and the lesser light to govern the night. He also made the stars. God set them in the expanse of the sky to give light on the earth, to govern the day and the night, and to separate light from darkness. And God saw that it was good. And there was evening, and there was morning – the fourth day. (Genesis 1:14–19)

On the fourth day, the stars, sun and moon are created. The writer deliberately does not mention the sun and moon by name, to avoid any confusion with other religions where the sun and moon are worshipped. In some other religions with which the Genesis writers would have been familiar, the stars were considered to be the controllers of human destiny, through astrology, but here the writer makes the point that the sun, moon and stars exist to serve God and to serve humanity by marking the days and the seasons.

And God said, 'Let the water teem with living creatures, and let birds fly above the earth across the expanse of the sky'. So God created the great creatures of the sea and every living and moving thing with which the water teems, according to their kinds, and every winged bird according to its kind. And God saw that it was good. God blessed them and said, 'Be fruitful and increase in number and fill the water in the seas, and let the birds increase on the earth'. And there was evening, and there was morning – the fifth day. (Genesis 1:20–23)

On the fifth day, now that all the necessary conditions have been created, there is the creation of living beings (plants were clearly not held to be in the same category). Living creatures are made, with the capacity to continue to procreate. The sequence of creation moves from the creatures furthest away from humanity (the mythical creatures), to the water-creatures and the birds.

And God said, 'Let the land produce living creatures according to their kinds: livestock, creatures that move along the ground, and wild animals, each according to its kind'. And it was so. God made the wild animals according to their kinds, the livestock according to their kinds, and all the creatures that move along the ground according to their kinds. And God saw that it was good. (Genesis 1:24–25)

According to Genesis, each different species of animal was created instantly, fully formed.

This is followed, on the sixth day, by the creation of land animals, which are indirectly made from the creative force of the earth. The land animals are divided into three groups: cattle, reptiles, and wild animals.

> *Then God said, 'Let us make man in our image, in our likeness, and let them rule over the fish of the sea and the birds of the air, over the livestock, over all the earth, and over all the creatures that move along the ground'.*
>   *So God created man in his own image,*
>   *in the image of God he created him;*
>   *male and female he created them.*
>
> (Genesis 1:26–28)

The creation of humanity is made more impressive by being preceded by a divine resolution: 'Let us make man'. The Hebrew word used is *adam,* meaning humanity, which is a collective noun and therefore never used in the plural. Humanity is to be made in God's image. The word 'image' literally means a 'duplicate'. It is difficult to know exactly what was meant, although some scholars suggest that to spiritualise this verse, to make it imply that humanity is in God's image in terms of its dignity or moral sense, is to over-interpret it. Perhaps the writer meant to claim that people actually look like God. The writing certainly does not limit this likeness to any particular aspect of humanity; rather, it suggests that humanity in its totality is in the image of God. The implications of what being in the image of God might mean are only sketched; what is made far more explicit is that humanity has a purpose. This is the commission to rule, and to dominate the world, especially the animals. Humanity is God's representative, to maintain and enforce God's power over the created world. Therefore humanity, while created by God, also has a task to perform, and a special responsibility towards God. Sexual distinction is created by God; there is the idea that humanity gets its full meaning through the existence of both men and women. They are blessed, and encouraged to procreate as a manifestation of being made in God's image and receiving God's blessing.

> *God blessed them and said to them, 'Be fruitful and increase in number; fill the earth and subdue it. Rule over the fish of the sea and the birds of the air and over every living creature that moves on the ground'. Then God said, 'I give you every seed-bearing plant on the face of the whole earth and every tree that has fruit with seed in it. They will be yours for food. And to all the beasts of the earth and all the birds of the air and all the creatures that move on the ground – everything that has the breath of life in it – I give every green plant for food'. And it was so.*
> (Genesis 1:29–30)

People and animals alike are given plants to eat, which is significant because it shows that killing did not originally form part of the created order. Animals did not kill each other for food, and the human domination of the animal kingdom is limited; they can rule the animals, but the Bible does not say that they can eat them.

Michelangelo painted a scene depicting the creation of Adam on the ceiling of the Sistine chapel.

God saw all that he had made, and it was very good. And there was evening, and there was morning – the sixth day. (Genesis 1:31)

God approves of the whole of the created order, now that it is completed. It could also be translated as 'completely perfect'. No evil, therefore, was put into the world by God's hand. There was no opposing power threatening God's omnipotence.

Thus the heavens and the earth were completed in all their vast array. By the seventh day God had finished the work he had been doing; so on the seventh day he rested from all his work. And God blessed the seventh day and made it holy, because on it he rested from all the work of creating that he had done. (Genesis 2:1–4)

On the seventh day, God rests, and the Sabbath is created, because the work is completed. The Sabbath is seen as being for God as well as for humanity; and it is important to note that, according to this story, creative work was finished at this point. God stopped creating the world because it was all done. Once created, the world has a life of its own, independent of God, and the creatures within it act according to their own free choices.

This might suggest that God stopped playing an active part in the world, once creation was finished – that he settled back to watch what would happen next, without bothering to do anything else, other than allow nature to take its course. However, the Bible makes it clear that this was not the case. God continues, after he has created the world, to be involved with his creation, and in particular to care about the well-being of humanity. He creates opportunities for them to exercise their free will, and cares about how they respond. He teaches them, with rewards and punishments, about right and wrong. Although humanity disobeys God, God responds with infinite love and patience, and (according to Christianity) ultimately steps into the world in the form of Jesus to bring about human salvation.

The book of Genesis continues in chapter 2 with the story of the first people, Adam and Eve. It shows their creation, the roles that they were given by God, their freedom of choice and what they decided to do with that freedom. It also shows the consequences for humanity of their actions.

Here we are presented with a rather naïve narrative. It contrasts with Genesis 1 in a number of ways, and many people have come to the conclusion that these are two distinct creation stories from different sources, brought together at a later date. The type of literary style is different: in Genesis 1 we had a poem or a hymn with a different verse for each day, and here is a continuous prose narrative. The name for God changes, translated as 'God' and 'Lord God', suggesting that this writing comes from a different source. There are some differences in the order in which things are created: for example, in the first account, the animals were created before humanity, but in the second account, humanity comes first. In this second account, the world is established around people, set up for our use, whereas in the first account, humankind was the culmination of the rest of creation, put into the picture to complete a scene which had been set. However, Henry Morris, an American creationist commentator on Genesis (see pages 191–4), writes of the second chapter: 'It does not in any respect contradict the account in the first chapter, but instead is complementary to it' (*The Genesis Record*, Baker Books, 1995), and this is the view taken by many Christians and Jews.

It is difficult to know whether the original writer meant this to be a historical narrative, detailing events which actually took place on a particular day in the past with real people. There is some evidence to suggest that the story is meant to be mythological, but this is nowhere made explicit. The characters in the story do not have personal names, but are called Adam, meaning 'humanity', and Eve, meaning 'life'. There are magical trees, a talking serpent, and a guard of cherubim. Robert Davidson, in his commentary on the first 11 chapters of Genesis, writes: 'The whole purpose of the narrative is not to describe what once happened but to explain certain puzzling features of life and human experience known to the narrator. We are in the realm of story myth'. Davidson agrees with the suggestion that the story comes from different sources, woven together, using creation accounts from other myths which also had accounts of trees and so on.

This is the account of the heavens and the earth when they were created.

When the Lord God made the earth and the heavens – and no shrub of the field had yet appeared on the earth and no plant of the field had yet sprung up, for

the Lord God had not sent rain on the earth and there was no man to work the ground, but streams came up from the earth and watered the whole surface of the ground – the Lord God formed the man from the dust of the ground and breathed into his nostrils the breath of life, and the man became a living being.
(Genesis 2:4–7)

The picture given of the earth before God began creation is very different from that of chapter 1. Here, there appears to be a dry wilderness instead of waters, and there was no rain but instead a flood (or possibly a mist) which used to rise up periodically and water the ground; perhaps this is using the same idea of the earth sitting above a mass of water. This idea is just given sketchily, to set the scene for the formation of humanity.

In verse 7, where the man is 'formed', the writer uses a verb most often descriptive of a potter shaping clay. God shapes an inanimate creature from the dust of the ground, and then breathes into it the breath of life. Some translations have used the word 'soul', but this is not what the Hebrew implies, there is no sense of ensoulment setting humankind apart. The word refers to vitality, God giving humanity the spark of life. Elsewhere in Genesis, the same word for the breath of life is used in the context of other animals, so there is no need to read into this text any implication of humanity having been set apart by the gift of a soul.

The picture given here of God is quite anthropomorphic; God is described as having breath, blowing into the man's nostrils. This indicates the special relationship between humanity and God, similar to the idea of 'image' and 'likeness'.

Now the Lord God had planted a garden in the east, in Eden; and there he put the man he had formed. And the Lord God made all kinds of trees grow out of the ground – trees that were pleasing to the eye and good for food. In the middle of the garden were the tree of life and the tree of the knowledge of good and evil.
(Genesis 2:8–9)

Humankind is placed by God into the Garden of Eden. The two trees, the tree of life and the tree of the knowledge of good and evil, are difficult to interpret, although they are central to the story. Some commentators have suggested that there are interwoven myths here, because the trees appear here at the beginning, and then are ignored until later. The tree of life disappears again until chapter 3, perhaps suggesting that the story has been muddled with one about humanity's search for immortality (although a reader who wanted to take the Bible more literally would not accept this view). Many have suggested that the purpose of these trees in the story is to show that, from the outset, humanity was given the responsibility to choose whether to live under the authority of God, or to disobey and to try to be more autonomous. The tree of the knowledge of good and evil has been given a variety of interpretations. Frequently it has been suggested that it is about sexuality: the man and woman do not feel any shame about being naked until they eat, they lose their innocence, and Eve's punishment is pain in childbirth. This does not seem to be a warning against sex in general, but against its misuse in fertility rites, a seeking to gain power and magic through the kind of sexual rites that were prevalent in Canaanite society in biblical times.

Probably a better explanation is that the 'knowledge of good and evil' is a broader concept, to mean 'knowledge of everything'. People are being warned not to think themselves omniscient; they should recognise the greater wisdom of God, and should not try to assert their independence outside the authority of God. Otherwise they will be doomed to die.

To think about

Does this suggest that, before the Fall, there was to be no death, and that humanity would be immortal?

A river watering the garden flowed from Eden; from there it was separated into four headwaters. The name of the first is the Pishon; it winds through the entire land of Havilah, where there is gold. (The gold of that land is good; aromatic resin and onyx are also there.) The name of the second river is the Gihon; it winds through the entire land of Cush. The name of the third river is the Tigris; it runs along the east side of Asshur. And the fourth river is the Euphrates. (Genesis 2:10–14)

At this point, the writer is quite specific about the location of the Garden of Eden. The writer seems to envisage Eden as a place on the map (and the passage has led many people to try to find out its exact location, searching for the sources of the rivers mentioned). However, elsewhere in the same story, Eden seems to be used as a religious idea rather than a geographically locatable spot (rather like Hades, representative of the underworld rather than something which might be reached by digging in the right spot).

The Lord God took the man and put him in the Garden of Eden to work it and take care of it. And the Lord God commanded the man, 'You are free to eat from any tree in the garden; but you must not eat from the tree of the knowledge of good and evil, for when you eat of it you will surely die'. (Genesis 2:15–17)

Here, God presents his created man with a choice. He can do as he is told, and leave the tree alone, or he can disobey God and eat from the forbidden tree. This passage has raised many puzzling questions. Why did God place this tree in the garden, if the man was not to eat from it – what purpose did it serve? Was God deliberately tempting the man, testing him to see what he would do – and if so, why did God need to give a test? The implication is that God did not know in advance what would happen, and this raises more questions about how, if at all, God can be said to be omniscient.

The Lord God said, 'It is not good for the man to be alone. I will make a helper suitable for him'. Now the Lord God had formed out of the ground all the beasts of the field and all the birds of the air. He brought them to the man to see what he would name them; and whatever the man called each living creature, that was its name. So the man gave names to all the livestock, the birds of the air and all the beasts of the field. But for Adam no suitable helper was found. So the Lord God caused the man to fall into a deep sleep; and while he was sleeping, he took one of the man's ribs and closed up the place with flesh. Then the Lord God made a woman from the rib he had taken out of the man, and he brought her to the man. The man said,
'This is now bone of my bones
and flesh of my flesh;
she shall be called "woman",
for she was taken out of man'.
For this reason a man will leave his father and mother and be united to his wife, and they will become one flesh. The man and his wife were both naked, and they felt no shame. (Genesis 2:18–25)

This section begins with the recognition that the man on his own is incomplete. He needs a partner. Then follows the story of God forming, out of the ground, all the wild animals and birds. Some people take this to show a different order of creation from that of chapter 1; others understand it to be filling in the details, letting the reader know that meanwhile, God had made the other creatures. Adam gives each animal a name, as a means of showing his power and control over them.

Possibly the story shows a series of unsuccessful experiments by God, where God suggested different animals to keep Adam company, but none was suitable. More probably, it underlines the sense of the loneliness of man before he has a suitable partner. Then God puts Adam into a deep sleep or trance, and forms Eve, using one of Adam's ribs. Davidson describes this as 'delightfully naïve', and says that the unlikeliness of the story should not blind us to its spiritual significance, while Morris, the creationist writer, says that God must have had a good reason for forming Eve in this way, rather than out of the dust of the ground like Adam and the animals, even if we cannot be certain what that reason is.

The passage gives a reason for the institution of marriage; 'For this reason a man will leave his father and mother and be united to his wife'. Many scholars have concluded that parts of this story are what is called an aetiological myth. An aetiological myth is a story which seeks to explain why things are the way that they are (rather like the

Rudyard Kipling *Just So Stories* of 'How the leopard got his spots', 'How the elephant got his trunk', etc). They suggest that this story of the creation of Eve can be seen as an aetiological myth. It explains why people want to leave their parents and set up with a new partner of their own: because they are originally of the same flesh, and need a partner in order to find completeness and fulfilment.

> *Now the serpent was more crafty than any of the wild animals the Lord God had made. He said to the woman, 'Did God really say, "You must not eat from any tree in the garden"?'. The woman said to the serpent, 'We may eat fruit from the trees in the garden, but God did say, "You must not eat fruit from the tree that is in the middle of the garden, and you must not touch it, or you will die".' 'You will not surely die,' the serpent said to the woman. 'For God knows that when you eat of it your eyes will be opened, and you will be like God, knowing good and evil.' When the woman saw that the fruit of the tree was good for food and pleasing to the eye, and also desirable for gaining wisdom, she took some and ate it. She also gave some to her husband, who was with her, and he ate it. Then the eyes of both of them were opened, and they realized they were naked; so they sewed fig leaves together and made coverings for themselves. (Genesis 3:1–7)*

In chapter 3, the serpent is introduced and everything starts to go horribly wrong. The serpent here does not seem to be anything other than one of the creatures which God had made; he is different only because he is 'more crafty' than any of the other animals. There is no suggestion here that he is to be equated with the Devil, although that was certainly an idea which came into Jewish and Christian culture later (probably as a way of coping with the problem of why a creature with the capability and inclination to do evil was part of the original Garden of Eden). The unanswered question is raised here, of how the serpent came to be more crafty in the first place; was this the way that he was created? The writer is so concerned with the guilt of humanity that he plays down this part of the story and does not deal with the question.

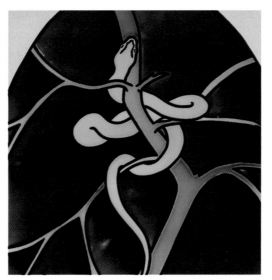

How did the crafty serpent come to be in a place which God had made?

The serpent begins with a question, asking Eve if God had really forbidden her to eat from the trees in the garden, implying that God has been unnecessarily authoritarian. Eve springs to God's defence, showing the serpent that they are given nearly everything except that they are forbidden to eat from the tree in the middle of the garden. (Here the narrative again seems to have a slight contradiction; they were forbidden to eat from two trees, but Eve only mentions one.) The serpent slyly suggests to Eve that God is just trying to keep something valuable from humanity; they are not as well off as they could be. Eve moves from a position of accepting obedient innocence, to one where she begins to judge God from her own perspective and questions God's motives. She has already begun to fall away from perfection. Eve notices how tempting the fruit looks, and she eats some. Adam follows her example, and immediately their innocence disappears; they discover that they are naked, and they cover themselves. It is interesting that it is not the serpent who makes Eve or Adam eat the fruit; he suggests to Eve that she might know better than God, and she is brought to a point where she decides for herself.

Then the man and his wife heard the sound of the Lord God as he was walking in the garden in the cool of the day, and they hid from the Lord God among the trees of the garden. But the Lord God called to the man, 'Where are you?'. He answered, 'I heard you in the garden, and I was afraid because I was naked; so I hid'. And he said, 'Who told you that you were naked? Have you eaten from the tree that I commanded you not to eat from?' The man said, 'The woman you put here with me — she gave me some fruit from the tree, and I ate it'. (Genesis 3:8–12)

God is depicted anthropomorphically here. He is 'walking in the garden', and Adam and Eve can hear him as he moves around. Possibly this verse suggests that before the Fall, God was much more accessible to humanity, to emphasise how distanced the people are about to become. Perhaps, before Adam and Eve disobeyed God, God was available to the human senses, to be seen and heard, although it is difficult for us to imagine how this could be. It also contrasts with the traditional view of God as omnipresent, where he is beyond space and able to be in all places at all times.

Adam and Eve experience the first guilt. They know that they have done wrong and they try to hide; they try to evade the truth and they try to pass the blame on to each other and also onto God ('You gave me this woman in the first place'). The writer shows that immediately, sin has become part of their nature, repeated in everything they do.

Then the Lord God said to the woman, 'What is this you have done?' The woman said, 'The serpent deceived me, and I ate'. So the Lord God said to the serpent, 'Because you have done this,
> *Cursed are you above all the livestock*
> *and all the wild animals!*

Key term

omnipresent – present everywhere, not confined by space.

You will crawl on your belly
and you will eat dust
all the days of your life.
And I will put enmity
between you and the woman,
and between your offspring and hers;
he will crush your head,
and you will strike his heel'.
To the woman he said,
'I will greatly increase your pains in childbearing;
with pain you will give birth to children.
Your desire will be for your husband,
and he will rule over you'.
To Adam he said,
'Because you listened to your wife
and ate from the tree about which I commanded you, "You must not eat of it",
Cursed is the ground because of you;
through painful toil you will eat of it
all the days of your life.
It will produce thorns and thistles for you,
and you will eat the plants of the field.
By the sweat of your brow
you will eat your food
until you return to the ground,
since from it you were taken;
for dust you are
and to dust you will return.'

Adam named his wife Eve, because she would become the mother of all the living. The Lord God made garments of skin for Adam and his wife and clothed them.

And the Lord God said, 'The man has now become like one of us, knowing good and evil. He must not be allowed to reach out his hand and take also from the tree of life and eat, and live forever'. So the Lord God banished him from the Garden of Eden to work the ground from which he had been taken. After he drove the man out, he placed on the east side of the Garden of Eden cherubim and a flaming sword flashing back and forth to guard the way to the tree of life.
(Genesis 3:13–24)

Judgement follows, and here again there is a strong element of aetiology, showing that the Fall is the explanation for many puzzling questions. The Fall of humanity is seen to be responsible for the perpetual struggle between one species and another, where Eve and the serpent are set against each other. Pain comes into the world for the first time, as well as the struggle for survival against the elements. The ground becomes 'cursed', producing thorns and thistles to make it difficult for the man to grow food except through hard work. The link is made here between the behaviour of humanity and the environment itself: the elements have to be struggled against because of human sin. People, then, have tried to become godlike, to gain the knowledge of good and evil, but instead they will be returned to the dust which formed them.

One of the many questions raised by this passage is: did God decide upon this punishment, out of a number of possibilities, or is what happens to people the inevitable result of their actions? (Rather like the difference between a mother telling her child that if he plays with the fire he inevitably will get burnt because that is the nature of fire; or her saying that if he plays with the fire, she will stop his pocket money, which is her choice.) This is a significant question, because if the punishment is inevitable, then humanity could be blamed for the evil and suffering in the natural world; but if God chose the punishment, then God can be blamed, as he could have chosen something else instead, or perhaps decided to forgive them.

Adam names his wife Eve, showing his authority over her. God clothes the people with animal skins, demonstrating that God still cares for people and provides for their needs even though they have disobeyed him. God decides to expel the people from the Garden of Eden, because they have eaten from the tree of the knowledge of good and evil, and 'become like one of us', and there is the danger that they might also eat from the tree of life and gain immortality. This is a strange verse, as it suggests that there could be a whole pantheon of gods, and it also suggests that God might have been jealous of his own position and wanting to guard against the possibility of having equals, as if this were a real possibility.

Did God know, when he created humanity, that people would disobey him?

The Genesis stories create interesting questions about God's omniscience. They imply that God did not have much idea of what people might do, and had to protect himself against possibilities. The people leave the garden, and the tree is guarded by cherubim (legendary figures, half man, half beast) with a sword, as though God could not be certain whether or not the people would try to fight their way back in.

To think about

Does the text imply that God knew from the start that people would disobey him? Or does it imply that God never intended the Fall to happen?

How does the creative God of the Bible compare with Aristotle's Prime Mover?

In many ways, the God of the Bible contrasts sharply with the Prime Mover proposed by Aristotle. The biblical God creates on purpose, choosing what to make (and, presumably, what not to make), whereas the Prime Mover does not have intentions or make decisions, because it is unchanging. The Prime Mover moves other things by drawing them towards itself, but remains unaffected by them, whereas God in the Bible takes action in order to create. The God of the Bible fashions things like a craftsman, giving them the form he wants them to have and shaping them until they satisfy him.

The God of the Bible takes an interest in his creation and makes decisions about it, which the writers describe using the imagery of a craftsman.

In Aristotle's thought, the Prime Mover could not have any bodily form or perform any bodily movements, because it had to be immaterial (otherwise it would be corruptible). However, the God of the Bible does, in places, seem to act in the way that someone with a body would act. He fashions creatures out of clay from the ground; he breathes into Adam the breath of life; he can be heard walking in the garden; he speaks to Adam and Eve with a voice and they can hear and understand what he says. However, it could be that the writers of the Bible never intended us to think that God actually has a body. These could have been meant simply as poetic ways of describing spiritual events that would otherwise have been difficult to put into words.

The God of the Bible and the Prime Mover of Aristotle also contrast in terms of their knowledge. The Prime Mover knows only itself, and thinks only of itself. It is completely unaware of the physical world, and completely unaffected by it. However, the biblical God is very much aware of the world. He is pleased with what he has made; he gives people rules about how to look after it all; he is affected by their behaviour when they choose to disobey.

Although the God of the Bible and the Prime Mover are different in many ways, both are considered to be responsible for the existence of the universe. Both God and the Prime Mover are described as the reason why the universe is here at all – why there is something, rather than nothing. Neither depends on anything else for existence, but exists 'necessarily'.

Practice exam questions

(a) Explain how the Bible portrays the creativity of God.

Questions like this can appear easy, because it might seem that you simply have to re-tell the creation stories in your own words. However, at AS level the examiners will be looking for several different points about the creativity of God; you should make reference to biblical texts to illustrate those points, but telling the whole story is not necessary. You should aim to include explanation of the concepts of *creatio ex nihilo;* creation by God's word; God as a craftsman; God creating the world for the benefit of humanity, with people as the supreme creation made in the image of God; God as involved with creation, particularly in terms of morality. When you discuss these concepts, try to give a specific example or quotation to support your answer.

(b) 'The creative God of the Bible is similar to Aristotle's Prime Mover.' Discuss.

You will already have explained the idea of the biblical God's creativity in part (a), so there is no need to repeat material. However, you will need to show understanding of Aristotle's concept of the Prime Mover, as well as making a comparison. Because this section assesses your evaluative skill, aim to make critical comment rather than simply describing. Be explicit about the similarities between the two ideas (such as that both are believed to be the reason for the existence of the universe), and the differences (such as that the God of the Bible is interested in creation whereas the Prime Mover is in every sense Unmoved); avoid just describing the two and leaving the examiner to work out what the similarities and differences are. Make sure that you arrive at a conclusion to show where your own opinion lies.

The goodness and love of God

The Bible presents God as a perfectly good being. Everything he does is good and done out of love; he is the source of all goodness and love; his nature is goodness and love. The Psalmists celebrate the goodness of God in hymns of praise:

They will celebrate your abundant goodness
and joyfully sing of your righteousness.
The Lord is gracious and compassionate,
slow to anger and rich in love.
The Lord is good to all;
he has compassion on all he has made.   (Psalm 145: 7–9)

For the Lord is good and his love endures forever;
his faithfulness continues through all generations.   (Psalm 100:5)

To think about

If God is perfectly good, does this mean he is unable to do wrong? If he is unable to do wrong, can he still be omnipotent?

The biblical writers illustrate the goodness of God in a number of ways:

God's goodness is revealed in the creation and the sustaining of the world. In the Genesis story, everything that God makes is 'very good'. He chooses and forms the different plants and animals that will live in the world, and he provides them with things to eat and water to drink. When the writers of the Bible praise God's goodness, it is often because God provides for the needs of his creation, giving the seasons and the harvest. Many religious believers claim that there is evidence of the goodness of God in the world around us. Through looking at the beauty of nature and the ways in which the Earth seems to be designed for the benefit of the people in it, God's goodness can be seen:

Sing to the Lord with thanksgiving;
make music to our God on the harp.

He covers the sky with clouds;
he supplies the earth with rain
and makes grass grow on the hills. (Psalm 147:7–8)

God as lawgiver and judge

In contrast with Plato's Form of Good, the God of the Bible is interested in moral behaviour. The Form of the Good is an idea or concept, which is incapable of taking an interest in anything, but the God of the Bible is concerned that humanity should make the right choices and aim to be good. As soon as humanity is created, God gives them moral rules to follow: they are to take responsibility for the planet as its stewards, and they are not to eat from the forbidden tree. When God chooses the Jews as his special people, again they are given rules to follow, and these rules illustrate that God does not just care about being worshipped, but is also interested in the way in which people treat one another. He gives them rules about family life, for example, telling them how they should treat their parents:

Honour your father and your mother, so that you may live long in the land the Lord your God is giving you. (Exodus 20:12)

In the Bible, God gives people the freedom to make moral choices, but also makes clear what is the right thing to do. He does not force people to obey the rules; but he does punish them when they disobey him.

To think about

Do you think a good God should have given people free will to choose whatever actions they want to take? Or should God have made people so that they were only capable of doing good?

When God becomes angry with people, it is not because of their failure to perform religious rituals correctly, but because of their moral behaviour. They constantly fail to live up to the standard of God's goodness in failing to show love towards one another. When God is particularly angry, it is because people have been callous towards the poor, ignoring those in need of their help. The prophet Amos, for example, warns the people of impending punishment because they have exploited the weak and failed to do anything to help those in trouble:

They trample on the heads of the poor
as upon the dust of the ground
and deny justice to the oppressed. (Amos 2:7)

The God of the Bible, then, is not simply the creator of goodness and the perfect example of goodness. God gives people laws to follow because of his relationship with the world he has created. Unlike Aristotle's Prime Mover, who thinks only of himself and his own nature, the God of the Bible is ultimately concerned with human behaviour. He knows people's inmost thoughts, he sees their every action, and he gives them laws to make sure that they understand how to distinguish a right action from a wrong one.

God gives these laws as written rules, for example as the Ten Commandments on the tablets of stone brought down by Moses from Mount Sinai; he also gives laws through the words of the prophets, spoken to the people and recorded by the writers of the Bible.

There is also the suggestion in the Bible that God gives people a conscience, a kind of inner law-giving voice helping them to discern right from wrong. Different Christian thinkers through the centuries have presented different understandings of how the conscience operates; in the Bible, the prophet Jeremiah looks forward to a time when there would be no need for written laws and teachings because people would know 'in their hearts' what God wanted them to do, and so there would be no need for judgement (Jeremiah 31).

Alongside the concept of God as lawgiver is the view that there will be consequences for people if they disobey God's commands. Although there is a popular conception that the New Testament is about forgiveness rather than judgement, the parable of the sheep and goats in Matthew's gospel echoes Amos' message of punishment for those who ignore the needy:

When the Son of Man comes in his glory, and all the angels with him, he will sit on his throne in heavenly glory. All the nations will be gathered before him, and he will separate the people one from another as a shepherd separates the sheep from the goats. He will put the sheep on his right and the goats on his left.

Then the King will say to those on his right, 'Come, you who are blessed by my Father; take your inheritance, the kingdom prepared for you since the creation of the world. For I was hungry and you gave me something to eat, I was thirsty and you gave me something to drink, I was a stranger and you invited me in, I needed clothes and you clothed me, I was sick and you looked after me, I was in prison and you came to visit me.'

Then the righteous will answer him, 'Lord, when did we see you hungry and feed you, or thirsty and give you something to drink? When did we see you a stranger and invite you in, or needing clothes and clothe you? When did we see you sick or in prison and go to visit you?'

The King will reply, 'I tell you the truth, whatever you did for one of the least of these brothers of mine, you did for me.'

Then he will say to those on his left, 'Depart from me, you who are cursed, into the eternal fire prepared for the devil and his angels. For I was hungry and you gave me nothing to eat, I was thirsty and you gave me nothing to drink, I was a stranger and you did not invite me in, I needed clothes and you did not clothe me, I was sick and in prison and you did not look after me.'

They also will answer, 'Lord, when did we see you hungry or thirsty or a stranger or needing clothes or sick or in prison, and did not help you?'

He will reply, 'I tell you the truth, whatever you did not do for one of the least of these, you did not do for me.'

Then they will go away to eternal punishment, but the righteous to eternal life.
(Matthew 25: 31–46)

This passage, and several others, suggest that God's judgement will be for people after death, or at the end of time, when those who have obeyed God will gain an eternal reward, while the others will be sent away to eternal punishment. In the New Testament, the judgement of God is linked very much with beliefs about the afterlife; however, in the Old Testament, God's judgement was often seen as the explanation for present events. Good fortune was seen as a reward for obedience to the laws of God, and bad luck such as defeat in battle was seen as God's punishment to the whole people, collectively, for their disobedience.

> *Tell the righteous it will be well with them,*
> *for they will enjoy the fruit of their deeds.*
> *Woe to the wicked!*
> *Disaster is upon them!*
> *They will be paid back*
> *for what their hands have done.*
> (Isaiah 3:10–11)

In Christianity, although God is believed to punish those who disobey, this is always seen in the context of goodness and love. God punishes because he wants his people to learn how to behave, in the same way that a good parent or teacher will exercise authority and discipline.

God's goodness is shown in his forgiveness and compassion. He takes pity on people when they are suffering. For example, Hannah was married to a man named Elkanah, who also had another wife. The other wife, called Peninnah, had children, but Hannah was infertile. This was a cause of friction between them; Peninnah would boast of her children and upset Hannah, who eventually turned to God and asked him for a son.

She promised God that if only she could have a son, that son would be dedicated to God's service; and God took pity on her, resulting in the birth of the prophet Samuel.

For Christians, God's goodness is exemplified in the person of Jesus and his sacrifice on the cross. In Christian belief, God chose to come to the world as a man, to live, to suffer and to make choices in the same way that people have to, and to pay the price for the sins of the world:

> *For God so loved the world that he gave his one and only Son, that whoever believes in him shall not perish but have eternal life.* (John 3:16)

Christians believe that Jesus was the 'pattern' of moral goodness for humanity, showing people the right way to treat each other and to behave towards God. Through parables and miracles, he taught his followers not to repay evil with evil, but to love each other and to forgive their enemies. He taught them to look for 'treasure in heaven' rather than storing up material wealth in this world, and to give their riches to the poor. He taught them to put themselves last in the service of others, to be willing to give up their lives if necessary, and to recognise the 'image of God' in themselves and in other people.

Christians believe that because God sacrificed himself on the cross, they can have certain knowledge of the ultimate goodness of God, even when they encounter difficulties, tragedies and pain in their own lives. They may not always be able to understand why God allows certain events to happen, but because of Jesus' death on the cross, they can be confident of the eternal goodness of God.

Does the God of the Bible really show perfect goodness?

Some people argue that the God of the Old Testament is not particularly good, and they point to passages in the Bible that seem to show a God whose decisions and actions are difficult for us to appreciate as examples of 'goodness'. Richard Dawkins, in his book *The God Delusion,* claims that the Bible is meant to be a source of morality in that it gives people rules to follow, and also presents God as a role model for people to copy. He does not think that either of these ways of guiding moral behaviour is acceptable:

> *Both scriptural routes, if followed through religiously (the adverb is used in its metaphorical sense but with an eye to its origin), encourage a system of morals which any civilized modern person, whether religious or not, would find – I can put it no more gently – obnoxious. (Richard Dawkins,* The God Delusion, *Bantam 2006)*

To think about

Do you think that Dawkins is making a fair point when he claims that the God of the Bible is immoral? How would you attack or support Dawkins' position?

Dawkins gives several examples of stories from the Bible which he finds morally objectionable, but the one he chooses as the worst is the story of Abraham and Isaac. In this story, God commands his faithful servant Abraham to kill his beloved son Isaac, as a sacrifice. Abraham is prepared to obey God's word, and takes his son to the mountain where he makes an altar and gets a fire ready. It is only at the last minute that God allows an angel to intervene and stop Abraham, revealing that it was a test of faith which Abraham had passed. In Dawkins' view, this shows a God who is immoral; he puts both Abraham and his son through a terrible ordeal, just to satisfy his own curiosity.

Other critics have pointed out that the God of the Old Testament can be jealous and angry; that he appears to have favourites; that he appears to use people as a means to an end, and that he often not only condones but commands and encourages killing:

When the Lord your God brings you into the land you are entering to possess and drives out before you many nations – the Hittites, Girgashites, Amorites, Canaanites, Perizzites, Hivites and Jebusites, seven nations larger and stronger than you – and when the Lord your God has delivered them over to you and you have defeated them, then you must destroy them totally. Make no treaty with them, and show them no mercy. (Deuteronomy 7:1–2)

There are also times where God's punishments seem less than just. When King David has Uriah killed so that he can marry Uriah's wife Bathsheba, God punishes David by killing his baby son, but he allows David himself to live and to carry on as king. However, in a different incident, Lot's wife commits the comparatively minor offence of looking back over her shoulder to the city from which she was escaping, and she is turned into a pillar of salt.

The Euthyphro dilemma

The problem known as the 'Euthyphro dilemma' is attributed to Plato, although it may have been a popular puzzle with which Plato was familiar, rather than his own invention. In his work *Euthyphro,* from which the puzzle gets its name, Plato raises the question: 'Is piety loved by the gods because it is pious, or is it piety because it is loved by the gods?' In other words, does piety only become good because it happens to be what the gods like – so that it has no intrinsic goodness of its own – or do they love it because it is intrinsically good, regardless of the gods' opinion? When Socrates debates the issue with Euthyphro, they are trying to understand the nature of piety and the relation that it has with the will of the gods.

In Christianity, Islam and Judaism, the question is still important, although it is altered slightly to apply to monotheistic belief. Is something morally good simply because God commands it, or does God command it because it is good?

Difficulties arise whichever option is chosen. If something is morally good simply because God commands it, then there are problems. This choice suggests that there is no sound reasoning for thinking that some actions are better than others, except for the arbitrary whim of God. If God decided that murder was good, or cruelty, or theft, then these things would be good. If God decided that compassion was bad, or honesty, or love, then these things would be bad. It implies that we only have the moral standards we recognise as good through chance. A further difficulty with this option is that it makes a nonsense of the idea of calling God 'good'. If something is morally good because God commands it, then to call God good is to say nothing meaningful at all.

However, if we choose the other option, in which God commands things because they are good, this also raises a problem. It implies that there is some kind of external measure of goodness against which God can be judged along with everything else. God is not in control of morality, but subject to it.

To think about

When God commands people to go to war, is going to war the right thing to do because God commands it? Or does God command going to war because it is good?

When reading the Bible and considering God's moral commands and actions, the difficulty can be seen. Are the Ten Commandments random choices made by God, without any intrinsic goodness apart from the fact that God commanded them? If, perhaps, instead of forbidding murder, God had commanded that people always wear yellow on a Tuesday, would wearing yellow on Tuesdays therefore have been morally right, and wearing other colours instead have been a sin? This does not seem to be consistent with other biblical teaching, or with our moral intuitions. It would appear that God gave these commands because they are good, rather than just arbitrarily.

However, the Bible does not appear to support the view that there is some kind of external standard of goodness against which God can be judged and to which God is subject. When God creates the world, everything he makes is 'very good'; the implication is that in the creative act, God determines goodness, creating it as he creates the universe. Things are good because God commands them; so when Eve takes and eats the fruit from the tree in the middle of the garden, in direct disobedience to the commandment of God, she is doing wrong. Eating the fruit was wrong because God had explicitly told her not to do it; there is nothing intrinsically wrong with eating fruit. Similarly, in the story of Abraham and Isaac, Abraham is praised and rewarded for his goodness in following God's command. Willingness to sacrifice Isaac was good simply because God commanded it, and not because it was good 'in itself'.

Different Christian theologians have considered the problem raised by the Euthyphro dilemma and tried to provide a Christian response to it. The most popular and influential view came from Thomas Aquinas in the thirteenth century. Aquinas argued that the Euthyphro dilemma was not a real problem for Christianity, because both parts can be accepted without there being any contradiction. God commands things because they are good; but he knows what to command with perfect knowledge, because his nature is entirely good. So God would never command something like murder or cruelty. God is Goodness-Itself, and as goodness is part of his character, God's moral commands are and will always be expressions of the goodness of his nature.

Practice exam questions

(a) Explain biblical ideas about the goodness of God.

In this section, to achieve high marks you need to make several different points, and support them with examples and quotations. The question is explicitly about the goodness of God in the Bible, so aim to keep closely to biblical ideas and avoid becoming side-tracked by other issues. You could include ideas such as: the goodness of God shown in creation (as expressed in Genesis); the goodness of God shown in his sustaining the world (as expressed in the Psalms); the goodness of God in giving moral guidance (as in the Ten Commandments); the goodness of God in punishing those who oppress the weak (as in the prophets); the goodness of God in sacrificing his son (as in the gospels).

(b) Assess the claim that some of God's actions in the Bible are morally wrong.

For this section, you could make reference to thinkers such as Dawkins who claim that the morality of God is 'obnoxious'. Show that you understand why people might say this, perhaps using examples from the Bible. Give your own assessment of this opinion, either supporting it or rejecting it, and explain your reasons. You might want to include reference to the Euthyphro dilemma, because perhaps, if God does something, then it can only be morally right.

Traditional arguments
for the existence of God

How far is it possible to demonstrate the existence of God? Traditionally, believers have tried to show, through personal stories of religious experience, through the way they live and through philosophical debate, that God does exist; and other people have tried to show, with counter-argument, that he does not.

One obvious problem with trying to demonstrate the existence of God is that God is not available to the senses. If God exists at all, then he cannot be seen, heard, tasted, smelled or touched in the same way as other existent beings. Perhaps 'exists' is not the right word to use of a being which is so very different from the physical world available to sense experience. According to Christian understandings of God, God is unique – an infinite spirit who created everything out of nothing, who is uncreated himself, who is eternal, omnipotent and omniscient, who is love itself, almighty and yet personal, capable of having relationships with his creation. Yet this kind of 'existence' is hardly the same as the existence which we have and which other physical objects have. The philosopher Bertrand Russell suggested that the word 'exists' was being used in such a different way, when we speak of God, that questions of the existence of God are not proper or answerable questions. Nevertheless, we usually assume that we understand the question 'does God exist?' even if we are understanding 'existence' in a radically different way from the way that we use the word if we are discussing, for example, the existence of the Loch Ness Monster.

The theologian Paul Tillich also raised the same issue of whether 'does God exist?' is a real question, but, unlike Russell, Tillich argued from a theist position. According to Tillich, 'existence' is something which relates to things that are created. Therefore, if people say 'God exists', they imply that God is on the same level as a finite, created object in the world. In Tillich's understanding, God is not a 'thing'. If an inventory could be made of all the 'things' in the universe, God would not be on that list – but that does not mean that there is no God. Tillich argued that God is not a *being* but is *being-itself*, the ground of all existence and the reason why everything finite has come into existence and remains in existence. To emphasise his point, when Tillich wrote of God, he used the term 'Being-Itself' instead of 'God'. So for Tillich, the question 'Does God exist?' makes about as much sense as asking 'Does existence exist?'

To think about

Would you agree with Tillich in his view that 'exists' is the wrong word to use of God? Why, or why not?

When people say that unicorns don't exist, they mean that if you could look at all the things in the world, you would not find anything which matched our understanding of 'unicorn'. However, if God is not one of the 'things in the world', but something different entirely, what does it mean to say that God does or doesn't exist?

In spite of objections such as those of Russell or Tillich, people have nevertheless attempted to show, using argument, that God does exist, and that the faith of believers is reasonable and logical.

Inductive and deductive arguments

Before we look at specific arguments for the existence of God, it is useful to have some understanding of what an argument is, and what it might be expected to achieve. When we use the word 'argument' in conversation, we often mean a disagreement: 'You were flirting with my boyfriend …' 'No I wasn't …' 'Yes you were!' and so on. But in philosophical terms, an argument is not the same as a string of contradictions with a few insults thrown in. An argument has a conclusion (or several conclusions), and these are supported by reasons in an attempt to persuade someone that the conclusions are true.

Many arguments are based on **inductive** reasoning, and others are based on **deductive** reasoning.

Inductive reasoning

Inductive reasoning is when people make inferences and draw general conclusions from particular examples. We see things happening a lot, and we conclude that (probably) they always, or usually, happen. The person doing the reasoning uses observation, and bases his or her thinking on previous experience, to make general rules or predictions:

The inductive argument leads to a conclusion which may be true, but could be wrong.

Inductive reasoning led Europeans to the conclusion that all swans were white, because all the swans they had ever seen were white. They realised that this conclusion was wrong when they discovered black swans in Australia.

Inductive arguments can be stronger or weaker as arguments, depending on the quality of the reasoning and the amount of reliable data available. If an inductive argument is based on only very little observation to draw a general conclusion, then it is a very weak argument; for example:

There were two robberies in my neighbourhood last month. Both were committed by black teenagers. Therefore, all crime is committed by black teenagers.

One type of inductive reasoning is **analogy**. Analogy is where similarities between two different things are used to support the conclusion that, if they are similar in ways A, B and C, then they are likely to be similar in way D as well. Some analogies are weaker than others:

Tigger and Marmaduke are both cats. They both like rabbit-flavoured cat food, tuna, chicken and lamb. Tigger likes beef, so Marmaduke will probably like beef as well.

Kate and Isabel both like shopping for shoes. They are both vegetarian, in their twenties, and both are architects. Kate supports Arsenal; therefore Isabel probably supports Arsenal too.

The human eye is like a camera: both have facilities to regulate the amount of light that enters, a lens which adjusts the size of the image, and a light- and colour-sensitive surface to receive the image. Cameras were made by intelligent designers; therefore eyes must have been made by an intelligent designer too.

The strength of analogy in an argument depends on how closely similar the two things really are, and whether they are similar in ways which are relevant to the conclusion. In the examples above, the analogy between one cat and another cat is strong, because different cats are similar in many different ways, and we can observe through experience that food preferences is one of these ways. In the second example, the reasoning is weaker, because although these young women share similarities, their football team of choice is not relevant to the other similarities. The third example, of the human eye being like a manufactured machine, is often used as part of one of the traditional arguments for the existence of God; it will be up to you to decide whether it is a good enough analogy to support the conclusion.

Deductive reasoning

Deductive reasoning is the kind where, if the premises (starting-points) of the argument are true, then the conclusion must also be true. The conclusion is a logical consequence of the premises. An example of deductive reasoning might be:

All cows are mammals. Tabitha is a cow. Therefore, Tabitha is a mammal.

With an inductive argument, the conclusion could be false even if the premises are true. The group of friends in the earlier example might have been sick because of the

Key terms

analogy – when similar things are compared as a way of clarifying or supporting a point.

amount they drank at the restaurant rather than because of the food. But with a deductive argument, the conclusion is an inevitable result of the logic of the premises. It is not based on observation or experience, but on logical processes.

Develop your knowledge

Detailed discussions of different ways of arguing and of evaluating arguments can be found in books about critical thinking skills, such as:
Critical Thinking: An Introduction by Alec Fisher (Cambridge University Press, 2001)
Critical Reasoning: A Practical Introduction by Anne Thomson (Routledge, 2002)
For a briefer outline in the context of the philosophy of religion, pp.40–44 of:
Philosophy of Religion: Thinking about Faith by C. Stephen Evans (Intervarsity Press, 1985)

A *priori* and a *posteriori* arguments

Another very similar way of classifying arguments is into two categories: *a priori* arguments, and *a posteriori* arguments. *A priori* arguments, like deductive arguments, are those which rely only on the processes of logic to prove a point. You do not need to have any particular experiences or provide any evidence, in order to make the proof; the proof can be made solely through the logic of the argument. *A posteriori* arguments, in contrast, are those which depend on some kind of evidence to support them. They derive from experience, they come after or 'are posterior to' experience of the way that things are. These sorts of arguments look at the world, and say that we experience X to be the case, and that therefore Y must be true. Examples of *a posteriori* arguments for the existence of God are design arguments, the moral arguments, the cosmological arguments and the arguments from religious experience.

Can God's existence be demonstrated through argument?

Someone who does not believe in God is not going to change his or her opinion because of the arguments of reason and logic, even if these are sound. There is more to religious belief than just agreeing to a set of statements: it goes beyond the bounds of reason. This does not mean that it has to be unreasonable; but religious belief consists of more than simple agreement that an argument appears to work. It involves commitment to a new way of looking at the world and of behaviour.

Religious belief, like being in love, is much more than just an intellectual acceptance of certain assertions. It involves emotions, intuitions and commitment. It does not depend on the strength of a logical argument, and can sometimes seem to fly in the face of common sense. Just as someone in love might still be in love even when the other person's faults are glaringly obvious, so too the religious believer might continue in complete faith in the existence of God even when obvious flaws in the philosophical arguments have been clearly demonstrated. Whether this faith is therefore misplaced remains debatable.

Faith in God seems to demand an element of uncertainty, and a willingness to take risks in spite of an absence of concrete proof. What would happen if God could be proven beyond all reasonable doubt – if God made himself known in a way that everyone would accept? Many people would argue that God has already done this, through revelation; Christians might argue that the experiences recorded in the Bible, for example, are proof of God's existence, and that the life and resurrection of Jesus were a clear demonstration of God showing people once and for all that he truly exists. But others do not accept these examples as proof.

Believers often point out that God must remain partially hidden from the world, in order to maintain **epistemic distance**. By this, they mean that the world should remain 'religiously ambiguous'. It is right that there should be no conclusive evidence for the existence of God, just as there should be no conclusive evidence against it. People should be able to see and explain the world purely in naturalistic terms, or as coming from and sustained by God, and have the freedom to decide for themselves which position to take. Only with this epistemic distance, it is argued, is it possible for humans to have a genuinely free will to exercise faith and moral judgements. If God's existence were undeniable, faith would mean nothing, and people would have no choice but to believe.

To think about

What would God have to do to make himself known to people so that his existence became unquestionable?

Most of the writers who have attempted to show the existence of God through reasoned argument recognised that their arguments do not constitute incontrovertible proof. However, what they do try to show is that belief in God is *reasonable*, and even *probable*; it can be accepted logically that God exists. Theism is an option that a sensible person might take, and religious belief is not a sign of madness, weakness or stupidity.

Key term

epistemic distance – a distance in knowledge or awareness.

Ontological arguments

Ontology is the branch of philosophy that explores the whole concept of existence. It is important to recognise that there are different kinds of existence. For example, you and I exist in a physical sense – we take up space, we can be seen and heard and presented as Exhibit A – but prime numbers exist in a different sense, in the realm of mathematical concepts, even though they are not available to the senses and have no physical properties. Forgiveness, boredom and jealousy exist, but in a different sense again. Sometimes scientists have to assume that something exists in reality in the physical world, even if they have never come across an example of it, because a combination of factors indicate that there must be X, even if we have not found it yet, in order to explain other things. Discoveries on the fringes of physics, for example, often work on assumptions that some things exist even before we have any real evidence of them.

The field of ontology, then, explores what it means for something to exist.

The ontological argument for the existence of God is an *a priori* argument, working from first principles and definitions in an attempt to demonstrate the existence of God. It is also a deductive argument, using logic rather than depending on the evidence of sense experience. In this way, then, the ontological argument is different from other attempts to argue for the existence of God.

According to the ontological argument, almost everything which exists does so in a contingent way; it depends upon other factors. We, as individuals, are contingent beings, because we would not exist if our parents had not existed before us, and we would not continue to exist if we had no food, water or oxygen. Everything else (apart from God) exists contingently too. It exists because of other circumstances, and under some conditions it would cease to exist.

This pencil has contingent existence. There was a time when it did not exist; there are things that could happen to stop it from existing.

To think about

What does grass depend on, to come into existence? What does it need to keep it in existence? What could happen to cause grass to stop existing?

Think about some other things which exist, and ask yourself the same questions of it.

Can you think of anything, apart from God, which exists but which does not depend on anything else for its existence?

God, however, it is argued by religious believers, is *necessary* rather than *contingent*. God is not a 'thing'; God has not come about because of anything; there was no time when God did not exist, and there is nothing that could happen which would cause God to cease to exist.

When Paul Tillich argued that God does not 'exist' in the way that the things in the universe exist, he was making the same point. God's existence is different from the existence of anything else.

Key point

- Supporters of the ontological argument claim that God's existence is different from ours, because we are contingent beings, whereas God has necessary existence. In this way, the ontological argument has close similarities with design arguments and cosmological arguments, because each depends on the idea that the existence of God is different from any other kind of existence.

Anselm and the ontological argument

St Anselm (1033–1109) was an Archbishop of Canterbury and a Benedictine monk. He produced the ontological argument from the perspective of 'faith seeking understanding' rather than in an attempt to convert unbelievers, although the argument is phrased in such a way that it presents a challenge to the atheist and the theist alike.

Anselm believed that faith was more important than reasoned argument. He presented his ontological argument as 'faith seeking understanding'.

Anselm set out his argument in his book *Proslogion*. It is usually agreed that Anselm gives his argument in two different forms, although some people believe that it is all part of the same train of thought. In the first form, Anselm starts by defining God as 'that than which nothing greater can be thought'. We all, he argued, would agree that this is what we mean by God (whether we actually believe in him or not). God is understood to be the highest sum of all perfections, where absolutely nothing could ever surpass God in any way.

To think about

Do you agree with Anselm's definition of God? If there were a God, is this what God would have to be like?

Anselm argued that if we have an idea of a God who is perfect in every way, where nothing could possibly be greater, then this God must exist in reality – because a God who just exists in our heads, as something we imagined to be great but did not actually exist, would be inferior to a real God – and we have already agreed that God cannot be inferior to anything in any way. So God must exist, in order to meet our definition of 'that than which nothing greater can be thought'.

Key point

- Anselm's ontological argument says that as God cannot be surpassed, the concept of God without real existence is a contradiction in terms; there must be an actual, existent God which surpasses the concept.

Supporters of Anselm use analogies to make their point. What would be greater, they say – a huge heap of cash that exists in your imagination only, or that same heap of cash on your kitchen table? Which would you prefer – the daydream of a beautiful summer day on a beach of soft sand with sparkling blue shark-free waters, or being at that same scene in reality? Existing in reality, they say, is far better than only existing as an idea.

It could be argued, of course, that there are some things which we would prefer not to exist: we might think, for example, that the best possible kind of boy band is one which does not exist at all in reality. However, these are always things which (in our opinions) are bad or undesirable things, whereas for Anselm, God's goodness is an aspect of his greatness. In Anselm's understanding of God, no one could seriously argue that a non-existent God would surpass an existent God in greatness.

1. Anselm's first form of the ontological argument, in summary, follows the line of argument that:

God is that than which nothing greater can be thought.

A real, existent being would be greater than an imaginary, illusory being.

Therefore, the concept of God is surpassed by an actual, existent God.

2. In the second form of his argument, which is closely linked to the first, Anselm argued that it was impossible for God not to exist. The argument goes like this:

God is that than which nothing greater can be thought.

Contingent beings (those which come in and out of existence, and which depend on other things for their existence) are inferior to beings with necessary existence (which are eternal and depend on nothing else for their existence, and of which the only example is God).

Because God is unsurpassable in every way, God must have necessary existence.

Therefore God exists – necessarily.

Here, Anselm argued that God must exist, because a necessary being cannot fail to exist – only contingent beings do that. Necessary existence is, in Anselm's view, part of the whole definition of God. It made no sense to Anselm to talk of a God who does not exist, because then he would not be God.

> ## Key point
>
> • Anselm was arguing that God, by his very nature, must exist, and must exist necessarily.

For Anselm, then, the existence of God is not something which needs to be demonstrated by referring to evidence. It is something which we can know simply by considering the concept of 'God', and working out what this means.

Analytic and synthetic propositions

In order to fully understand the ontological argument, it is necessary to draw a distinction between two different kinds of proposition (a proposition is a statement which 'proposes' something, or says that such-and-such is the case).

One kind of proposition is the **analytic proposition**. An analytic proposition is one which is true by definition: the usual example given is 'bachelors are unmarried men'. There is nothing we need to do to test this proposition – it can be arrived at through deduction. As long as we know what a bachelor is, then we can accept that he is an unmarried man, because the concept of being a bachelor includes the concepts of being unmarried and being male. If he were married, or not a man, then the word 'bachelor' would not apply. Anselm, in his ontological argument, was claiming that the statement 'God exists' is analytic – in other words, that the concept of God includes the concept of existence, and without existence, the term 'God' would not apply.

The other kind of proposition is a **synthetic proposition**. A synthetic proposition is one which adds something to our understanding, beyond the definition of the word, and we need more than just deduction to know whether or not it is true – we also need experience. So, for example, 'The corner shop sells newspapers' is a synthetic proposition, as the concept of a corner shop does not include the concept of selling newspapers. It might be a florist's or a butcher's shop – you would have to go to the shop and see if they had any newspapers and if they were prepared to let you buy one, if you wanted to know the truth of the proposition.

> ## Key point
>
> • Anselm held that 'God exists' is an analytic *a priori* statement. The concept of existence is part of the concept of God, he argued.

Anselm made reference to Psalm 53:1:

The fool says in his heart,
'There is no God.'
They are corrupt, and their ways are vile;
there is no-one who does good.

He found it difficult to understand how anyone could have the concept of God as 'that than which nothing can be conceived' without also realising that God must exist. As soon as someone understands what God is, then God's existence is surely obvious. Anselm asked:

Why, then, did the fool say in his heart 'God is not', since it is so obvious to the rational mind that you exist supremely above all things? Why, because he is a dim-witted fool … How was the fool able to 'say in his heart' what he was unable to conceive? (from Classical and Contemporary Readings in the Philosophy of Religion, *ed. John Hick, Prentice Hall, 1989)*

Gaunilo's criticisms of Anselm

Gaunilo was a French monk who was a contemporary of St Anselm, and he was the first to raise objections to Anselm's idea that God exists by definition. Gaunilo, then, like Anselm was a Christian, but he believed that Anselm's argument was not logical and therefore needed to be refuted.

Gaunilo claimed that the flaws in Anselm's logic would be made obvious if we go through the argument again, replacing the idea of God with the idea of an island. In his writings *On Behalf of the Fool*, he explained that we could imagine the most excellent Lost Island; we understand the implications of the phrase 'the most excellent island' and therefore this notion exists as a concept in our understanding. We might then, using Anselm's logic, go on to say that for such an island to exist in our minds means that this is inferior to the same island existing in reality. If our island is truly the most excellent, it cannot have the inferiority that comes from it being a concept only – it must therefore exist in reality. But clearly, there is no such island in reality. We cannot bring something into existence just by defining it as superlative.

Gaunilo argued that if we replace 'God' with 'island' in Anselm's argument, we can see how the argument falls down.

Gaunilo writes:

> *When someone tells me there is such an island, I easily understand what is being said, for there is nothing difficult here. Suppose, however, he then goes on to say: you cannot doubt that this island, more excellent than all lands, actually exists somewhere in reality … I would think he were joking; or if I accepted the argument, I do not know whom I would regard as the greater fool, me for accepting it or him for supposing that he had proved the existence of this island with any kind of certainty. (Classical and Contemporary Readings in the Philosophy of Religion, ed. John Hick, Prentice Hall, 1989)*

Anselm was impressed with Gaunilo's argument, and included it in later versions of his own book, along with his reply. Anselm argued that, although Gaunilo was right in the case of an island, the same objections did not work when the ontological argument was used of God, because an island has contingent existence, whereas God's existence is necessary. The argument works only when applied to God, because of the uniqueness of God and the unique way in which he exists – which was part of the whole point of the ontological argument.

Aquinas' criticisms of Anselm

Thomas Aquinas (1225–74) also argued against Anselm, even though he was firmly convinced of the existence of God himself. One of his points was that God's existence cannot be regarded as self-evident. He said that if we take, in contrast, such a statement as 'Truth does not exist', then we can see it is a nonsensical statement, because no one can accept the truth of 'truth does not exist' unless truth actually does exist after all. It is impossible to have a mental concept of the non-existence of truth because it is a contradiction in terms. It is not, however, impossible to have a mental concept of the non-existence of God, because people quite clearly manage it, including the fool who says in his heart 'There is no God'. If we can imagine a state of godlessness, then it cannot be a contradiction in terms, despite Anselm's claim.

Aquinas also questioned whether everyone would accept Anselm's definition of God as 'that than which nothing greater can be thought'. Aquinas believed that although we can approach an understanding and awareness of God, God will always remain unknowable to the finite human mind. He also raised doubts about whether this concept, even if universally shared, could indicate that such a being existed in reality:

> *Perhaps not everyone who hears the name 'God' understands it to signify something than which nothing greater can be thought, seeing that some have believed God to be a body. Yet, granted that everyone understands that by this name 'God' is signified something than which nothing greater can be thought, nevertheless, it does not therefore follow that he understands that what the name signifies exists actually, but only that it exists mentally.* (Basic Writings of Thomas Aquinas, *ed. Anton Pegis, Random House, 1945)*

Aquinas argued that there had to be more than just a definition in order to show the existence of God; it was necessary to provide firm evidence, rather than just argument, and this evidence was, he hoped, explained in his Five Ways (see pages 85–90).

Descartes' version of the ontological argument

Although Aquinas had argued that one reason the ontological argument does not work is that we do not know what God is, René Descartes (1596–1650) disagreed. Descartes was a very influential mathematician, philosopher and scientist, who reformulated the ontological argument in his work *Meditations*.

Descartes, like Anselm and Plato before him, believed that people were born with innate ideas – in other words, that there are some concepts which are imprinted on our minds from birth and which are universally shared by all of humanity. (This is an idea that has been revisited by psychologists such as Jung. Descartes thought that we understand such concepts as equality, cause, shape and number from birth; and he also believed that we are born with an understanding of what God is. We understand God to be the supremely perfect being, with all the perfections as his attributes. By 'perfections', Descartes meant the traditional attributes of God such as omniscience, omnipotence and omnibenevolence.

Descartes explained his understanding of how this innate idea demonstrated the existence of God, by using the analogy of a triangle, and also the analogy of a mountain. Descartes claimed that existence is part of the essence of God, just as three angles adding up to 180 degrees are part of the essence of a triangle, and a valley is part of the essence of a mountain:

Key terms

Cartesian – relating to Descartes and his thought.

Existence can no more be separated from the essence of God than can its having three angles equal to two right angles be separated from the essence of a triangle, or the idea of a mountain from the idea of a valley... (Descartes, Meditations V, trans. E. S. Haldane and G. R. T. Ross, Cambridge University Press, 1911)

Descartes recognised that the analogies have their limitations. While we might not be able to think of a mountain without also thinking of a valley, this does not mean that the mountain-and-valley combination in our imaginations actually exist in the real world. God, however, in Descartes' view, is different, because his nature involves not angles or valleys but perfections – and, for Descartes, existence is a perfection. Because God has all the perfections, and existence is a perfection, God therefore exists. Descartes goes on to say that as God is perfect, he must be unchanging, and so he must always have existed and will always continue to exist for eternity.

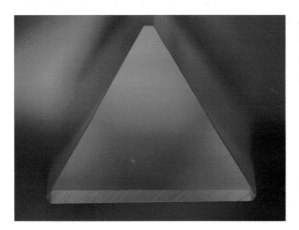

Descartes argued that just as three angles are an essential part of triangularity, so existence is an essential aspect of God.

Kant's critique of ontological arguments

Many thinkers believe that Kant's criticism of ontological arguments for the existence of God finally demolished such arguments. Kant argued that 'existence is not a predicate'; in other words, existence is not a characteristic or an attribute of something. Predicates of something describe what that thing is like – it might be green, or tall, or round, or sharp. But 'existence', Kant argued, is not the same as a predicate, it does not tell us anything about the object that would help us to identify it in any way. When we say that something 'exists', we are not saying that it has this or that quality or characteristic. What we are saying instead is that this concept, with all its characteristics, has been 'actualised' – that there is at least one example of something with these characteristics in real life.

Kant's point, when applied to ontological arguments, is that when we are thinking of

God, whether it is as Anselm's 'that than which nothing greater can be conceived' or Descartes' sum of all the perfections, we are thinking of a concept. Whether or not that concept is actualised is an issue, but not an issue that can be resolved simply by adding 'existence' to the different predicates we are ascribing to our concept. We can predicate of a triangle that it has three sides, and that its angles add up to 180 degrees, but we would have to investigate to find out whether the triangle we are picturing in our minds has been actualised. We can predicate of a unicorn that it is like a horse and has a single straight horn in the middle of its forehead, but adding 'exists' to our description will not make any difference to whether or not the concept 'unicorn' is actualised so that we could go and find one.

It could be argued, of course, in response to Kant, that God's existence is different from the existence of anything else, because other things exist contingently whereas God exists necessarily. Perhaps necessary existence is a predicate – but it can only be predicated of God. This argument, however, is unlikely to impress the sceptic, who may respond by saying that this makes the ontological argument circular: we have to accept that God exists necessarily, in order to come to the conclusion that God exists necessarily.

Modern versions of ontological arguments: Malcolm and Plantinga

Although many believe that Kant's criticisms of the ontological argument are fatal to it, nevertheless the argument has been revived in the twentieth and twenty-first centuries.

Norman Malcolm (1911–90) accepted that Kant was right to say that existence is not a predicate. However, Malcolm believed that the idea of God's necessary existence, from the second formulation of Anselm's argument, could still be used to provide a successful ontological argument. Malcolm argued that in order to be God, God must have necessary existence; he could not come into existence if he did not exist already, and he could not stop existing if he already exists. If God exists at all, then he exists in this eternal, necessary way. Malcolm's argument takes the following steps:

1. If God does not exist today, then he never can and never will – his existence must be impossible.

2. If God does exist, then he must exist necessarily.

3. God's existence is therefore either impossible or necessary.

4. God's existence is not impossible. It is not logically contradictory to have the

concept of a God who exists – it is an idea that we can entertain without any logical absurdity.

5. Therefore, given that God's existence is not impossible, it must be necessary – so God exists necessarily.

Malcolm's argument has not been generally accepted. One objection made is that there can be things that do not exist, without their existence being impossible. It might be illogical to say that 'sometimes there is a God, and sometimes there isn't' (if we accept that a God would have to be eternal), but it is not illogical to say 'maybe there is a God, and maybe there isn't'. Malcolm's argument, like other versions of the ontological argument, rests on our acceptance that God's existence is not the same as other kinds of existence.

Malcolm did concede that his argument would not convince atheists, but felt that it was nevertheless worthwhile because the believer would understand completely the necessity of God's existence, and therefore the truth of 'God exists' would make perfect sense for the theist. However, this seems to reduce the ontological argument to the point where it is saying no more than that God is true for those who believe in God – and many theists would want to claim that God exists in reality, whether we believe in him or not.

Alvin Plantinga's ontological argument uses something called 'modal logic', in which he employs the concept of 'possible worlds'. In modal logic, philosophers consider not just what exists and occurs in the world we have, but also what could exist or could occur in a possible world out of an infinite number of possibilities. They use these ideas to try to make sense of what is self-contradictory, possible or necessary in this actual world that we live in.

In his work *The Nature of Necessity* (Clarendon Press, 1974), Plantinga proposes an ontological argument for the existence of God. He writes of a being of 'maximal greatness', by which he means a being with all the perfections described by Descartes and which would fit Anselm's description of 'that than which nothing greater can be conceived'. Such a being would have to exist necessarily, rather than contingently, because a contingent being depends on other factors for its existence and so would not be maximally great, whereas a necessary being exists and can continue to exist independently.

Plantinga argues that the maximally great being's existence in a possible world is either necessary or impossible – those are the only two choices. The maximally great being's existence is only impossible if it is self-contradictory, in other words if there is something about the concept of a maximally great being that makes it illogical and incoherent as a concept. The maximally great being's existence is not impossible in an infinite number of possible worlds, and therefore it is necessary, in all worlds including ours.

Plantinga's argument, like Malcolm's, has its flaws. Perhaps the major flaw is that if the argument is turned on his head, and the concept of 'no maximality' is considered, then Plantinga's logic could be used to demonstrate that God does not exist in any possible world.

Develop your knowledge

The following books are recommended to extend your knowledge of ontological arguments:

The Puzzle of God by Peter Vardy (Fount, 1999)
Philosophy of Religion by Peter Cole (Hodder Murray, 1999)
Philosophy of Religion by Brian Davies (Oxford University Press, 1993)
Philosophy of Religion: Thinking About Faith by C. Stephen Evans (Intervarsity Press, 1985)
The Question of God by Michael Palmer (Routledge, 2001) is very thorough and explores the arguments for the existence of God in a depth that goes beyond A level.

Practice exam questions

(a) Explain Anselm's version of the ontological argument.

The question asks explicitly for Anselm's version of the ontological argument, so you do not need to go into detail about any other versions, although you could mention them in passing. Make a brief plan of the main features of Anselm's ontological argument: his purpose in writing it; his definition of God; his distinction between necessary and contingent existence; the differences between analytic and synthetic statements; the way in which he arrives at his conclusion. There is plenty of opportunity here for you to demonstrate your skill with key terms and specialist vocabulary. Remember that in part (a), you are showing knowledge and understanding, so you can save your criticisms of Anselm's argument until later.

(b) To what extent does Gaunilo's criticism of Anselm's argument succeed in demonstrating that the argument fails?

In this part you need to show that you understand Gaunilo's criticism. You should also demonstrate understanding of Anselm's response to it. However, the question is testing your skill in assessment rather than description, so make sure that you include evaluative comment rather than just a presentation of what Gaunilo said. Do you think Gaunilo was making a fair point? When Anselm replied to Gaunilo, did he give a satisfactory response or does Gaunilo's criticism still stand? You might want to argue that there have been other criticisms (such as those of Kant) that have been more successful than Gaunilo's; this would be a valid line of argument, as long as you also deal with the issues explicitly raised in the question.

Cosmological arguments

The basis of the cosmological argument is that the universe cannot account for its own existence. Why do things exist at all – why is there something, rather than nothing? There must be a reason, the argument says, for the existence of the universe, and this reason has to be something which is not part of the physical world of time and space.

This argument has a very long history. Plato, in *Timaeus*, argued that everything must have been created by some cause. Aristotle argued that behind the series of cause and effect in the world there must be an Unmoved Mover, and the Kalam argument in Islam is an attempt to show that the universe must have a cause and is not the result of an infinite regress (an endless chain going back for ever).

Cosmological arguments ask: why is there something, rather than nothing? Why is the universe here at all? They conclude that there must be a cause for the existence of everything – and that cause must be God.

Aquinas and the cosmological argument in the Five Ways

In the Middle Ages, cosmological arguments were used by Thomas Aquinas in his 'Five Ways' *(Quinque viae)*, which were ways of demonstrating the existence of God through inductive argument, based on observation and evidence.

Aquinas (1224/5–74) is generally accepted to be the greatest of all the mediaeval philosophers and theologians. He lived at a time when the works of Aristotle had recently been rediscovered by Europeans – they had been forgotten, but preserved by Arab philosophers, and in Aquinas' time they had only recently come to light because of Christianity's contact with Islam. Aristotle's work was (and still is) immensely impressive, both because of its range and because of its common-sense appeal to logic. It was seen by many mediaeval church leaders as a threat, because it offered an alternative, and very attractive, way of understanding the world – a way which did not depend at all upon Christian doctrine. Aquinas was among the thinkers who believed that it was necessary to find out where Aristotelian thought and Christian thought could be compatible; he could see the dangers of putting believers in a position where they were forced to choose between Christianity and common sense. A key goal for Aquinas was to show how faith and reason could work alongside each other. He was an enormously intelligent man (and apparently an enormous man, too) with an attractive personality. He soon became well-known within the Church, working as an adviser to the Pope as well as producing a huge amount of writing.

In Aquinas' view, knowledge of God could be reached in two very different ways. One is through revelation, where God chooses to reveal the truth to people, for example through the words of the Bible. The other is through our own human reason (which Aquinas thought was given to us by God for this very purpose). Aquinas thought that if we applied reason to the evidence that we see around us, we can reach valuable truths.

Key points

- Aquinas was very much influenced by Aristotle.
- Aquinas believed that faith and reason could be combined in order to reach a better understanding of God.
- The 'Five Ways' explain Aquinas' arguments for the existence of God.

Aquinas presented five ways of showing that God exists, because he was convinced that although the existence of God was not self-evident, it could be demonstrated with logical thought. He wrote about the Five Ways in his book *Summa Theologica,* which was written for Christian believers rather than with the intention of persuading others to convert. The book, which was never finished, is over 4000 pages long, and only two of these pages are devoted to the arguments for the existence of God, but these have become some of Aquinas' most famous ideas.

Of Aquinas' Five Ways, the first three are different variants of the cosmological argument. Aquinas based his argument on two assumptions:

(a) the universe exists
(b) there must be a reason why.

All but the most sceptical would agree with (a); however, not all would agree with (b). Some people, such as Bertrand Russell and Richard Dawkins, are happy to accept that the universe just is, without moving to the conclusion that there should be some reason for it. Aquinas, however, took as a starting point the view that there must be some explanation of why anything exists at all.

First Way – The Unmoved Mover

In his First Way of establishing God's existence, Aquinas concentrated on the existence of change, or motion, in the world. He considered the ways in which objects move, or grow or change in state (for example, become hotter or evaporate). His argument, closely following that of Aristotle, was that everything which is in motion, or changing, has to be put into motion, or changed, by something else. In this way, Aquinas (and Aristotle before him) produced a kind of pre-Newtonian understanding of the physics of motion. Things stay the same unless some force acts upon them to make them change or move. As things are, to our observation, changing and moving, then they must have been set in motion by something; Aquinas thought that this sequence of one thing moving another could not be infinite, but that there must have been an Unmoved Mover to set the whole thing off.

Aquinas argued that nothing in the universe would be in motion unless it was being moved by something else.

Aquinas also argued that if a change is brought about in Thing A by Thing B, then Thing B must have the characteristics of the change it brings about. For example, if Thing B makes Thing A hotter, then Thing B must itself be hot, or if Thing B makes Thing A darker, then Thing B must itself be dark. Peter Cole, in his book *Philosophy of Religion* (Hodder Murray, 2004), explains: 'What is potentially x is not actually x, yet the actual x can only be produced by something that is actually x'.

This is how Aquinas writes it:

The existence of God can be proved in five ways. The first and more manifest way is the argument from motion. It is certain, and evident to our senses, that in the world some things are in motion. Now whatever is in motion is put in motion by another, for nothing can be in motion except it is in potentiality to that towards which it is in motion; whereas a thing moves inasmuch as it is in act. For motion is nothing else than the reduction of something from potentiality to actuality. But nothing can be reduced from potentiality to actuality, except by something in a state of actuality. Thus that which is actually hot, as fire, makes wood, which is potentially hot, to be actually hot, and thereby moves and changes it …

Therefore, whatever is in motion must be put in motion by another. If that by which it is put in motion be itself put in motion, then this also must needs be put in motion by another, and that by another again. But this cannot go on to infinity, because then there would be no first mover, and, consequently, no other mover; seeing that subsequent movers move only inasmuch as they are put in motion by the first mover; as the staff moves only because it is put in motion by the hand. Therefore it is necessary to arrive at a first mover, put in motion by no other; and this everyone understands to be God.

The emphasis of Aquinas' argument was on dependency, rather than going back in time until a beginning was found; he was using the idea that God sustains the universe, and trying to show that we would not have a universe of change, vitality and motion without a First Mover. The continued changes and movements are because of the continued existence of a mover 'which we call God'.

Second Way – The Uncaused Causer

This argument is very similar, except that it replaces the idea of change and motion with the concept of cause. Every 'effect' has a 'cause', Aquinas argued; **infinite regress** is impossible; therefore there must be a First Cause 'which we call God'.

Here, Aquinas concentrates on the idea of 'efficient cause', borrowing terminology

directly from Aristotle. Aristotle had been very interested in the question of why things exist – not only why they exist in the form that they take, but also why they exist at all – and Aquinas was enthused by the same ideas. When Aristotle had considered the nature of causation, he came to the conclusion that 'cause' works at four different levels, which he named the material cause, the efficient cause, the formal cause and the final cause. By 'efficient cause', Aristotle meant the agent which makes something happen – so, for example, the baker kneading the dough is the efficient cause of the bread, or the musician pulling the bow across the strings is the efficient cause of the music.

The second way is from the nature of the efficient cause. In the world of sense we find there is an order of efficient causes. There is no case known (neither is it, indeed, possible) in which a thing is found to be the efficient cause of itself; for so it would be prior to itself, which is impossible. …

Now to take away the cause is to take away the effect. Therefore, if there be no first cause among efficient causes, there will be no ultimate, nor any intermediate cause. …

Therefore it is necessary to admit a first efficient cause, to which everyone gives the name of God.

Aquinas used Aristotle's ideas about 'efficient cause', where Aristotle had said that for every cause, there is an agent which brings it about. The efficient cause of violin music would be the violinist.

Aquinas took up Aristotle's understanding of causes, to argue that things do not cause themselves in this way – they cannot be their own agents. Therefore, he said, there must be a first efficient cause, and this would be God.

Third Way – Contingency

Key term

contingent – depending on something else.

In his Third Way, Aquinas argued that the world consists of contingent beings, which are beings that begin and end, and which are dependent on something else for their existence. Everything in the physical world is **contingent**, depending on external factors for its existence. Things are contingent in two ways: they depend on something having brought them into existence in the first place (for example, volcanic rock depends on there having been the right minerals, sufficient heat and so on to form it), and they also depend on outside factors for the continuation of their existence (for example, plants depend on the light from the sun). Since the time of Aquinas, we have become more aware of the existence of 'eco-systems', and have learned more about how the existence of one species depends very much on the existence of another and on natural resources; some would argue that these discoveries add support to the points Aquinas made.

The third way is taken from possibility and necessity, and runs thus. We find in nature things that are possible to be and not to be, since they are found to be generated, and to corrupt, and consequently, they are possible to be and not to be. But it is impossible for these always to exist, for that which is possible not to be at some time is not. Therefore, if everything is possible not to be, then at one time there could have been nothing in existence. Now if this were true, even now there would be nothing in existence, because that which does not exist only begins to exist by something already existing. Therefore, if at one time nothing was in existence, it would have been impossible for anything to have begun to exist; and thus even now nothing would be in existence – which is absurd. Therefore, not all beings are merely possible, but there must exist something the existence of which is necessary. But every necessary thing either has its necessity caused by another, or not. Now it is impossible to go on to infinity in necessary things which have their necessity caused by another, as has been already proved in regard to efficient causes. Therefore we cannot but postulate the existence of some being having of itself its own necessity, and not receiving it from another, but rather causing in others their necessity. This all men speak of as God.

Aquinas is arguing here that we can agree that everything in the universe is contingent. Contingent things need something else to bring them into existence, so nothing would have ever started – there would still be nothing – unless there is some other being, capable of bringing other things into existence but being independent of everything else, or **necessary**. It would have to be a being which is not caused, and which depends on nothing else to continue to exist – and this, Aquinas thought, would be God.

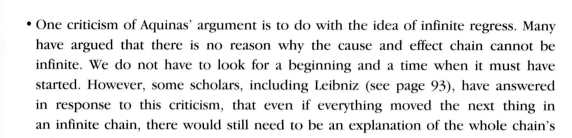

Key term

necessary – in this context, the word necessary is used to mean the opposite of contingent.
A necessary being has no cause and depends on nothing else for its continued existence.

Some criticisms of Aquinas' argument

- One criticism of Aquinas' argument is to do with the idea of infinite regress. Many have argued that there is no reason why the cause and effect chain cannot be infinite. We do not have to look for a beginning and a time when it must have started. However, some scholars, including Leibniz (see page 93), have answered in response to this criticism, that even if everything moved the next thing in an infinite chain, there would still need to be an explanation of the whole chain's existence.

- Some have argued against the idea that actual x can only be brought about by what is actual x – the philosopher Anthony Kenny wrote in his book *The Five Ways* (Routledge, 1969) that this is not always true; for example, Aquinas argued that for a stick to become hot, this had to be caused by actual heat, whereas Kenny argues that it could be caused by friction, and electric current can generate heat. Kenny makes this point by saying, 'it is not dead men who commit murders'. This part of Aquinas' argument is not true often enough to be sustainable. We might argue, using our own common sense, that we can be the cause of anger or jealousy in other people, without being angry or jealous ourselves.

- Some have criticised the idea of God as an uncaused causer, saying that the whole cosmological argument depends on the idea that nothing can cause itself, and then it is self-contradictory by saying that God does exactly what it just claimed was impossible. In answer to this criticism, which was being made during Aquinas' lifetime, he answered that this criticism makes the mistake of considering God to be a 'thing' like other objects in the universe, whereas God is not an object but different entirely. Aquinas argued that God is unique and exists in a unique kind of way.

- There is evidence to suggest that everything in the universe is contingent, but this does not necessarily mean that the universe as a whole is contingent. Some of the findings, or at least the theories, of science have suggested that matter, for example, may be eternal, or energy. However, these suggestions are still being explored by scientists; questions about the possible eternity of matter remain unanswered.

- Some writers, including Hume, argued that logically, the cosmological argument need not lead to one first cause; there could be a variety of different causes, and neither is there a logical reason to link this to the Christian God. The same criticism could be made of Aquinas' cosmological argument as can be made of teleological arguments.

Key point

- Aquinas' argument depends on his Aristotelian understanding of cause and effect. He assumes that everything must have a cause – but not everyone would agree.

The Kalam argument in Islam

The Kalam argument in Islam is a version of the cosmological argument. Muslim philosophers developed the Kalam argument using the thinking of Aristotle, just as Aquinas was to do from a Christian perspective. Kalam means 'speaking' in Arabic, and the Kalam tradition in Islam relates to seeking theological principles through debate and argument. Two thinkers in particular, called al-Kindi and al-Ghazali, studied Aristotle and saw how his ideas about cause could be applied within the Muslim faith.

The Kalam argument claims that everything which begins to exist must have a cause to make it come into existence. The universe must have had a cause, because there must have been a time when it began to exist: 'It is an axiom of reason that all that comes to be must have a cause to bring it about. The world has come to be. Ergo the world must have a cause to bring it about' (Al-Ghazali, *The Jerusalem Tract*, as quoted in William Lane Craig's *The Kalam Cosmological Argument*, Wipf and Stock, 2000).

Al-Ghazali argued that there must have been a real point at which the universe began, rather than an infinite regress, because although infinity is a mathematical concept, it cannot exist in actuality.

To think about

Supporters of the Kalam argument say that there cannot be an infinite number of days before today, because if there were, then we would never have reached today. And yet, here we are today. Do you think this is a good argument?

William Lane Craig, a modern American philosopher, is a supporter of the logic of the Kalam argument, although he writes as a Christian. He explains the view that an infinite regress (or an infinite anything) could not exist in reality, using the example of a library with an infinite number of books. If one of the books were loaned out, the library would still have to contain an infinite number – if every other book were to be taken away, the shelves would still have to be full … 'Suppose we add an infinity of infinite collections to the library … is there actually not one more single volume in the entire collection than before?' (William Lane Craig, *The Kalam Cosmological Argument*).

William Lane Craig argued in favour of the Kalam argument, using the example of a library with an infinite number of books, to show that infinity could not exist in actuality.

The Kalam argument continues by saying that we can now see that there must have been a time when the universe did not exist, as it cannot have existed infinitely long ago. This means that there was once the possibility of a universe coming into existence, or a universe not coming into existence – and there must have been something to have made the choice between those two possibilities. There must be some personal, intelligent agency to choose that the universe should exist, and this personal intelligent agent must exist outside space and time.

Criticisms of Kalam arguments

- Some people argue that the Kalam argument misunderstands the nature of infinity, and that infinity has to exist in actuality even if we cannot imagine it.
- It could be argued that there is no need for there to have been an agent making a choice between having a universe and not having one – the universe could just have begun, at random, by accident, without any conscious choice being made.
- Even if the Kalam argument is accepted, it does not provide evidence for the existence of a God with all the qualities and characteristics that theists claim God has.
- It might be argued that the Kalam argument is self-contradictory, since it denies the possibility of infinity existing in actuality, but uses this as part of an argument to demonstrate the actual existence of an infinite God.

Key points

- The Kalam argument is based on the view that infinity cannot exist in actuality, so that the universe must have had a beginning.
- Supporters propose that the universe came into existence as the free choice of a being beyond time and space.

Leibniz and the principle of sufficient reason

Gottfried Leibniz (1646–1716) offered an alternative form of the cosmological argument, in which he tried to avoid the problems raised by the suggestion of an infinite regression. He argued that even if the universe has always existed, this still does not give us an explanation of why it exists. According to Leibniz, everything has to have a **sufficient reason**. The principle of sufficient reason states that there must be reasons to explain facts, even if we do not know what these reasons are. There must be an explanation, known or unknown.

To think about

Do you think it is true that everything must have a reason to explain its existence? Could there be things which just exist, for no reason at all?

David Hume, however, argued that we could not logically move from the idea that everything in the universe has a reason, to say that the universe as a whole must have a reason. Bertrand Russell made a similar point in the twentieth century, by saying that just because every human being has a mother, this does not mean that the human species as a whole has a mother. It is overstepping the rules of logic to move from individual causes of individual things, to the view that the totality has a cause.

Hume also argued that we can imagine something coming into existence without a cause: it is not an incoherent idea. But others have objected that just because you could imagine something existing without a cause, it does not follow that in *reality* it could exist without a cause; the twentieth-century philosopher Elizabeth Anscombe gave the example that we can imagine a rabbit which had no parents and just existed, but obviously this would not be an actual possibility just because we could imagine it.

Key point

- The principle of sufficient reason proposes that everything must have a cause or an explanation, even if we do not know what the cause or explanation is.

Kant on cosmological and design arguments

Immanuel Kant (1724–1804) is usually regarded as one of the greatest philosophers of modern Europe.

Kant argued that our ideas about order and design and causality come from the way that we perceive the world around us. Our minds like to put things in order, and to see patterns and sequences. Perhaps the order in the world is something that we impose on it, when we perceive it, rather than something that is objectively there.

In his book *Critique of Practical Reason*, Kant rejected the views of thinkers such as Leibniz. Kant considered that the teleological and the cosmological arguments were essentially linked, because both arguments ultimately depend on the idea that God is necessarily existent – in other words, that God exists without a cause, does not come into existence or go out of existence and does not depend on anything else in order to exist.

The teleological argument depends on the view that there must be a Designer, existing outside the world in the same way as the First Cause or Unmoved Mover of cosmological arguments. These arguments, when followed to their logical conclusions, make the assumption that there is a God who 'necessarily exists', by definition. But Kant did not think that this was sound reasoning. (See Kant's criticism of ontological arguments, pages 80–81).

Key point

- Kant believed that the existence of God could not be discovered through the use of human reason, but was a matter for faith.

The radio debate between Russell and Copleston

In 1948, the BBC Third Programme brought together two eminent philosophers with very different views, to debate live on radio some of the issues of the existence of God. Frederick Copleston (1907–94) was invited to argue the case for theism. He was brought up as an Anglican, but converted to Roman Catholicism and became a Jesuit priest, leading philosopher and scholar. Copleston was well known for his immense and erudite nine-volume work, *A History of Philosophy*, and also for the publication of several other works including a biography and appraisal of Aquinas (Pelican, 1955).

In opposition to him was Bertrand Russell (1872–1970), an aristocrat who had made a name for himself as a philosopher of mathematics, and who went on to become a renowned opponent of war and of nuclear weapons. Russell took an atheist position, although he said that strictly speaking he was agnostic. He followed the thinking of the logical positivists, arguing that discussion of God was beyond the scope of human reason or experiment, and was therefore meaningless.

Copleston argued that, unless one accepts the existence of a first cause, an Unmoved Mover, there is no explanation for the existence of the universe at all (he combined the thinking of Aquinas and Leibniz in his argument). He said that without such an explanation, the universe is 'gratuitous', using the words of Jean-Paul Sartre: 'Everything is gratuitous, this garden, this city and myself. When you suddenly realize it, it makes you feel sick and everything begins to drift ... that's nausea' (Jean-Paul Sartre, *Nausea*, 1938).

Russell replied that he did not accept the need to find an explanation for the existence of the universe; he rejected Leibniz's principle of sufficient reason, stating firmly: 'I should say that the universe is just there, that's all'. Russell went on to explain his point of view in his 1957 book *Why I am not a Christian*. Copleston's view of Russell's position was to suggest that Russell was denying the importance of the argument: 'If one refuses even to sit down at the chess-board and make a move, one cannot, of course, be checkmated.'

In the radio debate, Copleston defended the cosmological argument, using points made by Aquinas and Leibniz.

In the debate, Copleston presented an argument which was very similar to that of Aquinas seven hundred years before.

1. Copleston argued that each object in the universe is dependent (contingent) on the existence of other things, and relies for its existence on 'a reason external to itself'. He gave the example of himself, dependent for his existence on the previous existence of his parents, and on the continued existence of air and of food. He argued that since nothing in the world contains the reason for its own existence, there must be an external explanation, something outside the objects in the universe which accounts for their existence and for the existence of the universe as a whole. In order for this explanation to be found, there must be 'a being which contains within itself the reason for its own existence'.

2. He asserted that, despite the views of those who disagree, it is meaningful to talk of a 'necessary being' whose essence involves existence.

3. He also claimed that it is meaningful to talk of there being a cause of the universe.

4. Copleston agreed with Leibniz, saying that every existent thing must have a sufficient reason for its existence. Copleston said: 'God is his own sufficient reason; and he is not cause of himself. By sufficient reason in the full sense I mean an explanation adequate for the existence of some particular being.' God is his own sufficient reason, but everything else is contingent.

Russell's position in the debate was to argue that concepts such as 'cause of the universe' and 'necessary existence' held no meaning.

Russell's responses to Copleston included these points:

1. The concept of a 'necessary being' had no meaning for him; the term 'necessary' cannot be applied to things, only to statements in logic, where B necessarily follows from A because it is part of the definition (for example, if Peter is a bachelor, then

Peter is necessarily an unmarried man, because that is the definition of bachelor). Russell said that 'necessary' in this sense is appropriate only for statements of definition, and that it does not make sense to talk of God as 'necessary'.

2. Also, the concept of the universe as a whole having a cause was meaningless for Russell. His view was that we cannot grasp the concept of the entire scheme of things, and then hope to find an explanation for it.

3. Russell said that the concept of cause is not applicable to the universe: 'I should say that the universe is just there, and that's all.'

4. He also claimed that scientists (in 1947) were discovering 'first causes which haven't in themselves got causes.' So the whole notion of everything having to have a sufficient reason and a Prime Mover was undermined.

By the end of the debate, Russell and Copleston concluded that they had very little ground in common, and could not even agree on whether they were discussing a question that had any meaning – so they might as well move on to another issue.

To think about

Whose view is closer to your own opinion – Russell or Copleston? What do you think are the strengths and weaknesses of each side of the argument?

 ## Develop your knowledge

A transcript of the radio debate between Russell and Copleston can be found in *Classic and Contemporary Readings in the Philosophy of Religion*, edited by John Hick (Prentice Hall, 1989).

Will science be the end of the cosmological argument?

In recent years subatomic physics has suggested that things can exist without a cause, and that motion does not have to be the result of a mover. Investigations in quantum physics suggest that electrons can pass in and out of existence without any apparent cause; although some would say there seems to be no cause because of our limited understanding, rather than that such things are causeless in reality.

Peter Atkins, Professor of Chemistry at the University of Oxford, dismissed the cosmological argument for the existence of God:

*There is of course one big, cosmically big, seemingly real question: Where did it all come from? Here we see most sharply the distinction between the methods. Religion adopts the adipose answer: God made it – for reasons that will forever remain inscrutable until, perhaps, we become one with Him (that is, until we are dead). Such an answer, while intrinsically absurd and evil in its implications, appears to satisfy those for whom God is a significant part of their existence. Science, in contrast, is steadily and strenuously working toward a comprehensible explanation. Witness the extraordinary progress that has been made since the development of general relativity at the beginning of the twentieth century. Though difficult, and still incomplete, there is no reason to believe that the great problem, how the universe came into being, and what it is, will not be solved; we can safely presume that the solution will be comprehensible to human minds. Moreover, that understanding will be achieved this side of the grave. (*Free Inquiry *magazine, Volume 18, Number 2, 1998).*

The cosmological argument, then, is by no means closed, but continues to be debated in universities. It does not present a proof of the existence of God, since there is the possibility that the universe is a brute fact and ultimately unintelligible; but it supports the possibility that the universe does have an explanation, and that this explanation could be God (although it need not necessarily be the God described by major world religions).

Practice exam questions

(a) Examine the cosmological argument for the existence of God.

Notice that the question asks you to 'examine' rather than just 'give'. You need to look carefully at the different aspects of the argument, and explain key terms and key concepts, such as the concept of an 'infinite regress' and the difference between 'necessary' and 'contingent' existence. For high marks, you should make reference to some different thinkers who have supported cosmological arguments – Aquinas and Copleston would be obvious choices. This question assesses your skills of knowledge and understanding, rather than your evaluative skill, so the key here is to show that you know and understand the logic and structure of the cosmological argument. Try to demonstrate that you understand clearly how the argument is structured and how the conclusion is supported.

(b) Comment on the view that the cosmological argument is convincing.

Here, your critical ability is being assessed. You need to show that you can sustain an argument, draw a conclusion based on that argument, and show that you are aware of different points of view. In order to do this, you should think about why some people found cosmological arguments convincing, and why others have rejected them (Hume would be an obvious choice here). However, if you simply explain 'some people think this … because … while other people think that … because …', then you are really just giving more description and explanation, rather than evaluating. Instead, when you show awareness of different points of view, try to make some critical comment about them. Do you find yourself agreeing with one view or another, and if so, why? For example, you could say '… and this is a valid criticism to make of the cosmological argument, because it shows that there are alternative plausible explanations for the existence of the universe other than God', or '… however, this criticism is weak because it assumes that we have to choose between scientific and religious accounts of the origins of the universe, whereas there are no strong grounds for dismissing God as the cause of the Big Bang'. When you give your own opinion, try to show how your outlook has been formed by the strength of one of these points of view, rather than simply listing different possible points of view and then adding your own to the list.

Key term

teleological – looking at the 'tail end', or end result, in order to draw conclusions.

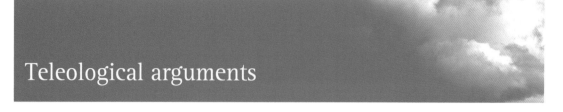

Teleological arguments

Design arguments for God's existence are often known as 'teleological' arguments. 'Teleological' comes from the Greek word for 'tail', or 'end' – the end results are important. They are the goal or purpose, and are used in order to draw one's conclusions.

These arguments are inductive arguments and *a posteriori* arguments – they look at our experience of the world, and draw inferences from it. Because they are inductive arguments, they reach conclusions which are statements of probability rather than conclusive proofs. It is up to us to decide whether we agree with the premises, and whether we think that the force of the argument is sufficient to persuade us to accept the conclusion.

Design arguments follow a pattern like this:

1. Whenever we see things made by people, which are ordered in a pattern, or beautiful, or particularly complex, which work particularly well to achieve a goal, we can infer that they must have been designed that way by an intelligent designer.

2. Order, beauty, complexity and/or purpose do not arise by blind chance.

3. We can look at the natural world and see that there is order, complexity and beauty in it, and things which work particularly well to perform a function. The resemblance to human inventions is close.

Design arguments propose that the orderliness in the universe points to an intelligent designer, which is God.

4. Therefore the natural world, like machines, must have been created by an intelligent being.

5. God is that intelligent being, and therefore, God exists.

Different versions of this argument stress different aspects of the apparent design of the world. One version is that design can be seen in the regularity of the universe, the movements of the planets and the seasons within them; another is that design can be seen in the way in which objects in the world suit a purpose; and another uses the beauty of the natural world from which to draw the conclusion that there must be an intelligent creator.

One of the most ancient teleological arguments comes from Cicero's *De Natura Deorum (On the Nature of the Gods)*. Cicero was a pre-Christian Roman philosopher (106–43 BCE). In this writing, a character called Lucilius Balbus asks, 'What could be more clear or obvious when we look up to the sky and contemplate the heavens, than that there is some divinity or superior intelligence?' Belief in God, he argued 'is drawn from the regularity of the motion and revolution of the heavens, the distinctness, variety, beauty and order of the sun, moon and all the stars, the appearance only of which is sufficient to convince us they are not the effects of chance.'

The Bible, too, suggests that it is obvious from looking at the world that God must have made it. Psalm 19, for example, begins 'The heavens tell out the glory of God, the vault of heaven reveals his handiwork.'

In medieval times, teleological arguments had the support of science, which assumed (following the thinking of Aristotle) that all natural objects had a purpose and a reason for their existence. In the eighteenth century, too, teleological arguments were particularly popular as they appeared to be supported by Newtonian physics.

Teleological arguments appeal to our aesthetic sense. The argument is not sophisticated; it appeals to our sense of wonder at the beauty of the natural world, the awe we feel when observing the intricacies of animals and plants or when watching the night sky through a telescope. The argument has an emotional pull as well as an appeal to logic, and this perhaps accounts for its enduring attractiveness.

Key points

• Design arguments are often known as teleological arguments.
• Design arguments say that features of the natural world point to the existence of a God who must have designed it.

Aquinas' design argument

The last of the Five Ways is the one which takes up a version of the design argument for the existence of God. In the Fifth Way, Aquinas said that nature seems to have an order and a purpose to it. We know, he suggested, that nothing inanimate is purposeful without the aid of a 'guiding hand' (he uses the example of an archer shooting an arrow at a target). Therefore everything in nature which is moving but which has no intelligence must be directed to its goal by God. Aquinas says that there is order and purpose in the world, but adds to this that inanimate objects (for example, the planets), could not have ordered themselves, as they do not have any intelligence with which to make plans or patterns. Therefore, they must have been given an order by a being with intelligence (which would be God).

Aquinas used the example of archery to illustrate his belief that purpose in the universe is evidence for the existence of God.

This is how Aquinas writes it:

The fifth way is taken from the governance of the world. We see that things which lack knowledge, such as natural bodies, act for an end, and this is evident from their acting always, or nearly always, in the same way, so as to obtain the best result. Hence it is plain that they achieve their end, not fortuitously, but designedly. Now whatever lacks knowledge cannot move towards an end, unless it be directed by some being endowed with knowledge and intelligence; as the arrow is directed by the archer. Therefore, some intelligent being exists by whom all natural things are directed to their end; and this being we call God.

To think about

Is Aquinas right when he says that nature has a purpose to it?

William Paley and the eighteenth-century design argument

It was in the seventeenth and eighteenth centuries that design arguments were at the height of their popularity. These were times of great strides in the fields of science – astronomy, botany, zoology and anatomy were all developing at an exciting pace. Those people who wanted to show that the existence of God could be demonstrated through looking at the world had plenty of material to illustrate their point of view. They could show that scientists were discovering every day how, for example, different plants were suited to their different habitats – some having leaves which allowed maximum water retention in dry countries, while others produced airborne seeds which could be spread by the wind. Different animals were made in different ways so that they could live in different climates and conditions. Physicists were discovering the rules governing forces, motion and gravity, and these rules appeared to work uniformly in all kinds of circumstances, revealing an order in the way inanimate objects operated. The invention of the microscope allowed scientists to observe the intricate structure and function of cells invisible to the naked eye. The more people learned about the world, the more clear it seemed to be that there was an intelligent creator and designer behind it all.

William Paley (1743–1805), who was Archdeacon of Carlisle, put forward what is probably the most famous version of the design argument, in his book *Natural Theology*.

To illustrate his argument, he used the analogy of someone coming across a watch on a heath (this was probably not Paley's own analogy, but one which was popular and which he chose to repeat). Imagine, he said, if someone was out walking on a heath, and looked down and saw a watch lying on the ground. The person finding the watch would notice how well the watch worked in order to tell the time, and would conclude that someone must have made the watch, rather than that the watch had just happened there by chance, or by the random orderings of atoms. Paley said that looking at a watch was similar to looking at the world, or at the human body, and noticing how it all works together – so intricately that one can only infer that there must have been a divine intelligence ordering it. Paley argued that we do not have to have ever seen a watch being made in order to realise that there must have been a maker; the watch does not have to work perfectly for us still to realise that it must have been designed. He went on to say that the world itself was even more impressive than a watch in its workings: '… the contrivances of nature surpass the contrivances of art, in the complexity, subtility, and curiosity of the mechanism.'

Paley argued that the mechanism of the universe could be compared to the mechanism of a manufactured object such as a watch.

In his book *Natural Theology*, Paley discusses many different examples of the suitability of the bodily structure of animals to the conditions of their life. He argued that not only is everything clearly designed, but it is designed for a purpose; and it is designed to an infinite degree of care. Even on the smallest scale, there is evidence of craft and skill, and despite the number of different kinds of things in the world, the same care seems to have been taken with the design of each. Paley concluded that this was not only evidence of intelligent design, but of God's care – if God cared enough about each insect to design it with such attention to detail, then surely people can be confident that God will care for them too:

The hinges in the wings of an earwig, and the joints of its antennae, are as highly wrought, as if the Creator had nothing else to finish. We see no signs of diminution of care by multiplicity of objects, or of distraction of thought by variety. We have no reason to fear, therefore, our being forgotten, or overlooked, or neglected.

Paley was not the only eighteenth-century thinker to have produced a teleological argument for the existence of God, but his view became the most famous. Charles Darwin studied Paley's writings as a compulsory part of his university education at Cambridge, and was greatly impressed by them; and many Christian ministers have been trained using the sorts of arguments that Paley put forward.

Key points

- William Paley used the analogy of a watch to argue that the natural world shows evidence of design.
- He argued that the more we learn about different animals and plants, the more clearly we can see evidence of intelligent design.

Hume's criticisms of design arguments

David Hume (1711–76) was a hugely influential Scottish philosopher, who is often referred to as a **sceptic**. He was not willing to accept popularly held beliefs without questioning and challenging them. His book, *Dialogues Concerning Natural Religion*, considers the reasoning put forward by proponents of teleological arguments. Hume wrote this book in the form of a discussion between fictional characters, so that one character (Cleanthes) argues the point of view of the design argument and another (Philo, who like Hume is a sceptic) argues against it. Hume wrote his criticism of design arguments 23 years before Paley gave his famous analogy of the watch. Paley was probably aware of, but not convinced by, the criticisms Hume made.

In his dialogues, Hume made several different criticisms of the idea that design in the world gives strong evidence for the existence of God:

1. One criticism was that the analogy between a watch and the world is weak. Hume said that it cannot be assumed that it is obvious to everyone how the world, like a watch, is formed regularly and for a purpose. Characteristics of purpose and design might be obvious in a watch, but they are not nearly so obvious in the world. We only make watches because the world is not like a watch; we would only stop and pick up the watch on the heath because it is so unlike the objects which occur in nature. We would conclude that the watch had been designed because we would think it could not have come about naturally, as such design is not seen in nature. It is not right, Hume thought, to draw these comparisons between the world and machines and use them as analogies when there is really very little similarity.

2. Hume also argued that order in the world does not necessarily mean that someone must have had the idea of the design. Even if we do see order in the world, that does not enable us to leap on to the idea of a Divine Orderer. We do not know, for a fact, that all order comes about because of an intelligent idea. All we can say is, yes, there is order in the world. The recognition of order, too, has its limitations, because we do not have other worlds to compare with this one, to see if this one is more ordered than another. We have no other standard by which to judge it. Perhaps there are other worlds, a great deal more ordered than this one, which, if we knew about them, would lead us to the conclusion that there is very little order in our own.

3. Order, Hume believed, is a necessary part of the world's existence. If everything were random and nothing suited its purpose, the world would not be here any more. Any world, he thought, will look designed, because if it were chaotic, it would not survive. It is not enough to show that the world is orderly for the conclusion to be drawn that God must have designed it. We also have to be able to prove that this order could not have come about except by God, and this is impossible to show. This self-sustaining order, it is argued, could have come about by chance. This was the kind of idea that Darwin's findings seemed to support, although of course Hume lived too early to know about Darwinism: the creatures we have around us are suited to their purpose only by chance, because the ones which were not suited (and there were plenty of them) did not survive.

4. Hume also criticised design arguments because of their assumption that if we look at the effects (the world), we can infer the cause (God). Aquinas had claimed that this was possible – that, in looking at the evidence around us, we can work backwards and see that God must be the cause of it. But Hume attacked this reasoning, saying that cause and effect does not operate as simply as this.

5. Hume said that even if we can assume a creator (and he was not sure that we could), there is no reason to suggest that this creator is the Christian God. We have a finite and imperfect world; there is no need to assume that there must be an infinite, perfect God behind it. Hume uses the example of a pair of scales, with one end hidden from view. The end we can see contains a weight that we know – a kilogram, for example –

and we can also see that the other end outweighs it, but we have no means of knowing by how much. We cannot infer with any confidence that it must contain a hundred kilograms, or nine, or a tonne; and we certainly could not claim with any authority that it had an infinite weight on it. Similarly, when we look at the world, we have only the effect to look at – the cause is hidden from us. We do not know, looking at the world, whether God is clever, or good or loving. He could have been stupid, only copying someone else's ideas, or he could have accidentally stumbled on this design after countless trials and errors.

6. There is no reason, either, to assume from looking at the world that it was made by just one God (we would not assume, if we found a watch, that it must have been made by the very same person who made the watches we were wearing). Hume argued that there are all sorts of other possibilities that are equally likely; the world could have been made by a committee or a team of gods – or even a team of demons:

> *And what shadow of an argument, continued Philo, can you produce, from your hypothesis, to prove the unity of the Deity? A great number of men join in building a house or ship, in rearing a city, in framing a commonwealth: why may not several Deities combine in contriving and framing a world?*

When we see a machine, we do not know whether one person made it, or whether there was a whole team. Hume said that if we look at the world, we have no reason to assume that it was made by just the one God.

7. Hume argued that the universe is unique, so we are unable to say what it is like, what it could have been like, or how it must have come into being, because we cannot have experience of any other way that things might have been. We do not know how worlds are usually made, or what degree of order to expect, and so on; and with no other experience, we cannot draw any firm conclusions.

Hume's criticisms of teleological arguments were based on reason and logic; he argued that you cannot make great leaps and assume that B follows from A as a proof, when there could be a variety of other possible explanations.

Key point

- Hume argued that if there is order in the world, there are plenty of different possibilities that could be offered to explain it. Order in the world does not demonstrate that it must have been put there by divine intelligence.

John Stuart Mill's criticism of design arguments

John Stuart Mill (1806–73) was one of the leading thinkers of the nineteenth century. He was known as a radical; his thinking explored theories of politics and economics as well as ethics, where he is particularly well known for his work on the ethical system of Utilitarianism. Mill was one of the first thinkers to consider the nature and scope of inductive reasoning and to look at the value of conclusions which were reached on the basis of probability rather than hard fact.

Mill took a different approach in his criticism of arguments from design. He did not address the issue of whether design arguments are logical, as Hume had done. Instead, Mill suggested that if we look at the world and the rules which govern it, then we see cruelty, violence and unnecessary suffering. In his essay *On Nature* (1874), he argued that if the world has been deliberately designed, then it indicates something very different from a loving creator God.

Living things, including people, inflict cruelty on each other, and seem to be designed for that purpose. Many animals are made with special features to enable them to be efficient killers – they have sharp claws and teeth, or excellent eyesight or hearing to help them spot their prey. Some live as parasites on other creatures. Even plants often have features which help them to suffocate other plants in order to gain maximum light and nutrients. The world, if it is designed at all, is designed so that some species can only exist by destroying others.

Nature seemed, to Mill, to be unnecessarily cruel.

Nature itself causes suffering, through natural disasters. Volcanoes, earthquakes, bush fires and floods are often natural occurrences, caused as an inevitable result of the structure of the earth. Mill argued that if there is a God who created and designed the world, then it must be a God who wants his creation to be miserable – it does not make sense to use the world as evidence of the existence of a good God. He argued in *On Nature* that we cannot want to worship a God who would design such a world – if people behaved in the way God seems to have behaved, then we would think of them as the worst kind of criminal:

> *… the order of nature, in so far as unmodified by man, is such as no being, whose attributes are justice and benevolence, would have made with the intention that his rational creatures should follow it as an example … In sober truth, nearly all the things which men are hanged or imprisoned for doing to one another are nature's every-day performances. Killing, the most criminal act recognised by human laws, Nature does once to every being that lives; and, in a large proportion of cases, after protracted tortures such as only the greatest monsters whom we read of ever purposely inflicted on their living fellow creatures …*

> *Next to taking life (equal to it according to a high authority) is taking the means by which we live; and Nature does this too on the largest scale and with the most callous indifference. A single hurricane destroys the hopes of a season; a flight of locusts, or an inundation, desolates a district; a trifling chemical change in an edible root starves a million of people. The waves of the sea, like banditti, seize and appropriate the wealth of the rich and the little all of the poor with the same accompaniments of stripping, wounding, and killing as their human antitypes. Everything, in short, which the worst men commit either against life or property is perpetrated on a larger scale by natural agents.*

To think about

Do you think that Mill is right when he argues that if the world is designed, it must have been designed by a creator who wants us to be miserable?

Mill argued that if we look at the way the natural world is designed, we see that it is full of pain and cruelty. If God designed the world, this indicates a cruel God who wants creatures to suffer.

Mill's argument, then, is based on the observation that the world is more than just imperfect – in his view, it is gratuitously cruel. He did not say that the world could not have been designed; his view was that if it has been deliberately designed, then it does not point to a perfectly good and loving designer.

Key point

- Mill's argument was that the design of the world involves cruelty and suffering – so if it was made by God, it must have been made by a cruel God.

Design arguments and Darwinism

The work of Charles Darwin is considered by many people to have presented design arguments with their greatest challenge. For people like Paley, the complex features of different plants and animals provided clear evidence of a divine designer. But what if these features had not always been there? What if there was evidence to suggest that they had only developed gradually, and that there had been plenty of creatures with poor design which had not survived?

Darwin's famous work *The Origin of Species* caused a huge storm when it was first published, but his theory of evolution did not come completely out of the blue. Fifteen years before Darwin published *The Origin of Species*, a book called *Vestiges of the Natural History of Creation* was published anonymously (1844). This caused a great deal of excitement, and the identity of the author was the subject of much society debate. This book suggested that there had been some kind of evolution, and that the existing species had ancestors which were different from themselves. The book was also keen to point out that God had made the early creatures, and God had made the laws governing their evolution.

This anonymous book, although the subject of discussion, was not treated as a serious threat to design arguments, because the ideas in it were presented as hypotheses, as guesses, without supporting evidence. The author, a man called Robert Chambers, was an amateur naturalist, and scientists were quick to spot and expose the mistakes in his reasoning.

However, when Darwin's work was published, it was supported by a mass of collected evidence and examples, and was therefore considered to be far more threatening to orthodox Christian beliefs. Chambers' views could be dismissed as wild guesses, but Darwin's theory that natural selection had been the cause of the origins of the different species was supported with data and seemed, to many, to be convincing. Darwin's theory was also supported by the new science of geology. Sir Charles Lyell's work suggested that the world was millions of years old, not just six thousand as suggested by the Bible; and geologists were beginning to find the fossilised remains of creatures which no longer existed.

Darwin's theory of evolution through natural selection was seen as an important challenge to design arguments.

Key term

natural selection – the process by which evolution is said to take place, through the survival of the fittest who pass on their genes to the next generation.

According to Darwin's theory of evolution through natural selection, the different species we can see in the world today have not always existed in their present form. When life first began, it was in a very simple molecular form. As it reproduced itself, the offspring were not identical. Those with stronger characteristics, more suitable for survival, lived for longer and were able to produce more offspring to continue the strong characteristics, while the weaker traits became extinct. Over many generations, different species evolved. Complexity was one of the characteristics which led to a greater chance of survival, and so more and more complex plants and animals were formed, with different characteristics to suit different habitats. Darwin's work was supported by the discoveries made in genetics by Gregor Mendel.

To think about

Some people argue that the theory of evolution shows that God is even more intelligent as a designer than people had imagined. God did not just make the creatures, but he made them with the ability to evolve. What do you think of this argument?

Darwin did not attack design arguments explicitly, but his views are important because those who supported design arguments were saying that such complexity and suitability for purpose *could only* have come about by the agency of God. Darwin provided an alternative explanation which to many people seemed (and still seems) more plausible than the existence of God.

Develop your knowledge

There is plenty of further material available to read about Darwin and the effect of his theories on Christian thought. As an introduction, try *Religion and Science* by Mel Thompson (Hodder Murray, 2000), pp. 31–5.

Richard Dawkins, a modern Darwinist

Richard Dawkins is a modern supporter of Darwin, and a strong critic of design arguments for the existence of God. According to Dawkins, Charles Darwin was one of the greatest thinkers of all time, and Darwin's work, he believed, has shown that design arguments such as those presented by William Paley are unacceptable to the modern mind. Dawkins writes:

Paley's argument is made with passionate sincerity and is informed by the best biological scholarship of the day, but it is wrong, gloriously and utterly wrong. The analogy between telescope and eye, between watch and living organism, is false. All appearances to the contrary, the only watchmaker in nature is the blind force of physics, albeit deployed in a special way. A true watchmaker has foresight: he designs his cogs and springs, and plans their interconnections, with a future purpose in his mind's eye. Natural selection, the blind unconscious, automatic process which Darwin discovered, and which we now know is the explanation for the existence and apparently purposeful form of all life, has no purpose in mind. It has no mind and no mind's eye. It does not plan for the future. It has no vision, no foresight, no sight at all. If it can be said to play the role of watchmaker in nature, it is the blind watchmaker. (Richard Dawkins, The Blind Watchmaker, *Penguin Books Ltd, 1986)*

Richard Dawkins argues against religious belief, because in his view religion is an excuse not to investigate scientifically. According to Dawkins, religious belief encourages people not to think. Theists assume that there are inexplicable elements to the world, and are satisfied with attributing the lack of any explanation to God, which discourages them from investigating further until they find the truth. Dawkins argues that a religious mentality is an obstacle to humanity. It invites people to leave the universe unexplored and to be satisfied with not knowing.

Many of Dawkins' books are devoted not only to the explanation of scientific principles but to arguing against religious claims that there is a creating and designing God. The book *The Blind Watchmaker*, the title of which immediately challenges Paley's famous analogy in support of the teleological argument, is subtitled: *Why the Evidence of Evolution Reveals a Universe without Design*. In this book, Dawkins argues that as scientists come closer to an understanding of how everything works, there is less and less need to resort to God to explain things. Dawkins believes that the discovery of DNA by Crick and Watson has been a major step forward in the discrediting of religious faith.

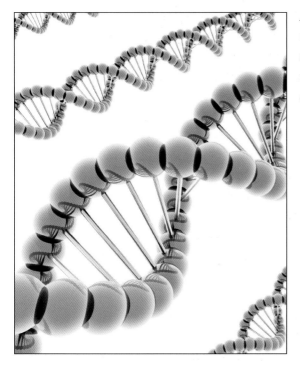

Dawkins argues that the discovery of DNA provides an explanation for the existence of humanity; there is no need to assume the existence of God to account for human life.

One of the points which Dawkins puts forward in *River out of Eden* (Phoenix Press, 1996) is that there is no fundamental and deep distinction between living and non-living material. This is one of the implications of Crick and Watson's breakthrough when they uncovered the mysteries of DNA; it appears that there is no mysterious 'spark' which distinguishes life. Dawkins writes that in the final analysis: 'life is just bytes and bytes and bytes of digital information.' This point, then, for Dawkins, finishes the idea of religious believers that life could not have just come from material elements, and that there must have been a creator, a First Cause at some point to 'breathe life' into the planet. DNA can explain the most fundamental causes of life.

The chapter 'Do Good by Stealth' in *River out of Eden* argues against the view that fitness for a purpose cannot have happened gradually. Christian 'creation scientists' often argue that it is wrong to suggest that the wing, for example, must have developed gradually; there would be no point, no use in half a wing or in an undeveloped wing that was halfway between limb and flying aid. But Dawkins argues, using examples such as the orchid which fools a wasp into pollinating it, that it is quite possible for animals and plants to become gradually better and better suited to their purpose, because the creatures with the successful genes are the ones which survive to reproduce in the classical Darwinian method. Those early orchids which only looked vaguely like the female wasp would have fooled the male wasps perhaps only some of the time, but this would be better than nothing, and gradually the wasp-resembling orchid could have evolved.

Dawkins also argues that survival advantages conferred on some genes cannot be ascribed to a caring agent, and that accidents and natural disasters cannot be blamed on any purposeful activity by supernatural forces; nature is neither cruel nor caring, but just indifferent. The processes of evolution cannot be ascribed feelings and purpose in this way.

Dawkins makes it clear in his books that he has no time for religious faith at all. He writes: 'It is often thought clever to say that science is no more than our modern origin myth' but he counters this kind of comment by saying 'Airplanes built by scientific principles work … airplanes built to tribal mythological specifications don't.' Science, he believes, has proved itself to be more than just another theory, because its principles can be put into practice and be shown to work, whereas beliefs about God cannot be tested at all and are therefore, in his view, worthless.

Key point

- Darwinism presents a challenge to arguments from design, because it suggests an alternative reason why creatures seem to be so well suited for their purposes. Darwinism suggests that evolution, and not God, is the cause of apparent design.

Criticisms of Dawkins

Dawkins assumes that the universe is a 'brute fact', but this is an assumption which cannot be proved true. If Hume were alive today to argue with Dawkins, he might suggest that 'brute fact' is one possibility as an explanation of the existence of the universe, but that there are also many other possibilities. Hume suggested, in his criticisms of teleological arguments, that we can only see one side of the (figurative) scales and that we have no way of knowing what is on the other side. His suggestion that there might be a God creating and designing the world, or there might be a whole pantheon of gods, and so on, still holds; we do not know, we can only guess. The same holds true for Dawkins' conclusion that the universe is a 'brute fact'.

Even if Dawkins could show the probability of the universe and the evolution of life being brute fact, it would still always remain only a probability. It could only be proved if it could be shown that the alternatives, such as the existence of God, are impossible, and Dawkins has not shown this. It is an argument using inductive reasoning, and as such, the conclusion could be wrong. Dawkins claims that science has demonstrated that chance is the cause of the universe and the life within it; but this is not incontrovertible. Randomness is not something which can be demonstrated – it is impossible to prove that something has happened by chance.

Dawkins' argument that 'airplanes built by scientific principles work' is not a sound argument with regard to the origins of humankind and of the universe. Aircraft can be tested through experiment, but the ways in which life began have to be worked out and guessed at through inductive reason rather than experimentation. Although evidence can be found to support theories such as the Big Bang, the experimental methods of science cannot do more than show probabilities about history.

Ian Barbour, in *Religion in an Age of Science* (Harper Collins, 1990), argues that if Dawkins objects to religious belief setting limitations on scientific discovery, then he should not allow science to dictate the usefulness of religion. Another critic of Dawkins, Alister McGrath, points out in his book *Dawkins' God* (Blackwell, 2004) that the point of view put forward by William Paley in his teleological argument is not typical of most Christian thought today – Dawkins is criticising an approach that is more than two hundred years out of date, and if Christians were to criticise the science of two hundred years ago, they would probably be able to find fault with that too.

 Develop your knowledge

Richard Dawkins' books and articles are written in an accessible way and are useful as supplements for your reading. Try *River out of Eden* (Phoenix Press, 1996) or *The Blind Watchmaker* (Penguin, 2006) where he assesses design arguments explicitly.

Alister McGrath presents an interesting counter-argument to Dawkins in his book *Dawkins' God* (Blackwell, 2004).

Tennant and design arguments

The theologian F. R. Tennant (1866–1957) was one of the first people to put forward a version of the design argument which included reference to and acceptance of the theory of evolution. According to Tennant, evolution is entirely consistent with design arguments, because of the way in which evolution itself seems to have a purpose. In the evolutionary process, creatures do not just randomly evolve this way and that, according to Tennant – progress is being made all the time, with the appearance on earth of life forms that are ever more complex, ever more intelligent and have an increasing amount of moral awareness. In Tennant's view, as he explained in his book *Philosophical Theology* (1930), evolution has a purpose, and is both created and guided by an intelligent God: 'the multitude of interwoven adaptations by which the world is constituted a theatre of life, intelligence, and morality, cannot reasonably be regarded as an outcome of mechanism, or of blind formative power, or aught but purposive intelligence.'

For Tennant, then, evidence supporting the theory of evolution was also further evidence of the existence of God. Tennant believed that if something is moving towards some kind of a goal, there must be a 'guiding hand' behind it, just as Aquinas had argued in his Fifth Way. Tennant saw evolution as movement, and therefore believed it to be evidence of the guiding hand of God.

Tennant and the anthropic principle

Tennant was the first to coin the phrase 'the anthropic principle'. By this, he was referring to the way in which the universe seems to be structured so that it was inevitable that life would develop. Physicists have discovered that there are a large number of 'coincidences' inherent in the fundamental laws of nature – and every one of these coincidences and specific relationships between different physical phenomena is necessary for life and for consciousness. If the laws of nature such as the law of gravity or the laws governing the balance of different gases in the atmosphere were even slightly different, human life (or any other form of life) could not have happened – and yet the laws of the universe are the way that we are, and we are here. For some people, including Tennant, the fact that we are here against all the odds is evidence of the existence of a God who fine-tuned the universe deliberately so that we could exist.

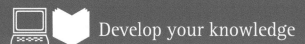

Develop your knowledge

An excellent but quite demanding book detailing these coincidences, the implications of them and the historical background of the anthropic principle is *The Anthropic Cosmological Principle* by John Barrow and Frank Tipler (Oxford Paperbacks, 1988).

Barrow and Tipler, in their book *The Anthropic Cosmological Principle*, explain for example a point made by the physicist Paul Davies, where he pointed out that if the relative strengths of nuclear and electromagnetic forces were even slightly different, carbon atoms could not exist in nature – and there would be no human physicists to study them. Roger Penrose, in *The Emperor's New Mind*, calculates the statistical improbability of the fine-tuning for the existence of the universe as one in 10 billion, multiplied by 123.

The anthropic principle can be held in a variety of different ways:

1. The weak anthropic principle: This just states that, given that we are here, the universe must have the properties and coincidences necessary for us to exist. This is useful in that it enables scientists to make further predictions about various aspects of the universe; but it gives no insight into *why* the universe is this way.

2. The participatory anthropic principle: Some, basing their views on quantum mechanics, which give an important role to the observer as well as to the observed, suggest that the universe would not exist unless there were observers to see it, which is a rather subtle philosophical view. However, others criticise this by saying that the universe shows evidence that it clearly did exist long before we were here, and also continues to exist in parts where we cannot observe.

3. The strong anthropic principle: This states that it is somehow *necessary* for the universe to have these special properties and coincidences. They do not just happen to happen, but are necessary; the universe was 'constructed' and could not have come into existence in any other way. This strong anthropic principle is used by Tennant and others to support modern teleological arguments – they argue that it was inevitable that human life should have come about, given the structure of the universe.

There have been various criticisms of the anthropic principle:

1. Some people think that the weak anthropic principle has no meaning at all, and that it is simply a tautology: *'We are here, therefore the universe is such that we are here.'* It does not tell us anything, it simply states the obvious.

2. Others believe that there could be an infinite number of universes existing, if existing is the right word, in parallel, in different kinds of time. We happen to live in one which is suited to life but have no access to the others. If this is the case, then the amazing coincidence that everything fell into place for the existence of life remains not very amazing, but something that was bound to happen given infinite possibilities.

3. Many people argue that it is illogical to argue that the universe is structured in the way that it is in order that human life can exist. The argument seems to give humanity a special status which is unwarranted (the word 'anthropic' comes from the Greek *anthropos*, meaning 'human being'). If the universe were structured differently, dung beetles would

not be here either, so the argument could equally well be made that the universe is designed for the existence of dung beetles – or even, that the universe is designed for the existence of cancer.

4. It might be highly unlikely that the structure of the universe allows for our existence, but everything that ever happens is highly unlikely, when considered alongside all the other possibilities of what might have happened instead. Think of the odds stacked against you being here reading this page. Of all the different people your parents might have met, they happened to meet each other; of all the numerous sperm and eggs that could have combined, it happened that you were conceived. Of all the different life choices you could have made, you have chosen to study this subject, and so on. For many people, this does not prove the existence of God, but is simply the random effect of chance.

When you throw dice, whatever score you achieve, the odds were against that particular outcome. Does this show a supernatural intelligence at work, making something happen against the odds? Or is it just the case that the dice had to fall some way or another, and they have fallen this way by chance?

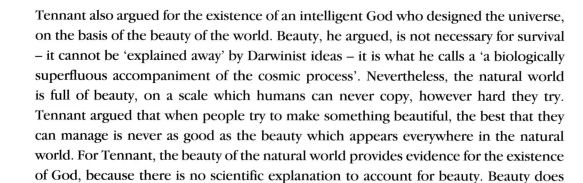

Tennant's aesthetic design argument

Tennant also argued for the existence of an intelligent God who designed the universe, on the basis of the beauty of the world. Beauty, he argued, is not necessary for survival – it cannot be 'explained away' by Darwinist ideas – it is what he calls a 'a biologically superfluous accompaniment of the cosmic process'. Nevertheless, the natural world is full of beauty, on a scale which humans can never copy, however hard they try. Tennant argued that when people try to make something beautiful, the best that they can manage is never as good as the beauty which appears everywhere in the natural world. For Tennant, the beauty of the natural world provides evidence for the existence of God, because there is no scientific explanation to account for beauty. Beauty does

Tennant argued that the beauty of the natural world cannot be explained by science. He thought the best explanation of beauty is that God made it, for his own enjoyment and for ours.

not perform a utilitarian function, so there is no reason for there to be so much of it in the world, Tennant argues, unless it is put there by God, for the purposes of human enjoyment and for God himself to enjoy when he looks at his creation.

Of course, not everyone would agree that the beauty of the world points to the existence of God. Some argue that beauty is not an absolute quality, but is a matter of opinion, so that beauty does not 'exist' in the sense that Plato's Form of Beauty might be said to exist, but is a value-judgement.

To think about

Do you think that beauty exists, in an objective way, or do you think that it is just a matter of opinion whether something is beautiful or not?

Key points

- Tennant's writing was intended to support design arguments in spite of Darwinist criticisms.
- He argued for divine design on the basis of the anthropic principle.
- He also argued that the beauty of the natural world is best explained if we accept the existence of God.

Swinburne's design argument

Richard Swinburne is a modern Christian philosopher of religion who supports teleological (and other) arguments for the existence of God. He believes that scientific discoveries provide good grounds for belief in God. In his book, *Is There a God?*, he argues that we need an explanation for the fact that the fundamental laws of nature operate with such regularity:

> … *not merely are there enormous numbers of things, but they all behave in exactly the same way. The same laws of nature govern the most distant galaxies we can observe through our telescopes as operate on earth, and the same laws govern the earliest events in time to which we can infer as operate today. Or, as I prefer to put it, every object, however distant in time and space from ourselves, has the same powers and the same liabilities to exercise those powers as do the electrons and protons from which our own bodies are made. If there is no cause of this, it would be a most extraordinary coincidence – too extraordinary for any rational person to believe.* (Is There a God?, p. 49)

For Swinburne, it stretches our credibility if we are asked to believe that the regularity of the laws of physics is just a coincidence. In his view, it is far simpler and more rational to conclude that these laws must exist because of a divine intelligence. Swinburne is impressed not only by the laws of physics themselves, but by the fact that these laws are easy for humans to observe. These laws, he argues, have important consequences for us. We can observe that seeds grow when they are planted and nurtured, and we can use this observation to grow our own food. We can observe that objects fall when dropped, and we can use this knowledge to avoid accidents. Swinburne says that this availability of scientific knowledge shows that God does not only exist, but cares for us: God gives us the freedom to make choices for ourselves and for other people. He also gives us the freedom to decide how much knowledge we want to have, and gives us the ability to make advances in science and technology.

Swinburne believes that Paley's argument is sound, in spite of the various criticisms made of it. He writes:

> *Paley's book is devoted to showing how well built in all their intricate detail are animals and humans, and so to concluding that they must have had God as their maker. The analogy of animals to complex machines seems to me correct, and its conclusion justified.* (Is There a God?, p. 58)

Develop your knowledge

Swinburne's arguments for the existence of God can be found in many of his writings, for example in his books *Is there a God?* (Oxford University Press, 1996) and *The Existence of God* (Clarendon Press, 2004).

There is a wide variety of material available to read about design arguments for the existence of God – some are more difficult than others. The following books are suggested as accessible:

Philosophy of Religion by Peter Cole (Hodder Arnold, 1999)
Philosophy of Religion by Brian Davies (Oxford University Press, 2003)
Philosophy of Religion: Thinking about Faith by C. Stephen Evans (Intervarsity Press, 1985)
Teach Yourself Philosophy of Religion by Mel Thompson (Teach Yourself, 2003)
The Puzzle of God by Peter Vardy (Fount, 1999)

Swinburne also argues in favour of Tennant's view that the beauty of the natural world is evidence of the existence of God. The main force of Swinburne's argument is that it is good scientific practice to look for the most simple explanation when trying to solve a problem. In his view, alternative explanations offered for the order of the universe are more complicated than belief in God. Although other possibilities have been given, these often depend on us accepting the occurrence of very unlikely coincidences, which, he believes, require just as much of a 'leap of faith' as belief in God requires.

Practice exam questions

(a) Explain Aquinas' version of the teleological argument.

Here, you need to concentrate on Aquinas' version of the teleological argument, and avoid confusing it with other arguments. Beware of attributing ideas to Aquinas when they came from other thinkers; if you want to make reference to other versions of the argument in your answer, be clear about which thinker made which point. In your explanation, you could include reference to the Five Ways (what was Aquinas trying to show here?) and mention his dependence on Aristotle. You could support your explanation with quotations from Aquinas, and explain the imagery he uses.

(b) 'The strengths of the teleological argument outweigh its weaknesses.' Discuss.

For this part of the answer, you need to consider the main strengths and weaknesses of this argument, and decide whether or not you agree with the statement. Strengths might include its popular appeal, and its reliance on evidence that we can all experience. Weaknesses might include the existence of evil in the world and the fact that there are other possible ways of explaining order in the world. For high marks, rather than simply listing strengths and weaknesses, you should argue that one side of the debate is stronger than the other, and reach a conclusion.

Moral arguments

Kant had dealt with the ontological argument. He did not think that God's existence could be demonstrated solely through *a priori* reasoning – God's existence could not be shown based solely on logical analysis on the concept of God ('theoretical reasoning'). However, in Kant's view, we could have knowledge of God based on practical reason, if we consider our sense of right and wrong, of duty and of what it means to be good.

Kant considered that the teleological and cosmological arguments were essentially linked with the ontological, because of their ultimate dependence on the idea that God is necessarily existent. The teleological argument depends on the view that there must be a Designer, existing outside the world in the same way as a First Cause or Unmoved Mover, and these arguments, when followed to their logical conclusions, presuppose that there is a God who exists by definition – as in the ontological argument. But Kant had already shown his conviction that the ontological argument did not work, not because God does not exist, but because 'existence is not a predicate'.

Therefore, for Kant, all the arguments for the existence of God which were based on reasoning, either inductive (starting from evidence and working backward) or deductive (working from first principles and definitions, as in the ontological argument), did not work. For Kant, then, the existence of God is not something that we can *know* through the powers of reason. Reason only works for the world of sense experience, but God's existence is beyond the grasp of the five senses. Kant wrote in *The Critique of Pure Reason* that we should 'deny knowledge, in order to make room for faith'.

Kant's 'moral argument', therefore, is more closely linked to the argument from religious experience (although not very closely), than to the cosmological, ontological or teleological. It is based on the premise that humanity ought to strive towards moral perfection. (see page 315).

Kant's thinking can be set out in a series of steps:

1. A good will, or a person with right moral intentions, seeks to bring about the Highest Good, the *summum bonum*, the perfect state of affairs. If we take our ethical nature

seriously, we can see that this is what we should aim to achieve. Kant was, however, adamant that people should not act virtuously in order to receive reward; he was convinced that an act is only truly moral if it is done for its own sake and without any selfish motive. People should do the right thing purely because it is the right thing, inspired by 'the good will'. If they are doing the right thing because they want a reward for it, rather than because it is right, then it is no longer a truly moral act; it becomes a situation in which we are treating others as a means to an end, for our own gain, rather than because of a good will. We should strive for the *summum bonum*, the perfect state of affairs, by acting morally and doing right for its own sake; the *summum bonum* is achieved when this virtue is rewarded.

2. Kant argues that 'ought implies can' – because we know that we ought to aim for the *summum bonum*, it follows that it must be achievable. Kant says it is 'a necessity connected with duty as a requisite to presuppose the possibility of this highest good.' In other words, because we are required by our sense of duty to try to bring about the Highest Good, it must therefore be a possibility, it must be attainable.

3. However, although the realisation (making real) of the Highest Good has to be a possibility, it is not within our power as humans to achieve it – because, although we can strive towards virtue in our thought and conduct, we cannot ensure that happiness is added to virtue to make the perfect state of affairs. On our own, we cannot ensure that we get what we deserve for our efforts, because we are not omnipotent.

4. Therefore, there must be a rational moral being, who, as creator and ruler of the world, has the power to bring moral worth and happiness together. Kant argues in *The Critique of Practical Reason*: 'the existence is postulated of a cause of the whole of nature, itself distinct from nature, which contains the ground of the exact coincidence of happiness with morality.' In other words, he says he is supposing the existence of a being outside nature who is capable of bringing together those who are virtuous with happiness.

5. As this reward for happiness clearly does not happen in this life, where the good sometimes have lives of tragedy and the wicked prosper, it must be attained in eternity.

Kant did not suggest that these arguments were conclusive, or arguments which would convince the unbeliever. Instead, he based his view on our common experience of a sense of duty. He claimed that we know, in ourselves, what is right, we know where our duty lies and what we ought to do. We have this experience of the universe as a place where morality is important, we know what good is, and we know that it should be rewarded; we instinctively want the good people to end happily in a story, and we feel satisfied with a happy ending for the virtuous and rather cheated if the bad people appear to win. This innate sense of a moral structure for the universe points to the existence of a God who can ensure justice. In Kant's own words: 'It is morally necessary to assume the existence of God.'

Kant's view was not that morality is pointless unless there is a God to reward it – his argument was subtly different. Things are right or wrong *per se*, in Kant's view, and therefore he concludes that there must be a God.

Criticisms of Kant's moral argument

Some people have criticised the reasoning of Kant, in his suggestion that the *summum bonum* is possible and that therefore there must be a God to make it possible. John Hick argues that Kant has moved from the idea of logical possibility to the assumption of actuality. Even if something is logically possible, like the achievement of the best possible state of affairs, it does not follow that it ever actually will happen. Hick also argues that there is a contradiction in Kant's argument. At one point, he says that people are under an obligation to achieve the *summum bonum*; but then he says that it is impossible for people to achieve this, because they cannot bring together virtue and happiness.

Some have argued that Kant's assumption 'ought implies can' is false. Usually, we assume that we ought to do only things which are possible; we would not tell our children, for example, that they ought to learn to fly. But it could make sense to aim towards something, even if it is not ultimately achievable; it could be worthwhile to make efforts in the right direction. Brian Davies argues this point, saying that it would not be meaningless to tell a not very able child 'you ought to learn French' even if fluency is not a possibility. Or someone might say that they are aiming for peace in the world, even though this is unlikely to be achieved. Kant jumps from 'it ought to be possible' to 'therefore it is possible'.

Some people claim that the moral arguments are somewhat similar to teleological arguments, that they are saying in effect: 'We can see that there are moral laws in the world; therefore we can point to the existence of a moral law-giver.' If this is a correct assessment of moral arguments, then the same criticisms could be used against it as were used against teleological arguments. Brian Davies uses the same arguments, against Kant, as Hume used against thinkers such as Paley: why do we have to postulate that, behind moral law, there must be the Christian God? There could be other possibilities; Davies suggests (using Hume's idea) that perhaps moral law-giving could be done by a whole group of angels.

According to some philosophers, there is no objective moral law, even though some writers claim that there is. We might have a sense of right and wrong, but, as Sigmund Freud suggested, this could just be the internalised voice of our parents or society (see pages 127–31). We could just be expressing a preference, and the sense of an external moral objectivity could be mistaken. If this view is taken, then the whole moral argument collapses, because it is based on the premise that we all agree that there are absolute standards of right and wrong. If there is no independent moral law, then there is no need to suppose an independent moral law-giver.

Some writers have argued that, far from religion being a necessary result of morality, in fact religion works in opposition to morality. Some, for example Bertrand Russell, have pointed out that much evil has been done in the name of religion (for example, the Crusades, the persecution of the Jews, the killing of 'witches', the martyrdoms of so-called heretics) and that true morality lies in the opposite direction from religion. The philosopher James Rachels argued that the whole concept of a God who is the object of worship goes against morality. In his view, worship requires the submission of one's own moral freedom, and a being who requires worship, and therefore the loss of moral freedom, is therefore not worthy of worship; God, therefore, cannot exist. Bertrand Russell argued the humanist case for morality. Humanists reject the idea that there is any sort of supernatural deity, and object to the idea that our morality must be the result of a divine law-giver. According to Russell, our morality is the result of humanity seeking to promote the satisfaction of desire for the majority of people; our moral codes exist for the well-being of our society and consequently for the individuals in it, rather than being the result of any outside cause.

Like the other arguments for the existence of God, Kant's moral argument appears to be inconclusive. There are people who can make a strong case for not accepting its premises; many people do not accept, for example, that we are all governed by moral laws. Kant believed that the *summum bonum* must be achievable in order to make sense of our experience of morality; in the eighteenth century, the predominant view was that the universe does make sense, that everything exists for a purpose and has its place in an order, that everything can be explained and had what Leibniz called a 'sufficient reason'. However, contemporary thinking does not necessarily accept this view. Perhaps the world just has no point; there does not have to be any external reason to explain our sense of morality; perhaps the good do often end tragically and the wicked prosper, and perhaps there is no reason to it. But, in general, it is our intuition that there is a reason for us to behave in a moral way, which is why we continue to act in the way that we do.

To think about

How convincing do you find Kant's moral argument as an argument for the existence of God?

How convincing do you find it as an argument for life after death?

Other moral arguments for the existence of God

Other writers too have reached the conclusion that the existence of morality implies the existence of God, and also reveals the nature of God as perfectly good.

Aquinas understood that God was revealed through the human recognition of right and wrong. Of Aquinas' Five Ways of demonstrating the existence of God, the Fourth Way is his discussion of how morality reveals God:

> *The fourth way is taken from the gradation to be found in things. Among beings there are some more and some less good, true, noble and the like. But 'more' and 'less' are predicated of different things, according as they resemble in their different ways something which is the maximum, as a thing is said to be hotter according as it more nearly resembles that which is hottest; so that there is something which is truest, something best, something noblest and, consequently, something which is uttermost being; for those things that are greatest in truth are greatest in being, as it is written in Metaph. ii. Now the maximum in any genus is the cause of all in that genus; as fire, which is the maximum heat, is the cause of all hot things. Therefore there must also be something which is to all beings the cause of their being, goodness, and every other perfection; and this we call God.*

Many scholars have considered this argument to be the weakest of the Five Ways. Aquinas argues that all qualities are caused by the thing that possesses the maximum amount of those qualities – for example, all heat is caused by the hottest thing there is, which is fire. But this does not seem to work in practice: large buildings, for example, are not caused by the largest building that exists, and neither are they built by the largest builders. Nevertheless, the point Aquinas was making demonstrates his belief that moral demands must come from a perfectly good being.

Cardinal John Henry Newman (1801–90), an Anglican convert to Roman Catholicism, wrote, in *Grammar of Assent* in 1870, 'If, as is the case, we feel responsibility, are ashamed, are frightened, at transgressing the voice of conscience, this implies that there is One to whom we are responsible, before whom we are ashamed, whose claim upon us we fear.' Newman, then, was arguing that the voice of our conscience can be recognised as the voice of God; because we know when we have done something wrong, this implies that there is someone telling us, someone who has made the rules about right and wrong and given us the ability to know whether or not we are keeping to those rules. In the same book he wrote: 'in this special feeling, which follows on the commission of what we call right or wrong, lie the materials for the real apprehension of a Divine Sovereign and Judge'. In Newman's view, the conscience reveals the will of God to each individual.

In the twentieth century, writers such as C. S. Lewis in *Mere Christianity,* and H. P. Owen in *The Moral Argument for Christian Theism,* have maintained the same argument, suggesting that our moral sense shows that there is a God requiring certain standards from us. Owen wrote, in the 1960s, 'It is impossible to think of a command without also thinking of a commander …'.

Illtyd Trethowan took the same stance, but preferred not to talk about the moral argument, because he did not think this was a series of logical propositions leading to a conclusion. He wrote instead, in his book *Absolute Value* (Allen and Unwin, 1970) about our moral *experience,* claiming that through morality we have direct experience of God, and therefore of his existence. Our awareness of our obligation towards each other is an awareness of God. Trethowan also went on to argue that we have value, and recognise value in others, because we are given that value by God. What we are recognising in each other is that we are made in the image of God and are valuable to God.

Freud's challenge to moral arguments

Sigmund Freud (1856–1939) grew up in a Catholic town in Moravia (now in the Czech Republic), where he was one of a very small number of Jews. He claimed to have grown up without any belief in God, and never to have felt the need for it, although he was certainly familiar with all the Jewish customs and festivals, and was surrounded by practising Catholics.

There were at least two possible influencing factors in Freud's anti-religious feeling: he was strongly influenced by the teaching of his Catholic nanny, who was keen to impress him with the ideas of heaven and hell and who was very fond of ritual; and also he was faced with anti-Semitism, made to feel inferior and an outsider because he was Jewish.

Freud entered university at the age of 17, and chose to follow the medical profession, where the current opinion was that everything could be reduced to physical and chemical elements. The feeling was very much against the Greek idea that people have a 'vital spark', and against the idea that people are endowed a soul by a Creator, with ultimate purposes and an everlasting destiny. Instead, the view was that everything that we are can be reduced to the physical, and that we can discover what we are by scientific method.

Freud did not particularly enjoy clinical medicine (dealing directly with patients), and began to move into scientific and medical research, studying especially the human nervous system. He opened a private practice in human nervous disorders, and was financially able to marry after four years of waiting; he and his wife had exchanged more than 900 love letters (an irrelevant piece of information, but rather sweet). Freud began to take an interest in the treatment of what was known as hysteria in Victorian times, and in hypnosis as a healing method.

Freud saw hysteria and its symptoms as the product of emotional trauma. The patient had to rediscover repressed emotions, under hypnosis if necessary, in order to be able to reach a cure. This was called the cathartic method, bringing the individual to confront the causes of his or her complex. Freud became particularly interested in his discovery that behind the manifestations of neurosis there were often sexual disturbances. This line of investigation made him unpopular with many other scholars and psychologists, who saw his insistence on learning about a patient's sexuality as unnecessary and improper.

What made Freud so important among psychologists, even though many of his theories have now been largely discredited, was that he was the first to recognise that people have layers of mental strata, some of which are not immediately recognisable. He was the first to look scientifically at the human psyche, and to acknowledge that people have an 'unconscious' as well as conscious mental processes. Today, we accept that the thoughts that are in the front of our minds are not all there is to it; we know that there are memories, associations and so on hidden in deeper levels which might take some investigation to uncover. Freud arrived at the belief that the human mind could be seen as being made up of three layers:

1. **The ego** – this is the part of the mind which is obvious to us, the conscious self. We are aware of it, we know what we are thinking about, we know our own opinions about issues, our tastes, what makes us angry, and so on.

2. **The id** – this is the unconscious self, the part of us which is not immediately obvious, made up of memories which might have been forgotten or repressed, unconscious desires, repressed wishes that we do not admit to ourselves, and so on; the areas which can sometimes be brought out when someone is under hypnosis.

3. **The super-ego** – this could be equated with the conscience. It is the driving moral force, the internal voice which tells us that we should do some things and not others. Freud firmly believed that these moral imperatives come from our society as we grow up. We learn what is right and wrong from our parents, our siblings and our communities, and we internalise these imperatives until it feels to us as though we have an 'inner voice' telling us what to do. But for Freud, this feeling that morality comes from some kind of supernatural moral law-giver is entirely illusory.

The thinking of Freud therefore presents a strong challenge to moral arguments for the existence of God. In response to those who claim that our moral sense must lead us to conclude that a divine law-giver exists, Freud presents a different explanation: our moral sense exists because we learned as we grew up that there were right ways and wrong ways to behave. We were rewarded when we were 'good', and punished when we were 'bad', until a sense of right and wrong became a second nature to us. Freud did not, of course, prove that God does not exist, but he did show that God is not the only possible explanation for the human sense of morality.

Freud worked from the presupposition that the origin of religion is psychological – in other words, he assumed from the start that religious belief, religious experiences and religious impulses come from within the mind and not from any external, supernatural being.

To think about

Do you think Freud is right in thinking that our sense of morality comes from our parents and not from God?

He was very much influenced by other popular thinkers. Philosophers such as Hume and Rousseau had already suggested, before Freud, that religion was a distortion of human reason. Darwin had greatly excited the public imagination with his suggestion of evolution, and it became fashionable to apply evolutionary theory to other aspects of life as well as the development of the species. Many people were wondering how religion itself had evolved, and took it for granted that it had. Darwinism itself was, at least in part, responsible for the nineteenth-century interest in anthropology; it was very popular to study so-called 'primitive' peoples in the hope of learning how more developed civilisations had evolved their ideas and social systems.

One anthropologist, William Robertson Smith, considered that religion had developed around the idea of a totem; the clan regarded itself as related to a particular object or animal, which was the totem, and this totem should not be killed or injured; but once a year the totem was symbolically killed and eaten and its strength passed on to the clan. Freud was very enthusiastic about this idea of the origins of religion and developed it in his own writings.

Freud was convinced from the outset that religious rites are similar to neurotic obsessions (repeatedly saying the rosary, for example, could be regarded as similar to obsessively washing one's hands). In his book *Totem and Taboo* (1913) he argued that religious attitudes of 'primitives' are similar to neurotic obsessions, and concluded that religion is a universal obsessional neurosis.

While looking for the emotional traumas that might have been the reasons for the problems of his patients, Freud was led to investigate the lost memories of childhood, and looked at his own experiences in the process. He discovered in himself an early passion for his mother (who was 20 years younger than his father; Freud was the eldest of eight and so perhaps particularly close to her) and a subsequent jealousy of his father. He considered that this was a universal human characteristic, which he termed the 'Oedipus complex', referring to the myth of King Oedipus, who had unwittingly killed his father and married his mother. Freud believed that all boys nurse a subconscious desire to get rid of their fathers and have their mothers to themselves.

Freud developed a theory that the Oedipus complex is behind religion. People know that this basic desire to kill their father is socially unacceptable, and so the desire is repressed and translated on the conscious level to making an effort to respect and love a symbol which really represents the person's own father. Belief in God is, by this analysis, just a way of over-compensating for negative feelings towards a father. The origin of religion is therefore explained psychologically.

Freud depended heavily on Feuerbach when he argued that religion is an infantile illusion, rooted in 'conflicts of childhood arising from the father-complex'. Religion is an illusion, a desire for wish-fulfilment.

We shall tell ourselves that it would be very nice if there were a moral order in the universe and an after-life; but it is a very striking fact that all this is exactly as we are bound to wish it to be. (The Future of An Illusion)

Psycho-analysis has made us familiar with the intimate connection between the father-complex and belief in God; it has shown us that a personal God is, psychologically, nothing other than an exalted father, and it brings us evidence every day of how young people lose their religious beliefs as soon as their father's authority breaks down. Thus we recognise that the roots of the need for religion are in the parental complex. (Leonardo da Vinci and a Memory of His Childhood)

Key points

Freud argued that:
- Religion is for people who lack the maturity to live comfortably as adults without their parents.
- Religion is invented to help people come to terms with the 'Oedipus complex'. They have feelings of guilt towards their fathers and therefore imagine a great invisible cosmic father-figure whom they can worship.
- Religion is an 'infantile neurosis' that people would be better off without.

Did Freud successfully demolish moral arguments for the existence of God?

Hans Küng, in his book *Does God Exist?* (1980), criticised Freud's interpretation of religion in a number of ways.

1. He argued that Freud's interpretation of early religion is highly fictional; there is very little evidence to suggest that the kind of totemism described by Freud was ever actually practised by any society. Freud could have been carried away by the tide of enthusiasm for evolutionary ideas, looking for historical phases and making assumptions without the supporting evidence.

2. Freud could also be criticised for setting out to find a theory which supported his view, rather than forming his view on the basis of the evidence. For example, he took for granted Feuerbach's projection idea and worked from that, with an assumption from the outset that there is no objective God. It is therefore hardly surprising that he comes to the conclusion that religion is false, as this was also his starting-point.

3. Freud's atheism, like that of Marx and Feuerbach, is in the end a hypothesis, with no more conclusive evidence for it than there is for theism.

4. Even if it can be shown that religion can be wish-fulfilment, an infantile expression of an illusion, this does not mean that it always is. Humanity's profound desire for God and for eternal life does not prove that these things exist, but it does not prove they do not exist either. Perhaps, if there is a God, it is not unlikely that he would satisfy our needs.

5. Belief in God can be very much influenced by a child's relationship with his or her father, but this does not mean it always is, or that God therefore does not exist.

6. The assertion that the super-ego is something which comes from society and is internalised by the individual is just an assertion. Freud could be right, but he has not proved that he is right. He does not demonstrate with evidence that the moral consciousness must come from society and cannot have come from God, although it is a reasonable suggestion.

 Develop your knowledge

Brian Davies' book *An Introduction to the Philosophy of Religion* (OPUS, 1993) has an excellent chapter on the relationship between morality and religion.

Practice exam questions

(a) Explain Kant's moral argument for the existence of God.

For this part of the question, you need to give a clear explanation of the main points of Kant's moral argument, using key vocabulary such as *'summum bonum'* where appropriate. Kant's argument is quite subtle in places, so take care not to oversimplify. For high marks, give as detailed and accurate an account as you can.

(b) 'Kant was wrong to suggest that we all share a sense of right and wrong.' Discuss.

Part of Kant's argument was based on the premise that we all instinctively know what our duty is, and we realise that we ought to do our duty. This question asks you to assess whether that claim is fair. You might agree that a moral sense is common to all humanity, and that even when people commit wrong acts, they nevertheless know what they ought to do. Or you might disagree, and argue that different people have completely different moral standards with little in common between them. Support your argument with examples where possible, and try to reach a conclusion based on the arguments you have outlined.

The problem of evil

When people want to give counter-evidence against belief in the existence of God, the most obvious place to begin is with the problem of evil. The problem of evil is this: if (as Christians claim) there is a God who is omnipotent and omniscient and who is all-loving, then why do evil and suffering exist in the world? Surely, they argue, a wholly good and loving God would want to prevent evil, if he could; and if God can do anything at all, then he can both eliminate evil and prevent it from happening. Yet there is clear evidence of evil and suffering in the world. Therefore the God described by Christianity cannot exist. The writer J. L. Mackie gives a neat summary of the problem in his book *The Miracle of Theism* (Oxford University Press, 1982): 'A wholly good omnipotent being would eliminate evil completely; if there really are evils, then there cannot be any such being.'

The problem of evil is sometimes known as 'the inconsistent triad'. There are three proposals that we are asked to accept:

1. That God is perfectly good.
2. That God is all-powerful.
3. That evil and suffering exist.

This 'triad' of three ideas is 'inconsistent' because, it is alleged, we cannot believe all of them at the same time without contradiction.

It is argued that, if God created the universe and everything that is in it, then he could have made the world in any way he chose. He could have chosen to make a world where earthquakes, floods, cyclones and volcanoes never happen. He could have made a world where people have no inclination or capacity at all to hurt one another. He could have made a world where animals were able to survive by some means other than killing each other; or a world where killing was painless and where no-one felt grief. Yet instead, this is the world we have: a world where some creatures survive by preying on others; where people go to war; where there are famines, fires and diseases, torture and crime, disappointments and injustice. How could an omnipotent God fail at the task of creating a perfect world and keeping it perfect? If the world has gone wrong and deviated from God's purposes, then why does God not use his omnipotence to make it right again?

To think about

Do you think that an all-loving God would eliminate evil from the world if he could?

It is also argued that, if God is omniscient, he must have known what the world was going to be like when he made it; and he must have known how humans would behave, given that he made human nature. If God meant the world to be this way, then he cannot be all-loving. A human parent's love is infinitely small in comparison with the love of God, and yet no human parents would ever want their children to suffer terrible pain: therefore a perfectly loving God cannot want the world to be the way that it is. Yet, if God intended that the world should be different, and it has all gone wrong, then this casts doubts on God's omniscience. Why did God not anticipate genocide, or hurricanes, or cancer? Why did he not make a world that would never go wrong?

To think about

Do you think that an omniscient (all-knowing) God should know the future as well as the present and the past – if he doesn't know it, does that mean he is not omniscient? Or do you think that because the future has not yet happened, it cannot be known, even by God?

The problem of evil is not just an intellectual problem. It is not simply a puzzle of logic which religious believers should try to solve for the fun of it, like sudoku. It presents genuine and immediate difficulties. Some people feel that the existence of evil in the world means that they can never accept the existence of a wholly good God. Other people sometimes lose a faith which was once strong when they are faced with great suffering; a father whose child has died, or someone who is paralysed in an act of terrorism, or a mother who cannot feed her baby because of famine, might conclude that there cannot be an omnipotent loving God after all.

'Natural' and 'moral' evil

Traditionally, evil and suffering in the world have been divided into two kinds: 'natural' evil (or sometimes 'non-moral' evil), and 'moral' evil. Natural evil refers to the suffering and harm which comes from the natural world and the way that things are made, rather than through any human agency – for example, the pain of childbirth, the suffering and loss caused by earthquakes or drought, or by congenital health problems such as cystic fibrosis, and the fact of death. Moral evil, in contrast, is that which results from human wickedness, such as murder, rape, terrorism, theft, deceitfulness or bullying.

Earthquakes are considered a 'natural evil', as they are caused by the structure of the planet rather than through any fault of humanity.

Natural evil is taken to mean those forms of evil and suffering which are not the direct result of free acts of human beings. There are several different areas which could be described as natural evil, and Peter Vardy in *The Puzzle of Evil* (Fount, 1999) lists them as including:

• animal suffering
• the suffering caused by natural disasters, such as floods, earthquakes, volcanoes
• pain resulting from disease
• pain resulting from apparently poor design of the human body (for example, pain in childbirth, and pain in the way in which parts of our bodies appear to give up working properly before our life-span is over)
• psychological illness.

Unless people try to claim that natural evil does not really exist, the believer who wants to maintain that God is omnipotent and all-loving is left with two possibilities: either a case must be made which shows evil to be the fault of humanity or the Devil, and not of God, or it must be shown that although God created natural evil, he had a good reason for doing so.

Some philosophers, such as Augustine and Aquinas, have argued that the evil in the natural world was not intended by God, but it is a necessary inevitable part of the existence of good. Evil does not have a separate existence of its own, but is a falling away from goodness, a measure of the distance that something is, away from perfection. All contingent beings have the capacity to be less than perfect, to fall short of their true nature, and therefore evil is a necessary part of the created, contingent world. Augustine argued that 'evil' in nature is part of the variety of the world.

Moral evil, in contrast to natural evil, is the kind which is caused by humanity. People deliberately inflict suffering on each other – they bully each other, steal from each other, commit acts of vandalism, violence, war and terrorism. People are unfaithful to their partners, and break their promises to their children. Sometimes they cause their own pain, for example when they suffer the consequences of smoking or drinking.

Moral evil might seem easier for theists to explain. They can argue, and often do, that the suffering resulting from moral evil is not God's fault, but our own. God lovingly gave us freedom of choice when he made us, and unfortunately we often choose to do wrong. However, there are still difficulties with this position. Did God not know, when he gave us free will, that we would choose the wrong things? Why did God create us with the ability and the inclination to do wrong? Why does God not stop us, when we make wrong choices – if God can see that someone is about to ill-treat a small child, why does he not step in?

'Moral evil' is the name given to the evil and suffering caused by humanity's own deliberate choices.

Although natural evil is often seen as being different from moral evil, in that it is not the direct result of human sin, Brian Hebblethwaite points out in his book *Evil, Suffering and Religion* (Hawthorn Books, 1976) that the two often overlap. He writes that the free will defence:

> *only partly explains the suffering actually caused by human wickedness, for example, by a protracted and cruel war such as the world wars of our century or the war in Vietnam. Granted that these evils are brought about by human action, it remains the case that it is the nature of the physical world and the structure of conscious and sentient beings such as ourselves that render the consequences of evil actions so terrible. Part of the problem of evil is the fact that, the structure of our bodies, nerves and brains being what it is, physical and mental torture (as well as disease and accident) can take such horrific forms.*

In other words, even though moral evil can be blamed on human failure, we still need an explanation of why we are made in such a way that we feel physical pain, bereavement, anger and grief. The question for those who believe that the world is wholly dependent on a good and omnipotent God is why God made a world which contains the possibilities for so much pain – instead of making a wholly good world, or even no world at all.

What is a theodicy?

Key term

theodicy – an attempt to justify God in spite of the existence of evil and suffering.

The accepted name for the whole idea of trying to resolve the problem of evil with the existence of a good and omnipotent God is **theodicy**. The word, first used by the philosopher Leibniz, comes from two Greek terms: *theos*, meaning God, and *diké*, meaning justice. A theodicy, therefore, is an attempt to justify God, to show that God can still have the character which is claimed by believers, even if the world does contain both natural and moral evil.

Some theologians, for example the Christian theologian Anders Nygren in his *Commentary on Romans* (Augsburg Fortress, 1978), have argued that it is wrong for religious believers to attempt any sort of theodicy. It is irreligious, they say, to imagine that humans with their small fallible minds can attempt to understand God. We should not be trying to make God explain himself to us; we should be far more concerned with explaining ourselves to God, or else be like Job in the Bible and fall silent in the awareness that God is so much greater than we are and incomprehensible to us.

John Hick, in his book *Evil and the God of Love* (Palgrave Macmillan, 1985) argues against this. He suggests that it is possible to try to understand the existence of evil and suffering in the world, without this necessarily being in the spirit of challenging God. It can be done in the spirit of genuine enquiry. Hick argues that Christians have to try to understand evil, because it is central to other aspects of faith, such as the notion of sin and redemption, and the concept of Christ as saviour. People cannot understand the basics of the Christian message without some consideration of sin and evil, and therefore some kind of a theodicy has to be an allowable subject of investigation.

Theodicy only presents a problem for people who believe in a certain kind of God, one who is both loving and omnipotent. People with no religious faith do not have the same kinds of questions to answer. For some, such as Bertrand Russell, as we saw in the discussion of the cosmological argument on pages 94-97, the universe needs no explanation; it just is the way that it is; and this includes evil and suffering, which just happen.

For the Christian, the Jew and the Muslim, however, who have a different picture of God and who believe that each individual has only one life, some attempt must be made to reconcile evil and suffering with the existence of a good God.

Jewish responses to evil and suffering

The Jewish Bible ('Old Testament' to Christians) does not present a consistent answer to the question of whether or not God is to be blamed for natural evil. Sometimes, for example in Genesis, the suggestion is that God created everything good, and that the whole world has been perverted by misuse of free will. At other times, God seems to be shown to be in control of the world, able to change natural rules and laws of logic when they suit his purpose, for example, sending the flood in the time of Noah, the plagues at the time of the Passover, and parting the Red Sea – so it might seem as though 'natural disasters' are the deliberate will of God.

For the most part, the writers of the Bible do not tackle the question of why there is suffering in the world. It is simply accepted as a fact of life. However, the book of Genesis does attempt to provide some explanation, with the story of the Fall of Adam and Eve in Genesis 2. In this story, God forms a man from the dust of the ground, and breathes life into him. God realises that the man needs a partner, and so a woman is created, using one of the man's ribs while the man is sleeping. The man and woman are given a garden in which to live, and are put in control of the other species as stewards of the earth. They are told not to eat from the tree of the knowledge of good and evil; but the serpent persuades Eve to try the fruit, and she does, before giving some to Adam. When they eat, they realise that they are naked, and are ashamed. They try to hide from God, but God questions them about what they have done. Because Adam and Eve have disobeyed God's command, they are punished, and from that point they and their descendants cannot live in Eden but have to struggle to make a living.

According to the book of Genesis, evil was brought into the world through the disobedience of Adam and Eve.

The Fall of humanity is seen to be responsible for the perpetual struggle between one species and another. Eve and the serpent are set against each other as enemies. Pain comes into the world for the first time, as well as the struggle for survival against the elements. The ground becomes 'accursed', producing thorns and thistles to make it difficult for the man to grow food except through hard work. The link is made here between the behaviour of humanity and the environment itself; the elements have to be struggled against because of human sin. Humanity, then, has tried to become god-like, to gain the knowledge of good and evil, but instead will be returned to the dust from which Adam was formed.

From the outset, humanity was given the responsibility to choose whether to live under the authority of God, or to disobey and to try to be more autonomous.

People are being warned not to think themselves omniscient; they should remain in recognition of the greater wisdom of God, and should not try to assert their independence outside the authority of God – otherwise they will be doomed to die. Does this suggest that, before the Fall, there was to be no death, and that God's plan was that humanity would be immortal?

Key point

- The book of Genesis teaches that evil came into the world when humanity made a deliberate decision to disobey God.

The Genesis story raises many questions: Why did the serpent want to persuade Eve to disobey God? Was the serpent created evil from the start, or did he somehow become evil even though he had been created good? Why did God allow the serpent to behave in this way?

The serpent in Genesis does not seem to be anything other than one of the creatures God had made, different only because he was 'more crafty' than any of the other animals.

There is no suggestion here that he is to be equated with the Devil, although that was certainly an idea which came into Jewish and Christian culture later (probably as a way of coping with the problem of why a creature with the capability and inclination to do evil was part of the original Garden of Eden). The unanswered question is raised here, of how the serpent came to be more crafty in the first place: was this the way that he was created? The writer is so concerned with establishing the guilt of humanity that he plays down this part of the story and does not deal with the question. However, it is an important issue to be considered, because if God gave the serpent its craftiness, and also gave the people their inclination to be disobedient, then it might still be argued that God is to blame for the existence of evil.

One of the many questions raised by this passage is: did God decide upon this punishment for humanity, out of a number of possibilities, or is what happens to people the inevitable result of their actions? (It is rather like the difference between a mother telling her child that if he plays with the fire he will get burnt, which is inevitable; or that if he plays with the fire, she will stop his pocket money, which is her choice.) This is a significant question, because if the punishment is an inevitable result of disobeying God, then humanity could be blamed for natural evil; but if God chose the punishment, then God can be blamed, as he could have chosen something else instead, or perhaps decided to forgive them.

Passages which occur later in the Jewish Bible also raise the problem of evil and suffering. These passages do not offer any kind of explanation, but express human emotions about the way the world is, and raise questions the writers wish God would answer for them. The prophet Jeremiah, for example, asks God to explain why the world seems so unjust. His problem was not just that innocent people suffer, but that wicked people seem to get away with wrongdoing, and it offended Jeremiah's sense of justice that God should allow this; he felt that God should be rewarding the good and faithful, and punishing the hypocrites:

> *You are always righteous, O Lord,*
> *when I bring a case before you.*
> *Yet I would speak with you about your justice:*
> *Why does the way of the wicked prosper?*
> *Why do all the faithless live at ease?* (Jeremiah 12:1)

The writer of Psalm 82 also felt that God's justice was difficult to understand:

> *How long will you defend the unjust and show partiality to the wicked?*
> *Defend the cause of the weak and fatherless; maintain the rights of the poor and oppressed.*
> *Rescue the weak and needy; deliver them from the hand of the wicked.*
> (Psalm 82: 2–4)

The book of Job

The book of Job, in the Old Testament, is often considered to be the most puzzling book of the Bible, both philosophically and historically. Historically, it raises all sorts of issues about when it might have been written and how it evolved into the book that we have today; whether the prologue comes from a folk tradition outside Judaism; and whether the epilogue was part of the original text. These issues keep biblical historians happily employed. Philosophically, it presents a whole different set of questions, as it addresses the problem of evil and suffering in a way which, for some, raises more difficulties than it solves.

The book of Job addresses the question of why good and innocent people sometimes suffer more hardship than they seem to deserve.

At the beginning of the story, the reader is introduced to a man named Job, who lived in the land of Uz. Job is presented as a wholly innocent man, as good and as dutiful to God as humanly possible. He works hard, he takes care of his family and he fulfils all his religious obligations – not only that, but he performs sacrifices on behalf of all his sons and daughters too, just in case they should have committed a sin. Then, the writer tells us, the time comes for God to meet with the angels, and among them is Satan. God and Satan begin to talk, and God asks Satan what he has been up to lately. Satan replies that he has just been wandering about the world a bit, here and there, and then God asks if Satan has happened to notice Job:

'Have you considered my servant Job? There is no-one on earth like him; he is blameless and upright, a man who fears God and shuns evil.' (Job 1:8)

It is as if God is boasting to Satan about Job's faithfulness. Satan answers that of course Job is a faithful man; it is only natural, God has given him everything he could possibly want, he has no cause to be anything other than good. Satan suggests that God puts Job to the test, and that Satan should be allowed to take away from Job the good things that he has – then they could see whether Job remained faithful, or whether he turned away from God. And God agrees.

Disasters begin to happen to Job and his family, in quick succession. His servants are lost. The roof falls in on his children and they are killed. His cattle die, and he is afflicted with sores. Poor Job is in a terrible state, but nevertheless he does not sin and turn against God: 'In all this, Job did not sin by charging God with wrongdoing' (Job 1:22).

Job's three friends, Eliphaz, Bildad, and Zophar, come along to help him, and are so appalled by his suffering that they follow the Jewish mourning custom of sitting Shiva with Job for seven days without speaking. They then try to find an explanation for Job's suffering, using well-rehearsed arguments. They suggest to him that God is correcting him for some fault, and urge him to search his conscience for a sin he might have committed which could explain this punishment:

So listen to me, you men of understanding.
Far be it from God to do evil,
from the Almighty to do wrong.
He repays a man for what he has done;
he brings upon him what his conduct deserves.
It is unthinkable that God would do wrong,
that the Almighty would pervert justice. (Job 34:10–12)

Job, however, cannot find a reason why God is allowing him to suffer so much, and after some time, he has heard enough from his friends. Job demands an audience with God. He wants to know what it is that has made God treat him in this way.

Oh, that I had someone to hear me!
I sign now my defence – let the Almighty answer me;
let my accuser put his indictment in writing. (Job 31:35)

Finally, Job gets his way and he does meet with God. However, God does not answer Job's complaints with any self-justification. Instead, he tells Job to be silent, and says that God is the one who will be asking the questions.

Then the Lord answered Job out of the storm. He said:
'Who is this that darkens my counsel
with words without knowledge?
Brace yourself like a man;
I will question you,
and you shall answer me.' (Job 38:1–3)

God asks Job rhetorical questions, in some of the most beautiful poetry of the Bible: Are you omnipotent? Did you create the world? Can you perform any of the feats that I can? Do you understand any of the things that I can understand?

Does the rain have a father?
Who fathers the drops of dew?
From whose womb comes the ice?
Who gives birth to the frost from the heavens
when the waters become hard as stone,
when the surface of the deep is frozen?
Can you bind the beautiful Pleiades?
Can you loose the cords of Orion?
Can you bring forth the constellations in their seasons
or lead out the Bear with its cubs?
Do you know the laws of the heavens?
Can you set up God's dominion over the earth? (Job 38:28–33)

'Who gives birth to the frost from the heavens when the waters become hard as stone, when the surface of the deep is frozen?'

Job recognises that he is in the wrong to call God to account. He comes to realise that God's omnipotence and omniscience are far beyond his own understanding, and that he is too small and too limited to be able to expect any answer to the problem of his own suffering. God can see the whole picture, the whole of creation, and he cannot; therefore he will never understand the greater context of what has happened to him. He is ashamed of himself for having demanded an explanation.

> *Then Job replied to the Lord:*
> *'I know that you can do all things;*
> *no plan of yours can be thwarted.*
>
> *'You asked, "Who is this that obscures my counsel without knowledge?"*
> *Surely I spoke of things I did not understand,*
> *things too wonderful for me to know.'* (Job 42: 1–3)

Once Job has reached this point, God restores everything to him. He has servants and cattle even more impressive than he had before, and he has ten more children to replace the ones he lost (so no harm done there!).

The answer to the problem of evil given in the book of Job, then, is that there is no answer, or at least not one that we can expect to understand. For some believers, this is acceptable. They will say that they do not know why they or their loved ones are suffering: but they do know that God is all-loving and omnipotent, and that God does not make mistakes, and this is enough for them. For other people, however, the story resolves nothing. It suggests that God uses people as his playthings, experimenting with them to see what they might do next with no concern for their feelings. Although, for some, God's answer to Job is an important reminder of humanity's smallness in comparison with the greatness of God, to other people it is too reminiscent of the obnoxious Mr Wormwood, father of Roald Dahl's character Matilda, who says (in the film of the book) to his unfortunate daughter: 'I'm big, and you're small. I'm smart, and you're dumb. I'm right, and you're wrong. *And there's nothing you can do about it!*

To think about

Some people agree that the book of Job is right in its conclusion that people cannot expect to understand the mind of God. Others argue that this is not good enough and that we have a right to know why we suffer. What is your own view?

Jewish theodicy

Moses Maimonides, a great Jewish philosopher of the twelfth century, wrote about the problem of evil and suffering in his work *Guide for the Perplexed*, where he distinguished three types of evil:

1. There is evil and suffering that happens to people just because they are physical beings, such as old age, illness, death and bereavement, and the suffering that comes about through the natural physical properties of the world, such as avalanches, storm damage and earthquakes. Maimonides argued that these evils do not challenge the goodness of God, because they are an inevitable part of physical existence, and we would not be here without them.

2. There is evil that people inflict on each other. This is humanity's own fault, although not always the fault of the victim in individual cases.

3. There is evil that people inflict upon themselves, or which they bring upon themselves as a punishment for their own wrongdoing; so again, they have only themselves to blame.

Later rabbis developed Maimonides' view, and concluded that suffering can be seen as a way of atonement for sins – both the sins of the individual, and the collective sin of the people as a whole. There was also the view that God does not give to people more suffering than they can bear.

However, the twentieth-century Holocaust put the question of why God allows suffering into painfully sharp focus. Among the millions who were killed, six million Jews were systematically murdered because of their faith, and there was no miraculous sending of plagues upon the Nazis to force them to let the people go. How could this happen? Had God abandoned his people, whom he had promised to care for as his kingdom of priests and his special possession? During and after the Second World War, Jews around the world tried to cope with the obvious questions raised, and came up with a variety of responses:

• Some people abandoned their faith altogether, concluding either that there was no God at all, or that if there was a God, they wanted nothing more to do with him.
• Others viewed the Holocaust as a punishment for sin, arguing that God had inflicted similar punishments in the past (for example, when the Jews had gone into exile in Babylon) and drawing comparisons. However, it is still difficult to understand the apparent indiscriminate suffering of a whole people, including the faithful and small

children, especially as those who escaped or collaborated with the Nazis were not notably less sinful than those who had died.

- Some regarded the Holocaust as a test of faith, just as Job had been tested, to see whether they would be able to remain faithful to God in the face of great hardship. However, this raises the question of why God would have needed to test the people at all – did he not already know whether they were faithful or not? And could the satisfaction of God's curiosity really be a justification for genocide?

- There is also the view that the Holocaust was necessary in order for the State of Israel to be established, and that although there had been great suffering, the restoration of the Promised Land would make it all worthwhile.

The twentieth-century Holocaust raised questions about evil and suffering which, for many, were impossible to answer.

John Bowker, in his book *Problems of Suffering in the Religions of the World* (Cambridge University Press, 1970), comments:

In a way, the outsider has no right to intrude on grief such as this – or at least, those who lived through those years find it hard to do so. Perhaps in the perspective of history it will be easier, but so close to the event there is no comment that can usefully be made. The scale is so vast, the enormity of evil so great, that it defies comprehension.

Develop your knowledge

Holocaust Theology: A Reader edited by Dan Cohn-Sherbok (New York University Press, 2002) provides a comprehensive, although quite demanding, discussion of different Jewish responses to the Holocaust.

After the Evil: Christianity and Judaism in the Shadow of the Holocaust by Richard Harries (Oxford University Press, 2003) is an accessible consideration of philosophical problems raised by the Holocaust, written from a Christian perspective.

Beliefs about evil and suffering in Islam

In Islam, the problem of suffering is understood within the belief that Allah is all-powerful. Allah is believed to be omnipotent, in the sense that everything within the world and outside the world is under his control – therefore, it follows that when people suffer, it is not because Allah has lost control, but because there is some divine purpose to the suffering. Because Allah is in charge of everything, it is Allah's will that some people die young, and that others live to a great age. It is even Allah's will that some become senile and lose the abilities that they once had. The Qur'an says:

O mankind! if ye have a doubt about the Resurrection, consider that We created you out of dust, then out of sperm, then out of a leech-like clot, then out of a morsel of flesh, partly formed and partly unformed, in order that We may manifest our power to you; and We cause whom We will to rest in the wombs for an appointed term, then do We bring you out as babes, then foster you that ye may reach your age of full strength; and some of you are called to die, and some are sent back to the feeblest old age, so that they know nothing after having known much, and further, thou seest the earth barren and lifeless, but when We pour down rain on it, it is stirred to life, it swells, and it puts forth every kind of beautiful growth. (Surah 22.5)

The key to Islam is in its name, which means 'submission'. For the Muslim, the way to cope with suffering is to submit to the will of Allah without committing the sins of doubt, complaint or scepticism. In the Muslim view, Allah is the omnipotent creator of everything, who has the right to do what he likes with his creation. If he chose to punish everyone, then this would be perfectly just, as all people fall short of the ideal. However, Allah is merciful and compassionate, and therefore people do not always receive the punishment they deserve.

When Muslims speak of Allah, they emphasise his nature as the most merciful and compassionate.

Free will forms a major part of the Muslim understanding of evil and suffering. This life is viewed as a test, in preparation for the life to come. When people die, they will be judged, and in order to acquit themselves well, Muslims should recognise that suffering is part of God's purposes for them, which they should bear with courage and faith.

Key point

• Islam teaches that Allah is merciful and compassionate, and that suffering is a test. Because Allah is omnipotent, suffering is always under his control and part of his purpose for humanity.

Hindu and Buddhist approaches to evil and suffering

The Eastern traditions of Hinduism and Buddhism do not have the same questions to deal with when considering evil and suffering, because neither religion claims that there is an all-loving, perfectly good God. Buddhism does not accept the existence of God at all (although some branches of Buddhism accept the existence of supernatural beings); and Hindus believe that God, or the various deities, exhibit characteristics of both good and evil.

In Hinduism, the deities contain elements of both good and evil. Shiva, for example, is a god of both creation and destruction. There is not a problem reconciling evil with the existence of God, because God is believed to contain both good and evil.

In both of these Eastern traditions, suffering is seen as something which is an inevitable part of the physical world of *samsara* – the endless cycle of birth, death and rebirth. For the Buddhist, all physical life is suffering (*dukkha*) because everything is in a constant state of change. Even when we are sublimely happy, we know that the moment cannot last.

Hindus and Buddhists believe that one of the keys to understanding suffering is the doctrine of **karma**. According to this doctrine, all volitional actions (in other words, all actions that we make a conscious decision to perform) have 'fruits', or consequences. If we do something good, then good will be caused by this action, and if we do something bad, then we cause more harm to happen as a result. The law of karma is not seen as reward or punishment inflicted by the gods, but as a natural law of nature – something that inevitably happens.

Clearly, in the space of a lifetime, people do not get what they deserve. People who act generously or kindly do not always find that others are generous and kind to them in return; sometimes people suffer hardship or illness even when they seem to have done nothing to deserve it. There are also those people who are thoroughly unpleasant, corrupt or criminal, who seem to live comfortable wealthy lives and never suffer for their behaviour. And what about babies who are born with health problems – how can their suffering be considered a result of their actions, when they are suffering before they have had time to do anything?

Hindus and Buddhists explain this with the belief that each person lives not just one life but many. Evil and suffering might be the results ('karmic fruits') of actions performed in a previous life. Therefore, no suffering and no privilege can be con-sidered undeserved, even if the person has no memory of the previous life.

For Hindus and Buddhists, the apparent injustices of life are the result of karma. People reap what they sow, either in the present life or in the future. If someone is suffering, it must be because of something they did in a previous existence – a beggar in this life might have been selfish and lacking in compassion in a previous life.

Although it might seem that this attitude to misfortune could make Hindus and Buddhists callous, as each person's suffering would be his or her own fault, in practice members of both religions are keen to show compassion to the poor and the weak. This is partly because the doctrine of rebirth leaves open the possibility that the beggar in the street might have been your own mother or your own child in a past life; and partly because people who ill-treat the poor will be storing up bad karma for themselves in the future.

Key point

- For Hindus and Buddhists, the doctrine of karma and rebirth helps to explain the existence of suffering. There is no problem of innocent suffering to tackle, and no concept that God is perfectly good.

Christian approaches to evil and suffering

For Christians, the problem of evil and suffering is particularly difficult, because of the emphasis on God's nature as all-loving. Christians have to try to reconcile belief in an omnipotent and perfectly loving God with the existence of evil and suffering in the world, and a variety of different responses have been given.

Evil as the work of the Devil

One way that Christians have tried to account for the existence of evil in the world is to blame it on the Devil. This is known as a dualist approach, because of the idea that there are two distinct and different elements involved.

Christian dualism suggests that there is a power of evil in the world (called the Devil, or Satan, by Christians) as well as a power of good (God), and that these two powers are in a constant battle. In the Bible, there are passages which suggest that there is a power of evil which deliberately tries to spoil the goodness of creation. This idea occurs from time to time in the Old Testament (for example, in the story of Job, where the Devil appears as a personal power, subordinate to God but still a force in his own right and the cause of the pain which afflicts Job), but it is much more prevalent in the New Testament. Jesus is tempted in the wilderness by the Devil, who shows him all the worldly power which could potentially be his:

'Then Jesus was led by the Spirit into the desert to be tempted by the devil. After fasting forty days and forty nights, he was hungry. The tempter came to him and said, 'If you are the Son of God, tell these stones to become bread.' (Matthew 4:1–3)

Demons afflict people who come to Jesus to be healed, and they are cast out:

'The whole town gathered at the door, and Jesus healed many who had various diseases. He also drove out many demons, but he would not let the demons speak because they knew who he was.' (Mark 1:33–4)

In the parable of the wheat and tares, it is explained that the Devil sows the weeds, and there is warning of the fires of hell for those who are evil:

Key term

dualism – belief in two distinct principles; they are often opposites, but this depends on the context in which the word 'dualism' is used.

151

Then he left the crowd and went into the house. His disciples came to him and said, 'Explain to us the parable of the weeds in the field.'

He answered, 'The one who sowed the good seed is the Son of Man. The field is the world, and the good seed stands for the sons of the kingdom. The weeds are the sons of the evil one, and the enemy who sows them is the devil. The harvest is the end of the age, and the harvesters are angels.

'As the weeds are pulled up and burned in the fire, so it will be at the end of the age. The Son of Man will send out his angels, and they will weed out of his kingdom everything that causes sin and all who do evil. They will throw them into the fiery furnace, where there will be weeping and gnashing of teeth. Then the righteous will shine like the sun in the kingdom of their Father. He who has ears, let him hear.' (Matthew 13: 36–43)

According to Luke, Judas was possessed by the Devil when he decided to betray Jesus:

Then Satan entered Judas, called Iscariot, one of the Twelve. And Judas went to the chief priests and the officers of the temple guard and discussed with them how he might betray Jesus. (Luke 22: 3–4)

There is seen to be a constant battle between the forces of good and evil; however, this view is not without its difficulties. If God created the world and everything in it, then surely God is responsible for the existence of the Devil, because God must have made this being with such great capacity for evil. Alternatively, the Devil, like God, could have always existed; but this casts doubt on God's omnipotence. It suggests that God's power is equalled by the Devil's, and that God lacks the ability to destroy the Devil.

Some Christians believe that there is a personal power of evil, the Devil, who tempts people to sin and disrupts the order of the natural world.

Augustine believed that the Devil, and other fallen angels, had been created good by God, but had exercised their free choice and had fallen from their original position, just as humanity did. Some of the angels had committed the sin of pride, by seeking equality with God, and had become fixed in sin and caused havoc in the material universe. Most modern theologians have rejected this idea of fallen angels, but there are some who still believe that it has some value. C. S. Lewis, for example, in *The Problem of Pain* (Geoffrey Bles, 1940) and *The Screwtape Letters* (Geoffrey Bles, 1942), suggested the possibility of malevolent forces at work in the world, and believed that this idea helps us to understand why there is pain.

The American philosopher Alvin Plantinga (b. 1932) also claims that we must at least accept the possibility of the Devil or demonic agencies. Natural evil, he argues, could be the result of the Devil's free decision to fall: 'It is possible that all natural evil is due to the free activity of non-human persons'. The Devil made a free decision to turn away from God, to tempt humans to sin and to disrupt the natural world, and God could not intervene to prevent this without removing from the angels, as well as from humans, the ability to act freely. Plantinga also comes to the conclusion that evil may be something which, like Job, we have to accept that we cannot understand, and that Christians should aim to develop the faith to realise that God is ultimately a mystery.

To think about

Belief in the Devil as a personal force for evil has become less fashionable among Christians. Why do you think the idea might have fallen out of favour?

If it is to be accepted that there are forces of evil in the world, then this implies that God cannot be omnipotent in the sense that God is in complete control and can do anything he wishes. The New Testament certainly does not give the impression of a God who has unchallenged power; instead, there is a constant struggle between the forces of light and darkness. Peter Vardy takes this approach in *The Puzzle of Evil*, arguing that God cannot be omnipotent in the sense of being able to do anything; he could choose to overthrow the forces of darkness, but only at the expense of freedom of choice for his creation, and so God's omnipotence is limited by his own decision to give freedom the highest priority.

There are problems, however, in the view that natural evil, pain and suffering are the work of the Devil. One objection, if the concept of the Devil is taken fairly literally, is the difficulty of understanding how the Devil or the angels came to fall in the first place. There must have been something in them, some kind of pride, which led them to want to seek equality with God; it must have been a flaw in the way in which they were created.

If the idea of a perfect world before the Fall is taken literally, it is also difficult to fit this with the twenty-first century world view, which finds no physical evidence for a perfect world ever having existed.

Another problem, if Plantinga's view is followed, is understanding the part that angels play in the created world. Belief in the existence of angels tends to contradict at least some of the biblical picture, in which humanity is God's supreme creation (although there are also many references to the existence of angelic beings). If there were angels as part of the created world, then humanity would not have the kind of special status suggested in the Bible, because there would be higher beings too. And what exactly are angels? Do they have a physical form, and if so, where do they live? Do they already have eternal life with God, without ever having had to be born into the world – and if so, why did God not make us all like that?

Some people find it difficult to believe in the Devil because of the implications for the uniqueness and power of God. The idea seems to suggest another being, perhaps not the equal of God but certainly a power rivalling God, and a power which God is unable to stop but can only fight against. God, instead of being Anselm's 'being than which nothing greater can be conceived' (see page 74), loses status; we could conceive of a better God, who was not limited by the Devil and in a constant battle, a God who had no rivals.

Belief in the Devil, then, might explain the agency of evil, but does not explain the existence of evil in the first place, and raises a lot of difficult questions which might seem to make the problem more challenging rather than resolving it.

Key point

- Some Christians believe that evil and suffering can be attributed to the work of the Devil, but this raises questions of how the Devil came into existence, and why God continues to allow the Devil to act in the world.

The Augustinian approach to the problem of evil

This approach is named after St Augustine of Hippo (354–430), whose thinking reflects the thinking of the great Greek philosopher Plato. Plato believed that everything in existence had its Ideal, or Form (so that there would be an Ideal Table, Ideal Beauty, Ideal Justice, and so on) and the things we see in the world are imperfect copies of these concepts. Imperfection, for Plato, was a feature of the physical world, and Augustine took up this idea and expanded on it in a Christian context.

Augustine was born in what is now Algeria, and worked as a Christian teacher and writer in Africa, under the rule of the Roman Empire. His autobiographical writings enable us to know a lot about his personal life and spiritual journey.

Plato thought that imperfection was just a part of the way that things are, but Augustine could not accept this, because in his view the world was created by God, and Augustine did not believe that God would deliberately create something imperfect. In his earlier life, Augustine had been a member of a cult which rivalled Christianity, called Manicheism. The Manichees believed that the universe was held in a cosmic battle between the forces of good and evil (with themselves naturally on the side of the good); they believed that people did wrong when the evil forces were winning, and could not be held responsible for their own moral actions as they were entirely at the mercy of these supernatural beings. But when Augustine became a Christian, he rejected these beliefs, and could not accept that there was any other power that could possibly rival God.

God's creation is explained in the Bible as 'good', and Augustine took this as the starting point for his theodicy: 'God saw all that he had made, and it was very good' (Genesis 1:31).

When Augustine tried to answer the problem of how an omnipotent and perfectly good God could exist given that there is evil in the world, his response had to rule out the possibility that evil is in the world because God made it – so he came to the conclusion that evil is not a real, positive quality. It is what he called a *privatio boni*, a privation of the good. In Augustine's view, evil did not have its own separate existence, but was a falling away from goodness, just as shadow falls when one moves further away from a source of light. According to Augustine, it is part of the goodness and perfection of the created world that it has so much variety in it, so many different plants and animals, and different kinds of people, and above them, angels, in a kind of hierarchy. Each part of creation is good in its own right; even though a tree cannot walk, for example, this is not an evil, but a part of the good diversity of creation. It is inevitable that, if the world is to be rich and varied, its constituent parts will be different, but God could still create a tree that was perfect for a tree, or a worm that was perfect for a worm even if it wasn't a butterfly. Difference is a good thing, and the necessary result of difference is that some creatures will be more limited than others.

To think about

Do you agree with Augustine's view that the variety of abilities between different creatures is a good thing?

In Augustine's view, evil first came into the world through the 'fall' of the angels. He said that the angels were all created perfect, but that some received less grace than others, as a part of the variety of things. They fell away from God as a direct result of their misuse of free will. They were trying to become 'lord of their own being' instead of relying on the goodness of God; and then this was repeated in the fall of Adam and Eve as representatives of humankind in the Garden of Eden, when they were tempted by Satan, the chief of the fallen angels. All the evil in the world, Augustine thought, has followed on from here, with the kingdom of the angels who remained perfect fighting for the good, while those who are fallen try to pervert the world. In Augustine's own words, in his *Confessions*: 'Free will is the cause of our doing evil ... thy just judgement is the cause of our having to suffer the consequences.'

This involves some interpretation of the story of the Garden of Eden in Genesis 2 and 3. Angels are not mentioned in the Bible story, except as guards of the tree of life once Adam and Eve have been expelled, and the Bible does not say that the serpent was Satan in disguise, it just says that it was a serpent.

Key point

• Augustine's theodicy claims that humanity was created perfect, but fell away from God through the misuse of free will. This sin was the cause of suffering throughout the natural world.

Criticisms of Augustine's theodicy

1. To many people, evil appears to be much more definite than a *privatio boni*. Deliberate cruelty towards a child or animal, for example, seems to be much more than just a lack of goodness on the part of the tormentor. A religious group called the

Key term

grace –
grace is defined by the *Oxford Dictionary of the Christian Church* (Oxford University Press, 3rd edn, 1997) as: 'the supernatural assistance of God bestowed upon a rational being with a view to his sanctification.' In other words, it is the help given to us by God to enable us to become holy. This view has been particularly influential for Catholics, because it was taken up by Thomas Aquinas, one of the key thinkers who influenced Roman Catholic doctrine.

Christian Scientists take up this idea of the non-reality of evil, trying to explain evil as some kind of illusion: sin, sickness and death would, according to the philosophy of the founder, Mary Baker Eddy, disappear if they were understood to be nothingness and in total contrast to the 'allness' of God. However, it is hard to deny that pain, cruelty and sickness really exist. Even if they are ultimately illusions, the illusion is real enough and has real symptoms (such as the death of the very ill) which cannot be satisfactorily ignored.

It can be difficult to accept that acts of criminality or terrorism come from nothing more than a lack of goodness, or that pain is nothing more than a lack of good health. Evil seems, to most of us, to have a definite force of its own, and to be more than mere absence of goodness.

2. Augustine's view still gives us no explanation of why God gave some of the angels too little grace, so that they fell into disobedience. John Hick writes: 'The idea of an unqualifiedly good creature committing sin is self-contradictory and unintelligible. If the angels are finitely perfect, then even though they are in some important sense free to sin they will never in fact do so.'

3. Even if we do accept that evil is a lack of perfection, this does not explain why God allowed this lack of perfection into the world in the first place. Friedrich Schleiermacher, in the nineteenth century, argued coherently against this part of Augustine's theodicy, showing that it is impossible to find a cause or a motive for the angels to sin, unless they were created imperfectly.

4. Augustine's theodicy raises some important questions about the nature of God's omniscience; if God knows everything in the sense that he can see into the future and knows what we will do, then why did he create the world, knowing that we would use our free will and freely choose to sin? Even if the choice to sin was wholly ours, God still made the choice to create the world knowing in advance what would happen, and could be blamed for making that choice. Or else, perhaps God did not know what angels or people would do and cannot tell the future; but we are left wondering whether God can really be all-wise if he never guessed that giving his creation the ability to sin was a recipe for disaster.

Practice exam questions

(a) Explain how Augustine approaches the problem of why people suffer.

In this answer, you should show that you understand the nature of the problem of evil and suffering. You should aim to give a clear and accurate account of the Augustinian approach, including ideas about evil as a privation of good rather than a force in itself, and ideas about variety. For high marks, your answer should be full and should make use of key terminology.

(b) 'Augustine's theodicy clearly demonstrates that God is not to blame for human suffering.' Discuss.

This question asks you to decide whether Augustine's theodicy is successful. You might consider whether, in attempting to justify God, Augustine raises other difficulties, such as doubt about God's omniscience or omnipotence. You could compare the Augustinian theodicy with others, particularly if you want to say that another theodicy is better, but make sure that the main part of your answer has a firm focus on the question. Try to work towards a conclusion by supporting a line of argument throughout, rather than describing different points of view and then surprising the examiner with your own.

The theodicy of Irenaeus

Irenaeus lived earlier than Augustine, from about 130–202, and was brought up in one of the earliest Christian families. According to many sources, Irenaeus heard the preaching of Polycarp, who knew John the Gospel writer; so Irenaeus lived at a time when Christianity was still very new, and he helped to form the New Testament with his opinions of which writings genuinely deserved a place in the Bible. Persecution of Christians because of their faith was something that was still at the forefront of people's minds in Irenaeus' time, and so the issue of how a God of love and power could allow such suffering was naturally a topic to which Christian thinkers would turn.

Irenaeus did not attempt to show that evil and suffering do not really exist, and he admitted that God appears to allow them to continue. His argument was that God allows evil and suffering to have a place in the world, and that the world was deliberately created with a mixture of goodness and evil, so that we can develop and grow as human beings into a mature and free relationship with God.

Irenaeus argued (as did Augustine later) that there had to be evil in the world, for us to be able to appreciate good, just as we might not appreciate warm summer days unless it were cold in the winter, or at least we knew what it was like to feel cold. Many of the good things in life that we take for granted only exist as 'good' because there are other things in the world which are not as good. Good is a qualitative judgement, a comparative, so there have to be other, less good, things, for the goodness to exist at all. All of our most admirable human qualities are relative to other things: people are generous, or brave, or inspiring or good-tempered in comparison with other people.

To think about

Would there still be such a thing as 'kindness' if everybody were equally kind?

But Irenaeus also argued that we have to have evil in the world in order for us to develop as individuals. If everything always went our way, we would never learn anything. We grow as individuals (he thought) through tackling problems, making mistakes, persevering and being patient.

Key point

• For Irenaeus, evil and suffering in the world are not just mistakes which happened even though God planned things a different way; they are part of the whole design, part of God's original intention. Evil and suffering are put in the world by God, for a reason, to enable us to exercise our freedom and develop as humans.

According to Irenaeus, and to others such as Hick and Swinburne who have developed their own Irenaean theodicies, when God made people 'in his own image and likeness' (Genesis 1:26), this had to include giving them free will. They had to have, like God, the freedom to make choices of their own – whether to be selfish, or whether to care for each other; whether to do something useful with their lives or whether to waste them; whether to develop a loving relationship of obedience to God, or whether to ignore him or try to compete with him. If God had not given them this free will, then they would not have been in his image. They would have been like puppets, only able to do the things that they were made to 'choose'.

Irenaeus drew a distinction between God's image and God's likeness. He believed that God made us in his own image, but that we have to grow into his likeness. In God's image, we have the freedom of choice that enables us to be moral agents. As Kant was to argue in the eighteenth century, we can only act morally if we have freedom of choice. We cannot be blamed for doing wrong if we were forced to do it, and neither are we admirable for doing good if we had no other option. In order to become the likeness of God, we have to develop and mature, and reach our potential. This can only be achieved, Irenaeus thought, if we learn to overcome difficulties, cope with our own imperfections and limitations, and resist real temptation to do wrong.

Irenaeus thought that if God simply gave us goodness when we were made, like a good fairy in 'Sleeping Beauty' bestowing gifts, then this goodness would not mean anything. Part of being good is an effort of will. If God stepped in every time someone made a wrong choice, and put right the evil that had been committed or prevented suffering from being the result, then this would be tantamount to removing the freedom of choice, as well as removing the potential for people to learn from their mistakes.

It might be asked why God did not make us in his own image and likeness, right from the beginning. Irenaeus anticipated this question, and answered it by giving the analogy of a mother feeding a new-born child. The child is not developed enough, right at the start, to be given an adult diet:

> *For as it certainly is in the power of a mother to give strong food to her infant (but she does not do so), as the child is not yet able to receive more substantial nourishment; so also it was possible for God Himself to have made man perfect from the first, but man could not receive this (perfection), being as yet an infant. And for this cause our Lord in these last times, when He had summed up all things into Himself, came to us, not as He might have come, but as we were capable of beholding Him. (Irenaeus,* Against Heresies 4:38:1)

Humanity is not capable, in this world, of being in the likeness of God – this only happens after death. It was an essential part of Irenaeus' theodicy that everyone should live after death, and that everyone should eventually complete his or her spiritual development and maturity in order to become the likeness of God.

Irenaeus argued that when people were created, they were in a state of immaturity and had to learn to grow into the 'image of God'. He used the imagery of a mother giving a small baby milk, and only introducing it gradually to more adult food.

Irenaeus, then, saw evil and suffering as a necessary part of God's plan for humanity. He used the example of the biblical story of Jonah, and argued that although Jonah suffered by being swallowed by the whale, it was all for the good. Jonah needed to endure this in order to be brought closer to God and to do the work that God had planned for him, in preaching as a prophet to the Ninevites:

For as He patiently suffered Jonah to be swallowed by the whale, not that he should be swallowed up and perish altogether, but that, having been cast out again, he might be the more subject to God, and might glorify Him the more who had conferred upon him such an unhoped-for deliverance, and might bring the Ninevites to a lasting repentance, so that they should be converted to the Lord. (*Irenaeus,* Against Heresies, 3:20:1)

Similarly, Irenaeus thought, suffering that other people endure should be seen in the same way. Even if we cannot see the reason for it, we should understand that suffering is necessary to bring us closer to God and to enable God to complete his purposes.

John Hick, a modern Irenaean

John Hick, a modern philosopher of religion, takes the same approach as Irenaeus, arguing that if we never experienced any difficulties or challenges, we would not be able to grow as personalities, we would not learn anything morally: 'A world which is to be a person-making environment cannot be a pain-free paradise but must contain challenges and dangers, with real possibilities of many kinds of accident and disaster, and the pain and suffering which they bring.'

Hick describes the world as 'a vale of soul-making' (borrowing the words from the poet John Keats), where things happen to us for our own good. In Hick's view, although we do not necessarily understand what happens to us now, everything will be resolved after death – he calls this an 'all-important aspect' of this kind of theodicy.

This approach depends on a belief in life after death – present hardships can only be justified if there is the promise of better things to come after death.

The fulfilment of the divine purpose, as it is postulated in the Irenaean type of theodicy, presupposes each person's survival, in some form, of bodily death, and further living and growing towards that end state. Without such an eschatological fulfilment, this theodicy would collapse.

Hick is saying that there has to be life after death for this theodicy to work. If someone dies young after a long and painful illness, or a baby is killed in an accident or dies because of abuse, then it cannot be seen to be 'all for the good' unless in the end it somehow works out for the best – so there has to be a long-term 'in the end' that goes beyond death in this world. Hick does not use this as an argument for the existence of life after death, but says that the theodicy would not work unless you are prepared to believe in this afterlife. In Hick's view, during the after-life, people continue with their growth and development towards a relationship with God and, in the end, everyone will be saved.

 Develop your knowledge

Evil and the God of Love by John Hick (Palgrave Macmillan, 1985) is a large and very comprehensive account of Hick's views on the subject of the problem of evil, where he criticises an Augustinian approach and proposes his own Irenaean views instead.

The Puzzle of Evil by Peter Vardy (Fount, 1999) is written for a more general audience and likely to be more accessible than Hick. It deals with different approaches to evil and suffering.

Criticisms of an Irenaean approach

1. One argument against this kind of view might be that some people suffer a lot more than others; does this mean that God wants some people to grow to spiritual maturity, but does not care about the other ones who lead peaceful and contented lives?

2. Some people seem to be made worse by their suffering, rather than better and stronger; it does not always teach people valuable lessons, but can make them lose their faith or become bitter, or even drive them to mental illness where they can no longer think and act rationally.

3. It could be argued, against Hick's view, that if everyone is saved in the end, then what is the point of the pain and suffering? We could equally well be saved without it, even if it did take us longer to learn lessons.

4. Some people are unable to benefit from suffering but they still experience it. For example, someone with severe learning difficulties might be hurt in a fire, or a tiny premature baby might have a painful infection, and they would not be capable of gaining new insights from their experiences. Animal suffering, too, is hard to explain using this view, if it is believed that the human soul is special and unique to humans, and that there is no life after death for animals.

5. Some people argue that the suffering people experience is too extreme, and that God could have taught the same lessons but with a lesser degree of pain. For some people, even if suffering is worthwhile in terms of the lessons it might teach to people, it would have been better still if God had never made the world. Dostoevsky, in his novel *The Brothers Karamazov*, presented the argument that the price we are expected to pay for our freedom of choice is just too high. In the story, Ivan Karamazov speaks to his brother, Alyosha, who is a novice monk, and points out to him examples of innocent suffering: the cruel treatment of animals, for example, and the torture of a child. Ivan says that it is not God that he doesn't accept, it's just that he 'returns his entrance ticket'; he wants no part in a world where the price is so high. He asks his brother if he would have created a world which was perfect except that it demanded, for its existence, the suffering of just one tiny child, and Alyosha has to admit that, no, he would not have created a world on those terms.

The best of all possible worlds

One of the main differences between the thinking of Augustine and that of Irenaeus on the problem of evil and suffering is that in Augustine's view, the world was created perfect but was spoiled by the misuse of free will on the part of the angels and subsequently by humankind; whereas, for Irenaeus, evil has always been part of the world and exists for a reason. It is not that God wanted to have evil in the world, but that evil is logically necessary if there is to be good. This fits in with the view that God's omnipotence is limited to that which is logically possible; God could not have created a world in which there was bravery but no fear or danger, for example, because this is not a logical possibility.

Some thinkers, most notably the seventeenth-century French philosopher René Descartes, have argued that the omnipotence of God must mean that he can do anything at all, in an unlimited way. According to Descartes, God's omnipotence means that God could, for example, make a square circle, or make $2 + 2 = 5$. The whole point about the power of God was that it encompassed absolutely anything. God created the rules of logic, and can suspend them at any time if he wishes.

However, most other thinkers have come to the conclusion that the omnipotence of God has to be confined to that which is logically possible. This does not place a limitation on God, because it still means that God can do everything that can possibly be done. If God's omnipotence is to be understood in this second way, and God is limited by logic, then some possible answers can be found to the problem of evil. It could still be held, for example, that evil was necessary logically for the existence of good.

Key point

- Some thinkers argue that God's omnipotence can only involve being able to do what is logically possible – and they say it would not be logically possible for God to produce a world in which we had freedom but in which there was also no evil.

Some scholars, such as Leibniz and the modern philosopher Richard Swinburne, have used this second understanding to argue that this world, although not perfect, is the best of all possible worlds. Swinburne suggests different possibilities which God could have chosen to create; he could, for example, have created immortal beings who only had a limited amount of work to do in the world before it was perfected; but this would have been a 'toy world' with no real freedom, and the end result would have been a foregone conclusion so that the beings would have only had a partial freedom. Swinburne claimed that the world which we have – with both birth and death, and an infinite amount of work which needs doing in the world before it is perfect, with each individual able to do something for good or for evil but not able to affect everything in a major way – was the best possible way in which God could have created things. Evil is necessary for our freedom, so that we can make real choices, and is also necessary so that we can have virtue. We would not be able to have the virtues without any evil; there could be no bravery without danger or fear, there could be no compassion without different fortunes for people, there could be no generosity if everyone had enough and was contented with what they had, no self-sacrifice, no need to put other people first. Swinburne argued that God could have just given us knowledge without any need to learn for ourselves, but that this would have made God's existence too obvious and would have removed the need for people to make their own discoveries.

Some people argue that unless there was suffering in the world, people would not be able to exercise compassion and generosity. However, others argue that this kind of suffering is too high a price to pay for freedom of choice. Is this the best of all possible worlds?

John Hick argued a similar case. In his view, we are put in the world to learn, to face evil and suffering and to become better through encountering it. Hick recognised that evil and suffering seem to be unfairly distributed, but in his view everything will be resolved after death. Hick is of the view that human freedom is so important that it is worth paying the price of natural and moral evil in order to have it.

Swinburne and Hick seem to be taking a consequentialist view when they are presenting their theodicies: the means which God uses might be unpleasant, but they are justified by the ends (which are our freedom of will). However, consequentialist views have been criticised in human ethics, and these criticisms could equally be applied to God. The philosopher Kant, for example, took as a fundamental principle the view that humans should not be used as a means to an end – but it would appear that God does this when he allows suffering.

Not everyone is of the same opinion. D. Z. Phillips, another twentieth-century philosopher, has argued against Swinburne and Hick. In his view, it is not right to suggest that God not only allows evil and suffering, but actually planned it to happen, and worked it into his design for the world before the world was even made. He argues that this would be an evil God, who was prepared to let so many people suffer in order that there should be freedom.

It can be argued, then, that even if the only possible world which could have been created involved suffering as well as freedom, there was still no need for God to have created a world at all. If this world is the only kind of world possible, then God should have left it uncreated.

To think about

If a world which contains evil and suffering is the best of all possible worlds, then should God have made the world at all?

The free will defence

The 'free will defence', as the name suggests, is the argument that God had to allow evil and suffering into the world as a logical consequence of giving us freedom to make our own moral and spiritual choices. There had to be a real possibility of our choosing to do wrong, if we were to have genuine freedom, and we had to suffer real consequences if we made the wrong choices. Both Augustine and Irenaeus base their theodicies around free will, as do more modern thinkers such as Swinburne and Hick. But as

Key term

process theology –
a theology which proposes that God moves along the same time-line that we do, does not know the future and cannot force people to behave in a way which compromises their free will.

we have seen, some argue that this is not sufficient as a defence. Perhaps God could have given us free will but with less devastating consequences – there could have been a small amount of suffering, but not quite so much. Or perhaps, as Dostoevsky suggests, God should not have made the world at all.

Practice exam questions

(a) Explain the main weaknesses of Irenaeus' theodicy.

At first glance, this question might look as though it ought to be a part (b), but in fact it is testing your abilities to describe and explain. You need to think carefully about how to answer this. As you have been asked for the main weaknesses, it would be unwise to spend too much of your answer explaining Irenaeus' theodicy in detail. Instead, give a short summary and then explain the weaknesses. For example, one weakness might be that the theodicy fails to account for the disproportionate amount that some people suffer compared to others.

(b) 'The strengths of Irenaeus' theodicy outweigh the weaknesses.' Discuss.

In the evaluation, you need to consider whether the weaknesses you have been outlining are serious problems. You also need to explain the strengths of the argument (for example, the way that it allows for human free will), and give your own opinion about the success or otherwise of Irenaean approaches to the problem of evil.

Process theology

Process theology developed from the 'process philosophy' of the philosopher A. N. Whitehead (1861–1947). This theory is based on the idea that God is not outside time at all, but present in the world with us, acting and responding, loving, rejoicing and suffering as we do. God is a part of the world as well as being outside it, and so, up to a point at least, God's power is limited because of the laws of physics that are a necessary part of the world's existence.

In this way of thinking, God does not know the future, but only knows what possibilities there are, and people have real free will. God offers people different options, but they can exercise their freedom in choosing, and God does not force people to choose one thing rather than another just to fit in with his preconceived plans. This is not simply because God prefers to give us freedom rather than exercise his power – it is because, according to process theology, God actually cannot force our choices.

David Griffin, Charles Hartshorne and other proponents of process theology have maintained that it is not logically possible for God to bring about the keeping of a covenant (an agreement) by himself. They argue that God can make moral demands of people, and give them laws, but he cannot enforce the keeping of those laws. It takes both sides to co-operate; one side cannot keep the rules of the agreement alone, even if that one side happens to be God. So if people choose to commit sin (moral evil) there is nothing God can do to stop them. Some process theologians have called the idea that God can prevent moral evil the **omnipotence fallacy**.

Key point

- In process theology, God is not responsible for moral evil, because he can only do what is logically possible, and it is not logically possible to force free individuals to obey moral laws.

God cannot force people to be morally good, and neither can he change the natural laws and developments of the physical world. He is involved in them, but is unable to choose to step outside them and make them any different. The tsunami of 2004, for example, was not something that God could have stopped. All God could do was suffer with those who were suffering, and offer people the freedom to make the most moral choices under the circumstances as they happened.

Jürgen Moltmann, a process theologian

Jürgen Moltmann (b. 1926) was born in Hamburg and drafted in the German army at the age of 18, towards the end of the Second World War. He surrendered to the first British soldier he met, in a Belgian wood in 1945, and became a prisoner of war for the next three years, where he had little to do but hear news reports of the liberation of German concentration camps and reflect upon the war. His captors nailed up photographs taken in the camps, for their prisoners of war to look at. Moltmann claimed that, at the time, he would have preferred to have died in the war than to be associated with German culture and the things that Germany had done.

Moltmann was encouraged to read the New Testament, and he became a Christian, impressed by what he was learning about a God who was with him even when he was behind barbed wire. One of the prisons where Moltmann was held, near Nottingham, was run by the YMCA, and the organisers allowed Moltmann to read theology books. He was particularly inspired by the thinking of a theologian called Reinhold Niebuhr.

Moltmann, a process theologian, was profoundly affected by pictures of the Nazi death camps, and this led him to write books about a suffering God.

By the time Moltmann was released, he was 22. He went home to his native Hamburg, to find it in ruins from Allied bombing. He was disappointed at first to see that people were trying to rebuild the country the way it had been before, instead of taking the opportunity to move forward, and decided to work on a new theology of hope, meant for the survivors of the war. He was aware of the great debt he owed to other Protestant theologians for the way they had helped to shape Christian thought, but he was also very critical of them for having said so little about the political situation during the war and in the years leading up to it.

Theology of Hope (1964), *The Crucified God* (1972) and other works established Moltmann as one of the leading Protestant theologians of the later twentieth century. The key theme of Moltmann's writing is hope for the future, based on the cross and resurrection of Christ. Moltmann was unable to avoid dealing with the problem of evil in his writing – how could a God of love, a God who would die on the cross to save people from sin, allow the sort of pain and evil that had happened during the war?

In *The Crucified God*, Moltmann proposed the view that God does not look on the earth from a long way away, allowing people to suffer as a means to a greater end while remaining unaffected. In arriving at this view, he describes how he was profoundly affected by a passage in Elie Wiesel's autobiographical *Night*. Wiesel, a Jew being held in a concentration camp, recounted an occasion in the camp when three people were sentenced to death by the guards – two adults, and one still a young boy:

For Moltmann and other process theologians, the key to the problem of evil and suffering is in the pain and death of Christ. God, he believes, does not stand by and let people suffer without caring, but joins them on earth and suffers with them.

This time the Lagerkapo refused to act as executioner. Three SS replaced him. The three victims mounted together onto the chairs. The three necks were placed at the same moment within the nooses.

'Long live liberty!' cried the two adults.

But the child was silent.

'Where is God? Where is He?' someone behind me asked.

At a sign from the head of the camp, the three chairs were tipped over. Total silence throughout the camp. On the horizon, the sun was setting.

'Bare your heads!' yelled the head of the camp. His voice was raucous. We were weeping.

'Cover your heads!'

Then the march past began. The two adults were no longer alive. Their tongues hung swollen, blue-tinged. But the third rope was still moving; being so light, the child was still alive ...

For more than half an hour he stayed there, struggling between life and death, dying in slow agony under our eyes. And we had to look him full in the face. He was still alive when I passed in front of him. His tongue was still red, his eyes were not yet glazed.

Behind me, I heard the same man asking:

'Where is God now?'

And I heard a voice within me answer him:

'Where is He? Here He is – He is hanging here on this gallows ...'
(Elie Wiesel, Night, *1958)*

Key point

- In process theology, the key to understanding evil and suffering is the belief that God is not detached from the world, but is here and is suffering with us, feeling our pain as we feel it.

Moltmann took this answer that had presented itself to Wiesel, and considered it in a Christian context, coming to the conclusion that although people may not always be able to rationalise suffering or reach an acceptable theodicy, Christians can have the comfort and the hope that comes from knowing that God suffers alongside them: 'God's being is in suffering and the suffering is in God's being itself, because God is love' (Jürgen Moltmann, *The Crucified God*, Harper and Row, 1974).

In Moltmann's view, the hope offered by Christianity should not just be seen as a hope for the future, in heaven after death. It should be taken as a hope for the present, carrying with it the obligation for Christians to transform the world that they live in.

Moltmann's understanding of the place of God in human suffering was not the understanding that was reached by Wiesel himself, however. Wiesel, like Ivan Karamazov in Dostoevsky's novel, found that the suffering of the innocent, and especially the innocent children in the gas chambers, was enough to cause him to abandon his faith forever.

Criticisms of process theology

1. The idea of a suffering God contradicts belief in God as omnipotent, and this seems unacceptable to many people. God should be able to do anything – people do not just want God to suffer alongside them, they want God to step in and remove the suffering altogether. Process theology seems to suggest a weak God who is powerless to stop evil and who is not worth worshipping or praying to. In contrast, most Christian thinkers have preferred the description of God proposed by St Anselm, where God is 'that than which nothing greater can be conceived' (see page 74).

2. As well as making God seem limited in power, process theology also makes God seem unfair. People are left to suffer because of the wrong choices of others, and only a few gain any benefit from the process.

3. Some process theologians, such as Griffin, are unclear about the existence of an afterlife. Rather than God making everything right in heaven, rewarding the good and compensating those who have suffered, instead there is just the comfort (if it is a comfort) of knowing that the good parts of life outweigh the bad – and this is not true for each individual; perhaps it is not even true for humanity as a whole.

4. Process theology does not seem consistent with the teaching of the Bible. In the Bible, God does have power over the laws of nature, because he created them. He put the sun and moon in the sky and gave them their patterns of movement; he can part seas, make shadows move backwards, cause the sun to stand still, calm storms and walk on water. God is omnipotent, as described in the book of Job. If process theology is to be accepted, then Christians need to take a very different view of how the Bible is to be understood.

Religion and science

The different methods of science and religion

Humanity is proud of its achievements in science. We tend to think of scientific knowledge as something that has a definite truth, that gives us a certain and reliable knowledge. If advertisers offer us a product that has been 'scientifically proven' to give us clearer skin or a cleaner bathroom, then many of us feel justified in spending our money on it. We also tend to trust what scientists tell us, even if we have very little scientific knowledge ourselves with which to test their claims. We are happy (mostly) to get into aeroplanes, trusting that the engineers who designed them knew what they were doing and that we will survive the journey without falling out of the sky. We take advice from our doctors, and swallow the medicines they prescribe for us, even when we have no understanding of the chemicals involved, because we trust that the medicine has been through a long process of tests before being prescribed for human consumption.

One of the main reasons for our faith in science is that scientists use methods of observation, reason and experiment. Their conclusions have been repeatedly tested and they are capable of being tested again independently by other observers. Carl Sagan, the astronomer, compared science with democracy in order to explain our confidence in it – both are transparent, so that everyone has the opportunity to look at the data and know that they are not being cheated or misled. Of course, with science, most of us rarely do look at the data for ourselves or conduct our own experiments to see if scientists are telling us the truth, but the important thing is that we know we could if we wanted to. Scientific method is regarded as having five key steps:

1. **Observation** – someone notices something and begins to wonder about it. For example, Newton observed that objects fall to the ground when dropped, rather than just hanging in mid-air. The person decides to make more observations, to keep records of what has been observed and to classify them.

2. **Hypothesis** – the scientist has an idea about what might explain whatever phenomena he or she has observed. Perhaps objects fall to the ground because there are little monsters with powerful magnet-like objects just under the surface of the earth.

Repeatable experiments are an essential part of scientific method.

3. **Experiment** – the scientist tests the hypothesis to see if it is true. Experimental digging reveals no such little monsters. So the hypothesis has to be revisited and modified, or perhaps rejected altogether in favour of an entirely new hypothesis. Scientific experiment is generally of the kind that is repeatable, so that it can be checked and verified by others. In general, the data from such experiments is made available to other scientists so that they can check it too, which reduces the possibility

of bias on the part of the scientist who might inadvertently be influencing the experiment in order to achieve the desired result.

4. **Law** – once enough experiments have been conducted (and it is difficult to know how many count as 'enough'), a 'scientific law' might be produced. This is a general rule which seems to account for the results of the experiment and confirm the hypothesis. As far as scientists know, this general rule can now be used to make predictions and to inform other observations. But this might possibly apply only until something else is observed which breaks (or 'falsifies') that rule, in which case a new hypothesis and more experiments are necessary.

5. **Theory** – scientists may develop a theory which links several laws together on the basis of an underlying principle. It might account for why the laws operate in the way that they appear to.

Scientific knowledge, then, is based on inductive reasoning (see pages 67–9). There is always the possibility that the conclusions drawn may be wrong, and most scientists welcome scepticism as a necessary and healthy part of the scientific process.

Possible problems with scientific method

• There are some people, of course, who are so pleased with their laws and theories that they refuse to acknowledge the validity of any counter-evidence. If they encounter new experimental evidence which contradicts their laws and theories, they are not prepared to allow it as evidence. Thomas Kuhn (1922–96), a scientist and philosopher of science, argued in *The Structure of Scientific Revolutions* (University of Chicago Press, 1962) that this attitude is more common than people usually admit.

• There is always the potential for difficulties when scientists have preconceived ideas of what they are expecting to observe, and of which factors are going to be relevant to the experiment. If, for example, doctors want to conduct experiments to discover what predisposes some people to a particular disease, they are likely to choose to look at factors such as diet, smoking, exercise, age, income group and gender. But they are unlikely to consider factors such as whether the patient has a blue front door or a favourite football team. This could affect the outcome of the experiment: if it is the case that supporting Newcastle predisposes people to dementia, this will remain undiscovered because the football team of preference was ruled out before the experiments began. (So if, for example, scientists do not consider religious belief to be a factor when they are looking at mental health issues, they are not going to reach the conclusion that religious belief is beneficial to mental health.)

• Perception can be fallible. Sometimes we can see things which are not really there, especially if we want them to be there. Sometimes we can miss things, because we do

Key term

not expect to see them. Our human senses, and our powers of reason, are not unlimited.

However, in spite of the potential for problems, science nevertheless has great strengths. In particular, it has the strength that it is (nearly) always open to challenges and willing to reject previously held beliefs.

Religion, of course, is often accused of the very opposite. Non-believers become frustrated with theists because of the theists' refusal to admit the possibility that they could be wrong and that there might not be a God after all. Even in the face of counter-evidence, such as when a theist prays for someone's recovery from an illness but the person gets worse and dies, the theist will not often accept that he or she must have been wrong all the time to believe in God. (See pages 231–34 for Antony Flew's discussion of this.)

Despite all the different arguments for the existence of God, most religious believers do not base their belief on reason and logic. They do not work out, on the balance of probability and in the light of the evidence, that it seems likely there is a God, and proceed after that to have religious faith. Neither do they conduct experiments to find out whether God exists, and use the results as a basis for faith. Religious belief does not seem to depend on reason very much at all, but on faith. Believers argue that they 'just know' that God exists and that God is involved in their lives. They might also 'just know' that the words of their holy scriptures are true, so that the scriptures themselves can become a reliable source of knowledge about God and about the world.

Augustine wrote that 'faith is to believe what you do not see; the reward of this faith is to see what you believe'. To some people, sceptical of religion, this simply proves their point. They claim that religious believers fool themselves to the extent of seeing what they want to see and imagining that the God they would like to believe in really does exist. But religious believers argue that God makes himself available to them in a way that goes beyond reason, through faith. It is only through faith that people can be given genuine evidence of the existence of and activity of God. Those who lack this faith will always be unable to recognise the evidence for what it is.

How can we know what is true?

One of the questions which has been discussed by philosophers throughout history is that of the nature of knowledge. What can we know, and are there any certain, absolute truths? Different philosophers have taken widely different views on the subject.

Peter Vardy, in *The Puzzle of God* (Fount, 1999) considers other ways of answering the question 'What is truth?'. He divides opinion into **realist** and **anti-realist** views. The realist believes that there are actual facts 'out there', which we get right or wrong in our search for understanding. A statement is true if it corresponds to an objective reality. Realists will always allow the possibility that they could be wrong, even if this is very unlikely – it could turn out that the world is cuboid after all, or we could wake up and find that reading this page was all a dream.

The anti-realist view, in contrast, holds that all truth is relative, and that something can be true for one person but not true for another – the world was flat for the people who lived in biblical times, but it approaches being spherical for us today. In the anti-realist view, something is true if it is coherent and fits with the rest of our understanding. An anti-realist would be quite happy with the idea that something could be true for some people and false for others.

Most of us have a view of the world which falls in between these two positions. We might consider that there are some facts 'out there' which are objectively true or false (apart from 'analytic' statements of definition, which are not open to verification and falsification in the same way), such as that Rebecca is taller than Vicky; and there are other statements which could be considered relative, such as 'Giotto was a better artist than Michelangelo'. However, it is very difficult to draw a dividing line and decide which statements fall into which category. The problem becomes more acute when discussing questions of religion, such as the existence of God. A statement such as 'God exists' would be considered by a realist to be talking about whether there is, 'out there', a corresponding reality which meets the definition 'God'. An anti-realist, in contrast, might claim that the statement is true for believers, but false for non-believers: as long as what is being said fits a person's world view and works for them, it can be said to be true.

Descartes is probably the philosopher most famous for considering the nature of certainty, the extent to which there is anything that can really be known without any doubt. His concern with certain knowledge began a debate which lasted for at least the next 150 years. He used the method of systematic doubt, reducing everything he thought to be true to that which he knew, beyond any doubt at all. He decided to 'reject as absolutely false anything which gave rise in my mind to the slightest doubt' (*Discourse on Method*), and on this basis he rejected sense experience because it can sometimes be mistaken. We can think we heard someone at the door, when there is no-one there, or believe that the room is cold when the thermometer tells us otherwise. Reason, too, with the use of logic, can also be mistaken, as people make mathematical errors or jump from one point to another without justification.

In his *Discourse on Method*, Descartes maintained that nothing could be accepted as true knowledge unless we could clearly perceive it without any possibility that we

Key term

rationalism – the belief that the mind is the source of knowledge, and truth can be induced using the powers of reason. Sense experience is secondary, and what really counts is the way in which we interpret our experiences of the world. A rationalist would hold that all data which can be gained through the senses is fallible; the only certainties come through the mind. The senses can be mistaken; for example, we can see someone in the street and mistake them for someone we know, and then realise that it is a complete stranger. Rationalists follow in the tradition of Plato.

might be mistaken. How can we be certain that our whole lives, and all our experiences within that life, are not a dream? Descartes realised that even if everything were doubted in this way, the fact that he was there doubting it was incontrovertible, and he therefore came up with his famous saying: *Cogito ergo sum*, 'I think therefore I am'.

Descartes adopted a method of extreme scepticism in an attempt to determine what we can know.

Descartes' view was that this knowledge had come through intuition, and not through any experience of the material world. Therefore knowledge which comes through ideas has to be superior to knowledge gained through the senses. This led Descartes to support the ontological argument for the existence of God (see page 72). Descartes believed that, because we have the concept of a perfect entity, that concept counts as certain knowledge of the existence of God. However, at this point many other philosophers would disagree with Descartes.

The question of what is truth, and how we can know what is true, is a difficult one and the subject of a vast amount of philosophical discussion. For example, **John Locke** (1632–1704) argued that there are no such things as innate ideas, and that all our knowledge comes from our experience of the world. There are 'primary qualities' which objects have 'out there', such as number, size and so on. There are also 'secondary qualities' such as colour or taste, which depend on the perceiving person. An apple only tastes sweet when we are eating it; it cannot be said to taste sweet when it is sitting in the fruit bowl minding its own business.

George Berkeley (1685–1753) went further and suggested that objects only exist by being perceived; the tree only exists when someone is perceiving it, for example. Although things clearly do continue to exist when they are not being perceived, Berkeley argued that this is because they are being perceived by God.

Bertrand Russell argued that common sense tells us that there is a real, external world which gives rise to our sense experience (a tree might not be perceived by us, but if we walk straight into it because we have not perceived it, we can soon tell that it exists independently).

This discussion is enormous, and important contributions have been made to it from Plato, Aristotle, Hume, Kant, and many other of the great philosophers. It is too vast a subject to be covered adequately here, but it is important to recognise that there are many different views of the nature of reality and the nature of truth, and therefore those scientists such as Richard Dawkins who adopt a strictly empiricist view of the world are choosing to take just one of a number of possible approaches. Dawkins holds that knowledge is gained through sense experience (empiricism) and that the only meaningful knowledge is that which can be tested.

Most people would argue that there is a fundamental difference between knowledge and belief. Belief, perhaps, is giving assent to something which may or may not be true, where there is not, and perhaps could never be, evidence to support it beyond reasonable doubt. Knowledge, in contrast, could be said to be belief which is supported with evidence, where our experience of the world is sufficient to justify our belief.

Can religion and science be compatible?

Some people argue, and many people assume, that scientific empiricism and religious faith are opposites. An empiricist values the knowledge which can be gained through sense experience, and some empiricists, such as Richard Dawkins and Peter Atkins, argue that this (alongside inductive reasoning) are the only kinds of knowledge worth having. However, empiricism can be compatible with religious belief, as long as the empiricist is willing to accept that there could be other forms of knowledge as well as empirical knowledge. It is only the reductionist form of empiricism which is incompatible; this is the kind of empiricism which says that things are no more than their component parts. Other empiricists are happy to hold that a whole can be more than the sum of its parts. For example a society is more than just the number of people in it; a painting is more than oil and canvas; a symphony is more than just a collection of notes measured in hertz and placed in a particular order. In the same way, a human person can be more than just the physical elements that make up his or her body, human life is more than just the struggle for survival of 'selfish genes', and the universe is more than just an accidental collection of matter.

John Polkinghorne, for example, is a scientist whose career depended upon empirical testing, but he writes of the knowledge of God which he believes he gained through the sacraments, through the Bible and through the example of other Christians. He does not see the different kinds of knowledge as opposed or conflicting, but complementary, giving different insights into the nature of reality.

Other people with a scientific background, for example William James (see pages 248–55), have supported the view that knowledge can be gained through religious experience, arguing that this is a valid kind of experience alongside sense experience, and that the knowledge gained should not be rejected out of hand; and Swinburne argued, with his Principles of Credulity and Testimony, that there is no obvious reason to reject religious experience *per se*.

Not only have people argued that religious experience should be counted alongside empirical experience as a means of gaining knowledge; there have also been many who have argued that empirically available knowledge can support religious belief, for example, those scientists who support the anthropic principle (especially Paul Davies), and those who have used teleological arguments for the existence of God.

An answer to questions of how far empiricism is compatible with belief, therefore, might argue that reductionist forms of empiricism are incompatible, but that in other ways people have found that they can take empirical knowledge seriously alongside other forms of knowledge.

The creation of the universe

The Big Bang theory

The Big Bang theory is the name given to the most popular of the scientific theories put forward by cosmologists to explain how the universe came into being. The theory began as the result of the observation that other galaxies are apparently moving a way from us at great speed, and also moving away from each other. The universe seems to be expanding, with the stars and planets getting further and further apart, in the same sort of way that dots drawn onto a deflated balloon will move away from each other when the balloon is blown up.

The science of cosmology asks questions and tries to provide explanations about the origins of the universe.

Scientists realised that they could use this observation to gain insights into how the universe began. By imagining the expansion of the universe in reverse, they concluded that there must have been a time when matter was very tightly packed together in an unimaginably hot, small zone of 'infinite density', as what scientists call a 'singularity'. Using Einstein's theory of general relativity, the conclusion was reached that matter had to have been thrown outward by a massive inflation of energy and heat, about 14 billion years ago. Before the Big Bang, there was nothing – no space, and no time. The Big Bang did not send matter out into pre-existent space, but (according to many expert physicists, such as Stephen Hawking and Richard Penrose) both space and time were caused at the same instant as the Big Bang.

No one is sure why the Big Bang happened at all – why this singularity should have started to expand, rather than remaining as a singularity. What caused this change, and why at that moment? In some ways, this is a nonsensical question, because there was no 'before' the Big Bang, according to the theory. There was no time in which anything 'before' could have happened. Space and time came from within that singularity. It is a difficult idea for us to comprehend. Some conclude that the Big Bang just happened, causelessly, while others are drawn to the conclusion that there must have been some kind of reason for it.

The Big Bang is supported by fairly strong empirical evidence. Astronomers and physicists generally agree that the evidence for the universe having some kind of beginning is convincing. Edwin Hubble (1889–1953) observed the speeds at which galaxies are moving away from us, which supports the idea that the universe is expanding, and the hypothesis that in the beginning matter was extremely hot is supported by the discovery of cosmic background radiation.

To think about

Do you think we could ever reach a definitive answer to questions of how the universe began? Why, or why not?

Other theories about the origins of the universe

The Big Bang theory is not the only possible explanation for the origins of the universe, although it is the most popular. In the 1940s, the steady state theory was developed, proposing that the density of the universe remains constant as it expands because of the continuous creation of a minute number of atoms. This does not fit very well with the First Law of Thermodynamics, but neither does the Big Bang theory. The discovery of cosmic background radiation can be accommodated by steady state theories, but it fits more easily into Big Bang models. Steady state theories became less popular during the twentieth century, but new observations of accelerating galaxies have caused scientists to look at them again.

Inflationary universe theories, developed by Alan Guth and others in the 1980s and 1990s, are attempts to find new ways of looking at the origins of the universe without falling into many of the difficulties encountered by the Big Bang theory. This theory concentrates on what might have happened about 10–35 seconds after the beginning of time, where the universe expanded for a tiny instant at a much greater speed than the Big Bang theory would allow, filling the universe with something called vacuum energy.

In 1957 Hugh Everett published a theory that this is not the only universe, but that there are 'multiverses'. According to this theory, every universe that can possibly exist actually does exist, which would mean that we live in just one of a great number of universes. After all, if the Big Bang (or whatever else) caused the birth of one universe, why could it not have happened many times, as a result of random fluctuations in a quantum vacuum. If this is just one of a multitude of universes, then arguments for God as the designer of order in the universe would fail. The multiverse theory, however, is still only a hypothesis, and no empirical evidence has yet been produced to support it. Keith Ward, a Christian philosopher, argues in his book *Pascal's Fire* (Oneworld Publications, 2006) that belief in the existence of multiverses demands a greater leap of faith than belief in God.

Big Bang explanations, then, are by no means the definitive answer to questions of how the universe began, although they are used by the majority of scientists, for the time being, as a basis from which to proceed.

Have the discoveries of physics removed the need for God?

Some scientists, such as Richard Dawkins and Peter Atkins, claim that scientific theories which account for the origins of the universe have in some way removed the need for God. They argue that it might be difficult for us, at the moment, to understand how and why the universe came into existence, with exactly the right combination of elements and forces to allow for the existence of human life. However, this difficulty does not mean that we need to assume the existence of God, or use the concept of God as part of the explanation. We may not have found the right scientific explanation yet to account for the universe, but we can be confident that one day, we will work it out without having to resort to the supernatural, just as we have worked out the answers to other difficult scientific questions.

The cosmological argument depends on the notion that the existence of the universe and everything in it is contingent, and therefore there must be something with necessary existence to bring it all into being, and to provide an explanation of why anything exists at all. However, the argument of Dawkins and Atkins is that we now know with some degree of certainty how the world came into being. We have discovered the cause, which is a physical cause explicable in scientific terms, and we have no need of the idea of God.

The phrase 'God of the gaps' has frequently been used to signify the kind of belief which puts in 'God' as an explanation for those questions to which we have not yet found an answer. Some Christians, particularly in the nineteenth century, claimed that although scientists were finding answers to previously unexplained phenomena, these answers would never be more than partial, and only God could really understand how everything came to be. But this line of argument has resulted in a shrinking God, needed to plug fewer and fewer gaps until eventually, perhaps with the dawn of the

Grand Unified Theory (a theory which has not yet been developed, to explain how all the physical laws we have are linked together), God is no longer necessary at all.

The challenge of evolution

Evolutionary theory is often cited as being the biggest threat to traditional religious belief. There are people who assume (often without knowing much about either evolution or religion) that Darwin 'disproved' Christianity. There are also Christians who believe that evolutionary theory is so wrong that it should not be taught to children in schools.

The mood before Darwin

The eighteenth century was an age when people had great confidence in the powers of human reason, and when there had been many developments in philosophy during what is known as the Enlightenment. To most people, it seemed as though the world was a static whole which followed ordered rules and patterns, and it seemed that we were gradually learning more and more about it and about ourselves. Eventually, perhaps, we would have it all worked out, and we would understand exactly how everything fitted together. People had great confidence that the universe functioned like a well-ordered machine; and to some people (such as William Paley) the more people learned about the natural world around them, the more obvious it was that it had all been designed by an intelligent being who had everything under control.

However, the nineteenth century brought with it such rapid developments that it became no longer obvious that the world was static. Instead, it seemed that everything was changing more quickly than people could keep up with. People had been used to living in the ways of their parents and grandparents, but the fast-moving pace of the nineteenth century meant that old lifestyles and skills were disappearing, to be replaced with the new. There was a sense of progress, but also a sense of nostalgia.

Many writers of the Victorian era, such as Thomas Hardy, wrote with nostalgia of a lifestyle they could see was fast disappearing.

Many different factors were involved in the process of change, including:

- **The Industrial Revolution:** steam power, electricity and other new forms of power meant that labour could be mechanised, and goods could be mass-produced in factories. Working lives became more divided and specialised, and people moved away from the places of their birth to towns and cities where they could be employed in factories rather than in agriculture. Cities grew rapidly in order to meet the needs of the expanding population, and families became more fragmented.

- **Medicine:** developments in medicine, including the discovery of vaccination, meant that, at least among the wealthy, children were more likely to survive infancy. There was a rapid growth in population, leading to predictions by some (for example, Malthus) that the country would soon not be able to provide the resources needed to sustain the people.

- **Developments in communications:** before the nineteenth century, most people were born and died in the same town or village, and made contact with only a small number of people during their lives. The introduction of the railway, of telephones, and of the postal system, changed all of this, and gave people the opportunity to see other parts of the country or of the world, to consider the possibility of living away from their families while remaining in contact, and to talk to people whose ideas and beliefs were different from those they had always accepted.

- **Divisions between rich and poor:** there had always, of course, been rich and poor people, but in the nineteenth century this became increasingly obvious, especially in the cities, where many people were living in overcrowded slum conditions, often without the support of the extended family to help with the care of the children and the elderly. This contrasted sharply with those who were making new fortunes in industry, and who were beginning to be able to introduce electric lighting into their homes and to travel. These inequalities led some to begin to question the role of the Church, and to ask themselves whether it was true that God had ordained each person's station in life.

The nineteenth century, then, was an age of transition, and those people who lived in it were very much aware of this. Novels of the nineteenth century show a nostalgia for a past age and a changing landscape and a concern that progress for some meant degradation for others.

When Charles Darwin began his work, therefore, he did not introduce the idea of evolution out of the blue, into a world which had never considered such a possibility. Concepts of progress, of society moving forward, leaving old ways behind and being in a constant process of change, were already embedded in popular thought. The philosopher Hegel, for example, had introduced ideas about the ways in which progress is made when people catch on to one idea (which he called a thesis) and then turn away from it and go to the opposite view (the antithesis) until eventually the 'pendulum' comes to rest at a middle point (the synthesis) – after which, the process begins again and ideas are carried forward. Karl Marx took up Hegel's way of looking at progress when he described his predictions that large differences between rich and poor would eventually lead to revolution. Other people, then, besides Darwin, were considering the idea that humanity does not stay the same, following rules of nature in a uniform and unchanging way. The concept of humanity as part of an ever-changing process was already there.

Sir Charles Lyell and the challenge of geology

Sir Charles Lyell, who was born in 1797, twelve years earlier than Darwin, presented one of the first major challenges to a literal view of the Bible, because of his study of geology, one of many new sciences. At the start of the nineteenth century, most people accepted Bishop James Ussher's calculations that the world had been created in 4004 BCE. Ussher had worked this out, in the years leading up to the English Civil War, by matching the dates given for different events in the Bible, the ages different characters were said to have reached before they died, and other dates that were already well-known through archaeology and ancient writings. He reached the conclusion that the date of the creation of the world could be very precisely placed at nightfall on the eve of 23 October 4004 BCE. Other scholars, such as Lightfoot, made similar calculations, and although there were some slight differences in their conclusions, depending on the version of the Bible they had used, it was nevertheless taken as a fact that the world had been in existence for no more than about six thousand years.

Lyell's discoveries challenged this assumption. James Hutton, who died the year Lyell was born, was the pioneer of geology as a science, and Lyell followed his methods to develop a theory called *uniformitarianism*. This theory claims that the earth was formed gradually, through natural and slow processes. This seems obvious to us today, but before Lyell, the theory had been one of *catastrophism*, in which the earth was formed all at once six thousand years ago; any changes which could be seen in the evidence of rocks was attributed to occasional and sudden catastrophes, such as the Flood described in the Bible.

Lyell supported his own uniformitarian theory, by showing how geological processes such as erosion, uplift, glaciation and sedimentation had altered the earth's structure, in a process which must have taken place over millions of years. It began to seem that there was firm, scientific evidence to support the view that the planet was much older than the Bible described.

As well as introducing uniformitarianism, Lyell also developed a method of studying the earth's strata (layers of rock), and classifying them according to age and origin. In the newer rocks closest to the surface he discovered fossils of creatures which still existed, but in the deeper levels there were fewer examples of fossils of living species, and instead there were the remains of animals which were now extinct. Other scientists, too, began to uncover fossils of dinosaurs and of other creatures which had no mention in the creation stories of Genesis.

Lyell's discoveries in the field of geology challenged the view that the earth was only six thousand years old.

Lyell's work was scientifically convincing, and some of the public as well as some scientists began to believe in a long process of change, rather than an immediate miracle, as an explanation for the way in which the world appears. However, Victorian scientists and theologians who were adamant that the biblical account of creation was historically accurate, in spite of geological evidence, came up with different suggestions of how biblical and geological ideas could be reconciled:

• it was suggested sometimes that God had put the fossils into the rocks at the time of creation in order to test the faith of humankind (this was a view held by Philip Gosse)
• some said that the word 'days' described in Genesis was meant to signify 'long periods of time' rather than a literal 24 hours.

Darwin's theory of natural selection

Darwin's voyages on the *Beagle* led him to observe that there is variation within all species. Even within the same species of bird, or flower, or moth, there are some that are bigger than others, or lighter or darker in colour, which have bigger feet or longer stems and so on. Darwin used this observation to form a hypothesis. His idea was based on seeing that each species has a limited supply of food, and that there is competition for nutrition both within the species and with other species that inhabit the same environments. When there is not enough food to go round, some will be the winners and others the losers. The particular animals or plants that end up getting the food, and also avoid being eaten by their predators, are the ones whose characteristics are the most advantageous to them. The giraffes with the longest necks can reach the leaves that other giraffes cannot reach, so they have more food. The birds with the best camouflage against their environment are less likely to be eaten by predators, who go for the ones they can see more easily. In this way, the strongest and the most advantaged members of the species survive for longer.

Because they survive for longer, they are able to reproduce more often. Their offspring tend to inherit the advantageous traits: they are more likely also to have long necks or better camouflage. Those members of the species with the less advantageous traits do not get to reproduce very much, because they starve or are eaten. Gradually, the species changes and the advantageous traits become more popular; a greater proportion of the species now has longer necks, better camouflage, or whatever. This, of course, means that the competition for food has grown. Once again, the survivors who go on to reproduce the most are the ones with unusual characteristics that set them slightly apart from the crowd – and so the process goes on, as evolution through natural selection. Over time, evolution can result in species which are particularly suited to a niche environment, and even completely new species.

Darwin's illustration of beak variation in finches records his observation of different inheritable characteristics.

How Christian belief was threatened by Darwinism

It is central to Christian belief that human beings were created with the purpose and capacity for direct communion with God. God created humankind deliberately, in his own image, and made people unique from other animals in giving them a soul, and the means by which to love God freely through divine grace. The first pair, Adam and Eve, disobeyed God and lost humanity's innocence and capability for direct contact with God. The work of Christ set right this catastrophic disobedience, atoning for the sin of Adam, and redeeming humankind. Edward Pusey, a church leader in Victorian times, wrote:

It lies as the basis of our faith that man was created in the perfection of our nature, endowed with supernatural grace, with a full freedom of choice such as man, until restored by Christ, has not had since.

Darwin's ideas therefore seemed to threaten the whole edifice of Christianity:

- It appeared as though humankind was not God's supreme creation at all, but an accident, a chance happening.
- If humankind had not been deliberately created in a ready-made form, but had evolved by the chance processes of evolution through natural selection, then the idea of God having a purpose in creation appears to be challenged.
- If the distinction between humankind and the rest of the animal kingdom is blurred, then it appears as though humankind does not have a unique place or a unique soul, and is not in the image of God; it seems unlikely that there came a point during evolution at which people developed souls.
- If Adam and Eve were not real historical people, and the Fall was not a historical event, it makes the redeeming work of Christ seem unnecessary and incomprehensible.
- The concept of God as a designer is challenged, and the wonders of the natural world appear to be attributable not to God but to random chance; the idea that the hand of God can clearly be seen in the works of his creation is undermined, as are the teleological arguments for God's existence.
- The authority of the Bible as the revealed word of God is diminished, because it appears to be mistaken. Instead of seeing God revealed in the Bible and in the world around us, both of these traditional sources of God's revelation are threatened.

Darwin himself was aware that the theories he was putting forward would present these challenges. In a letter to his friend and colleague Asa Gray, who was an American botanist, he wrote:

With respect to the theological view of the question. This is always painful to me. I am bewildered. I had no intention to write atheistically. But I own that I cannot see as plainly as others do, and as I should wish to do, evidence of design and beneficence on all sides of us. There seems to me too much misery in the world. I cannot persuade myself that a beneficent and omnipotent God would have designedly created the Ichneumonidae with the express intention of their feeding within the living bodies of caterpillars, or that a cat should play with mice. ... On the other hand, I cannot anyhow be contented to view this wonderful universe, and especially the nature of man, and to conclude that everything is the result of brute force. I am inclined to look at everything as resulting from designed laws, with the details, whether good or bad, left to the working out of what we may call chance. (Charles Darwin's Letters, a Selection, ed F. Burkhardt, CUP, 1996)

Darwin always insisted he was an agnostic rather than an atheist.

Darwin delayed publication until Alfred Russell Wallace, another evolutionary theorist, put him in a position of wanting to be credited for his data. However, he felt that publication was 'like confessing to a murder'; he knew that he would be in trouble, but he did not want to obscure what he believed to be scientifically convincing.

The debate between Wilberforce and Huxley

Darwin's theories of the origins of species were criticised widely. The usual conception is that the arguments were between scientists, on the side of Darwin, and the church, but in fact much of the opposition to Darwin came from other scientists, who were unwilling to accept Darwin's conclusions. It was not the case that Science, as a body, supported Darwin whilst Religion was opposed.

However, there was a debate less than six months after the publication of *The Origin of Species* (1859), which made the confrontation between the established church and Darwinism very public.

Samuel Wilberforce (1805–73), bishop of Oxford and a renowned eloquent speaker, decided to lead the attack on Darwin, in an article in a periodical called the *Quarterly Review*, and in a meeting of the British Association, held in Oxford in June 1860. In the article, he stated that Darwin's theories showed: 'a tendency to limit God's glory in creation', that 'the principle of natural selection is absolutely incompatible with the word of God', and that 'it contradicts the revealed relations of creation to its Creator'.

What happened at the meeting in Oxford is less clear, and has been fuelled by stories which may or may not be true, so that the popular account of events could well be legendary rather than factual. Darwin himself did not attend the meeting, as he suffered from ill health for many years, possibly because of a tropical disease picked up on his travels.

Legend has it that Wilberforce (known as Soapy Sam because of his unpleasantly sarcastic and pretentious manner) was defeated by the sincerity of the young Thomas Huxley, Darwin's advocate. According to legend, the church tried to dictate to the scientists which conclusions they were allowed to reach, but the strength and simplicity of Huxley turned the tide against religion and relegated it to the realms of superstition, where it is gradually being eliminated by all enlightened people. However, some reputable historians, such as Owen Chadwick, suggest that reports of the debate should be treated with some caution, as they are not entirely consistent and may well have been embroidered with the passage of time.

Popular history has it that Wilberforce said to Huxley that someone might be willing to trace his descent through an ape on the side of his grandfather, but would not accept it on his grandmother's side; an appeal to the Victorian sentimentality about women. Huxley is alleged to have replied that he would prefer to be descended from an ape than from someone who spent his talents misrepresenting those who seek the truth.

Wilberforce's arguments seem to have been centred around the gaps in Darwin's theory; he could not give any evidence for evolution through these different stages (although later discoveries of fossils made Darwin's ideas seem much more credible). Wilberforce argued that Darwin was presenting only a theory, not a proof; and he pointed out that in our experience, species tend to revert to type: when there is deliberate selective breeding of, for example, racehorses or pedigree dogs, there is a tendency for offspring to revert to the original rather than to continue to develop the required characteristics. This suggested to Wilberforce that species, although variant, were fixed and fundamentally stable.

At the time of the debate, the most eminent naturalists were on the side of Wilberforce, on scientific grounds rather than for religious reasons. Darwin himself was impressed by the way in which Wilberforce managed to find the parts of his argument which were the weakest, and went back to work on substantiating those.

Creationism

The reaction to Darwin was by no means universal. Some abandoned religious faith as superstition; some tried to find ways of compromising; others rejected the possibility that the theory of evolution could be right, and maintained their belief in the literal truth of biblical accounts of the origins of humanity. This third group of people are known as creationists – those who believe that the Genesis accounts are historically accurate and factual. Creationist views were not limited to the Victorian age, but are still prevalent today, particularly in America, where groups campaign against the teaching of theories of evolution in schools.

The main points which are made by creationists are:

- The belief that nature is 'all there is', that everything has to be empirically testable, is an assumption, and a step of faith. Scientists who reject the literal truth of the Bible are placing their faith in naturalism; creationism makes the assumption that there is a creator God. If scientists are to be allowed their assumptions, creationists should not be denied the right to assume as a starting point the truth of the Bible.

- Large-scale change from one type of organism into another has never been verified, and there are plenty of scientists who believe that it is impossible. Variation within one kind of organism, such as the example of the dark and light moths, is accepted by creationists, but it is not accepted that there can be change from one species to another, for example from a reptile to a bird.

- Fossil evidence suggests evolution could have been produced in a single abrupt event, such as the biblical Flood, rather than gradually accumulating.

- The belief that the atoms produced by the Big Bang eventually brought themselves together, by chance, and resulted in people after years of evolution, takes an enormous amount of faith to accept; it is a belief which demands acceptance of the extremely improbable and is far less credible than belief in the creator God of Genesis.

- The Bible comes from God, and God does not get things wrong. Therefore, if science and the Bible disagree, scientists are mistaken, because they are fallible.

Creationists hold that scientific theories of evolution are only theories, and can be challenged; there is evidence against them, which means that they depend on belief. Creationism rests on the assumption that the theories devised by people can never disprove the truth of the Bible. Scientific ideas can be measured against the Bible, to see how far they are consistent with it, but the Bible does not have to match any human theory in order to be considered worthwhile, because of its unique status as the word of God.

Creationism has remained popular among evangelical Christians, particularly in America, although it would be wrong to suggest that it represents the opinions of most Christians or Jews. Ronald Numbers, an American writer, cited in his article 'Creationism in 20th Century America' (*Science*, 1982) an opinion poll which showed that 44 per cent of Americans said that they believe that God created human beings in their present form within the last ten thousand years. However, as Numbers points out in his article, there are various shades of opinion within creationism itself, from those who are 'strict creationists' who believe that the days of Genesis should be taken literally, to those 'progressive creationists' who believe that the days are immense periods of time. Some strict creationists believe in one single act of creation in 4004 BCE, while others believe in a number of creative acts.

Many biblical literalists have tried to overcome the problems of geological evidence, by identifying two separate creations. The first, described at the beginning of Genesis, was 'in the beginning', possibly many millions of years ago, and then the second took place in six actual days approximately four thousand years before the birth of Christ. Most fossils, they argue, come from the first creation and are relics of creatures who were destroyed before the arrival of Adam.

The Scopes trial

The Scopes trial in America is probably the most famous example of conflict between creationism and evolutionary science. In 1925, John Thomas Scopes, an American high school teacher, confessed to having broken a recently made law in Tennessee banning the teaching of human evolution in state schools. His subsequent trial focused international attention on the anti-evolution crusade. Scopes was eventually found guilty as charged, but there was little cause for celebration among the creationists, because they had received very little sympathy from the press. In particular, it had come to light that the creationists, or fundamentalists as they had come to be called, could not agree on a theory of creation even amongst themselves.

The Scopes trial brought the conflict between science and religion into the news.

Although the Scopes trial could hardly have been considered a great success for creationists, the aftermath was a continued, although much more low-key, pressure by fundamentalists on the state schools, public libraries, local press and other media to reject evolutionary theory and promote creationism.

Modern creationism

Henry Morris (1918–2006), an American Christian, was a leading supporter of a literal interpretation of the Bible, and is seen by many as one of the founders of the twentieth-century creationist movement. He was a prolific writer who, with his son, produced a range of books arguing that the world was created exactly as described in Genesis, and that scientists who disagree with this conclusion are seriously mistaken in their understanding of their data. *The Genesis Flood* (P & R Publishing, 1960), written with Old Testament scholar John Whitcomb, attempted to use scientific arguments and geological evidence to support the Genesis accounts of creation and the flood. *Biblical Creationism* (Baker, 1993) was written with the intention of showing how the story of the creation of the world in six days is supported throughout the Bible.

Morris begins his argument from the starting-point of belief that the Bible is the inerrant word of God. He states explicitly:

> *I had become convinced that the Bible was the Word of God, inspired and inerrant in every word … The Bible taught clearly and explicitly that all things were made by God in a six-day week of natural days. There was no room for evolution or the long geological ages at all. (Henry Morris,* Biblical Creationism*)*

In the view of creationists, the Bible is completely correct in every detail about how the universe came into being.

In Morris's view, there is no convincing 'compromise' theory which allows for a belief in evolution alongside belief in the historical accuracy of the biblical text. He points out how the biblical text is quite explicit in its details, and argues that God does not make mistakes. Scientists are fallible and with the best will in the world can easily misinterpret data; they were not present at the origins of the world and can only speculate. God, on the other hand, made the world and also wrote the Bible, Morris claims; therefore we can have complete confidence in the biblical accounts, because they were recorded by the only being who has certain and infallible knowledge of what happened.

Where, for example, the Genesis account mentions the 'days' of creation, Morris argues that a close reading of the text does not allow for an interpretation where a 'day' means 'an era'. In Genesis 1, the word used for 'day' is *yom*. Morris argues that this always means a 24-hour period, and a different word entirely is used for 'era': '... there should be no uncertainty whatever that God intended the account to say that the creation of all things had taken place in six literal days' (*Biblical Creationism*).

Morris argues that the Genesis account must have been written either by God himself on a tablet of stone, in the same way that the Ten Commandments were written for Moses, or else by Adam, who would have been given the gift of the ability to write, and also a special revelation by God so that he would know the details of events that happened before his own existence. Once Adam was created, he would then be in a position to tell the rest of the creation story from his own experience, guided by the Holy Spirit to ensure its accuracy. This dual authorship would account for the appearance of two creation stories in Genesis. The first story, outlining the six days of creation, would have come directly from God, whereas the second came from Adam's perspective (although it would still have been directed by God and guaranteed to be without mistakes). Although some critics claim that there are two different creation stories in the book of Genesis, Morris does not accept this. Everything was made in the order described, by God himself, in Genesis 1. Creation was completed with the arrival of humanity, after which God rested. The second creation account, beginning in Genesis 2, is where Adam describes the order in which he became aware of the rest of creation around him.

Some people argue that the passage where Adam gives names to the animals cannot possibly be literally true, because there are so many different kinds of animals – over a million different species, according to many sources. However, Morris answers this point by saying that verse 20 of Genesis 2 refers only to Adam naming those animals which were to be his closest companions, the livestock and the birds.

> *Now the Lord God had formed out of the ground all the beasts of the field and all the birds of the air. He brought them to the man to see what he would name them; and whatever the man called each living creature, that was its name. So the man gave names to all the livestock, the birds of the air and all the beasts of the field.* (Genesis 2:19–20)

Adam's intellect would have been far greater than our own, Morris argues, and God would have assisted Adam in naming the animals; therefore there is nothing in this account that is impossible: 'this project would not have occupied more than about half a day.'

Unlike some creationists, who claim that fossil evidence of dinosaurs was planted by the devil to deceive human minds, Morris does not deny the existence of dinosaurs at some point in history: 'even the animals that have since become extinct – such as dinosaurs – were made on the fifth and sixth days of the creation week.'

Morris argues that references in the Bible to the 'behemoth' might be references to dinosaurs such as the diplodocus.

Morris does, however, reject the claim that dinosaurs lived millions of years ago, and that most species of dinosaur were extinct before humans arrived on the planet. This would not be consistent with the biblical account. He and other creationist writers point out passages in the Bible which refer to 'behemoth' and 'tannin': both words to describe 'monsters'. 'Behemoth', according to Morris, is used to describe gigantic beasts such as elephants, hippopotami and brontosaurus, and 'tannin' refers to sea-monsters such as blue whales, walruses and plesiosaurs.

Look at the behemoth,
which I made along with you
and which feeds on grass like an ox.
What strength he has in his loins,
what power in the muscles of his belly!
His tail sways like a cedar;
the sinews of his thighs are close-knit.
His bones are tubes of bronze,
his limbs like rods of iron.
He ranks first among the works of God,
yet his Maker can approach him with his sword. (Job 40:15–19)

For Morris, a literalist interpretation of scripture is not only reasonable but necessary.

Creationism, or creation science as it is sometimes called by its supporters, seems to see the relation between science and religion in terms of conflict. Ian Barbour, in his book *Religion in an Age of Science* argues that it is not legitimate for the creationists to try to put limits on what a scientist can be allowed to discover. Religious belief should not be allowed to dictate the conclusions which scientists are allowed to draw, and therefore Barbour argues that it is wrong for creationists to try to limit what can be taught in schools. However, Barbour argues, it is equally wrong for some scientists, most notably Dawkins, to try to make science dictate what people should believe in religious terms.

Pierre Teilhard de Chardin (1881–1955)

Pierre Teilhard de Chardin was the strange combination of palaeontologist and Jesuit priest, whose ideas were very popular in the 1950s and 1960s, particularly amongst his fellow Catholics. He aimed to show that science and religion could live compatibly together, and that the discoveries of the one could and should enhance the other. However, Teilhard de Chardin's ideas were not always very much welcomed by the Catholic Church of his time, because he was not concerned only with peacemaking between science and religion; he aimed to use scientific ideas to reshape Christian thought for modern people, and was therefore considered too radical by many. He was seen by the Vatican as something of a threat, and was forbidden to have his religious writings published, as they were seen to be too closely linked to the 'modernism' of which the Catholic Church disapproved. He took up a research position in China, where he was engaged in the discovery of 'Peking man' as well as philosophical reflection.

Teilhard de Chardin proposed a new and original way of combining evolutionary ideas with Christianity.

Many people today consider Teilhard de Chardin's ideas rather outdated; some of the things he said about science have not found much favour with other scientists, and some of his religious thinking has been considered to be too fanciful and mystical to appeal to many. However, he had an impact in his day, and is still considered to be useful for study in many Roman Catholic secondary schools.

Teilhard de Chardin was a prolific writer, and his style is often rather difficult to follow, as it is unsystematic and tends to go off at tangents.

One of his objectives was to show that the material world of plants, rocks, animals and so on is not just the neutral subject for scientific investigation, but is the setting for mystical visions of God; the subject matter of science, he argued, is the mirror in which the reflected face of God can be seen.

Teilhard de Chardin was very impressed by the theories of evolution, and believed that this was the key to religion as well as to science. His most important work was called *The Phenomenon of Man* or *The Human Phenomenon*, depending on how the French is translated, and this dealt with the concept that evolution is the key to understanding the whole world and all the systems within it. According to Teilhard de Chardin, evolution is a process with a purpose, through which the energy and matter of the universe has continually changed in the direction of becoming ever more complex. He argued that when humanity emerged through the evolutionary process, a new dimension entered. The biosphere (the layer of living things which cover the earth) became surrounded by a new layer, which he called the noosphere, and this was a mind layer of human consciousness surrounding the earth. As the process of evolution continues, this gives rise to ever higher levels of mind and spiritual consciousness, until eventually the 'Omega point' is reached; and this can be equated with God. God-Omega attracts humankind towards himself through his love, most eminently seen in the person of Christ, and the whole evolutionary process is shown to have direction rather than being random.

Teilhard de Chardin saw scientific endeavour as itself a part of evolution, a way forward in the human move towards the Omega Point, and part of the means by which God could be reached.

His thinking was found attractive by many, because it was a way in which evolution could be seen to be not contradictory to religion but part of it, a religious process in itself. God, in this way of thinking, is not pushed to the edge as a last resort means of explaining those questions which science has not yet resolved; instead, God is at the centre of science, its fundamental objective. Scientific discoveries are movements towards an uncovering of God; as people understand more about the world they evolve a step nearer to the Omega Point.

However, Teilhard de Chardin's thinking was also criticised. It was considered by the church to be incompatible with traditional Christian doctrine in many respects, contradicting central beliefs such as the Fall of humankind, and seemed to be replacing the teachings of the Bible with a new and apparently made-up understanding of the purposes of the world. It seemed as though Teilhard de Chardin was replacing the biblical accounts, even if they were myths, with new myths of his own invention. Scientists did not take this thinking very seriously, because the ideas of the noosphere and the Omega point were not considered to be in any sense scientific; they were wholly unverifiable and unfalsifiable.

To think about

In your opinion, how far is Teilhard de Chardin's work consistent with biblical teaching?

Nevertheless, the work of Pierre Teilhard de Chardin is still read and admired as a genuine attempt by someone with a scientific background to try to bring together religious belief with evolutionary thinking.

Intelligent Design and irreducible complexity

'Intelligent Design' is the name given to the view that the existence of the universe and the features of different things within the universe are best explained if it is accepted that there is an intelligent being who designed it all. This is proposed not only as a religious belief but as a scientific theory. Those who support Intelligent Design believe that the cosmological and teleological arguments for the existence of God have strength, and that other explanations which remove any question of God leave many issues unresolved. Mysteries such as why the Big Bang ever happened in the first place can be answered with reference to God, as can questions about the evolutionary process.

One aspect of the Intelligent Design approach is the argument from irreducible complexity. This argument claims that there are serious flaws in Darwinist models of evolutionary theory, and that, rather than trying to find ever more convoluted ways to explain them, it is far more obvious to look to God as the explanation.

The concept of 'irreducible complexity' as an argument against Darwinian models of evolution has been popularised by the writer Michael Behe. Behe's book *Darwin's Black Box* (first published in 1996) put forward the view that modern biochemistry has revealed features of life that have hitherto been mysterious (a 'black box'). In Darwin's time, he argued, nothing much was known at a level smaller than that of the cell, but now X-ray crystallography has enabled scientists to investigate further. The results of their investigations, Behe claims, cast doubt on the validity of Darwinism.

One of the most important points that Behe makes in his book is that some aspects of life are 'irreducibly complex'. He gives the analogy of a household mousetrap to make his point. A mousetrap consists of several different parts, all of which are necessary for the mousetrap to work at all. It has a flat solid base, a spring, a metal hammer and a sensitive catch. This, although an apparently simple device, is 'irreducibly complex', in that if you took away any of its parts it would not work at all. Also, if any of the parts had a fault – for example, if the hammer were feeble or the catch not sensitive – it would not do its job. The system as a whole needs to have a certain 'minimal function'.

Behe uses this analogy and applies the same principles to aspects of life. He picks out several processes and discusses in detail the way that they work, to illustrate that several different functions need to be present simultaneously for there to be any result at all. One of his examples is the clotting of the blood. Blood clots when we cut ourselves. Otherwise, even a small cut would cause our blood to leak out gradually until we had none left. But blood cannot continue to clot all the way through our bodies as part of the healing process – it has to clot just enough to heal the cut, and then stop, so that the rest of our organs continue to function as normal. This blood-clotting process, Behe argues, is irreducibly complex, requiring a complex interaction of different proteins in order to work at all. What, he asks, would be the evolutionary advantage to a creature of having just part of this process? It does not fit in with Darwin's ideas about natural selection.

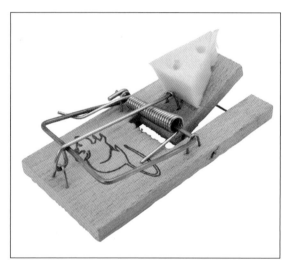

Behe argues that if a mousetrap did not have all its parts, it would not function.

He also uses the example of the eye, to show another instance of irreducible complexity. Darwin himself accepted that the eye presented a problem: it was difficult to see how simple light-sensitive cells that can be seen on some creatures could somehow evolve into fully functioning eyes:

To suppose that the eye with all its inimitable contrivances for adjusting the focus to different distances, for admitting different amounts of light, and for the correction of spherical and chromatic aberration, could have been formed by natural selection, seems, I confess, absurd in the highest degree. (Charles Darwin, The Origin of Species)

However, he went on to suggest a way in which it could be possible, if the simplest kind of 'eye' could be shown to have been of some use and advantage to the creature, and therefore he concluded that the apparent difficulties were perhaps not such a big problem.

Behe's conclusion, then, is that modern biochemistry has lifted the 'lid' of 'Darwin's black box'. Things that were a mystery to Darwin have been explored, and the observations scientists are now able to make are, in Behe's view, best explained if it is accepted that an intelligent God is in control of the evolutionary process.

Critics of Behe and of Intelligent Design in general argue that this sort of conclusion is not good science. The existence of God can never be tested with experiment or verified. It is a reversion to the 'God of the gaps' mentality, falling back on the notion that 'God did it' instead of continuing to investigate scientifically. Some critics use the analogy of the 'Flying Spaghetti Monster' and the 'Invisible Pink Unicorn' to illustrate their opinion of the Intelligent Design argument: it is simply postulating some supernatural, unfalsifiable cause as a lazy way of reaching a conclusion.

Paul Davies

Paul Davies is a modern physicist who has taken an interest in the philosophical questions raised by his studies of the origins of the universe and the possibility of the discovery of a grand theory of everything. His books include *God and the New Physics* (Penguin, 1990), *The Mind of God* (Penguin, 2001), and *The Goldilocks Enigma* (Allen Lane, 2006).

Davies' studies lead him to various conclusions:

1. There is something special about the universe and the way in which it works according to mathematical principles; this suggests to Davies that there is evidence for God. Although, in the book *The Mind of God*, Davies explains why each of the traditional arguments for the existence of God fails to convince, he still believes that the existence of the universe and the patterns within it point towards God. Although he appreciates the problems of the cosmological argument with its jump from the existence of the universe to an assumption of a supernatural cause, he still writes:

> The origin of galaxies, for example, has no satisfactory explanation at present. The origin of life is another baffling puzzle. But we can conceive of both these systems being deliberately engineered by an intelligent super-being, without any violation of the laws of physics.

2. Davies is a supporter of the anthropic principle; he looks at the probabilities against the different elements of the universe being so fine-tuned that we are able to exist, and concludes *The Mind of God* by saying, 'We are truly meant to be here'; because it is so unlikely that the different particles would just have fallen, by chance, into the right conditions for us to be here asking the questions, that it could not have happened by accident. This is an idea he develops in *The Goldilocks Enigma* where he argues that

the universe is so carefully fine-tuned that the likelihood of it having happened by random chance is remote:

If almost any of the basic features of the universe, from the properties of atoms to the distribution of the galaxies, were different, life would very probably be impossible. Now, it happens that to meet these various requirements, certain stringent conditions must be satisfied in the underlying laws of physics that regulate the universe, so stringent in fact that a biofriendly universe looks like a fix – or 'a put-up job', to use the pithy description of the late British cosmologist Fred Hoyle. It appeared to Hoyle as if a super-intellect had been 'monkeying' with the laws of physics. He was right in his impression. (Paul Davies, The Goldilocks Enigma*)*

Davies believes that the universe is 'just right', like the porridge Goldilocks stole when trespassing on the Three Bears.

3. Davies believes that scientific study cannot answer all of our questions or meet all our needs, and suggests that our knowledge can be enhanced through mysticism and religion in order to explain the purposes of our existence in the universe.

The ideas supported by Davies could be, and are, criticised from different quarters. Empiricists such as Dawkins and Atkins argue that finding patterns in the universe is acceptable, but asking why these patterns might exist is like asking about the colour of jealousy; it is an inappropriate and meaningless question to ask. There is no purpose, the universe has patterns and that is 'brute fact'. Similarly, in answer to Davies' support of the anthropic principle, they would argue that every possible shape that the elements of the universe might have fallen into is unlikely when compared with all the possibilities. There are so many possible combinations that any one has odds stacked against it. The fact that we are here is an accident, the result of randomness, not purpose.

John Polkinghorne, in his book *Science and Creation*, points out that Davies' concept of God is not the same as that of the Christian religion. Davies suggests a God who, to Polkinghorne, is a 'Demiurge', an agent at work in the world alongside many other agents, who is vastly superior in power and intelligence but who is limited by the materials already there for him to work with. Davies writes of this God organising pre-existent matter, but not able to create out of nothing as described in Genesis. Although Polkinghorne and Davies both consider that the discoveries of science lead towards rather than away from an understanding of God, they do not share an idea of what this God might be like. Polkinghorne's own understanding is very much more in tune with the traditional Christian understanding, and he is keen to distance himself from Davies.

John Polkinghorne

John Polkinghorne is an Anglican priest and also a theoretical physicist. He is the author of several books about the relation between science and religion, including *Belief in God in an Age of Science* (Yale University Press, 1998) and *Exploring Reality: The Intertwining of Science and Religion* (Yale University Press, 2005). In his books, he defends the view that science and religion can co-exist and complement each other, each contributing in its own way to human understanding of the world. His conclusions are many; some of his main points are:

1. Science cannot tell religion what to believe but religion cannot tell science what its results have to be; religious people have to take the results of scientific investigation seriously, and this investigation indicates that the planet has evolved over 15 billion years from an initial Big Bang.

2. Religious belief involves a leap of faith, but that does not have to mean a leap in the dark. Scientists have discovered that some aspects of the world do not work to the same logic that we are used to, and investigation of these requires similar leaps of faith, which often result in new discoveries. Faith is necessary for science as well as for religion.

John Polkinghorne is both a physicist and an Anglican priest.

3. Polkinghorne bases his belief on his encounter with Christ, met through the witness of the church, the accounts in the Gospels, and through the sacraments. He also finds suggestions of the power of God through his scientific enquiry. (A critic might say that this is not sufficient basis for belief, because there is no falsifiable evidence here.)

4. It is possible to take two approaches to the possibility of finding a total theory of everything. One approach assumes that the universe is brute fact, and the other assumes that there is a God. Both of these rest on unexplained assumptions.

5. Polkinghorne believes that the fact that human reason is capable of arriving at the same mathematical patterns as those which occur in the universe is highly significant. He believes that the reason we have within us, and the rational order of the universe, both come from a common source, which is the reason of the creator God. The world reveals the existence of Mind, and our thirst to understand the universe by arriving at a Grand Unified Theory will, he thinks, demonstrate the existence of God.

6. He considers that the fine-tuning of the universe to allow for human existence, the anthropic principle, is evidence of planning, and that it is much more reasonable to believe that our existence is deliberate than that it happened by chance. Arguments which support the idea that we are here by chance involve just as much speculation and are less likely.

7. Science provides information which raises questions which it is beyond the power of science to answer. The more we discover about the universe, the more evidence appears for purpose. (A critic might argue that, if it cannot be proved that something happens by chance, perhaps it cannot be proved that there is an unseen purpose behind things.)

8. About the origins of the world, Polkinghorne argues along with most other Christians that the 'how' of the beginnings are not important for theology; it is the reason that things exist at all which concern religious believers.

9. Polkinghorne cites the French biochemist Jacques Monod, who asserts that the universe happens by blind chance. Polkinghorne's answer is that God gives his creation independence, freedom to go which way it wants, and he implies that this freedom is not confined to the sphere of human free will but can be seen in all elements of the universe.

10. He also suggests that modern science has moved away from the Newtonian view that the world is mechanical and predictable. Instead, it is so sensitive that slight disturbances in one area can have unpredictable knock-on effects; and this new understanding is more receptive to theology, as science becomes more flexible.

Practice exam questions

(a) Explain the creationist understanding of the origins of life.

In answering this question, you need to concentrate on explaining what creationism is. You could include some background information about the history of creationism, but you need not go into great detail about events such as the Scopes trial; although you will probably want to contrast creationism with other views, in an examination you will not have time to go into a great deal of detail about Darwinism or the Big Bang. For high marks, you should summarise the main points made by creationists, with the reasons why they hold this point of view. You could give evidence of your reading, perhaps with reference to creationist thinkers such as Henry Morris.

(b) 'Science has proved that God did not create the universe.' Discuss.

This is a broad question, and you will have only a limited time to answer it, so you need to be selective about what you include. You might want to talk about the differences between different kinds of knowledge, and the way in which inductive reasoning cannot give certain proof. You could refer to thinkers on either side of the argument, such as Dawkins and Atkins or Davies and Polkinghorne. You should aim to present a coherent argument rather than just a range of viewpoints, and reach a justified conclusion.

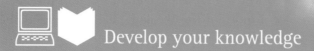

Develop your knowledge

There is a huge range of books available on the subject of science and religion. These are some that you may find helpful:

The Blind Watchmaker by Richard Dawkins (Penguin, 1986)

The God Delusion by Richard Dawkins (Bantam, 2006)

Dawkins' God by Alister McGrath (Blackwell, 2004)

Religion in an Age of Science by Ian Barbour (Harper Collins, 1990)

Darwin's Black Box, by Michael Behe (Free Press, 2006)

Science and Religion by Mel Thompson (Hodder Murray, 2000)

Belief in God in an Age of Science by John Polkinghorne (Yale University Press, 1998)

A2

A2

Religious language

How can people speak about God, when human language is made of words which relate only to this world and the things within it? If God is so different from us, is there any way that believers can speak of God so that what we say is both true and meaningful? Agnostic thinkers argue that God is something we can neither know nor speak about. Their view is that God is not available to reason, not accessible to experiment and testing, and none of the words in human vocabulary can communicate anything about God; therefore, they argue, there is no point in discussing God or in making statements claiming that God is like this or like that. Bertrand Russell held this point of view, and in his radio debate with Frederick Copleston about the existence of God (see pages 95–7) he tried to demonstrate these beliefs.

Theists, however, have always tried to communicate their understanding of God through language. In Islam, for example, there are ninety-nine names for Allah, whose descriptions include 'The Gracious', 'The Merciful', 'The Compassionate', 'The Light' and 'The Giver of Life'. In the *Bhagavad Gita*, the Hindu god Krishna is described as 'the goal of all knowledge', 'the cause of all causes' and 'the Supreme Lord of all beings.' Jews describe God as 'the creator', 'the king of the universe' and 'the father of all'. As well as trying to express an understanding of God, theists also try to communicate other aspects of belief which are outside everyday experience, for examples, beliefs about the afterlife, about the state of enlightenment and about the nature of the soul. Every religion uses language in an attempt to convey supernatural ideas, and the normal language of ordinary life can often seem inadequate.

To think about

Some experiences seem impossible to put into words – such as the emotions felt by a woman who has just given birth, or by someone who has achieved a lifelong ambition, or been bereaved. Can you think of your own examples of experiences which seem impossible to convey in language? Why do people nevertheless try to communicate these experiences? What methods do they use, when ordinary language is inadequate?

One of the issues for philosophers of religion is whether religious language can communicate ideas effectively, even when these are ideas which go way beyond our normal experiences in everyday life.

The uses and purposes of religious language

'Religious language' does not refer only to specialist vocabulary used in the context of religion. There are, of course, many specialist terms that religious people use, which might not be fully understood by those who do not know much about that religion. Christians, for example, might talk about 'the Eucharist', 'the Messiah', or 'justification by faith'; Muslims might talk about 'the sin of shirk', 'tawhid' or 'Shari'ah law'. One way of understanding religious language, then, is thinking that it refers to the kinds of words that might be found in the glossary of a book about religion. Another view is that 'religious language' involves old-fashioned words from traditional acts of worship, such as 'thou art' and 'blessed be he'. However, in philosophy, 'religious language' is a much broader concept than either of these.

Sometimes religious language is used in the context of **truth-claims**. In other words, religious people use language to make statements about what is, or is not, the case. They might say something like, 'There is no God but Allah, and Muhammad is his prophet', or 'Jesus is alive today'; they would be asserting that their religious beliefs are true (and, by implication, that the opposite is false). Much of the debate about religious language in the philosophy of religion is concerned with this kind of use of language. However, there are also other ways in which religious language can be used. When religious believers meet together for worship, for rites of passage and for festivals, they do not spend all their time making truth-claims.

Religious language can also be used to **express feelings and emotions**. Christians might repeat the words 'We are truly sorry, and repent of all our sins' before taking Holy Communion. Parts of the Bible show believers expressing their feelings:

How long, O Lord, must I call for help,
but you do not listen? (Habakkuk 1:2)

And Mary said:
'My soul glorifies the Lord
and my spirit rejoices in God my Saviour.' (Luke 1:46–47)

Some critics of religion point to its tendency to stir up emotions as evidence that religion is no more than hysteria, where people encourage each other to believe just because of the warm feelings it gives them, responding to their emotional needs. However, others argue that emotion is an important part of human life and that it has a rightful place in religion. Scholars such as Peter Donovan argue that religion encourages people to discipline their emotions in the right directions, to calm their anger against others, to control their jealousies, to feel compassion for the weak, repentance when they have done wrong and joy in the happiness and success of others. In a similar way, religious language can be used to evoke feelings of worship. Repeating the name of God in Sikh worship, or the *Aum* sound in Hindu meditation, helps to put the believer into a particular frame of mind, setting aside everyday concerns and focusing attention onto the object of worship.

Religious language can also be used **performatively**. The words announce that something has happened or is about to happen: 'I now pronounce you husband and wife together'; 'We now commit this body to the ground'; 'Let us worship God'. Often, the words have the same function as an action. People thank God by saying words of thanks, or praise God by saying words of praise – the speaking is the doing. The words used in a baptism, at a wedding or in an act of holy communion perform a particular function that is essential to the activity. Without the words spoken at a wedding, the bride and groom would not be married; without the words at an infant baptism, the baby would not be baptised but would just get wet.

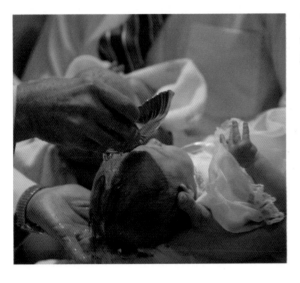

'I baptise you in the name of the Lord' is an example of religious language being used in a performative sense.

Religious language can also be used **prescriptively**, encouraging people to act in certain ways and not in others:

Honour your father and your mother, so that you may live long in the land the Lord your God is giving you. You shall not murder. You shall not commit adultery. You shall not steal. (Exodus 20:12–15)

And whatever you do, whether in word or deed, do it all in the name of the Lord Jesus, giving thanks to God the Father through him. (Colossians 3:17)

Religious language, then, involves much more than just making truth-claims. It is often best understood within the context of worship, where it might accompany particular actions (such as lighting candles) or particular events.

The *via negativa* as a way of speaking about God

Some writers have argued that it is only possible to speak about God properly if we use negative terms, and talk about what God is not. This is sometimes called the apophatic way, or *via negativa* (negative way). It involves speaking of God using only negatives, to emphasise the difference between God and humanity. God is described as 'immortal', 'invisible', 'inaccessible', 'timeless', 'incorporeal' and so on. These descriptions of God are plain statements of fact, argue those in favour of the *via negativa*. Those descriptions which try to give God positive attributes are misleading and should be avoided, they claim – if we say God is like a father, or like a shepherd, then we might give people completely the wrong idea, conveying the impression that God has a body, or is male, or has faults. Even if we say something like 'God is love', then we start making people think of human love with all its flaws and jealousies and inconsistencies. If we say 'God is good', then we start thinking about our own goodness, because it is the only goodness we know, and we imagine that God must possess a goodness like ours; but our own goodness is so flawed and temporary that it is wrong to use the same concept and try to apply it to God. As soon as we try to speak of God in positive terms and suggest that God has attributes which we recognise from the physical world, we start making statements which are so inaccurate that they damage understanding. People who support the *via negativa* believe that it is better to accept the mysteries of God than to try to pin God down by using flawed concepts; if we use these, we end up belittling God and imagining that our reason is capable of understanding divine mysteries.

Supporters of the via negativa *argue that if we use positive terms to speak of God, such as 'The Lord is my shepherd', then we immediately mislead.*

Pseudo-Dionysius the Areopagite, who was a sixth-century Christian mystic, argued that the *via negativa* was the only way in which we can speak truthfully about God, because God is beyond all human understanding and imagination. Pseudo-Dionysius was a theologian who wrote about religious experience as well as the religious language used to express it. He wrote about the need for the soul to become unified with God by going beyond the realms of sense perception and rationality, entering obscurity, a 'cloud of unknowing' from which God can be approached. Pseudo-Dionysius was a follower of Plato, believing in the division between the physical body and the spiritual soul, and believing that the soul's search for God can be held back by the demands of the body and the mind's desire for understanding. His ideas about God being beyond knowledge and beyond the realms of rational thought greatly influenced the author of the anonymous fourteenth-century book *The Cloud of Unknowing*, as well as other medieval Christians and mystics, including Thomas Aquinas.

For Pseudo-Dionysius, it was counter productive to speak of God as though God could be encountered by the senses or as though we could reach God through reason. It was only through recognition of the limits of humanity that spiritual progress could be made. People who are genuinely seeking God should put away their need to have the answers to everything, he thought; they should stop trying to use logic and arguments. Instead, they should allow God to speak to them in stillness, accepting that God will remain a mystery, and realising that until they are ready to accept this, they will miss the point and end up with an idea of God which is too small.

The great Jewish thinker Moses Maimonides (1135–1204) was also a supporter of the *via negativa*. Maimonides explained his beliefs that the attributes of God could be expressed in negative terms, whereby people come to an understanding of what God is not and therefore move closer to appreciating what God is. In his writing, Maimonides used the example of a ship to demonstrate what he meant:

There is no necessity at all for you to use positive attributes of God with the view of magnifying Him in your thought ... I will give you ... some illustrations, in order that you may better understand the propriety of forming as many negative attributes as possible, and the impropriety of ascribing to God any positive attributes. A person may know for certain that a 'ship' is in existence, but he may not know to what object that name is applied, whether to a substance or to an accident; a second person then learns that a ship is not an accident; a third, that it is not a mineral; a fourth, that it is not a plant growing in the earth; a fifth, that it is not a body whose parts are joined together by nature; a sixth, that it is not a flat object like boards or doors; a seventh, that it is not a sphere; an eight, that it is not pointed; a ninth, that it is not round shaped; nor equilateral; a tenth, that it is not solid. It is clear that this tenth person has almost arrived at the correct notion of a 'ship' by the foregoing negative attributes ... In the same manner you will come nearer to the knowledge and comprehension of God by the negative attributes ... I do not merely declare that he who affirms attributes of God has not sufficient knowledge concerning the Creator ... but I say that he unconsciously loses his belief in God. (Moses Maimonides, The Guide for the Perplexed, *trans. M. Friedlander, 1936)*

Not all philosophers would agree with that point of view. The writer Brian Davies, for example, criticises Maimonides. Davies writes:

> *Only saying what something is not gives no indication of what it actually is, and if one can only say what God is not, one cannot understand him at all. Suppose I say that there is something in my room, and suppose I reject every suggestion you make as to what is actually there. In that case, you will get no idea at all about what is in my room. Going back to the quotation from Maimonides … it is simply unreasonable to say that someone who has all the negations mentioned in it 'has almost arrived at the correct notion of a "ship"'. He could equally well be thinking of a wardrobe. (Brian Davies,* An Introduction to the Philosophy of Religion, *Oxford University Press, 1986)*

Davies, then, points out that Maimonides' method of arriving at the 'right answer' is unlikely to lead people in the right direction at all. Another objection that could be made to Maimonides' point of view is that when we try to arrive at something by process of elimination, we need to know before we start what the different possibilities are, so that we can know what we have left when the alternatives have been crossed off – so the *via negativa* might not work for someone who began by knowing nothing of God.

I am thinking of something. It is not any of the objects you can see here. What am I thinking of?

The *via negativa* is a prominent feature of the religious language of Buddhism. The nature of reality is described in the *Saddharmapundarika* in this way:

*For the Tathagatha has seen the word as it really is: It is not born, it dies not; there is no decease or rebirth, no samsara or nirvana; it is not real or unreal, not existent, or non-existent, not such, or otherwise, not false or not-false. (*Buddhist Texts Through the Ages, *trans. Edward Conze, Oxford University Press, 1954)*

In Buddhist texts, the *via negativa* is used in an attempt to convey central beliefs; the nature of nirvana, and the nature of the Buddha, are concepts which are notoriously difficult to describe. Although Buddhists do not believe in God, they still use the *via negativa* in attempts to convey the essence of ultimate reality:

There is, monks, an unborn, a not-become, a not-made, a not-compounded. If, monks, there were not this unborn, not-become, not-made, not-compounded, there would not here be an escape from the born, the become, the made, the compounded. But because there is an unborn, a not-become, a not-made, a not-compounded, therefore there is an escape from the born, the become, the made, the compounded. (Udana 80)

Key point

• The *via negativa* uses only negative terms to speak of God, as a way of avoiding belittling God by attributing human qualities to him.

Strengths and weaknesses of the *via negativa*

The *via negativa* has the advantages, then, of:

• being a way of recognising that we have to go beyond our normal everyday experiences in order to experience God. It does not place a limit on God by giving a point of reference that is within the physical world.

- being a way of conveying the essential otherness and mystery of God, and underlining the belief that God is not like us.

- being a means by which we can say something about God, or about reality, which is literally true and does not need interpretation. Unlike symbolism, analogy or myth, the *via negativa* applies equally well in different cultures and in different periods of history. If we do not use figurative language, which necessarily demands interpretation, we can say things which are understandable and which mean the same things across cultures and generations.

However, the *via negativa* also has disadvantages:

- If we speak of God only negatively, then it is still not very easy for the person who has no experience of God to know what we mean. To say that white is 'the opposite of black' does not give much help to the person who has never seen and has no concept of white. God cannot be reached by process of elimination, if he is outside our experience.

- Antony Flew in his essay 'Theology and Falsification' argued that if we try to explain God by saying that he is invisible, soundless, incorporeal and so on, there is very little difference between our definition of God and our definition of nothingness; we argue God out of existence by 'a thousand qualifications' (see pages 231–33).

- Many of the holy scriptures of the world's religions do make positive statements about God. For example, the Bible makes positive claims that God is a king, a judge, a father, a shepherd, a rock. If it is believed that holy scripture comes from God, then this would suggest that it can be right and appropriate to make positive claims about God.

Practice exam question

'The only way in which meaningful statements can be made about God is the *via negativa*.' Discuss.

For this question, the *via negativa* needs to be compared with other ways of making statements about God, so it would be useful to read the rest of the chapter before tackling the topic. A good answer to this question would include explanation of the *via negativa* and examples of different thinkers who have supported it to a greater or lesser extent. Useful reference could be made to Aquinas, Pseudo-Dionysius and Maimonides. Criticisms of the *via negativa* should also be explained and evaluated – to what extent are these criticisms valid? Do they mean that people should abandon the *via negativa* altogether, or should they use it with caution or only up to a point, or are the criticisms not worth taking seriously? Alternative ways of talking about God using positive terms could be explored, but this should not take up the bulk of the essay. For high marks, you should aim to present an argument rather than simply a presentation of different perspectives.

Analogy and its use in religious language

Some thinkers (most notably Aquinas) have argued that we cannot say anything positive that is literally true of God, because the use of ordinary human language automatically limits God, placing his attributes only within our experience and understanding. Aquinas used the term *via eminentiae* (the way of eminence) to show that what we say of God, and indeed what we know of God, is only partial – we should realise that the love of God, for example, is 'eminent'. Our own love and the love that we receive is partial and flawed, but God's love is the prime example of love. However, Aquinas suggested in *Summa Theologica* that there could be a way of making positive claims about God and conveying positive ideas, as long as we understand that the words we use have an analogical, rather than a literal, application.

Sometimes, we use words of two different things in a way that is **univocal** – which means the same words are used in exactly the same way, such as when we talk about a green hat and a green ball; in both cases, the word 'green' means the same thing as a reference to colour.

Sometimes, we use words of two different things in a way that is **equivocal** – which means when the same word is used in two completely different senses, such as when we talk about a fruit punch and a hole punch, or a dining table and a periodic table.

When words like 'bat' are used equivocally, they have completely different meanings.

In addition, we use words in a way which is **analogical**. This means that the same term is used, in not exactly the same sense, but in a similar or related sense. We use this kind of language in other contexts, besides in religious language. For example, we might talk about a smooth floor and a smooth wine; the wine is not smooth in the same way that the floor is smooth, but the word is used in a related way – it is the same kind of idea which is being expressed. Another example of analogical use of language is when we speak of a woollen blanket and a blanket of snow. Poetry often uses this kind of language as metaphor and simile; as well as the words having their obvious, denotative meaning, they also carry connotations which help our minds to associate them with other related concepts and gain greater insights.

Aquinas said that there were two main types of analogy:

1. Analogy of attribution, where there is a causal relation between the two things being described. For example, a seaside town might be called 'healthy' because it causes the people who live there to be healthy, while a sticky cake might be called 'sickly' because of the effect it has on the person eating it. In Aquinas' view, when we speak of God as 'living' it means that God is the cause of life, for example.

2. Analogy of proportionality, where the words relate to objects which are different in proportion. For example, we might speak of a clever dog and a clever scientist, and the words are used in proportion; the dog is clever as dogs go, and the scientist is clever in comparison with other people. In religious terms, then, Aquinas thought that we can use terms such as 'loving' and 'faithful' when we speak of God, but we have to recognise that God's love, faithfulness and so on are on an infinitely vaster scale than our own.

Some people (for example William Blackstone) have argued that this Thomist doctrine is unhelpful, because we have to translate the analogies into univocal language before they mean anything; we have to know how God's love relates to human love before we understand anything. This method of speaking about God still leaves us with an unclear picture, where we know something about the nature of God, but not a great deal.

C. Stephen Evans answers this by saying that there is nothing wrong with accepting that God is mysterious and that our knowledge of him is limited, as long as the believer understands enough to be able to worship. The 'otherness' of God, described by Rudolf Otto as *mysterium tremendum et fascinans* (a fearful and fascinating mystery) is something which our language ought to convey, not disguise.

A more modern version of the idea of speaking of God analogically comes from the philosopher Ian Ramsey, who explained his ideas in his 1957 book *Religious Language*. He tried to explain the way in which religious language could usefully describe God, by using the terms 'models and qualifiers'. According to Ramsey, we can use 'models' when we speak of God, using words such as 'righteous' or 'loving' – these are words which we understand because we have a reference point in our own human experience. However, to ensure that we do not limit God and that we recognise that his attributes are unlike our own, we also need to use 'qualifiers'. These are adjectives and adverbs such as 'everlasting' or 'perfectly'. In this way, we can anchor our ideas about God within our own experience, so that we at least know what we are talking about; and then we can show that God is different from us proportionally, by using the qualifier to point us in the right direction. We might not understand and comprehend exactly the nature of God, because qualifiers such as 'infinitely' or 'perfectly' are in many ways beyond our imagination; but it is a method of speaking about God positively which aims to avoid either limiting God or speaking incomprehensibly.

To think about

Scientists often use analogical models to help convey ideas, and to help them predict how things will behave. An example is the model of the atom with the nucleus at the centre orbited by electrons. It is not a model in the physical sense, but a conceptual model. Can you think of any other examples of scientific models?

Analogies are considered to be useful in many different contexts, especially when used to communicate complex or new ideas. They can help us to form pictures in our minds, and to associate ideas and draw conclusions. However, they are not completely without difficulties. It is not always clear exactly in what respects two different things are being considered similar – in what respects might the love or the justice of God resemble our own, and how are they different? In Aquinas' view, it was important to remember that God cannot be wholly understood, and that we never will reach a clear understanding where we comprehend exactly what God is.

The use of myth in religious language

This method of speaking analogically is only one of the possible ways of conveying meaning in religious language. Myth is another example of how positive truth-claims about God (rather than just saying what God is not) can be made, usually in the form of stories.

The definition of 'myth' is not always clear, partly because the word is often used in casual conversation to mean something that is just not true (for example, 'it is a myth that this county runs a decent bus service'). However, theologically, the word 'myth' is used to describe a story or a metaphor which is not necessarily historically accurate (although it may have some basis in history), but which nevertheless conveys important truths that might be difficult to express in other ways. The myth is intended to encourage a particular kind of attitude in the people who hear or read it – it may be an appreciation of the greatness of God, or a deeper understanding of moral behaviour and its consequences, for example.

The use of myth to convey religious ideas has its difficulties, particularly when the writer does not make it explicit whether the story is meant to be myth or whether it is meant to be an accurate account of history. The creation stories in the Bible, for example, are interpreted by some people to be myths, while for others, they are literally true, and this difference of opinion causes sharp divisions within both Judaism and Christianity. In the sacred writings of many religions, a story which might or might not be intended as a myth is presented without introduction, and it is left up to the reader to decide how the story is meant to be interpreted.

Myth as a means of conveying religious ideas can also have problems in that mythological imagery has a tendency to be culturally determined. Although myths can often be understood outside their cultural contexts, nevertheless they are likely to communicate the most to a specific geographical location and a particular time in history. Some elements of the myth might be 'lost in translation', where the ideas used might have particular significance in one culture but not in another – conversely, the ideas could take on a meaning that the writer never anticipated, distorting the original communication.

However, conveying religious ideas through myth also has many advantages. It gives people a visual way of understanding what are often abstract ideas, so these ideas can be more easily understood. Because the stories are often lively and memorable, they are passed on from one generation to the next, and can be so vivid that the myth is still remembered even when the religion has died out. Ideas can be expressed in myth which might be difficult to communicate in other ways, and sometimes several different meanings and layers of meaning can all be conveyed within the one story, so that people can return to them again and again and find new ways of relating the stories to their own lives. Through myth, believers are able to communicate something positive about God, without having to resort to the *via negativa*.

Some point out the mythological features of the Genesis creation stories: there are unusual trees with special powers, people being made from dust and from ribs, and a talking serpent. They point out the parallels with myths and folk tales from other cultures, and compare the biblical creation stories with scientific accounts of the origins of the universe and the evolution of the species, concluding that surely these stories are meant to be understood as myths. The stories convey the power of God and his purposes in creation; the responsibilities of humanity to act as stewards of the earth; the disobedience of humanity in the face of God's commands; the suffering that comes as a consequence of sin. The creation stories in Genesis have sometimes been described as 'aetiological' myths, which are myths that set out to explain the origins of puzzling features of the world. How did people get here? How did the animals get their names? Why is it that people leave their parents and go and find themselves husbands and wives? How did sin come into the world? Why do women have pain in childbirth, and why do men have to struggle against the natural world in order to grow their food? Those Jews and Christians who regard the creation stories as myth take the view that important truths are being communicated here, but that the stories do not have to be regarded as literally true – indeed, to take them as if they were historically and scientifically accurate misses their point.

Many people understand the stories in Genesis as myth; but there are also many others who believe them to be literally true.

Others, however, disagree about the interpretation of holy scripture as myth. Many believe that stories in the Bible and in the Qur'an are directly inspired by God and are to be accepted as entirely true. If the Bible says that Noah built an ark which contained two animals of every kind of species, then he did. If the Bible says that Jonah was swallowed by a big fish and survived the experience, then he did. For these believers, interpreting the word of God as 'myth' comes far too close to suggesting that the words of the Bible are false.

Within the Christian tradition, the view that elements of holy scripture might be interpreted as myth became more popular when scientific theories began to propose that the world was much older than the Bible seemed to suggest. Evolutionary theory put forward the idea that the different species might have evolved gradually through a process of natural selection, rather than have been created from the beginning in the form we see them today. By the nineteenth century, Christians were worried that advances in science seemed to be producing evidence that contradicted the Bible. While some Christians responded by reaffirming their faith in the infallible literal truth of scripture, others began to suggest that perhaps there were parts of the Bible which were never meant to be taken literally. Perhaps the writers intended them as myths, and they should be understood as such.

Perhaps some of the Old Testament stories, such as the story of Daniel in the lions' den pictured here by Rubens, were always intended to be understood as myth.

The Genesis creation stories seemed an obvious place to start, if some of the Bible were to be interpreted as myth. If the Genesis stories were understood as mythical ways of communicating important ideas, then intelligent and rational people could continue in their Christian faith while accepting the discoveries of science.

To think about

Do you think that there are some parts of the Bible that are best understood as myth, rather than being taken to be literally true? If so, which parts would you classify as myth?

Many Christians were able to accept the idea that the Old Testament was full of myth. Ancient stories which seemed bizarre to the modern mind, such as the turning of Lot's wife into a pillar of salt in Genesis 19, or the story of God making a bet with Satan at the beginning of the book of Job, became much more acceptable if they were understood as myth rather than as literal truth. Christians explained some of the more difficult Old Testament stories as having been written before Jesus came into the world to reveal the final and complete truth – the Old Testament writers had included obscure mythical elements in their writings because they had not yet received the revelation of God in Christ. These Old Testament myths were still the word of God, and were still true, it was argued, but they had a different kind of truth.

However, when it was suggested that there might be myth in the New Testament, many Christians found the idea much more difficult to accept. In his essay 'New Testament and Mythology' (1941), the German theologian Rudolf Bultmann argued that the writers of the New Testament were never trying to make a record of accurate historical fact, but that they had expressed their beliefs through the language of myth. The real point of the gospel message, for Bultmann, was the need for individuals to reach a personal decision about the direction they wanted their lives to take in relation to God. In Bultmann's view, the modern, intelligent, literate person could not take seriously the supernatural elements of the Gospel stories, such as visitations by angels, the virgin birth and miraculous events, but this did not have to mean that the whole of Christianity should be rejected. Bultmann advocated the 'demythologising' of the New Testament as well as the Old, to enable Christianity to hold what he saw as its rightful place as an essential, vital option in a fast-changing world.

The Myth of God Incarnate sparked much more controversy than its authors had anticipated.

In 1977, John Hick edited a book called *The Myth of God Incarnate*, to which several well-known theologians contributed chapters, and this book took up Bultmann's ideas about demythologising the New Testament. The theme of the book, as the title suggests, was that Jesus was not literally God in human form, but that the idea of Jesus as God incarnate was a myth. It was a pictorial way of expressing the importance of Jesus to God and of expressing Jesus' godliness, but statements such as that 'God was in Christ' were not literally true. The writers of the book described how the idea of God becoming human was to be found in other myths predating the New Testament, and they claimed that the early Christians used this mythology as an aid to expressing their own ideas, but that it was a mistake to take the incarnation literally. Hick writes:

I suggest that its character is best expressed by saying that the idea of divine incarnation is a mythological idea. And I am using the term 'myth' in the following sense: a myth is a story which is told but which is not literally true, or an idea or image which is applied to someone or something but which does not literally apply, but which invites a particular attitude in its hearers. Thus the truth of a myth is a kind of practical truth consisting in the appropriateness of the attitude to its object. That Jesus was God the Son incarnate is not literally true, since it has no literal meaning, but it is an application to Jesus of a mythical concept whose function is analogous to that of the notion of divine sonship ascribed in the ancient world to a king. (John Hick, The Myth of God Incarnate, *SCM, 1977)*

Hick and his co-authors argued that the way in which first-century Christians understood the world is inappropriate today, and that the mythological language they used to convey their beliefs might be a hindrance, rather than a help, to modern faith:

> *The Christians of the early church lived in a world in which supernatural causation was accepted without question, and divine or spiritual visitants were not unexpected. Such assumptions, however, have become foreign to our situation. In the Western world, both popular culture and the culture of the intelligentsia has come to be dominated by the human and natural sciences to such an extent that supernatural causation or intervention in the affairs of this world has become, for the majority of people, simply incredible.*

For many more conservative Christians, however, there are some central beliefs which should be taken literally, and not regarded as myth. Belief in the virgin birth, for example, or the literal physical resurrection of Jesus, as well as the incarnation, should not be treated as myth but should be accepted as literal fact. It is argued that if these ideas are treated as myth, then Christianity becomes not much more than general advice to be nice to other people. They argue that it should not be taken for granted that a rationalist, scientific way of looking at the world is the best way or the only way of understanding truth; if modern society has difficulty in accepting the literal truth of biblical ideas, then modern society should change.

Using myth as a means of conveying religious ideas, then, can create problems rather than resolving them. It is very difficult for people to know how far they should go in interpreting language as mythical rather than literal. It is also difficult to know how a myth is to be understood: what are the central, important truths that should be distilled from it, and what is the embellishment that can safely be stripped away?

Key point

- Myth can be a useful way of expressing the inexpressible, but it can be difficult for people to know when something is to be interpreted as myth and when it is to be understood literally.

Practice exam question

To what extent is myth an effective way of conveying religious truth?

In answer to this question, you need to show that you understand what is meant by the term 'myth'. You should show the advantages of using myth, such as its ability to stand the test of time (sometimes the myths of a culture are still well known even when the rest of the culture is forgotten), and you should be able to give examples of myth. You might want to consider debates about which parts of the Bible should be treated as myth, and you could refer to thinkers such as Bultmann and the contributors to *The Myth of God Incarnate*. In evaluation, you need to consider possible problems with myth, such as the difficulties of knowing what the writer meant us to understand, the problems of treating ideas as mythical when they have always been considered central to faith, and the problems of translating metaphors across cultures. You might want to compare the use of myth with other ways of conveying religious truth, as long as these other ways do not become the focus of the essay. By the end, you should have answered the question and made clear the extent to which you think myth is effective.

The use of symbols in religious language

Another possible way (as well as analogy and myth) of saying positive things about God is through the use of symbols.

All language, of course, is symbolic, in the sense that we use words to stand for other things. We use the shapes of the letters to stand for particular sounds, and we use groups of letters to make words to stand for different objects, actions, feelings and so on. Much language, both religious and non-religious is symbolic in the sense of being figurative; it is used in a metaphorical way rather than literally, and people recognise without needing to be told that when we say 'I'm going to kill my husband when I get home' or 'our French teacher went mad when we told her we hadn't revised for the test', we are using words figuratively rather than literally. Religious people often use language symbolically when talking about their relationship with God. They might say that God 'listened' to their prayers, although they believe that God has no body and therefore no ears; they might say that God 'walks with them' even though they believe that God is always everywhere and is beyond space. The figurative, symbolic use of language helps to create a short cut; but it can also cause problems of communication, if it is not clear whether a phrase was meant as a symbolic metaphor or whether it was meant literally.

People use symbols to describe God and their relationship to him, saying things like 'The Lord is my shepherd', or 'God is my rock'. They also use symbols instead of language, to convey meanings that cannot readily be put into words, or to evoke particular feelings, or to identify themselves as members of a particular group of believers so that they can be easily recognised by others.

Paul Tillich made a distinction between signs and symbols, arguing that signs are chosen arbitrarily to stand for something else, and as long as we agree on the meaning of the sign, it does not really matter what form the sign takes. A symbol, on the other hand, according to Tillich, 'participates in' the object represented. He uses the example of a national flag, which evokes feelings of loyalty and patriotism at the same time as it symbolises the country. Tillich claimed that all religious ideas and language were symbolic, pointing beyond themselves to 'being-itself', which was how he understood the nature of God.

Tillich argued that symbols 'participate in' that which they represent, as opposed to signs which are just arbitrarily chosen.

John Macquarrie, in *Principles of Christian Theology* (SCM, 1966) writes:

In the widest sense of the word, a 'symbol' is anything which is presented to the mind as standing for something else. In this broad sense, symbolism is all-pervasive of life, and there are almost innumerable kinds of symbols … We notice first that words (and even the letters out of which written words are made up) are symbols, so that in the broad sense all language has a symbolic character. When, however, we speak of 'symbolic language', we generally have a fairly definite kind of language in mind, a kind in which the words are not understood in their direct or proper reference but in which they, so to speak, bounce off that to which they properly refer so as to impinge at a distance on a more remote subject-matter, to which the speaker wishes to refer.

Macquarrie disagreed with Tillich's use of the term 'symbol', saying that it was not consistent with current English usage and was therefore misleading and unhelpful. He argues that we might say 'Clouds are a sign of rain', which is an example of how a sign can have an intrinsic connection with what it signifies, in contradiction to Tillich's claim that this is the function of a symbol, not a sign. Mathematical symbols are chosen arbitrarily without having obvious connection with, or 'participation in' what they stand for. Macquarrie preferred the idea of the conventional symbol and the intrinsic symbol:

The conventional symbol has no connection with what it symbolises other than the fact that some people have arbitrarily agreed to let it stand for this particular symbolizandum. The intrinsic symbol, on the other hand, has in itself a kinship with what it symbolises.

But, he argued, the two were not distinct categories, and it could often be difficult to identify whether something was one or the other; it might have elements of both.

Macquarrie claimed that the value of symbols is that they provoke in us an 'existential response' and an understanding in terms of 'similarity of relation':

• **existential response** – by this, he meant that symbols remind us of feelings such as loyalty or awe, and we can then recognise that we should have the same response to God (or Being, as Macquarrie uses it in this context). When religious believers experience dipping themselves symbolically into water, they are reminded of ideas and feelings about cleansing; so Hindus bathe in the Ganges, Muslims perform *wudu* (washing rituals) before prayer, Sikhs bathe in the Pool of Nectar at the Golden Temple in Amritsar, Christians participate in believers' baptism, and orthodox Jews use the cleansing symbolism of the *mikveh*.

• **similarity of relation** – symbols can work in the same way as analogies. If we are Christians, we can see that light is to the world as Christ is to us; the sheep are to the shepherd as we are to God. If we are Buddhists, we can see that the journey the lotus makes from the mud at the bottom of the pool to the surface of the water is like a personal journey from ignorance to enlightenment.

Different symbols can complement each other, although they may appear to contradict; they should not be treated like theories where one is true and therefore the others are false, but perhaps like poetry, illustrating different aspects of the truth. Because symbols invoke feelings and association of ideas, they can not only convey meaning but also leave room for the individual to add his or her own interpretations and feelings, and so they can be part of private as well as public religion.

It could be argued that the symbol can only be properly understood by those within a restricted community (see Wittgenstein's theory of language-games, pages 235–8). In order for people to have shared understanding of what a symbol means, they need to have similar presuppositions and beliefs. For some groups of people, the hammer and sickle might be a symbol of hope, strength and unity; for others, it might be a symbol of fear and repression. Perhaps this means that religious symbols, too, will

Symbolic actions, such as bathing in the Ganges, carry different levels of meaning for believers.

always be tied to particular cultures or times in history, and that their meanings can only be properly understood by those who are believers themselves.

The symbol of light, used to represent God, is perhaps the most universal of all religious symbols. It represents truth, knowledge and purity, because things can be so much more clearly perceived when there is light than when there is darkness. A flame can represent purification, prayer, the soul and remembrance of the dead. Water can be used as a sign of cleansing from sin, and of life-giving force. Religious people use symbolism not only in language, but also in art, in architecture, and in their body language: when they kneel for prayer, or prostrate themselves, or bow their heads, they remind themselves of their position in relation to God.

The symbol of a flame is used in Judaism to represent remembrance and honouring of the dead.

Logical positivism and the challenge to religious language

The verification principle

Much of the philosophy of religion deals with the questions raised by particular religious beliefs and concepts. These beliefs and concepts are investigated in an attempt to discover whether or not they are coherent, and whether there is evidence for or against them to indicate if they are true or false.

However, some philosophers have argued that religious statements, such as 'God exists', 'God is love' and so on are neither true nor false, but meaningless. We can only usefully discuss statements which mean something, and according to some, religious statements lack any kind of meaning at all. There is no point, according to some thinkers, of even raising these questions, because there is nothing to talk about (see page 97 and Bertrand Russell's response to the cosmological argument for the existence of God).

Philosophical discussion about meaning often identifies two different ways in which a word or phrase might mean something:

• **denotation** – this is when the word stands for something, as a label for it, such as the word 'window' standing for the part of the wall that has glass in it

• **connotation** – this is when the word carries other associations with it, so that 'window' might carry associations of opportunity, or of finding a space in a busy week. Connotation can carry meaning beyond the literal truth of the words, and sometimes words can convey meaning that was unintended by the speaker.

Ludwig Wittgenstein (1889–1951), one of the most remarkable philosophers of the twentieth century, raised the whole question of the meaning of language, and inspired debates across the world: people were talking about 'the meaning of meaning', how meaning is conveyed from one person to another, and what the necessary conditions for something to have any meaning at all might be.

Wittgenstein was a strong influence on the Vienna Circle, a group of philosophers who met after the First World War and carried on getting together into the 1920s and 1930s. They were led by a writer called Moritz Schlick (who, incidentally, was eventually murdered by one of his former students). Following the thinking of Auguste Comte (1798–1857), these people held the belief that theological interpretations of events and experiences belonged in the past, to an unenlightened age when 'God' was used as an explanation for anything that science had not yet completely mastered. Comte had said that the 'theological' era was replaced by the 'metaphysical', where concepts from philosophy were used as a replacement for the gods to fill in the gaps left by science; and finally, there was the 'positivist' age, where it could be seen that the only useful form of evidence for investigation was that which was available to the senses, which could be tested in a scientific way. Comte, then, held the view that a theological way of looking at reality was outdated, and the Vienna Circle took up this idea. They held that empirical evidence (that which is available to be tested using the senses) was the key to understanding what was, and what was not, meaningful.

Logical positivists claim that evidence is only useful if it is available to be tested using the senses.

In 1936, A. J. Ayer wrote a very influential book called *Language, Truth and Logic*, in which he set out the main principles of what is known as **logical positivism**. Taking up the ideas of Wittgenstein and of the Vienna Circle, he attempted to set down rules by which language can be judged to see whether or not it really means anything at all.

The main argument of logical positivism was the **verifiability theory of meaning**. This was a way in which statements could be tested to see whether there was any point in talking about them. As we saw in discussion of the ontological argument (pages 72–83), statements can be divided into two types, the analytic and the synthetic.

1. Analytic statements: These are propositions which define meanings of words. We do not have to go and check whether they are true, using our experience. Analytic statements just give us information about what words mean: a dictionary is full of analytic statements. These statements are true or false depending on whether the words in the statement actually mean what is suggested. 'A kilogram is a unit of mass' is a true analytic statement; 'pigs are flying insects' is a false analytic statement. The logical positivists also included some other kinds of statement in this group, for example tautologies (statements which say the same thing twice, such as 'Ice is icy'), and mathematical statements such as ('3 x 4 = 12').

2. Synthetic statements: These give information about reality, rather than just defining our use of language. For example, 'It is raining today' or 'This sandwich has got mayonnaise in it' are examples of synthetic statements.

The logical positivists decided that in order for synthetic statements to qualify as meaningful, they had to be verifiable using empirical evidence – in other words, it had to be possible to test the truth of the statement, using the experience available to the five senses. We can test whether it is raining outside with our senses of touch, vision, hearing and smell; we can test whether this sandwich has got mayonnaise in it using empirical evidence too – so both qualify as meaningful statements.

The verifiability theory, then, says that if a statement is neither analytic nor empirically verifiable, it says nothing about reality and is therefore meaningless. This way of thinking was taking up the ideas of Hume, who argued that if a statement did not contain any abstract reasoning (such as that found in mathematics) or any experimental reasoning, then it said nothing at all. Statements, if they go beyond giving mere definitions, have to be verifiable. They have to be capable of being tested, to find out whether or not they are true. We have to know the conditions this proposal would have to meet, in order for it to be true.

Friedrich Waismann, a philosopher of mathematics and one of the Vienna Circle, gave a neat description of the logical positivist position:

> *Anyone uttering a sentence must know under what conditions he calls it true, and under what conditions he calls it false. If he is unable to state these conditions, he does not know what he has said. A statement which cannot be conclusively verified cannot be verified at all. It is simply devoid of any meaning.*

A. J. Ayer agreed that, in order for any statement to be meaningful, it has to be in principle verifiable using empirical methods. This ruled out talk about God, amongst other things, because according to the logical positivists, claims such as 'God created the world', 'God has a plan for each of us' or 'the Lord is my Shepherd' cannot be shown to be either true or false using the senses.

To think about

This way of looking at the meaning of language also has implications for ethics, because statements such as 'it is right to defend the weak', or 'stealing is wrong' cannot be verified empirically either – does this mean that they, too, are meaningless?

Objections to the theory of verification

Not surprisingly, the verification principle of meaning was not universally welcomed.

Key terms

empirical – to do with evidence that is available to the five senses.

verifiable – capable of being shown to be true, through the use of evidence.

A. J. Ayer's work on the verification principle encouraged new discussion of the meaningfulness of religious language.

The most significant criticism was that statement of the theory itself does not pass the test as a meaningful statement. The verifiability theory cannot be verified by sense experience (we cannot tell, using the senses, if these are the only types of statement to have any meaning) and so is not a meaningful synthetic statement; and if it is analytic, it is giving a new sense to the word 'meaningful', a new definition which we do not necessarily have to accept.

The idea that all meaningful synthetic statements have to be empirically verifiable also causes practical problems. Many of the claims made by advances in science, for example, such as the existence of black holes, cannot be verified by sense experience; also many historical statements, of events that happened in the past, cannot be tested now using the senses. People experiencing psychological problems would not be able to explain their symptoms to a psychiatrist in a meaningful way, because of the private nature of the feelings they were experiencing. We would have to dismiss as meaning-less statements such as 'I had a weird dream last night', or 'I'm not looking forward to the exams', because there is no way of testing them using the senses, but statements such as these do have meaning to us.

Logical positivists accepted that there was a problem, and that they were disallowing too much as meaningless, so the theory was weakened to allow for 'indirect experience'. However, there was still a desire to dismiss as meaningless all talk of the supernatural, of God, of life after death, and of other theological concepts such as sin and salvation. Religious 'truth claims' such as 'God created the world' were ruled out.

Some philosophers, most notably John Hick, argued that religious truth claims are verifiable, because they are 'eschatologically verifiable'. By this, he meant that although we cannot test and see at the moment, in this life and this world, whether the good will be rewarded, or whether God really does exist and love us, after death these claims will be verified. (This raises an interesting issue about the meaningfulness of any claims about the future – would logical positivists count as meaningful the assertion 'in a thousand years, the first Wednesday in March will be a very wet day for Scotland'?) Critics of Hick have argued that 'eschatological verification' is not possible, because even if there is an afterlife and even if we do have physical senses in it with which to perceive things, they will not necessarily be the same senses that we have now; and if there is no afterlife, then there will be no one to do the verifying.

Eventually it became clear, and Ayer himself agreed, that the theory could not be adjusted so that scientific and historical statements were seen to be meaningful and yet religious claims were ruled out. However, there were and are still those who consider that there are some assertions which, because of the lack of any possibility of empirical evidence, are meaningless. The **falsification principle** was developed as a modification of the verification principle, once it had been accepted that the verification principle was unsound.

The challenge of Flew: the falsification principle

Falsification is a word usually associated with Karl Popper. He used the concept in his discussion of the scientific method, where he argued that in order for a statement to be 'scientific', it had to be falsifiable. This means that we have to understand and be able to demonstrate what it would mean for it to be false. For example, 'Polystyrene floats on water' is a scientific statement, because we know what would 'falsify' it: if we put some polystyrene on the surface of water and it sank, then we would have proved ourselves wrong. 'An emu can't fly' is a scientific statement, because we know it would be falsified if ever an emu took flight. Some statements are unfalsifiable, because we cannot observe or demonstrate anything that might falsify them, for example, statements about our personal taste or speculations about unremembered events long ago. Such statements are, in Popper's view, not meaningless, but they are also not scientific.

Antony Flew's article 'Theology and Falsification' (*New Essays in Philosophical Theology*, ed. Antony Flew and Alasdair MacIntyre, SCM Press, 1955), has become one of the best-known pieces of writing on the subject of religious language. In this article, Flew returned to the debate begun by the logical positivists, suggesting that instead of insisting that a statement should be verifiable, it should instead be falsifiable.

Flew began his article by referring to a parable from John Wisdom's paper 'Gods'. In this parable, two explorers come across a clearing in the jungle, and in the clearing there are both flowers and weeds. One of the explorers is convinced that there must be a gardener who comes to the clearing and looks after it, but the other disagrees. The two explorers decide to settle their argument by lying in wait for the gardener, but he never appears. The one who believes in the existence of the gardener suggests that perhaps he is an invisible gardener, so they set up all sorts of traps, but still no gardener is found. The Believer continues to qualify his assertion that there is a gardener, by saying that he is invisible, silent, intangible and so on, until eventually the sceptical explorer asks 'But what remains of your original assertion? Just how does what you call an invisible, intangible, eternally elusive gardener differ from an imaginary gardener or even from no gardener at all?'.

Just how does what you call an invisible, intangible, eternally elusive gardener differ from an imaginary gardener or even from no gardener at all?

Flew draws a parallel between the Believer and a religious person who makes claims such as 'God loves us as a father loves his children' and 'God has a plan'. According to Flew, when these beliefs are challenged, for example when evil and suffering are encountered, religious believers do not accept that they are wrong and that God does not love us after all, or that God has no plan. Instead, they qualify their claim by saying that God's love is not like human love, or that God's plans are a mystery to us. Every time something happens to challenge their belief, the religious person meets it with further modifications, until eventually there is nothing left of the original assertion. Flew concludes that the claims religious believers make about the nature and activity of God die a 'death by a thousand qualifications'; in the end the believers are saying nothing at all, because their statements are empty. They are neither meaningful nor meaningless but 'vacuous'.

For Flew, if a statement is to be scientific, it has to assert something, and at the same time deny the opposite of that assertion; saying 'x is y' has at the same time to say 'x is not not-y' in order to be scientific. An assertion has to rule out some states of affairs. C. S. Evans, in *Philosophy of Religion*, puts Flew's point of view as 'An assertion which does not rule out anything, but rather is compatible with any conceivable state of affairs, does not appear to assert anything either'. So, for example, if I said I was standing on a mountain, that would rule out some states of affairs – I would not be sitting down, for example, or lying on a beach, or reading in the bath. In asserting that I am standing on a mountain, I am ruling out some states of affairs. If you asked

'Under what circumstances would your claim to be standing on a mountain be false?' I could answer with some examples, 'If I were weeding my garden, my claim to be standing on a mountain would be false'. But, Flew argues, when theists talk of God and his attributes, they refuse to rule out any states of affairs. If asked, 'Under what circumstances would your statement that God loves us be false?' they would not be able to think of any. Whatever happened, however cruel or frightening, they would still cling to their original assertion, all the while qualifying it with claims that God's love is mysterious. For Flew, a claim which cannot be falsified is not really saying anything at all.

Responses to Flew's 'falsification principle'

In response to Flew, Richard Swinburne argues that we do not have to be able to specify what would count against an assertion, in order for that assertion to be meaningful. He argues, in *The Coherence of Theism* (Oxford University Press, 1977), that we cannot specify what would count against scientific theories of the beginnings of the universe, for example, because we do not know enough about the scientific theories involved; but this does not make the theories meaningless to us. This is because we accept that there is undoubtedly something which, hypothetically at least, could count against those theories, if only we understood what their implications were. For Swinburne's objection to work, we have to allow that something could count against the existence of God, or the nature of God as traditionally understood, even if we cannot specify what that might be.

To think about

If you are a religious believer, can you imagine anything that could happen to make you think that you were wrong to believe in God?

If you are an atheist, can you imagine anything that could happen to make you believe in God after all?

R. M. Hare responded to Flew (in *New Essays in Philosophical Theology*) with a parable of his own. He asked us to imagine a lunatic who is convinced that all university dons want to murder him. No matter how many kindly dons he meets, he is not shaken from his belief that they are only pretending to be kind as part of their plots to kill him. There is nothing that the dons could ever do to persuade him that he is wrong in his belief. Hare invents the word 'blik' to describe this man's unfalsifiable conviction. Hare's argument is that we all have our own 'bliks' with which we approach the world and make judgements about it; we all have unfalsifiable ways of framing our understanding of our experiences which help us to find meaning in the world.

The belief that everything happens by chance is just as much a 'blik' as the belief that things happen according to the will of God or that everything was 'meant to be'. Religious people have 'bliks', but so do atheists, and each finds meaning.

C. S. Evans, however, argues that this view is not very coherent, because Hare talks about bliks being right or wrong, sane or insane, without explaining how this might be. We do not know how we might judge them as right or wrong when they are unfalsifiable.

Nevertheless, it could be argued that Flew's confidence in empirical evidence as the final test of meaning is, in itself, unfalsifiable. Flew's article finishes with the question: 'What would have to occur or to have occurred to constitute for you a disproof of the love of, or the existence of, God?' The religious believer might want to respond to him with a similar question: 'What would have to occur or to have occurred to constitute for you a disproof of the all-importance of empirical evidence?'

Other thinkers have argued that religious language is not necessarily about making propositions, but that it can have truth and meaning in a much wider variety of ways. R. B. Braithwaite, for example, accepted that religious statements are not cognitive assertions, but went on to argue that they could still be meaningful; they could be giving moral imperatives, for example, or using important symbols about a way of life. One problem with Braithwaite's view is that people who make religious truth-claims often intend the words to mean exactly what they say. If they say 'God is love', then they mean that there is a God, who exists, and whose nature is love, they don't just mean that we should act lovingly towards one another. If that was what they meant, that is what they would say. The person making the statement should be allowed some knowledge of what they mean when they speak.

Paul Tillich argued that religious language is not cognitive (talking about things that can be known) but symbolic. Symbols are not the same as facts, and therefore it is wrong to criticise them as if they were. Symbols cannot be verifiable or falsifiable – if someone says 'My love is like a red red rose', it would not make sense to ask if this was true or false. Symbols need not be meaningless, even if they are unverifiable; they can be effective or ineffective ways of drawing religious believers to 'the power of being'.

In his book *Religious Language*, Peter Donovan outlines several ways in which religious language might have meaning without making propositional statements. For example, it includes commands, expressions of preference, questions and so on. Words are used performatively or to solemnise occasions, such as 'I baptise you in the name of the Lord', 'Go forth in peace', and 'The Lord be with you', and these are meaningful uses of language where it would not be appropriate to follow with the question 'true or false?' Donovan claims that religious language is not usually used to make truth-claims and assertions; these are one small part of religious language: 'The use of language within religious behaviour is generally not of the argumentative, fact-claiming kind.'

Since the days of the Vienna Circle, the philosophy of language has moved on, and shown that language is concerned with much more than just the making of statements which might or might not be literally true. The work of Wittgenstein did much to illustrate the different functions which language performs.

Practice exam question

How fair is the claim that religious language is meaningless?

For this question, you should show understanding of the views of those who have claimed that religious language is meaningless – especially the views of Ayer and Flew, with reference to the 'Parable of the Gardener'. In your evaluation of their claims, you need to assess whether they have made a valid case that religious language is meaningless. You also need to include the views of those who have challenged Ayer and Flew, and give an assessment of their counter-arguments. There are many different thinkers who have contributed to this debate, and it can be tempting to make a long list of 'who said what', but for high marks, you should aim to present an argument with a conclusion that gives your answer to the question of whether religious language is meaningless.

Wittgenstein's theory of language-games

Ludwig Wittgenstein was a fascinating character, whom many believe to be the greatest philosopher of the twentieth century. He was the youngest of eight children of a very wealthy and influential Viennese family; their father had become rich in the steel business, and Ludwig Wittgenstein inherited a fortune from him. All the children were intellectually gifted, and all were inclined to extreme self-criticism. Three out of Wittgenstein's four brothers eventually took their own lives; the survivor became a world-famous pianist, continuing his career even after he lost an arm in the First World War. Ludwig Wittgenstein went to school with Adolf Hitler, and according to some sources, Hitler's hatred of the Jews was sparked in his childhood by an intense dislike of Wittgenstein, whose parents were both of Jewish descent.

Wittgenstein thought that it was important to recognise this. There are many aspects of reality that we can experience with the senses, and that we can talk about using commonly understood terms. However, there are other aspects which we cannot experience, which we have difficulty understanding and which we find it hard to conceptualise – the nature of infinity, for example, or the concept of timelessness.

Wittgenstein and Hitler were at school together. It is alleged that Hitler disliked Wittgenstein because of Wittgenstein's superior intellect. Hitler is top right, Wittgenstein is bottom left.

In Wittgenstein's view, people should confine themselves to talking only about those parts of reality which can be conceptualised. Those other areas may have reality and truth, or they may not, but we will never know, and we will always be unable to talk about them meaningfully. Wittgenstein's best known saying relates to these ideas: 'Whereof one cannot speak, thereof one must remain silent.'

In his early work, to which he gave the rather uninviting title *Tractatus Logico-Philosophicus* (1921), Wittgenstein attempted to set out principles to demonstrate what could, and could not, be expressed in language. By doing this, he hoped also to show the scope and the limitations of philosophy and of human reason. It was this book which had such a profound effect on the Vienna Circle and on all of those logical positivists who embraced its ideas. However, although he was quite convinced at the time that he had found answers to many philosophical problems with this work, in later life, Wittgenstein began to think that he might have been wrong about the limitations of the meaningfulness of language, and that his criteria for determining meaningfulness might have been too narrow.

Wittgenstein's later work explored the ways in which language can have meaning in different ways and on different levels. He looked at how words can indicate more than one idea at a time, and how language is a process, developing and changing in different times. He also explored the idea of language usage in different contexts, showing how different groups of people, all engaged in the same activity, can use words with a meaning that they might not have in a different context. For example, physicists studying magnetism might use the word 'field' in a way that is very specific to what they are doing, and a listener would need to know something about magnetism in order to understand them properly, whereas a farmer might use the word 'field' in a very different sense. A cricketer might use the same word too – and all these different uses would be related, where the word 'field' is used to designate a particular area, while at the same time there must be an understanding of the community and the context before the full meaning is clear.

Wittgenstein saw language in terms of a game, where we know how to play it once we understand the rules. He was not implying that language is trivial, or that words are used as a way of playing tricks on people, but he thought that the analogy of a game would be useful as a way of highlighting and explaining the scope and limitations of language.

We can say that we know what a word means, once we can use it in context, he argued; learning a language is like learning a game, where we understand how and when to use particular words by seeing how they are used. We accept that words are used in certain ways because we recognise the role they have in the whole game. Wittgenstein uses the example of a chess piece; we might learn that a certain piece is called a 'king', but we will not really understand this until we have played chess and understood the significance of the king within it. There is no point in arguing about how language is used. It might seem unreasonable that we use certain words in certain ways, but if you want to play the language-game, you just accept the rules that have been agreed by everyone else.

Wittgenstein argued that language can be understood using the analogy of a game. When we participate in the game and learn how everyone plays it, the language all starts to make sense.

Another of Wittgenstein's illustrations is when he asks us to imagine being in the driver's cabin of a steam train. We would be able to see all sorts of different buttons, pedals and levers, but we would not really understand them properly unless we had a go at driving the train. Then we would understand which were the really important controls and which were secondary; which ones only worked if you used them in conjunction with others; which ones had to be handled with special care; which were only used in exceptional circumstances.

To think about

What might the word 'result' mean to a sports player? What might it mean to someone working in a medical laboratory? What might it mean to a student? Do you think Wittgenstein is right to argue that we can only understand meaning from within the language-game?

Wittgenstein, in *On Certainty*, showed that language makes statements which are groundless. We cannot justify the statement 'this is a piece of paper'; we cannot find reasoning to support why we call it this, it is just how we were educated to conceptualise the world. Definitions are 'groundless beliefs' but they shape the way in which we understand the world to an enormous extent. Wittgenstein argued that religious belief shapes the way the world is seen in a similar sort of way. Our beliefs about whether or not there is a Last Judgement, for example, will be groundless whether we believe it or not, but it will shape the way we think and the decisions we make to a large extent.

The Welsh philosopher D. Z. Phillips (1934–2006) took a Wittgensteinian approach, and argued that religious language was just a way of defining the rules of the game of religion. 'God is love', he argued, is not a description of an actual existent being, but a way of showing how the word 'God' is to be used. The same kind of argument can be made about religious experience: that it has to be seen within the context of the religion as a whole before it can be judged. The argument is made that religious language is meaningful for those who genuinely use it, and it does not need to be justified to those who do not participate in that particular language-game. Many of the terms and concepts only make sense within the context of participation in the 'game' of religion. Just as it would not make sense to speak of shoppers in Marks and Spencer being 'offside' or 'checkmated', it might also not make sense to talk of salvation, sin, enlightenment or communion outside the context of religious participation.

Peter Donovan, in his book *Religious Language*, takes up Wittgenstein's analogy of the use of language-games. He emphasises that philosophers are not suggesting that religions are games, but that this is a useful way of understanding how the language of religion has a special meaning:

It is only when we are engaged in the Jewish and Christian religious language-games that the question 'Was Jesus the Messiah?' can be properly understood, and as we know, it is answered differently within each of those two language-games.

… The same is true, equally, of the many actions, gestures and forms of worship which make up religious behaviour. They mean what they do because of their connections with other parts of the religious system and its thought-world. Statements in religious language, like moves in games, are context-dependent. It has thus become quite common amongst philosophers of religion to speak of the way language is used in a certain religious tradition as the 'language-game' of that religion. That way of speaking is a useful reminder that misunderstanding and confusion are likely to result if statements are taken away from their context, and analysed without regard to the usual circumstances in which they are uttered, the moves they are used to make, and the point of the game as a whole.

As with a game, the more people participate in religious behaviour, the more they will understand the language and the subtleties of its use. Other aspects of games can also be used in this analogy: with religion, as well as with games, there is the concept of developing skill, of having goals, of achieving success, of training and practice, of emotional commitment and loyalty.

Key point

- Wittgenstein put forward the view that the meaningfulness of language, including religious language, can be illustrated if we think in terms of 'language-games'.

 Develop your knowledge

Philosophy of Religion by Peter Cole (Hodder Murray, 1999), pp. 103–7
An Introduction to the Philosophy of Religion by Brian Davies (Oxford University Press, 2004), ch. 1
Religious Language by Peter Donovan (Hodder Murray, 2004)
Teach Yourself Philosophy of Religion by Mel Thompson (Teach Yourself, 2003)

Religious experience

What is a religious experience? Some people would class a religious experience as a rare supernatural event, for which there could be no scientific explanation; an experience in which someone had a direct encounter with God, perhaps in the form of seeing a vision. Others would take a much broader view, and consider religious experience to include more common occurrences such as feelings of peace, or of wonder at the beauty of nature. Some would think that if a person's whole outlook on life is religious, then all of their experiences will be religious experiences because they will interpret the things they see and do in everyday life as part of God's world, and have the sense that God has a guiding hand in the decisions they make. Whether religious experience happens at all, whether it happens to just a few individuals, or whether it is a common part of being human, depends very much on our understanding of what should be classified as religious experience.

To think about

How would you define a religious experience? What makes religious experience different from other kinds of experience, if anything?

Richard Swinburne, in his book *Is There a God?* argued that obviously, if there is a God, he would want us to have direct experience of him: 'An omnipotent and perfectly good creator will seek to interact with his creatures and in particular with human persons capable of knowing him' (Swinburne, *Is there a God?*, Oxford University Press, 1996). God might want to reveal himself in order to give support, or to answer prayer, or to set people straight and encourage them to co-operate with one another, Swinburne claims. If there is a God of the personal kind described by many of the world's religions, then we might expect that we would have experience of him, either as individuals or corporately (as a body).

However, the question is raised of whether religious experience can be counted as evidence of the existence of such a God. The 'experiential argument', or 'argument from religious experience', is a reason for faith that is often given by religious believers. Theists may say that they know that God exists because he has done this or that in their lives. Billy Graham (one of the first American Christian evangelists, very well known in the 1950s and 1960s) once said in an interview, 'I know that God exists because I spoke with him this morning.' After all, if we believe that a celebrity really does live in our local area because we have seen her shopping in the supermarket, why should we not believe that there is a God if we have had encounters with him?

Often, theists will relate some kind of conversion experience if asked to explain their belief in God. In fact, if questioned about why they hold their beliefs, people are far more likely to tell you about their own religious experience than to claim they were convinced by the design argument, for example. There are many people who, once they have had some kind of religious experience, will not be convinced by any alternative possible explanation for what has happened to them, and cannot be argued out of belief in God. Some people's religious experiences have been so convincing *to them*, that it has changed their lives and their outlook completely.

But can religious experiences tell us anything reliable about ourselves or about God? Are they occurrences which, as Swinburne suggests, should only be expected, given that there is a loving creator God at work in the world? Or are they 'mental events' which go on simply inside someone's head, like a dream or a memory? Do religious experiences show that there is a God 'out there', or do they show just that God is 'true for the believer' within that person's own world-view? Are reports of religious experience evidence of no more than over active imaginations, or even of the desire to fool other people for the sake of attention?

Religious experiences, like other kinds of experience, are unique to each individual. Even if two people go to the same concert, or share the same food, their experiences of it will not be identical, because they are two different people and will have different needs, tastes, expectations and interpretations of events. The same, then, applies to religious experience – each person who claims to have had a religious experience will give a different account of what happened to him or her, interpreted in his or her own particular way. Interpretation of these experiences may be coloured by the individual's cultural and religious background, so that a Hindu might understand that he has had an experience of Krishna, while a Roman Catholic might believe that she has encountered the Virgin Mary. However, there do seem to be some common features of such experiences, and several thinkers have tried to analyse what those features are and have tried to determine whether they can tell us anything significant about human nature; and perhaps, about God.

C. Stephen Evans, in his book *Philosophy of Religion* (Intervarsity Press, 1985) draws a distinction between what he calls 'the religious dimension of experience' and 'religious experience'. By the former, he means the habit of religious believers of interpreting their lives and the world around them in a religious way. They might, for example, experience the world 'as an orderly, purposeful reality' and so be drawn to teleological arguments for the existence of God and see the hand of God at work in the natural world around them. 'Religious experience' is the term we usually use for particular events which have been interpreted as encounters with the divine. Evans believes that these religious experiences generally fall into one of two types:

Key terms

monist –
the belief that
everything has an
essential unity.

numinous –
a word used by
Rudolph Otto to
mean the 'wholly
other'.

1. A monist experience, in which the individual becomes intensely aware of the essential one-ness of all things, feeling that he or she is in union with the divine and that God can be found in the self and in the natural world. This sort of experience is particularly typical of Hindu mysticism, and is described in the Upanishads:

When a man knows God, he is free: his sorrows have an end, and birth and death are no more. When in inner union he is beyond the world of the body, then the third world, the world of the Spirit, is found, where the power of the All is, and man has all: for he is one with the ONE. (Svestasvatara Upanishad 1)

Many Hindus meditate in an attempt to achieve a mystic, monist union with the divine.

2. A sense of the separateness or otherness of God, in which the individual becomes aware of the greatness and the mystery of God and aware of his or her own smallness in comparison. This was an idea explored by Rudolf Otto in his book *The Idea of the Holy* (Oxford University Press, 1923); Evans uses Otto's term in calling this kind of experience 'numinous'. It is the kind of experience described in Psalm 8, where the writer tried to capture his sense of the greatness of God in comparison with his own insignificance:

When I consider your heavens,
the work of your fingers,
the moon and the stars,
which you have set in place,
what is man that you are mindful of him,
the son of man that you care for him?' (Psalm 8:3–4)

Evans identifies three elements which he considers to be common to religious experience, although the emphasis might be different in the traditions of different religions, and in different individual experiences:
- a sense of unity with God and with the world
- a sense of dependence
- a sense of separateness.

Objectivist and subjectivist views of religious experience

An **objectivist** view of religious experience is that if a religious experience is true, it is evidence of the existence of a God who exists independently, outside the human mind, and who can be encountered through experience. However, some people argue that objective religious experiences are impossible, as we have no way of knowing whether the object of someone's religious experience is actually God, or whether it just seemed like God to that person. And how, they ask, can we know enough about what God is like to recognise him if we met him?

To think about

What would be the difference (if there is any difference) between having a dream about the Virgin Mary, and having the Virgin Mary really appear to you through a dream?

A **subjectivist** view of religious experience says that what is important about religious experience is the effect that it has on the believer. It is not necessary to think in terms of an actual, objective being which we call God (but God's existence is not denied either). The meaning of a religious experience is the meaning given to it by the believer. If someone genuinely believes that he or she has had a direct encounter with God, then the experience of God is true for that person.

It could be argued, however, that subjectivist views dilute religious experience, so that it does not matter whether they really are encounters between people and God or not (which many religious believers would say is the whole point of them). Subjectivist views might seem to reduce religious experience to the level of a particular personal mental state, like a dream or a strong emotion. This does not seem consistent with many reports of religious experience, such as the majority of those in the Bible, which are described with vividness as real encounters; it also does not account for corporate religious experience such as the story of Pentecost, where a group of people together all shared in the same event:

When the day of Pentecost came, they were all together in one place. Suddenly a sound like the blowing of a violent wind came from heaven and filled the whole house where they were sitting. They saw what seemed to be tongues of fire that separated and came to rest on each of them. All of them were filled with the Holy Spirit and began to speak in other tongues as the Spirit enabled them. (Acts 2:1–4)

Key terms

objectivist view – the view that if a religious experience truly happens, it demonstrates the existence of a God 'out there'.

subjectivist view – the view that religious experience can be true for the believer.

veridical – if an experience is described as veridical, it means that it is a genuine experience of something that is actually there.

Rudolf Otto: *Das Heilige (The Idea of the Holy)* (1917)

Rudolf Otto (1869–1937) was a Protestant theologian who used his vast knowledge of natural sciences, comparative religion and oriental traditions to try to analyse religion. In his book, *The Idea of the Holy*, Otto tried to identify what it was about a religious experience that made it religious, rather than just an experience. He wanted to show that it was fundamental to religion that individuals should have a sense of a personal encounter with natural forces, which he described as 'Mysterium Tremendum et Fascinans'. That encounter would bring a sense of awe and mystery, a feeling of strangeness. Otto said that the divine would be recognised as having three main qualities:

1. A mysterious quality, a realisation that God is incomprehensible, that God can be met and his work can be seen and yet that God can never be captured, fully understood or described.

2. God is recognised as being of ultimate importance.

3. God has a quality that is both attractive and dangerous. Otto tried to explain the feeling that God cannot be controlled, but that at the same time the individual feels a sense of privilege during a religious experience.

Otto made use of the term 'numinous', which he used to describe the feeling of awe-inspiring holiness. He said that ordinary language could not do justice to religious experience, because it is an experience unlike others within normal sense-experience. He argued that religious language is a 'schema', an attempt to find clusters of words which approach the idea being expressed, although the idea in itself is inexpressible.

Otto's book was important because for the first time someone tried to express and to understand the 'otherness' of religious experience.

Peter Donovan, in his book, *Interpreting Religious Experience* writes:

> *In* The Idea of the Holy, *Rudolf Otto portrays as central in all religions an apprehension of awesome, felt as a reality outside the self, which he calls the numinous. Arising directly from this experience is another which Otto describes as creature-consciousness: 'It is the emotion of a creature, submerged and overwhelmed by its own nothingness in contrast to that which is supreme above all creatures.' This two-fold experience, holiness and dread, sense of overpowering majesty and feeling of one's own worthlessness, is characteristic of the more dramatic types of conversion and regeneration.*

Just as awareness of holiness produces fear, terror and dread at a level far more profound than mere moral guilt or remorse, it also fascinates and attracts, arousing a longing for redemption and salvation. It is the presence of these emotions of numinous wonder and awe that characteristically makes religious conversions more than mere changes in lifestyle, or the 'turning over of a new leaf'.

Schleiermacher's thought

Otto was developing the ideas of Friedrich Schleiermacher (1768–1834), a theologian who claimed that the essence of religion was based in personal experience, and it was not enough just to agree to a set of doctrines, or commit oneself to a set of ethical principles. Schleiermacher believed that every person has a consciousness of the divine, but that in many people this is obscured by other concerns. Religious people are those who are aware of, and try to develop, this sense of the divine. His most famous book was called *On Religion: Speeches to its Cultured Despisers*.

According to Schleiermacher, religious experience is 'self-authenticating': it requires no other testing to see if it is genuine. He thought that doctrines such as the creed were attempts by individuals to understand their religious experience, which went against the thinking that experience had to be seen within the framework of existing doctrine. In the Roman Catholic tradition, the experiences of mystics had to be tested against the Church's teaching and against Scripture before they were considered to be genuine, whereas in Schleiermacher's view, the experiences should have priority and the statements of belief should be formulated to fit them.

Schleiermacher was reacting against the contemporary view of eighteenth-century Germany, that reason was of prime importance. He called religion 'a sense and taste for the infinite' and also 'the feeling of absolute dependence', and believed that feeling and experience were all-important. An individual's religious experience was based on the sense of being wholly dependent. In his view, religious experience could take a variety of different forms in different cultures, and the different religions of the world were reflections of this. He believed that Christianity was the highest of the religions, but not the only true one. Christianity was the highest because, in Jesus Christ, there was the only example of someone with complete 'God-consciousness', totally unobscured.

Those who criticised Schleiermacher's view thought that he put too much emphasis on the subjective, reducing religion to emotion and removing the possibility of showing that religious claims are based on fact. Some critics argued that there has to be the possibility of testing experiences against the Bible and the doctrines of the Church, otherwise any such experience would count as valid – even, perhaps, hallucinations caused by mental illness or drugs.

Different forms of religious experience

Visions and voices

These are probably the forms of experience that many people think of when they consider 'religious experience'. In visions, the person having the experience feels that he or she can actually see something supernatural, whether it is Mother Kali, the Virgin Mary, a ladder coming from the sky or an angel. It is not always clear, in reports of such experiences, whether 'seeing' is being used as a metaphor, or whether the people reporting the vision believe that they could see it in just the same way as they see things in their everyday lives. In the Bible, the vision of Isaiah in the Temple at the point when he was called to be a prophet is a particularly powerful example (Isaiah 6:1–8). Isaiah 'saw God' and was able afterwards to give a detailed description of the different heavenly beings he encountered. When people hear voices, this can be equally dramatic, and they give reports of exactly what was said to them. In the story of the boy Samuel in the Temple (1 Samuel 3), Samuel is woken from sleep by a voice, and he believes it to be his master Eli because the voice is so vivid, suggesting that this is not meant to be understood metaphorically but as a real sound available to the ears. In many reports, visions and voices are combined, when the person encounters someone who gives a message. For example, Saint Bernadette Soubirous both saw and heard the Virgin Mary at Lourdes. She could describe what Mary had been wearing, and recorded the words that had been spoken to her.

Numinous experiences

These are, by their nature, difficult to define, and they are reported by both theists and non-theists. According to Rudolph Otto, in *The Idea of the Holy*, numinous experiences are at the heart of all religious experience. Otto describes it as 'the distinctive experience of God, at once ineffably transcendent, remote, yet stirring a recognition that here is the primary source of beauty and love'. These are times when the individual gains a new and deeper understanding of reality, and feels as if he or she has touched on a different dimension, becoming filled with a sense of awe and wonder. It may be triggered by being out in the countryside in the early morning, or while witnessing a scene of beauty or the birth of a baby, but it can just happen out of nowhere in the most ordinary of circumstances. The experience itself may be fleeting, but the effects are lasting.

Conversion experience

Conversion experiences can be dramatic, or they can be gentler and slower to develop. This kind of religious experience tends to follow a basic pattern:

1. The individual is dissatisfied with his or her current 'system of ideas' (a phrase from *Our Experience of God* by H. D. Lewis, Allen & Unwin, 1959). People are not likely to be converted if they are quite content as they are.

2. The person searches, at both an intellectual level and an emotional level, for a basis on which to make a decision. For example, they may turn to the Bible, be persuaded to go to an evangelical meeting or a church service, or listen to stories of other conversions.

3. There is a point of crisis, which is a time of intense emotion, sometimes with physical symptoms as well as emotions. Often this is described as a sense of the presence of God, a sense of sinfulness and repentance. Sometimes the experience is described in terms of visions, bright light and voices.

4. This is followed by a sense of peace and joy, and a loss of worry. There is also a desire to share the new faith with other people, to talk about the experience.

5. In the longer term, the convert experiences a change of direction, a new sense of purpose in life, and sometimes a complete change of career.

Conversion experiences have been the focus of a number of sociological and psychological studies that have attempted to determine whether there are particular personality traits or other circumstances which might make some individuals more susceptible to conversion experiences than others.

In the 1960s, two American sociologists called John Lofland and Rodney Stark made a study of conversion experiences, concentrating in particular on conversions to the Unification Church (a sect commonly known as the 'Moonies'). Their 1965 study (published in the *American Sociological Review*, 30/6) suggested that conversion experiences follow a pattern which can be seen to be common in all kinds of conversions – not only religious conversions, but conversions from one political party to another, for example.

Conversion experiences can be the subject of controversy. All human behaviour happens within a social context, so it can be difficult to separate internal spiritual influences from external social causes, and it can be impossible to tell what a person might have done or how he or she might have felt without those outside influences.

Corporate religious experience

This is where several different people all have the same, or a similar, religious experience at the same time. It is quite unusual. Usually religious experiences occur privately to individuals, but there have been reports of groups of people all sharing the same feelings and receiving the same messages. A biblical example of this is the story of Pentecost in chapter 2 of the book of Acts, where everyone felt the same sensation of a rushing mighty wind, and saw the same tongues of fire appearing. The 'Toronto Blessing' is a modern phenomenon in the United States and Canada, first documented in the 1990s, where groups of people all worshipping together appeared to have the same experience of being overcome by the Holy Spirit, which caused them to weep or laugh uncontrollably and fall to the ground. A further example might be the experiences reported in the village of Medjugorje in Bosnia, where six young teenagers and children allegedly had visions of the Virgin Mary and received messages from her.

Corporate religious experiences can seem to have more evidential force than solitary ones. In science, the more times an experiment can be witnessed by different people, the more weight is added; so perhaps if several people all share the same religious experience, this might mean that it is more likely to be veridical. However, others argue that there may be elements of group pressure at work. Someone might say that they can see and hear something, and others might join in and agree that they can see and hear it too because they want to be included. In the case of the Toronto Blessing, many have suggested that the experiences are caused by whipped-up hysteria in a heightened emotional atmosphere, rather than by the Holy Spirit.

Develop your knowledge

In chapter 7 of Kenneth Grahame's book *The Wind in the Willows*, 'The Piper at the Gates of Dawn', Rat and Mole have a numinous experience of the god Pan while out on the river.

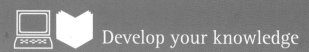

William James: The Varieties of Religious Experience

Probably the best-known book ever written on the subject of religious experience was produced by William James at the beginning of the twentieth century. *The Varieties of Religious Experience* was not originally written as a book, but as a series of lectures, called the Gifford Lectures, given in Edinburgh in 1901–2, with the sub-title 'A Study in Human Nature'. When the lectures were published as a book, it was immediately successful, not only because its anecdotes of religious experience were fascinating in themselves, but because of the sympathy and intelligence with which James discussed his insights.

In his book, James was not trying to hammer home an evangelical Christian message, and did not set out to dismiss the importance of religious experience or to prove that it had no basis. His aim was to take as objective a stance as he could, to take personal accounts of religious experience seriously, and to make observations about them which he hoped would lead to some significant insights.

William James' book The Varieties of Religious Experience *is regarded as a classic for its attempt to look at religious experience in an objective yet sympathetic way.*

William James (1842–1910) came from an outstanding family who lived in Boston, Massachusetts. His brother was Henry James, the novelist, and his father was a religious writer who was rich enough to be able to pursue his interests without having to work for a living. William James was brought up in an atmosphere of intellectual discussion and free thinking, where it was acceptable to question traditionally held beliefs. He chose a career in medicine and qualified as a doctor at Harvard, becoming professor of physiology, psychology and philosophy at Harvard University, so he was well trained in scientific method as well as having an understanding of the limitations of certainty when it comes to analysing human beings. James set out to study religious experience through scientific investigation, as far as was possible, by looking at a variety of sources and comparing reports of religious experience to see if they had any common features or characteristics that might add to human understanding.

James was not trying to make a value-judgement about religion as a whole, and not trying to prove religious experience to be true or false. He wanted to look at religious experience objectively. Of course, it is never possible for anyone to approach a subject of investigation without any preconceived ideas about what the results of the investigation might show, and it is impossible for anyone to make a study without their own personality creeping in as they decide which direction to take next and what to select as interesting from their findings. Some people will approach a study of religion from within, expecting to affirm beliefs they already hold, while others will approach from a position of scepticism, assuming that accounts of religious experience are based on illusion and can be explained away. James' own position, of being prepared to accept the possibility that religious experience might have some validity, also shows preconceived ideas, and so it could be argued that his book was no more 'objective' than a study from a Christian writer or an atheist. However, his intention was to avoid, as far as he could, colouring the results of his studies with his own interpretations, and he tried hard to allow the facts (as he saw them) to speak for themselves.

To think about

Do you think it can be possible for a person or group to make a completely objective study of anything?

James included in his book many first-hand accounts of religious experience, in the words of the people who told him their stories. James considers, for example, what is understood by 'conversion', and gives various accounts of different conversion experiences. His understanding is that the term relates to a process where someone who is 'divided', and conscious of being wrong and unhappy, becomes much more confident about what is right, and much happier, as a 'consequence of a firmer hold on religious realities'. James recognises that this can be a sudden or a gradual process.

One of the cases described by James is that of Stephen Bradley, who was an uneducated man. Bradley already considered himself a Christian from the age of 14, because of an experience in which 'I thought I saw the Saviour, by faith, in human shape, for about one second in the room, with arms extended, appearing to say to me, Come.' But nine years later, there was a religious revival in his village, and he realised that he was not as certain in his faith as other people seemed to be; he wanted this certainty. He went to hear a Methodist preacher, and although he 'trembled involuntarily', he 'felt nothing at heart'. Later that evening:

I began to feel my heart beat very quick all on a sudden, which made me at first think that perhaps something is going to ail me, though I was not alarmed, for I felt no pain. My heart increased in its beating, which soon convinced me that it was the Holy Spirit from the effect it had on me. I began to feel exceedingly happy and humble, and such a sense of unworthiness as I never felt before. … a stream (resembling air in feeling) came into my mouth and heart in a more sensible manner than that of drinking anything, which continued, as near as I could judge, five minutes or more, which appeared to be the cause of such a palpitation in my heart.

He goes on to describe how he felt the presence of angels, and it seemed as if his reading of the Bible was directly the word of God speaking to him. He felt a sense of commission to go and speak to his neighbours about religion, and he thought his faith had an unshakeable quality which it had lacked before.

James also presents the example of S. H. Hadley, who describes himself before his conversion as 'a homeless, friendless, dying drunkard'. Then 'I seemed to feel some great and mighty presence. I did not know then what it was. I did learn afterwards that it was Jesus, the sinner's friend.' Hadley decided to stop drinking, and took himself to a mission, where he was impressed by the preacher's conviction of faith. He heard testimonies of 'twenty-five or thirty persons, every one of whom had been saved from rum' and he went forward to be prayed for. Hadley describes how:

I said, 'Dear Jesus, can you help me?' Never with mortal tongue can I describe that moment. Although up to that moment my soul had been filled with indescribable gloom, I felt the glorious brightness of the noonday sun shine into my heart. I felt I was a free man.

Hadley said that he never wanted another drink, and he felt a new sense of commission. James reports that Hadley then 'became an active and useful rescuer of drunkards in New York.'

Other experiences include that of an Oxford graduate who was the son of a clergyman but who had not been interested in the church until he 'was converted in my own bedroom in my father's rectory house at precisely three o'clock in the afternoon of a hot July day (July 13, 1886).' This was straight after reading a book about religion.

Can experiences such as these be used as evidence for the existence of God? Many people would say not. The experiences, they argue, cannot be tested by others, and this makes them unsuitable for any kind of 'scientific' study. Although we have these accounts of experiences, in the person's own words, we have no way of recreating them for ourselves – even if we go to religious revivals, or give up alcohol, or read books about religion, it will not be the same, and we would not be surprised if nothing happened to us at all.

James, however, believed that up to a point at least, the experiences could be tested for validity. In his book he argues that the test of religious experiences was not the dramatic nature of:

super-normal incidents, such as voices and visions and overpowering impressions of the meaning of suddenly presented scripture texts, the melting emotions and tumultuous affections connected with the crisis of change' which 'may all come by way of nature ...', but 'the real witness ... is to be found only in the disposition

Key term

pragmatism – a way of thinking which says that the truth or meaning of something depends, at least in part, on its practical consequences.

251

of the genuine child of God, the permanently patient heart, the love of self eradicated. And this, it has to be admitted, is also found in those who pass no crisis, and may even be found outside of Christianity altogether.'

For James, then, a religious experience does not have to be marked by dramatic supernatural events, although it can be; the real test of what happened is the long-term change in the person. James is known as a pragmatist; that is, someone who holds that the truth of something can be determined by its practical effects and consequences. Other thinkers, however, have disagreed with this view. Bertrand Russell, in his radio debate with Copleston about the existence of God, stated quite firmly his view: 'The fact that a belief has a good moral effect upon a man is no evidence whatsoever in favour of its truth.' Russell argued that it might be possible, for example, for someone to be profoundly affected for the good by a story about a great hero, but this could happen even if the story were a myth and the hero were entirely fictional.

To think about

A child is told, and believes, that Santa Claus only brings presents to well-behaved boys and girls. The child makes great efforts not to talk with his mouth full, to be kind to others and to wipe his feet when he comes indoors. Does his improved behaviour provide evidence of the existence of Santa Claus?

Does James' 'test' show that religious experiences come from a real encounter with a God who exists 'out there' objectively, in other words, that religious experiences can be veridical? Or does it show only the force of the experience within the mind of that individual, subjectively?

James recognised that psychological interpretations of conversion would look to the subconscious mind for the origins of religious experience, whereas the religious believer would look to God, and he did not offer his own view to tell us which he thought was the better interpretation. He did, however, stress that religious experience can often have a power which takes over the individual's whole life and often changes it for the better.

The main arguments of *The Varieties of Religious Experience* are as follows:

1. In James' view, the spiritual value of religious experiences is not undone even if we can find a psychological explanation for the experiences. James particularly rejected the view that religious experience was the result of a repressed or perverted sexuality (which was the interpretation being offered by Freud and his followers). He said that this view was just an attempt to discredit religion by those who started with an antipathy

towards it; study of religious life shows that the context of religion is disconnected from that of sexual consciousness.

2. James did not agree that there was a single feature of religious experience that defines it, but he understood it to be 'The feelings, acts, and experiences of individual men in their solitude, so far as they apprehend themselves to stand in relation to whatever they may consider the divine.' He said that, in the human consciousness, there is 'a sense of reality, a feeling of objective presence, a perception of what we may call "something there"'.

3. The experiences of great religious figures can set patterns for the conventional believer to study. James gives examples of 'saintliness', lives which have followed from the conversion or mystical experiences described, and refers especially to St Teresa of Avila 'one of the ablest women, in many respects, of whose life we have the record.' He uses these examples to show that Christians can be strong people, who have helped society to progress and adapt. People can learn from the experiences of these saints whether or not they have similar experiences of their own.

4. James believed that religious experience was more important as a focus of study than religious practice or religious institutions such as the church. He thought that religious institutions were secondary, because they came about as a result of personal religious experience.

James identified four main qualities of a religious experience:

1. Ineffability: by this, he meant that the experience is impossible to express adequately in normal language.

2. Noetic quality: the experience gives the person an understanding of important truths, which could not have been reached through the use of reason alone. People who have had religious experiences often speak in terms of having had the truth revealed to them.

3. Transience: the experience is over quite soon, lasting no more than a few hours, even though the effect of the experience could last a lifetime.

4. Passivity: the person having the experience feels as if the experience is being controlled from outside themselves – they are the recipients of the experience, rather than the instigators of it.

On the subject of conversion experiences, James argues:

'To say that a man is "converted" means, in these terms, that religious ideas, previously peripheral in his consciousness, now take a central place, and that

religious aims form the habitual centre of his energy.' In other words, a religious conversion experience can change someone's whole outlook on life, so that before the experience they might just have been aware of the existence of religious ideas whereas afterwards, religious ideas are the person's starting-point for his or her interpretation of the world.

James thought that psychology can describe conversion, but it is unable to account for all the factors in any given case, and he asserted that the conversion experience can be tested by its results. He argues that the final test of an experience is not its origin, but the way it works, rather like the test of whether a medicine is a valid one. Christian believers might support James in this opinion; the Bible refers to the 'evidence' of the Holy Spirit as a way for Christians to test their experiences and the claims of others: 'But the fruit of the Spirit is love, joy, peace, patience, kindness, goodness, faithfulness, gentleness and self-control' (Galatians 5:22).

When James gives examples of different experiences, he notes how convincing these experiences are to the person having the experience. He says: 'They are as convincing to those who have them as any direct sensible experiences can be, and they are, as a rule, much more convincing than results established by mere logic ever are.' Some people have tried to use the strength of someone's belief that they have encountered God as evidence that it must have really happened; but other people reject this line of argument, saying that something is not necessarily true no matter how sincerely people believe it.

James concluded that although religious experience does not give proof of anything, it is reasonable to believe that there is a personal God who is interested in the world and in individuals. He recognised that this was what he called a hypothesis, but said that it was a perfectly reasonable hypothesis; and that it was *not* reasonable for scholars or ordinary people to reject clear evidence of religious experience just because they started from a position of scepticism.

Criticisms of James

In spite of the success of the book at the time, few philosophers have followed William James in his conclusions. Some later philosophers have argued that language analysis (such as that of the Logical Positivists, or the work of Wittgenstein, see pages 235–8) has made James' work obsolete. The British philosopher Antony Flew, for example, in his discussion of religious language in 'Theology and Falsification' (1950), concluded that statements which cannot be tested empirically (using the five senses) are meaningless. A statement such as 'I saw a vision of the risen Christ' cannot be tested in this way. James' test of religious experience through its results in the life of the individual would be rejected by Flew.

It seems that James is basing his thinking on a subjective understanding of religious experience, concentrating on whether the experience is true for the individual, rather than whether it relates to a God who exists in the 'real world'. This is a question James leaves unanswered, and many would agree that he was wise to do so. James might have established that the behaviour of an individual after a religious experience is consistent with what we might expect if God did exist, but this in itself does not show that there really must be a God. If we were to take the same approach that David Hume took with regard to the cosmological and teleological arguments for God's existence, we might consider whether there were also other possible causes of a religious experience. Perhaps it could be caused when the mind was in a particularly vulnerable state, for example during a serious illness or after fasting or a period of solitary confinement (James admits that the sensations of a religious experience can be duplicated by alcohol and other drugs). Perhaps religious experiences are created by a whole committee of gods, or even by demons, or perhaps by telepathic forces of some kind.

A modern study of religious experience:
Religious Experience Today: Studying the Facts by David Hay

This book was first published in 1990, and came out of the findings of a group of researchers at the Hardy Research Centre at Manchester College, Oxford; David Hay is one of the researchers, writing about how the research happened to begin and what has been discovered so far.

When Manchester College, Oxford was founded in 1889, its vice-principal was a man named J. Estlin Carpenter. Carpenter had a religious experience when out walking, where he suddenly became aware of the presence of God around him, even though he had not consciously been seeking any kind of understanding of God. In 1894, Carpenter went to the USA, where he met Edwin Starbuck, a pupil of William James. Starbuck was the first to construct a questionnaire which inquired about the prevalence of religious experience among ordinary people. When Carpenter returned to England, he brought some copies of the questionnaire to distribute among staff and students; and later, William James, having given the Gifford lectures in Edinburgh which provided the basis for *The Varieties of Religious Experience*, came to speak in Oxford at Carpenter's invitation. Carpenter was of the opinion that religious experience was a universal phenomenon, which could be found in all cultures and societies.

Later, Alister Hardy, who was born in 1896, and studied natural history at Oxford, became interested in bridging the gap between the zoology and marine biology that he was studying, with his own sense of the mystical. He wanted to use scientific means to explore the extent and nature of religious experience as a part of human life. Hardy's idea was to set up a special research unit in Oxford.

Eventually, in 1969 when Hardy was 73, the Religious Experience Research Unit was set up. Hardy appealed to the public for accounts of personal religious experience. At first he asked people through the religious press, but this proved to be disappointing, as the responses were mainly from elderly ladies. By advertising in the *Guardian,* the *Observer* and *The Times*, and through the BBC, as well as through articles in the United States, Australia and New Zealand, Hardy's unit received over 1500 responses, which then had to be classified. The examples of experience tended to fall into one of a variety of types:

1. A sense of the patterning of events, where individuals feel overwhelmed by a sense that their lives have an unfolding pattern to them, a sense that they are being guided by God and that the things which happen to them are not the result of chance.

2. A sense of the presence of God, often in the most ordinary of circumstances; the respondents described the sudden conviction of the reality and presence of God around them, which often took them by surprise because of its spontaneity.

3. Answered prayer – people who wrote to the research centre described occasions where they had actively looked for divine help in different circumstances, perhaps for healing, and went on to describe how they believed that their prayers had been answered. Not all of these prayers were in times of distress.

4. A presence not called God – some respondents were unhappy with conventional ideas of God, and preferred to write of sensing a presence which they were unwilling to describe as God, preferring to talk of a pervading power or just a presence.

5. A sense of the presence of the dead – some people who wrote in described an awareness of the presence of a dead person with them; quite often a close relative. Nearly a fifth of the population of Britain claim to have had this sort of experience. According to the research centre, these experiences seemed to be more common among the uneducated; they were often given a religious interpretation, where God had sent the dead person back to comfort the living.

6. A sacred presence in nature – this is often reported by better educated people; David Hay suggests that this is perhaps because of the respectability given to the idea by people like Wordsworth.

7. A sense of evil or occult forces – people wrote in and described occasions when they were overwhelmed by a sense of absolute evil.

8. An experience that all things are 'one', a sense of unity with other aspects of the world, a loss of identity and a sense of being part of the whole.

This report came to a number of conclusions:

- religious experience can often be 'triggered', for example by listening to music, or prayer, by the beauty of nature, by attending a church service, by watching little children playing or by reading the Bible
- between half and two-thirds of the adult population claim to have had some kind of religious experience
- these people are, on the whole, better educated than average, and are happier people
- a large proportion have never spoken to anyone about their experiences
- young and old people are equally likely to report religious experience
- many of these people have no connection with any formal or institutional religion
- patterns are similar in the UK, Australia and the USA.

Hay expressed the opinion that, while claims to religious experience were sometimes clearly connected with insanity, there were strong grounds to suggest that religious experience should be taken seriously. The facts, he said, did not bear out the suggestions that religious experience was the result of social or individual pathology.

Develop your knowledge

The Religious Experience Research Centre has now moved to Lampeter University in Wales. It has a website which is well worth a visit (http://www.lamp.ac.uk/aht/Home/home.html).

Swinburne's Principles of Credulity and Testimony

In his books *Is there a God?* (Oxford University Press, 1996) and *The Existence of God* (2nd edn, Clarendon Press, 2004), Richard Swinburne supports the argument from religious experience. He makes a case that we should treat reports of religious experience in the same way that we treat reports of other, non-religious experiences: unless we have a good reason to be suspicious of these reports, we should believe them and take them at face value.

To think about

If your friend told you that she had received an e-mail from an old friend yesterday, would you believe her, or would you want to check out her story before you decided whether or not she was telling the truth? If she told you that she had received a message from God yesterday, would your reaction be the same? Why, or why not?

Early one morning, when I was out walking my Labrador, I met another dog-walker. I had seen him a few times before. It was a frosty, late winter morning, and while the two dogs played chase with each other around the trees, the other walker pointed out to me where the snowdrops were growing, and the winter aconites, the catkins on the silver birches, and the new shoots that would later become a carpet of bluebells. We agreed what a beautiful morning it was. Then we called our dogs back and went off in our separate directions.

Do you believe me, that I genuinely met this man one morning? You might think, there is no good reason to suspect otherwise. This woman has written this book and someone has agreed to publish it, so we can make a fair assumption that she tells the truth at least some of the time. It is not an unlikely event: dog-walkers meet other dog-walkers on a regular basis, and the plants described are the ones which normally appear in late winter. So you might accept the story as true. Then again, you might treat it with scepticism. You might think, she has something to gain by telling us this story, so she might have made it up; perhaps she thought the book was going to be too short and just wanted to fill up the pages. You might think, I've never met this woman and it could be the case that she makes things up all the time – she might not even have a dog. Or perhaps she *thinks* that she went out for this walk, and genuinely believes it herself, but in reality she is in a maximum-security hospital and only let out occasionally …

However, the chances are that, as you were reading, you did believe me – because we usually accept what other people tell us about their experiences, unless we happen to be of a particularly suspicious nature, or unless we have good reason to think they are not telling us the truth.

Early one morning, when I was out walking my dog, I met with God. It was a frosty, late-winter morning, and while my dog ran about in the trees, God showed me a perfectly formed clump of snowdrops. He showed me where he had made frost to edge every blade of grass and every leaf, and how it glittered like diamonds in the sun. He showed me the catkins and the tiny buds and shoots, and reassured me that he was in control of the world he had made, that he had designed it all and that it was very beautiful. Then I called my dog back and set off for home to write this.

Now do you believe me? According to Swinburne, you should treat my second account in just the same way that you treated my first one: by believing me, unless you have a strong reason to doubt that I am telling the truth.

Swinburne explains his principles of credulity and testimony in his book *Is there a God?*, which was written largely as a response to Richard Dawkins' *The Blind Watchmaker*' (Penguin, 1986). Swinburne argues that, when people tell us of their experiences, we should accept that the person who has had the experience is in the best position to know what really happened, even if other people subsequently try to put a different interpretation on it.

The **principle of credulity** is very simple: it just says that experience is normally reliable, and the balance of probability says that experience can be trusted. Even if some experiences turn out to be misleading, we should take the more likely view, which is that we can trust experience. Swinburne is not saying that experience is infallible; he is saying that it is more likely to be true than not, and therefore we should accept it on balance, unless we have convincing reasons not to. We know that sometimes our senses mislead us, and our experiences lead us to draw wrong conclusions, for example when we think we see someone we know well in the street and then realise that it is in fact a stranger. But usually, when we think we recognise someone, we need to accept our own instincts, or we will get nowhere – if it looks like Grace, it sounds like Grace, it is wearing Grace's coat and has Grace's laugh, then we are better off accepting that it really is Grace rather than continuing in a state of suspicion and thinking that our perceptions might be wrong.

> *Initial scepticism about perceptual claims – regarding them as guilty until proved innocent – will give you no knowledge at all. Initial credulity is the only attitude a rational man can take – there is no half-way house. However, claims which can subsequently be shown unreasonable can be weeded out. But the onus remains on the challenger. Unless we take perceptual claims seriously, whatever they are about, we shall find ourselves in an epistemological Queer Street. Religious perceptual claims deserve to be taken as seriously as perceptual claims of any other kind. (Swinburne,* Is there a God?*, Oxford University Press, 1996)*

Interestingly, Swinburne is using the same sort of argument that Hume used when he was trying to discredit belief in miracles. Hume was saying that we should go with the more likely explanation (which for him was the non-supernatural one in every case), whereas although Swinburne is also saying that we should go with the more likely approach, this leads him to the view that we should accept experience, including religious experience, at face value unless we have a good reason not to.

The **principle of testimony** works in a similar way. We find that usually, people tell us the truth. Less often, they are mistaken or only joking or deliberately deceitful, but in most cases, we can believe what we are told. Therefore, we should go with the balance of probability when we are told something, and we should accept someone's account of their personal religious experience.

Bernadette Soubirous' reports of visions of the Virgin Mary at Lourdes led to the building of a centre for Christian pilgrimage. According to Swinburne, if she said that she saw the Virgin Mary, then she probably did.

Key point

- Swinburne argued that religious experience should be treated like other kinds of experience. If we have religious experiences, we should take them at face value, and if other people tell us of their religious experiences, we should be prepared to believe them.

J. L. Mackie, however, in *The Miracle of Theism* (Oxford University Press, 1983) disagrees. (*The Miracle of Theism* is an ironic title, meaning, it is a 'miracle' that anyone believes in God given the weight of the arguments against his existence.) He says, in response to the principle of testimony, that when people tell us things they could be telling the truth, they could be deliberately deceiving us or they could be mistaken. We might know that the person who speaks is usually trustworthy and unlikely to be deliberately deceiving when they give reports of religious experience, but they could easily be mistaken, by putting a wrong interpretation onto whatever they felt, and assuming it to come from God when in fact it came from another source entirely. For Mackie, the balance of probability suggests that the mistake is more likely than the supernatural explanation, and therefore we should go with the view that these people are mistaken, however sincere they might be.

Many atheists, too, would disagree with Swinburne – they would say that it is substantially more likely than not that God does not exist, and therefore the argument breaks down.

Swinburne's principles of credulity and testimony have been criticised by a number of scholars, including Caroline Franks Davis, Richard Gale and Michael Martin. Some, such as Gale, argue that religious experience is not the same as other types of experience, and that therefore usual rules about when to accept an experience at face value do not apply. It may be true that we should, as a general rule, accept that if we perceive something, it is as we perceive it to be; but they argue that this applies to everyday experiences available to the five senses only, and not to other kinds of experience. If we dream, for example, that there are monsters under our beds, then in a sense we 'experience' the monsters, but most people would argue that as a general rule we should not take 'dream experiences' at face value and assume that our dream perceptions are veridical. Caroline Franks Davis, in her book *The Evidential Force of Religious Experience* (Oxford University Press, 2004) argues that we take reports of any kind of experience at face value, unless there is some special importance attached to whether or not the reporter is telling the truth. So, for example, we would not take at face value the report of someone who claimed to have witnessed someone else committing a crime, without wanting to check that the reporter had good eyesight, that it happened in a clear light and so on. Davis argues that the question of the existence of God is not the sort of trivial matter where we would be happy to take someone else's word for it – it is a question of ultimate importance, and therefore needs investigating further. Swinburne perhaps needs to make a stronger case to support the view that religious experiences should be treated in the same way as other, more ordinary kinds of experience.

Some atheists, such as Michael Martin (*Atheism: A Philosophical Justification*, Temple University Press, 1990) claim that Swinburne's principles of credulity and testimony can also lead to the conclusion that there is no God. An atheist might be said to experience the world as godless, and to have a strong sense of the absence of God; using Swinburne's argument, perhaps we should conclude that the world is probably as the experience suggests and that there is no God. Caroline Franks Davis takes this further by referring not only to the absence of any religious experience, but to those who have definite experiences in which they feel that God does not exist or has abandoned them; experiences which are often known as 'dark nights of the soul'. Bertrand Russell, too, pointed out that:

… there are abundant recorded cases of people who believe that they've heard Satan speaking to them in their hearts, in just the same way as the mystics assert God … and I don't see that from what mystics tell us you can get any argument for God which is not equally an argument for Satan.

Swinburne, however, responds to this criticism by arguing that the principle of credulity cannot be applied in the negative. His principle of credulity, he argues, is that if it seems to a person that X is present, then X probably is present. However, this does not mean that if it seems to a person that X is not present, then X is probably not present. This would only work, he says, in circumstances where, if X were present, we should expect to experience X – but there is no reason to suppose that the atheist would experience God if he were present. The atheist is not likely to interpret his or her sensory perceptions in a religious way, so a religious experience is not likely to happen, whether or not there is a God. Perhaps people have to be receptive to the possibility of God before religious experience can happen at all – after all, people are not receptive to very high-frequency sounds, but their experience of the absence of these sounds is not evidence that the sounds are absent; a dog or a bat might be able to hear them.

It could be argued that if we are to believe that things are, usually, as they appear to be, then this has serious implications, especially for theodicy. By Swinburne's logic, if we experience innocent suffering and it appears to us that the creator and designer of the world is therefore cruel, we should accept that our experiences are probably correct. In response to this criticism, it might be said that there is a big jump between sensory perception such as seeing, and interpretation such as concluding that God is malevolent; but then, it might be argued that there is also a big jump between having a vision of God, and making the interpretation that God really does exist.

Richard Gale also criticises Swinburne's assumption that people believe things if it is more probable that they are true than that they are not (as Hume argued, in his discussion of miracle, where he said that 'a wise man proportions his belief to the evidence'). According to Gale, this is not how belief works. We can believe things even though we know that the balance of probability is against them. Gale writes:

I need not go back to Kierkegaard or Tertullian for an example, since I can appeal to my own case as a young boy when I believed with all my heart that the Giants would win the pennant, even though I believed that their chances were extremely remote; I wouldn't have bet my piggy bank on it. ('Swinburne's Argument from Religious Experience' in Reason and the Christian Religion, *ed. Alan Padgett, Oxford University Press, 1994)*

Supporters of Swinburne might respond to this by saying that Gale seems to equate 'belief' with 'blind faith', making belief into the opposite of reasoned knowledge, which is not necessarily the case. Swinburne is arguing in favour of basing beliefs on reasonable justification, but Gale argues that belief is not a matter of reasoned choice, and that we cannot choose what we believe or make ourselves believe something if we simply don't.

In conclusion, then, it seems that Swinburne's argument only succeeds if people are willing to accept that there is at least a fair chance that God does really exist, and if they are willing to accept that a supernatural explanation for an experience is not beyond the bounds of credibility.

Strengths and weaknesses of arguments from religious experience

Religious experience can be used as an argument for the existence of God. The argument has several weaknesses:

- In the view of many people, religious experiences are only authoritative for the people who have them. Other people might know you to be someone who usually tells the truth, who is not prone to exaggeration; they might see that your behaviour changes in some way after the experience that you tell them about, but in the end, only the person who has had the experience is going to be totally convinced. Religious experience cannot be tested by others in a way that might be said to provide conclusive proof. Because religious experience is totally individual and unique, no one else can look at it and see whether or not it is true.
- Critics sometimes point out that members of different faiths encounter God in a way that matches their previously held beliefs: a Roman Catholic might see the Virgin Mary, whereas a Hindu might see Lord Shiva. For some, this undermines the evidential force of religious experience and demonstrates that such experiences are no more than wish-fulfilment.
- Some experiments with electrical impulses, drugs and fasting have suggested that sensations usually associated with religious experience can be artificially created in the brain. V. S. Ramachandran and Sandra Blakeslee (*Phantoms in the Brain*, Fourth Estate, 1998), for example, describe experiments carried out on the temporal lobes of the brain which made patients feel a strong sense of divine presence. This sort of experiment has led some critics to argue that religious experience is not, therefore, veridical – it does not show that there is a real God, but instead shows that something is happening within the brain, which can be explained by science, and which people wrongly interpret to be God. Perhaps modern science can explain away religious experiences using modern scientific and medical knowledge; for example Francis of Assisi had religious experiences after severe illness, so perhaps he was hallucinating, and Hildegard of Bingen may have been suffering from migraine rather than experiencing God.

However, the argument from religious experience also has some strengths:

- Some people would disagree with the view that religious experience only carries authority for the individual who has it. Many claim to have been profoundly influenced by other people's experiences, which they would take to be authoritative. Hindus, for example, might be affected by the story of Arjuna's vision of Krishna in the *Bhagavad Gita*; Muslims take the religious experiences of Muhammad to be supremely authoritative.

- In response to the criticism that followers of different religions experience a God who conforms to their expectations, it could be argued that surely, if God wants his followers to recognise him when he reveals himself to them, he is going to choose to appear in a form that they will understand.

- There is no reason why God should not appear to people who have been fasting, or taking drugs, or undergoing experiments. Even if the artificially created 'religious experiences' of scientific experiment are not caused by God, other religious experiences outside the laboratory may still be caused by God.

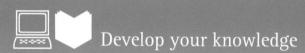
Develop your knowledge

All of these books are recommended for further reading:
Religious Experience by Peter Cole (Hodder Murray, 2005)
Is there a God? by Richard Swinburne (Oxford University Press, 1996)
Philosophy of Religion by C. Stephen Evans (Intervarsity Press, 1985)
The Miracle of Theism by J. L. Mackie (Oxford University Press, 1993)
The Evidential Force of Religious Experience by Caroline Franks Davies (Oxford University Press, 2004) is an in-depth consideration of the topic, and a very interesting book for those who wish to extend their knowledge beyond A level.

Conclusion

The power of religious experience is such that many people claim that they will not believe in God, or in miracles, until they have first-hand experience. They might be able to see the logic of one of the reasoned arguments, but this on its own will not give them a faith of their own and a relationship with God.

Religious experience, nevertheless, cannot be used as a 'proof' for the existence of God, because it is essentially private, and cannot be tested by others – it is difficult for anyone except the recipient to be totally convinced by it. Probably, for the unbeliever, the argument from religious experience is the weakest of all the arguments for the existence of God because it does not contain any premises which we would all accept, or even tip the balance of probability; but for the believer, it is the most convincing, as actual first-hand experience will always be more convincing than any argument.

The essentially subjective nature of religious experience need not mean that it is worthless. A lot of the most important aspects of human life, such as love, grief or beauty, cannot be tested or explained, and yet we often base the most important decisions of our lives on private feelings which cannot be tested by others.

Practice exam question

To what extent should we take seriously other people's reports of religious experience?

In answering this question, you have a wide range of material on which to draw. Remember that you are writing a critical argument as well as description, and that your answer (whether or not we should take reports of religious experience seriously) should run throughout the whole essay rather than be tagged on at the end. You need to demonstrate knowledge and understanding of a range of points of view, and use quotation or paraphrase to support them. Try to give evidence of your reading by referring specifically to named scholars and books, and try to use key vocabulary such as 'veridical' and 'credulity'.

Revelation through sacred texts

The term 'revelation' is used by theologians to mean knowledge that is gained through the agency of God. Revelation is therefore considered by many believers to be superior to knowledge discovered through reason or by empirical testing, because it is said to come from an infallible source. It is also direct and unconditioned by the usual human limitations of misunderstanding and bias.

Propositional and non-propositional revelation

'Propositional knowledge' is usually taken to refer to knowing that something is so. The 'mental library' of facts that people know is their propositional knowledge: a quiz would test someone's propositional knowledge. Examples of propositional knowledge might be knowing when your birthday is, knowing who wrote *Great Expectations*, knowing Boyle's Law or knowing the French for 'please'. Propositional knowledge is considered to have a 'truth value' – in other words, it can be true or false, or somewhere in between.

'Non-propositional knowledge' refers to other kinds of knowledge, for example knowing how to do something – the skills that we have. So examples of non-propositional knowledge might include knowing how to ride a bicycle, or how to whistle, or how to do a good impersonation of your teacher.

Non-propositional meaning can be conveyed in a variety of ways, for example through art, music and dance, and through the use of metaphors and symbols. Advertisers often use non-propositional ways of getting their message across, so that they can avoid being open to charges of giving false information. They imply, non-propositionally, that eating their yogurt will provide you with lots of opportunities for being with your family, smiling and running along beaches, without actually saying so.

Some theologians have emphasised the difference between 'propositional revelation' and 'non-propositional revelation'. Belief in non-propositional revelation is the belief that God is revealed through the things he has done – in the beauty of the world, for example, or in creating us, or in guiding us in one direction rather than another or giving us feelings of hope or of peace. In Christianity, God is considered to be revealed in the person of Jesus, not only in the things that Jesus said but also in the things that Jesus did and in his character. In Judaism, God is seen to be revealed through the workings of history, and in particular through the freeing of the Hebrews from slavery in Egypt at the time of the Passover. Those in the Jewish and Christian traditions might refer to Psalm 105:37–42 as an example:

> He brought out Israel, laden with silver and gold,
>   and from among their tribes no-one faltered.
> Egypt was glad when they left,
>   because dread of Israel had fallen on them.
> He spread out a cloud as a covering,
>   and a fire to give light at night.
> They asked, and he brought them quail
>   and satisfied them with the bread of heaven.
> He opened the rock, and water gushed out;
>   like a river it flowed in the desert.
> For he remembered his holy promise
>   given to his servant Abraham.

Belief in propositional revelation is the belief that God speaks to people in words, and passes on information to his listeners. This is information that they could not have gained through reason alone – for example, information about how God will save them from sin, or information about the moral standards demanded by God, or information about life after death.

Barth's understanding of revelation

Some theologians, most notably Karl Barth (1886–1968), have objected to the attempts of philosophers to understand more about the nature of God through human reason (this is called 'natural theology'). Barth argued that the only way in which people can gain true knowledge of God is through revelation.

Barth objected to natural theology because in his view, it leads to a picture of God which is not the same as the God of Christianity. Barth rejected the ideas of thinkers such as Aquinas who tried to combine faith with reason, because he thought that their views led away from the truth of the Bible. He consciously followed the thinking of the Danish theologian Kierkegaard, by saying that all efforts to discover truth about God apart from God's revelation to us in Jesus Christ were only likely to lead to error. Barth's thinking has two important implications:

1. Knowledge of God can only be found in Christianity, and other world religions therefore are considered not to have any truth except where they agree with Christian teaching.

2. The Old Testament is open to testing to see how far it meets the revelation of God in Christ. The New Testament is seen as superior in truth to the Old.

Barth's concept of revelation, explained in his enormous work *Church Dogmatics*, included the following points:

- God acts in revealing himself to us as and when he wants to; no human actions can facilitate the granting of revelation. (This goes against, for example, the ascetic practices of the mediaeval mystics who tried to put themselves into what they considered to be the most likely states in which to receive religious experience.)
- Divine revelation is not the same as human insight, and the difference must be recognised.
- Ordinary language is inadequate to convey revelation.
- Revelation is a personal disclosure of God's being and nature.
- Revelation is conveyed through the witness of the Bible; the Bible is not identical with the word of God, but it testifies to it – Scripture points to the word of God, rather than being literally the words spoken by God.
- Revelation is given only in Jesus Christ, who is God's full and final word to humanity; this does not mean that the revelation of Christ is all the revelation that there is, but it means that only Christians can experience the revelation of God in the natural world or through great art or music.

Ideas about propositional revelation raise important issues about the status of sacred writings. In Islam, the Holy Qur'an is believed to be a perfect record of the words of Allah, spoken to the prophet Muhammad, who recited them so that they could be written down. Each word of the Qur'an is believed to come directly from Allah; it does not reflect Muhammad's own personal opinions and concerns, because Muhammad was simply the mouthpiece for the words. He did not have a profound religious experience and then decide afterwards how best to put his new knowledge into words, for example. This would have meant that he had to decide for himself how to express ideas, which words to use, and which concepts to emphasise. Instead, according to Muslim belief, Muhammad was told each word directly, and this was faithfully and accurately recorded in the Arabic language that Allah had used when he spoke to the prophet. For this reason, Muslims study Arabic from an early age if it is not their native language, so that they can read, hear and understand Allah's very words. There are translations of the Qur'an in many other languages, but these do not have the same status as the Qur'an in Arabic, because a translation must inevitably involve slight changes in meaning and emphasis.

Muslims believe that the Qur'an was dictated to the prophet Muhammad, who recited it without error.

Because the Qur'an is believed to be the exact words of Allah, Muslims insist that it is not just for those people who were living in the culture of Muhammad's time, but is Allah's own truth for all generations and in all parts of the world. If society changes so that the Qur'an seems in places to be old-fashioned or uncomfortable, then it is society that should change in order to keep more closely to the Qur'an. It is out of the question for parts of the Qur'an to be disregarded or considered obsolete.

To think about

How might the belief that the Qur'an is the directly revealed word of Allah affect the ability of Muslims to assimilate into Western culture?

The Bible as the revealed word of God

What does it mean to Christians when they say that the Bible is the word of God? There are many different ways in which this could be understood.

According to some Christians, the Bible is the word of God in the same way that the Qur'an is the word of God for Muslims. God told the writers what to write, word by word, punctuation mark by punctuation mark, so that all the writers had to do was record. The writers' role was that of the amanuensis: a scribe who copies down someone else's words. It would be the same as the role played by someone who takes dictation from an examination candidate who has broken her arm and is unable to write. The ideas expressed, and the words chosen to express them, would come not from the mind of the person doing the writing, but directly from God, who takes over the minds of the writers and breathes his word into them as 'inspiration'.

To think about

If the Bible is the word of God in the sense that God dictated every word, does this mean that Christians should always read it in its original languages?

The relation between written Scripture and inspiration by the will of God is an issue that occupied the minds of even the earliest Christians. The author of 2 Peter, writing to early Christians in New Testament times, reassures his readers that when they read the words of the prophets, they can be confident that they are reading the words of God himself, rather than the prophets' own perceptions and commentary on life. God gave the prophets his Holy Spirit, and this told them what they were to say:

Above all, you must understand that no prophecy of Scripture came about by the prophet's own interpretation. For prophecy never had its origin in the will of man, but men spoke from God as they were carried along by the Holy Spirit. (2 Peter 1:20,21)

Then the Lord reached out his hand and touched my mouth and said to me, 'Now, I have put my words in your mouth.' (Jeremiah 1:9)

This raises the question, of course, of what 'counts' as Scripture. 2 Peter, like the books of the prophets, is also in the Christian Bible. When the author was explaining the point about writers being carried along by the Holy Spirit, was he too being guided by the Holy Spirit? Did he imagine or intend that his words would be taken by many to be the infallible word of God? For some scholars, the intention of the original author is something to be researched in order to gain important insights into the true meaning of the text. For others, the intention of the writer is not as crucial, because the Holy Spirit could have put layers of meaning into the words, even though the original writer had no idea of their significance.

Clearly, there are some advantages in holding the belief that the entire Bible is inspired directly and without mistake from God. It gives the Bible the status of an infallible source that believers know they can trust and rely on. Where the Bible makes claims about historical events, these can be taken as accurate accounts of exactly what happened, and there is no need to doubt a word:

After Noah was 500 years old, he became the father of Shem, Ham and Japheth. (Genesis 5:32)

Where the Bible makes statements about geographical features of the countryside, the age of the world, the position of the Earth in relation to the sun and moon, the workings of the human body – or any other statement about the world – they can be accepted as the truth because they are the revealed and perfect word of God, untainted by human error. In matters of morality, the Bible can be trusted to give the right answer whenever it provides ethical guidance, and whenever it gives advice about how to organise family life and religious life:

A woman should learn in quietness and full submission. I do not permit a woman to teach or to have authority over a man; she must be silent. (2 Timothy 11:14)

With this view of the inerrancy of Scripture, there need be no debate about whether miracles actually happen, whether the Virgin Birth should be taken literally, or whether there genuinely was a flood in the time of Noah, because the Bible is a source of certain knowledge. In this view, Adam and Eve lived as real people (rather than, perhaps, as metaphors for humanity as part of a myth); the world was created exactly as described in Genesis, and God created each separate species to be distinct from the beginning of creation. Jonah really was swallowed by a big fish and survived the experience; Daniel really did escape unharmed from his encounter with the lions; Jesus really did walk on water, turn water into wine and rise from the dead (see pages 191–4 for the writer Henry Morris' perspective on understanding the Bible).

The view that God dictated the Bible can also account for passages where the biblical writer seems to know details of events that he could not possibly have experienced, and where he could not have gathered the information from any human source either:

In the beginning God created the heavens and the earth. Now the earth was formless and empty, darkness was over the surface of the deep, and the Spirit of God was hovering over the waters. And God said, 'Let there be light,' and there was light. (Genesis 1:1–3)

One day the angels came to present themselves before the Lord, and Satan also came with them. The Lord said to Satan, 'Where have you come from?'
Satan answered the Lord, 'From roaming through the earth and going back and forth in it.' Then the Lord said to Satan, 'Have you considered my servant Job? There is no one on earth like him; he is blameless and upright, a man who fears God and shuns evil.'
(Job 1:6–8)

Although many Christians believe that the Bible has no mistakes, the view that every word of the Bible was spoken by God as dictation is not a mainstream Christian view. Many believe that the different books of the Bible were written as different believers were guided by the Holy Spirit to record their experiences and their relationship with God in their own words, including their own feelings and interpretations as well as being driven by God to say the right things. The Bible is, in this view, still 'inspired', but not in the sense of being inerrant in every syllable.

One of the difficulties with the 'amanuensis' view of the writers of the Bible is that there are passages where it appears that the voice of the human writer comes across strongly:

How long, O Lord? Will you forget me forever?
How long will you hide your face from me?
How long must I wrestle with my thoughts
and every day have sorrow in my heart?
How long will my enemy triumph over me?
Look on me and answer, O Lord my God.
Give light to my eyes, or I will sleep in death. (Psalm 13:1–3)

It could be difficult to imagine God dictating these words for someone to write down, without the human mind having any part to play. The words sound very much those of a human complaint, where the Psalmist is struggling with having to wait for God to answer his prayers in the way that he wants them answered. Some might argue that this is, nevertheless, the infallible word of God, where God is choosing this form of expression as a way of telling people that it is acceptable to take frustrations and anger to God in prayer; but perhaps a simpler explanation is that the words come from a human author, inspired by his relationship with God to express his feelings in his own way.

Also, within the Bible there are many different styles of writing, suggesting a variety of different human authors. The four Gospels, for example, are written in (at least) four distinct styles. Matthew's Gospel contains many allusions to Jewish culture and to the Jewish scriptures, giving the strong impression that not only was he Jewish himself but that he expected his readers to be Jewish. Luke, on the other hand, stops to explain some aspects of Judaism in case his readers are unfamiliar with them. For example, before he tells the story of the boy Jesus in the Temple, Luke pauses to explain to his readers why Jesus' parents were in Jerusalem with him:

> *Every year his parents went to Jerusalem for the Feast of the Passover. When he was twelve years old, they went up to the Feast, according to the custom.* (Luke 2:41–42)

It would have been unnecessary to explain this custom to a Jewish audience; it would have been obvious to them that this is what people always do at Passover. Details such as this suggest the involvement of different Christians in the writing of the Gospels, each wanting to tell the story of Jesus but each having individual interests and reasons.

Mark's Gospel is often considered to be written in rather poor Greek in comparison with the others, which does not suggest that God personally dictated the story; and John's Gospel has a much more mystical, theological flavour to it, perhaps indicating that the writer of John was more influenced by first-century philosophy than the other evangelists were. If God really did dictate every word of the Bible, it is difficult to understand why there are four gospels at all, rather than just one. It is also difficult to see why these gospels contain some passages that are almost identical; and why on occasion details of the stories are not quite consistent with each other.

Practice exam question

To what extent can the view that scripture is inerrant be defended?

For this question, you are being asked whether the Bible is inerrant, in other words whether it is without mistakes. This is not quite the same thing as saying that the Bible is literally true. For your answer, you need to explain why some people have taken this point of view (you could use Henry Morris' views as a basis for discussion), and also why others prefer to take a more liberal view (you could use Bultmann and others). You might want to use examples of where parts of the Bible appear to contradict each other.

Philosophical debates about miracles

Muslim pilgrims have been cramming into the home of a Bolton couple to examine the 'miracle aubergine' whose seeds spell out the name of their God, Allah. More than 50 worshippers crowded inside the terraced house on Essingdon Street, Daubhill, last night, after reading in the BEN how Ruksana Patel had cut into the vegetable and discovered the 'miracle'.

Ruksana, 23, made the discovery in the kitchen of her home. She and her husband, Salim, 25, immediately recognised the Arabic word spelling out Allah and rushed to their priest, Mr Abdullah Patel. Mr Patel, of the Masjid-e-Gosia Mosque on Auburn Street, Daubhill, confirmed the outline of the word and that 'a miracle' had occurred. (Bolton Evening News, *13 March 1996*)

What criteria does an event have to meet before it can be described as a miracle? Do miracles happen today? Were the miracles described in the Bible real historical events that could have been witnessed by anyone passing by at the time, or were they a poetic way of explaining people's beliefs? If God can and does perform miracles, what does this imply about his nature?

To think about

How would you define a miracle?

Miracle stories are a significant feature of the Bible. They are used as examples of God's saving power and personal interest in his people, for example in the miracle of the parting of the Red Sea at the Exodus:

Then Moses stretched out his hand over the sea, and all that night the Lord drove the sea back with a strong east wind and turned it into dry land. The waters were divided, and the Israelites went through the sea on dry ground, with a wall of water on their right and on their left. (Exodus 14:21–2)

For Jews, miracles are an essential part of their story as a nation. The miracles described in the scriptures are taken as evidence of God's care for his chosen people, and the stories of what God has done for his people throughout their history are repeated in homes and synagogues at festivals throughout the year.

In the Christian tradition, miracles are used as proof by the Gospel writers, to show that Jesus really was the Messiah that the Jews were expecting:

> *I will keep you and will make you*
> *to be a covenant for the people*
> *and a light for the Gentiles,*
> *to open eyes that are blind,*
> *to free captives from prison*
> *and to release from the dungeon those who sit in darkness.* (Isaiah 42:6–7)

They are used as illustrations of Jesus as the Son of God: they show that Jesus had God's absolute power over nature:

> *One day Jesus said to his disciples, 'Let's go over to the other side of the lake.' So they got into a boat and set out. As they sailed, he fell asleep. A squall came down on the lake, so that the boat was being swamped, and they were in great danger. The disciples went and woke him, saying, 'Master, Master, we're going to drown!' He got up and rebuked the wind and the raging waters; the storm subsided, and all was calm.* (Luke 8:22–4)

They are used as indicators of what the kingdom of God will be like, when the blind are made to see again:

> *The people were amazed when they saw the mute speaking, the crippled made well, the lame walking and the blind seeing. And they praised the God of Israel.* (Matthew 15:31)

Prisoners are miraculously set free, as a fulfilment of prophecy:

> *Suddenly there was such a violent earthquake that the foundations of the prison were shaken. At once all the prison doors flew open, and everybody's chains came loose.* (Acts 16:26)

They show Jesus' ability to give new life even to those who have died:

> *While Jesus was still speaking, some men came from the house of Jairus, the synagogue ruler. 'Your daughter is dead,' they said. 'Why bother the teacher any more?' Ignoring what they said, Jesus told the synagogue ruler, 'Don't be afraid; just believe.'*
>
> *He did not let anyone follow him except Peter, James and John the brother of James. When they came to the home of the synagogue ruler, Jesus saw a commotion, with people crying and wailing loudly. He went in and said to*

*them, 'Why all this commotion and wailing? The child is not dead but asleep.'
But they laughed at him. After he put them all out, he took the child's father and
mother and the disciples who were with him, and went in where the child was.
He took her by the hand and said to her, 'Talitha koum!' (which means, 'Little girl,
I say to you, get up!'). Immediately the girl stood up and walked around (she was
twelve years old). At this they were completely astonished.* (Mark 5: 35–42)

Many believe that the whole essence of the Christian message depends upon the
concept of miracle: the miracle of God becoming incarnate, born of a virgin; the
miracle of his taking on the sin of the world; and the miracle of his resurrection.
They might argue that to reject the view that God performs miracles is to reject the
whole of Christianity.

*Miracle stories, such as
that of the Feeding of
the Five Thousand, are
considered by many
Christians to be essential
to the gospel message.*

We will consider three main issues that arise in the discussion of miracles. Firstly, there
is the problem of definition: what do we mean when we use the word 'miracle' to
describe an event? This is an important issue, because other questions (such as whether
miracles happen today) cannot be answered without a shared understanding of what
a miracle is. Secondly, there is the issue of whether miracles actually happen: whether
interpreting an event as 'a miracle' is something that a reasonable person might
do. Thirdly, there is a need to consider the implications of the idea of miracle for
an understanding of the nature of God: is the concept of a God who occasionally
intervenes in the world to perform miracles consistent with other beliefs about the
nature of God?

Key point

- Miracles are often an important feature of biblical stories, but there are
  philosophical issues raised by the concept of miracle.

The problem of definition

What is a miracle? It is a word that is in common English usage. When an accident happens which had the potential to be much worse, people say 'It's a miracle that no one was killed.' If there is a terrible natural disaster, and someone is pulled alive from the wreckage when hope was fading, reporters talk about a 'miracle rescue'. More commonly, advertisers talk about 'miracle' cleaning products, 'miracle' hair restorers, and 'miracle' fertilisers for your plants – but what does it actually mean?

The word comes from the Latin *miraculum*, meaning 'wonder', but in religious understanding, a miracle is something more specific than any wonderful event or narrow escape. For the majority of religious believers, a miracle is something extraordinary (in comparison with the ordinary, expected course of things) which has been brought about by God for a particular purpose. The notion of miracle carries with it a religious interpretation of an event. Something must be more than just unexpected and in apparent violation of the laws of nature to be a miracle. It must have some kind of religious significance, and it must fit in with our understanding of God. We would not call some apparently supernatural event which did nothing but harm a miracle, even if it did defy the laws of nature as we know them; but we might call it a miracle if it did good. (This raises questions about 'miracles' such as the plagues in Exodus, which did good for some people but harm for others. The Hebrews might have looked on them as wonderful events, but the Egyptians who lost their drinking supply, their cattle and their first-born sons might not have seen it that way.)

Writers such as Stephen Evans, in his book *The Philosophy of Religion: Thinking about Faith* (Intervarsity Press, 1985), have argued that miracles are not just magic tricks: 'Obviously the miracles of a religion such as Christianity are not merely bizarre events or stunts. They have a function and purpose, and usually that function is a revelatory one.'

One famous definition of miracle comes from the eighteenth-century philosopher David Hume, who wrote about miracles in his *Enquiry Concerning Human Understanding*: 'A miracle may be accurately defined, a transgression of a law of nature by a particular volition of the Deity or by the interposition of some invisible agent.'

Hume here leaves open the possibility that a miracle could be performed by angels or demons, for example. Hume's definition led him on to argue that a reasonable person has no grounds for believing that miracles ever happen, as we shall see later.

John Macquarrie, in *Principles of Christian Theology* (SCM Press, 1966), took up the point that a miracle has to be something which is attributable to God, in addition to being a wonderful event. He writes:

In a minimal sense, a miracle is an event that excites wonder. Certainly every event that might be called a 'miracle' would do this, and there must be many such events, but it is evident that in a religious context the word 'miracle' carries more than just this minimal sense. It is believed that God is in the event in some special way, that he is the author of it, and intends to achieve some special end by it.

Macquarrie goes on to say that some nineteenth-century philosophers and theologians tried to argue that everything is a miracle, because everything is brought about by God. They wanted to argue this case because of the problems raised by the idea of a God who performs occasional miracles for a selected few. However, Macquarrie argues that the 'everything is a miracle' definition is not very helpful, because there are some events which stand out as being more important and significant than others. If we call everything a miracle, then the word loses any kind of meaning. Therefore we have to show in our definition of miracle that it refers to an event which has some kind of distinctiveness. Macquarrie writes:

Here we come up against the traditional view that a miracle has its distinctiveness because it is an event which breaks into the order of nature. By this it is meant that the so-called 'laws' or regular procedures of nature are on some occasions suspended, so that miraculous events take place without 'natural' causes and as the consequence of 'supernatural' agency; or, in some accounts of the matter, there is added to the natural causes operating in a given situation a supernatural cause, and the result produced is other than it would have been, had only the natural causes been at work.

So Macquarrie is saying that in the traditional view, when a miracle occurs, natural laws ('rules' of nature) could be suspended. Examples of this might be in the story where Jesus walked on the water, where Jesus did not sink under the water as would have been expected if only natural laws had been in operation; or at the feeding of the five thousand, where five loaves and two fishes miraculously filled five thousand hungry people, instead of satisfying only a few. Although this traditional view is one which is widely held within the Christian church, Macquarrie himself rejected belief that God sometimes suspends the laws of nature, because of the philosophical difficulties it raises.

Another thinker, R. F. Holland, also made the point that miracles might not have to break the laws of nature, and gave the example of a child playing on a railway line, just around a bend, so that the driver of the approaching train had no idea that the child was on the line. The child's mother, from a vantage point on the hillside, can see both the child and the train and is powerless to do anything about it. But just in time, the train stops a few feet away and the child is unharmed – the driver had fainted and the brakes had been applied automatically. The mother, no doubt, would see such an event as a miracle, even if other people might interpret it as just a happy coincidence.

It seems, then, that the majority of scholars are agreed on what a miracle is, although there are differences of opinion. A miracle has to be brought about by God; for many, it has to break the laws of nature in some way – there should be no natural, scientific explanation for what has happened; and it must happen for a reason, to fulfil God's purposes.

The issue of how to define a miracle came under discussion in recent years, following the death of Mother Teresa of Calcutta in 1997. Many of her followers and admirers within the Roman Catholic Church wanted her to be canonised (given the status of a saint), and they were pressing for this to happen even before she died; but in order for canonisation to be allowed by the Vatican, it had to be shown that Mother Teresa had performed at least two posthumous miracles. This, of course, raised the issue of what would qualify to be counted as a miracle – especially as hundreds of people came forward, claiming that Mother Teresa had performed some miraculous work for them after her death. Would a dream in which someone saw Mother Teresa and heard her voice be considered a 'miracle'? Probably not: anyone can have a dream about anyone else, without that other person having actually caused the dream. Also, anyone could claim to have had such a dream, but there would be no way of testing this claim and getting concrete evidence. In order for the 'miracle' to be counted, it had to be something which science could not explain, and which was open to verification by observers, who should be in a position to vouch for the facts of the matter both before and after the event. Many people claimed to have been cured of illnesses by Mother Teresa, and enquiries were set up to investigate these claims.

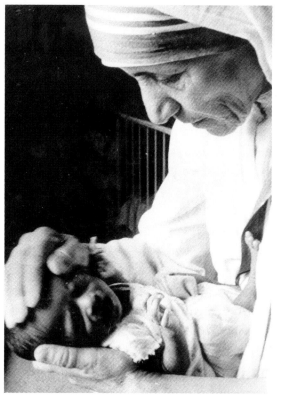

Hundreds of people have claimed to be the recipients of miracles brought about by the saintliness of Mother Teresa.

In 2002, Pope John Paul II signed decrees which accepted as authentic one of the miracles attributed to Mother Teresa. This acceptance gave Mother Teresa the status of beatification (having the title 'Blessed' in front of her name). This miracle involved a Bengali woman, Monica Besra, who had been suffering from a large abdominal tumour. It was claimed that on the first anniversary of Mother Teresa's death, a locket containing a photograph of Mother Teresa had been applied to Mrs Besra's abdomen by two nuns, prayers had been said, and this had cured the tumour. After months of investigation by Vatican officials, the Pope judged that the cure had genuinely been the result of supernatural intervention by Mother Teresa. A miracle had taken place which was directly attributable to her.

The case, however, raised controversy. Although some of the doctors who treated Mrs Besra said that there was no scientific explanation for her recovery, others disagreed, saying that the tumour was tubercular and had simply responded to an anti-tubercular drug – there was no reason to attribute the cure to Mother Teresa. Other people objected, too; not because they had opinions about whether this was or was not a miracle, but because they felt that the whole of Mother Teresa's work for the poor was evidence of her sainthood. They argued that God was clearly acting through Mother Teresa in her life and example. The concern that she had shown for the poor, her self-sacrifice, and her skill in attracting the attention of the world to the Christian message was, some said, miraculous in itself, and the call for posthumous miracles was missing the point and was insulting to her memory.

Develop your knowledge

Richard Swinburne's book *The Concept of Miracle* (Macmillan, 1971) gives an in-depth consideration and defence of miracles.

Aquinas on miracle

It seems that, for many, in order for something to be properly called a miracle, it must be outside the normal operations of nature and science, and it must be an occurrence where an alternative, natural explanation cannot be produced. This understanding stems from the work of Thomas Aquinas, who, in the thirteenth century, attempted to define different events which could be interpreted as miraculous, in his work *Summa Contra Gentiles*. Aquinas recognised that to call an event a 'miracle' is to put an interpretation onto what happened and express an opinion about it (just as calling an event a 'tragedy' is to interpret it):

Things that are done occasionally by divine power outside of the usual established order of events are commonly called miracles (wonders). We wonder when we see an effect and do not know the cause. And because one and the same cause is sometimes known to some and unknown to others, it happens that of the witnesses of the effect some wonder and some do not wonder: thus an astronomer does not wonder at seeing an eclipse of the sun, at which a person that is ignorant of astronomy cannot help wondering.

Aquinas went on to argue that for an event to be properly worthy of the name 'miracle', it has to be an event which is intrinsically wonderful, not just wonderful to this person but not to that one. (This would rule out, for example, calling the ordinary birth of a healthy baby a 'miracle' – it might appear miraculous to the new baby's delighted parents, but for most people, the production of babies is something normal, natural and to be expected from humans.) Aquinas also claimed that for an event to be a miracle, it must have a cause which is 'absolutely hidden'. The launching of a space shuttle, then, would not be a miracle even though the majority of us might not understand how it was achieved, because the cause is not completely hidden – those who made the shuttle and did the launching would, one hopes, be aware of how it was done.

Aquinas believed that miracles could be placed in rank order. At the top of his list, the highest order of miracles, are 'those in which something is done by God that nature can never do.' He gave some examples of this, from the Bible. One was from the book of Isaiah 38:7–8, where God made a shadow move backwards, as a sign to Hezekiah; another was from Joshua 10:12–14, where the sun and moon were made to stand still so that Joshua and his men had time to destroy their enemies the Amorites, and return to their camp in safety.

'Miracles of the second rank are those in which God does something that nature can do, but not in that sequence and connection.' For this second rank, Aquinas gave examples such as people being able to see after being blind (where, in the natural order of things, people see first and then become blind but the process does not happen the other way around, in his view); people living after being dead; and people being able to walk, after being lame or paralysed. Today we might argue that walking after being lame or even paralysed does sometimes happen naturally or with the help of medical science, and that restoration of sight is not uncommon, but these are examples given by Aquinas from within his thirteenth-century experience.

Finally, Aquinas argues:

A miracle of the third rank is something done by God, which is usually done by the operation of nature, but is done in this case without the working of natural principles, as when one is cured by divine power of a fever, in itself naturally curable, or when it rains without any working of the elements.

Here, Aquinas meant the sort of miracle in which a broken limb is mended in an instant. With the normal workings of nature, we would expect the break to mend gradually through the usual healing processes, but if it were a miracle, God could intervene and make the same thing happen while by-passing natural means.

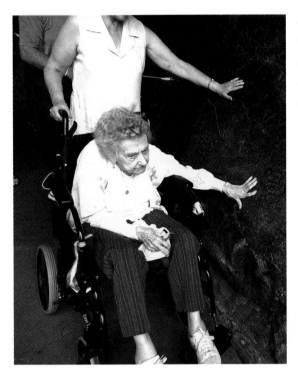

Most Roman Catholic pilgrims who visit the shrine at Lourdes go to worship and to seek inner peace. However, there have been reports of miraculous healings.

Hume's rejection of miracle

Probably the most important rejection of the idea of miracle comes from the philosopher David Hume (1711–76). Hume believed that miracles were, almost by their very definition, beyond the realms of reasonable belief – no sensible person could seriously believe that a miracle had happened, when other interpretations of the event would always be far more likely.

Hume was very pleased with his argument refuting reports of miracles. In his *Enquiry Concerning Human Understanding* he writes:

> *'I flatter myself, that I have discovered an argument of a like nature, which, if just, will, with the wise and learned, be an everlasting check to all kinds of superstitious delusion, and consequently, will be useful as long as the world endures.'*

According to Hume, wise and sensible people form their beliefs on the basis of evidence. A sensible belief will be proportioned to the evidence, so that it must be more likely that something is true than false, before a sensible person will believe it. Hume argued that, in the case of miracles, we should weigh the evidence, looking at which is the more likely; do we think that natural rules will have held good, or do we think that it is more likely that a miracle will have taken place? In Hume's way of thinking, our past experience has shown us that, for example, water does not turn into wine, and neither can people walk on it, and the whole weight of our past experience bears this out. Therefore reports that something different has happened should be treated with scepticism.

If someone tells you that he or she has witnessed a miracle, then you have several choices. You could believe the person – particularly if you know the person well and think that he or she is the sort of person who usually tells the truth. Alternatively, you could think that the person is mistaken, or is deliberately deceiving you. Hume argued that the reasonable person would opt for the most likely of the choices; and although it might be unlikely that this person is deceitful or joking, and it might be unlikely that he or she has made a mistake, it will always be even more unlikely that a miracle actually occurred. The balance of probability shows us in every case that it would be unreasonable to believe in the miracle.

Hume argued that, for a miracle to be called a miracle at all, it must be something that never happens in the normal world: and therefore, miracles do not happen, by their own definition. In his own words:

> There must therefore be a uniform experience against every miraculous event, otherwise that event would not merit that appellation. And as a uniform experience amounts to a proof, there is here a direct and full proof, from the nature of the fact, against the existence of any miracle.

Hume also claimed that stories of miracles tended to come from 'ignorant and barbarous places and nations' rather than from well-educated people; therefore the testimony of people who claimed to have been first-hand witnesses of miracles was not to be trusted. These were people who were likely to be gullible, and who were less familiar with more rational and scientific ways of looking at the world. We should take more notice of these reports if the alleged witnesses had a reputation to lose should their stories turn out to be untrue, or if they had nothing to gain. Hume went on to argue that people have a natural tendency to look for marvellous events, and to want to believe in the supernatural and paranormal, and that this desire might colour the interpretation of events. He said that there were no really well-supported cases where miracles had been witnessed by a suitable number of reliable people; no miraculous occurrences which were 'attested by a sufficient number of men, of such unquestioned good-sense, education, and learning, as to secure us against all delusion in themselves…'.

Hume argued that a sensible person 'proportions his belief to the evidence', and said that it was far more likely that a report of a miracle was false than that it was true.

Hume's final point was that the different miracle stories from different religious traditions tended to contradict each other, making the other seem less likely or cancelling each other out. A miracle story from Christianity aims to show the primary authority of Jesus, whereas miracle stories from Islam claim that it is Muhammad who has been given first authority by God. Hume's view was that each of these differing accounts weakened the other's evidential force.

Key point

- Hume argued that sensible people should not believe reports of miracles, because other explanations of the event are always going to be more likely.

Some answers to Hume

1. Hume's definition of miracle is often criticised. Many argue that Hume fails to recognise that the 'laws of nature' are descriptive, rather than prescriptive: in other words, they tell us about what has been observed, they do not tell nature what it may or may not do. Therefore if something happens which goes against the rules of nature, it just is different from events that have previously been observed; it does not break a rule which must be obeyed. A 'transgression of the laws of nature', then, is not an impossibility, it is an unusual occurrence which adds to our understanding.

—R. Swinburne

It is argued, against Hume, that his view of looking at the laws of nature operating in the world is one typical of the eighteenth and nineteenth centuries (and of course Hume could hardly be blamed for this outlook). We are far more likely, nowadays, to recognise that the so-called 'laws' of science are provisional; they work for us, for now, as descriptors of what has been observed, but we are willing to accept that we may come across exceptions to our rules which will lead us to revise what we had previously thought to be true. We are more willing to accept that events may possibly occur which are beyond our past experience; but we are still likely to think that there must be a scientific explanation for these events, even if we do not yet know what these are. Other writers, however, such as Stephen Evans and J. L. Mackie, say that Hume simply meant that a miracle was an exception to the normal processes of nature, and that this does not show a misunderstanding of the nature of laws of nature.

2. Modern thinkers, therefore, are likely to want to modify Hume's view: miraculous events are not necessarily impossible, but they are unlikely. Hume would still say that the sensible person would choose the likely interpretation of an event rather than the unlikely.

3. Some theologians would object to Hume's definition of miracle on the grounds that it misses out the point of a miracle, which is its revelatory purpose. A miracle is not just an exception to the normal course of nature, but is an event with a special significance and reason behind it. That reason is the revelation of God.

P. Tillich &
R. F Halland.

4. Modern liberal theologians consider that there is an element of myth in the Bible, and they might well agree with Hume that there are stories which seem so improbable that it is very hard for a rational person to believe in them; but this does not make the whole miracle story worthless. If the myth is removed (the story is 'demythologised', to use the terminology of Rudolf Bultmann) there is still truth there to be found; the point still remains. The miracle story may have been a way of saying that God is like *this*, that the kingdom of heaven is like *that*. We may no longer be able to accept a world-view that includes miraculous events, but this need not mean that we have to reject the revelation too. This is the view of John Macquarrie, Maurice Wiles and others. Their answer to the question 'is it reasonable to believe in miracles?' then, would be that it could be unreasonable to believe literally in all the miracle stories of the Bible, but that these stories do have a truth which remains once the mythology has been taken out. Stories of present-day miracles might be met with some scepticism, especially those which do not seem to have any particular point, such as accounts of statues which produce blood.

5. One of Hume's other arguments was that testimonies to miracles were invariably unreliable, coming from uneducated people who had an interest in having their stories accepted. One criticism of this view is that Hume does not consider the possibility of first-hand experience of a miracle; he assumes that we only learn of miracles by report. He writes of what a sensible person would do on hearing reports of a miracle, but not of what that person might do if miraculously healed; he writes of reports of miracles coming from far-away nations, but not of what his conclusions might be if an

apparent miracle happened on his own doorstep in Edinburgh. People have suggested that perhaps Hume's view might have changed if he had experienced a miracle himself.

6. Hume also does not consider that a miracle might leave evidence that could be seen by many, such as a healed man walking about again in his home town. Possibly Hume is right that many reports of miracles have been exaggerated or invented, but this does not mean that this is true of all of them. As Hume began from the belief that no reasonable person could believe in miracles, it was perhaps inevitable that he would consider those who report miracles to be ignorant.

7. Hume could also be criticised for making a jump from what is improbable to what is beyond rational acceptance. There are numerous reported incidents of very unlikely things happening, where the balance of probability was heavily weighted against their occurrence, but this does not mean that they did not happen. Most of us can think of instances in our own lives when something highly unlikely actually happened: the holidays we took in distant countries where we met our next door neighbours walking along the beach; the times we were just thinking about a friend we had been neglecting for months when she happened to telephone; the times when two people turn up at a wedding wearing identical outfits even though there are hundreds to choose from in the shops. Had we reported these events to Hume, he might have concluded that we were mistaken or deceiving him, because of the weight of probability against them having actually taken place – but we still know that they did.

8. Finally, Hume's point that different miracle stories from different religions count against each other is probably the weakest in his argument. It does not follow that if different belief systems make different claims, then they must both be wrong; it is quite possible that one could be true and the others false. It would be a more forceful criticism if it could be shown that reports of miracles from within one religion were contradictory – which perhaps they are.

Maurice Wiles and *God's Action in the World*

Maurice Wiles (1923–2005), a twentieth-century philosopher of religion, argued against traditional belief in miracles, but for a very different reason from the position taken by Hume. Wiles was part of a group of authors who wrote a controversial book called *The Myth of God Incarnate* (ed. John Hick, Westminster John Knox, 1977) in which they argued that some of the first-century ways of looking at the world are inappropriate for the present day. When Wiles wrote his book *God's Action in the World* (SCM Press, 1986) he wanted to explain how God could be seen as taking part in the affairs of people and showing concern for the events of history, but reinterpreting this in a way that could make sense to modern people rather than people of biblical times.

In *God's Action in the World*, Wiles describes how Christian teaching has always interwoven prophecy and miracle as the two key pointers to its main message: the incarnation of God in Christ. He writes that the early Christians did not see any difficulty in accepting the occurrence of miracle; for them, creation itself and all the regularities of the workings of nature were entirely dependent on the will of God, so there was nothing unacceptable in the idea that sometimes, God might will nature to work in a different way from usual in order to achieve his purposes.

Wiles does not reject the possibility of miracle for scientific, rationalist reasons, as he explains: 'Certainly the notion of miracle cannot simply be ruled out on scientific grounds as logically impossible, since the world we know is not a closed, deterministically ordered system.'

He does not see anything logically wrong with the idea that God could choose, if he wanted to, to dry up the sea, because God had, after all, made the sea in the first place and decided how it would operate. For Wiles, the problem was not one of logical inconsistency, but a problem of making sense of the morality and the wisdom of God. In his view, the real difficulty with the idea that God performs miracles is closely related to the problem of evil:

> *Miracles must by definition be relatively infrequent or else the whole idea of laws of nature, even of a broadly statistical sort, would be undermined, and ordered life as we know it an impossibility. Yet even so it would seem strange that no miraculous intervention prevented Auschwitz or Hiroshima, while the purposes apparently forwarded by some of the miracles acclaimed in traditional Christian faith seem trivial by comparison. Thus to acknowledge even the possibility of miracle raises acute problems for theodicy.*

Wiles argued that although God could perform miracles and suspend the laws of nature if he wanted to, it would be impossible for this to happen very often, otherwise we would not be able to have laws of nature at all. If the sea dried up every day to prevent people from drowning, or gravity stopped working every time someone fell from a dangerous height, or fire sometimes did no harm, then it would be impossible for us to live normal lives – we would never know what the natural world was going to do next.

But even so, Wiles argued, if we take a traditional view of miracle, then it is very difficult to see why God apparently did nothing miraculous to prevent the huge tragedies that are part of human history. Wiles asks here why nothing prevented Auschwitz or Hiroshima – today, we might ask why nothing prevented the planes from hitting the Twin Towers, or the tsunami from causing such damage in Asia, or the Pakistan earthquake from claiming so many lives. Wiles compares enormous tragedies, where there was no miracle, with some of the miracle stories in the New Testament, and says that it becomes very difficult to see why God would, for example, heal an individual blind man and give him his sight back, and yet let so many other people die horribly without doing anything to help.

For Wiles, it was impossible to accept that God occasionally intervenes in the world to perform miracles for a few individuals, but did nothing to prevent the devastation of Hiroshima.

Wiles' objection to the traditional view of miracles, then, is on moral grounds. He thought that if there is a God who sometimes performs these sudden miraculous interventions in the world, then it must be an arbitrary God – a God who has favourites, a God who can be unfair and who lacks compassion. For Wiles, the answer had to be that God works in the world in other ways, and not with these sudden random miracles just for a chosen few.

Key point

- Wiles argued against miracles on moral grounds. He thought that a God who performed occasional, arbitrary miracles was not worthy of worship, and that we should look at God's action in the world in a different way.

Criticisms of Wiles

- The main objection to Wiles' view, of course, would be that it is not consistent with the teaching of the Bible. Wiles might not like the concept of a God who performs occasional miracles, but nevertheless the Bible is quite clear that this is how God operates.
- Some might claim that Wiles is wrong to judge God's actions by human moral standards. If God wants to cure a blind man but not save the people of Hiroshima, they might argue, then because it is God's choice, it will be the right thing to do – even if we cannot understand it.

- It could also be argued that Wiles misses the point of miracles; they are not meant to be simply helping people in need, but have the purpose of revealing something about God, and therefore a comparatively small miracle might be more significant because of what it shows about God.

Practice exam question

'A God who performs miracles is not worthy of worship.' Discuss.

This question relates directly to the views of Maurice Wiles, and therefore your essay should focus on his work and a discussion of it. In your essay, you should explain the point of view expressed in the statement, and demonstrate that you understand why some people support it. You should also give some counter-arguments. You might want to extend the discussion to a consideration of other issues connected with miracles, before arriving at your conclusion.

The attributes of God

One of the most fundamental questions in the philosophy of religion is, what do people mean when they talk about 'God'? Theists are people who believe that God exists – but what exactly is it, that they are saying exists, and what are they asking other people to believe in? Are they talking about an object, one amongst all of the other objects in the universe? Are they, perhaps, talking about 'Existence-Itself', encompassing all of the universe within it? Or are they perhaps talking about a concept that exists in our mental perception of the world but would cease to exist if there were no one to think about it? What do they understand the nature of God to be?

To think about

Do you think people could ever come to an adequate understanding of the nature of God?

As we have seen, most philosophy of religion as we know it comes from within the Christian tradition. Because Christianity began and grew within the context of the Roman world, Christian understandings of the nature of God developed from the interweaving of biblical ideas and concepts from the ancient Greek philosophers. Christians inherited the language, symbolism and poetry of the Old Testament, in which God is anthropomorphised, involved with the world and unpredictable;

but the early Christian fathers also came from a culture in which classical ideas of a timeless and spaceless First Cause were very attractive. In particular, ideas from Plato and Aristotle were adopted and woven into Christian interpretations of the nature of God – sometimes successfully, and sometimes in a way that produces at least apparent contradictions. Philosophers of religion have to try to untangle these ideas and work out which, if any, make more sense.

Omnipotence

The idea that God is omnipotent, or all-powerful, is a familiar one in Christian thought. However, it has caused a considerable amount of controversy, where people have wondered whether the concept of God's omnipotence is compatible with other attributes ascribed to God, and also wondered whether omnipotence is in itself a coherent concept. For example, people have for years debated the questions of whether God can create a stone too heavy for himself to lift, or a knot which he cannot himself untie. People discuss whether God's omnipotence is compatible with his being all-loving, since it would be illogical for God to be both able to do evil (because he is able to do absolutely everything), and unable to do evil (because he is perfectly loving) at the same time.

To think about

Could God make a promise, and then break it?
Could God undo an event which has already happened, to change the course of history?

There are many passages in the Bible which support the view that God is omnipotent. For example, in the book of Genesis there is the story of Abraham and his wife Sarah, who showed kindness and hospitality to three strangers, bringing them water and preparing a meal for them to refresh them before they went on their way. As a reward, God told Abraham that he and Sarah would have the son they had always longed for – even though Sarah was well past child-bearing age. The idea was so ridiculous to her that she could not help laughing:

Then the Lord said, 'I will surely return to you about this time next year, and Sarah your wife will have a son'. Now Sarah was listening at the entrance to the tent, which was behind him. Abraham and Sarah were already old and well advanced in years, and Sarah was past the age of childbearing. So Sarah laughed to herself as she thought, 'After I am worn out and my master is old, will I now have this pleasure?' Then the Lord said to Abraham, 'Why did Sarah laugh and say, "Will I really have a child, now that I am old?" Is anything too hard for the Lord? I will return to you at the appointed time next year and Sarah will have a son.' Sarah was afraid, so she lied and said, 'I did not laugh'. But he said, 'Yes, you did laugh'. (Genesis 18:10–15)

There is a similar story in Luke's Gospel, where Mary the mother of Jesus hears from the angel that her cousin Elizabeth is pregnant with John the Baptist, despite the fact that Elizabeth, like Sarah, has passed the menopause and has never been able to have children: 'Even Elizabeth your relative is going to have a child in her old age, and she who was said to be barren is in her sixth month. For nothing is impossible with God' (Luke 1:36–37).

Even miracles which go against the laws of nature are within the powers of God. In the Abraham story, God asks a rhetorical question 'Is anything too hard for the Lord?', implying that God can do anything and everything that he wants to. It is this idea of 'everything that he wants to' that has given many Christian thinkers a way of solving the difficulties of God's omnipotence: if God is capable of doing anything that he wants to do, then he is omnipotent – but there are things which God would never want to do because they are against his nature, such as breaking the laws of logic, failing or doing something unjust.

In the New Testament, God's omnipotence is declared by Jesus in the context of the story of the rich young ruler:

Then Jesus said to his disciples, 'I tell you the truth, it is hard for a rich man to enter the kingdom of heaven. Again I tell you, it is easier for a camel to go through the eye of a needle than for a rich man to enter the kingdom of God.' When the disciples heard this, they were greatly astonished and asked, 'Who then can be saved?' Jesus looked at them and said, 'With man this is impossible, but with God all things are possible.' (Matthew 19:23–26)

Christian theologians have taken the view that if God did not have supreme power, he would not be able to do the things that are necessary for human salvation. Unless God had omnipotence, he would not be able to carry out his plans for the universe; he would not be able to save people from their sins; he would not be able to resurrect people from death; he would not be able to give them eternal life in heaven. Both Anselm and Descartes depended on this understanding of God when they formed their ontological arguments, claiming that God is 'that than which nothing greater can be conceived' (Anselm), and that God has all the perfections (including perfect power). If God were anything less than omnipotent, then we would be able to conceive of a greater, more perfect and more powerful being; so God, by definition, must be omnipotent.

When Descartes explored what it meant for God to be perfectly powerful, he therefore came to the conclusion that God can do absolutely anything, even that which is logically impossible. God is the source of logic and can therefore suspend logic or replace it whenever he wants to.

Could God create a rock so heavy that he could not lift it?

However, most scholars have believed that this kind of view turns God into an unpredictable and arbitrary tyrant, who might do anything (and therefore cannot be relied upon). If God is really all-powerful in the sense that he can do anything at all, then God has to be capable of doing evil, of being unforgiving, of turning against us, and of failing. He has to be capable of being self-contradictory.

The problem of whether God is or is not capable of doing evil, for example, could be answered by saying yes, admittedly it is contradictory that God should be both capable of evil because of his omnipotence, and incapable because of his love. However, because God is omnipotent, he can get around that logical problem (even if we, as humans without omnipotence, cannot see how). For some people, it is enough to accept that the human mind cannot comprehend the omnipotence of God; but for others, this kind of approach is just dodging the question, and is nothing more than a refusal to admit that religious belief does not make sense.

Descartes' view creates difficulties for theodicy. The theodicies which have been put forward by most Christian thinkers suggest that God could not act in any other way than the way he does, without depriving us of our free will; suffering is a price which has to be paid for us to make free choices and be autonomous moral agents. However, if Descartes is correct and God is capable of suspending the laws of logic to allow us to have free will without the consequent evil, then the existence of evil in the world becomes something which God could change if he wanted to, but which he just chooses to inflict on us even though there is no justification for it.

Could God prevent war without compromising human free will? If not, then is God still omnipotent?

To think about

Does this qualified view of the nature of God's omnipotence mean that God still meets Anselm's definition of 'that than which nothing greater can be conceived'?

Thomas Aquinas argued that God is completely omnipotent in being in charge of the whole world, creating it and keeping it in existence, and with everything in the world dependent on God for its existence. Aquinas said that God is omnipotent because 'he can do everything that is absolutely possible', qualified by saying that 'everything that does not imply a contradiction is among those possibilities in respect of which God is called omnipotent'.

From this, then, it follows that God cannot do anything which is inconsistent with his nature, because that would imply a contradiction. God is incorporeal (has no body) for example, and therefore cannot swim, or die, or become tired. God is perfectly good, and therefore cannot deceive, or do any other form of evil.

Peter Vardy, in *The Puzzle of Evil*, suggests that God's omnipotence is much more limited than many Christians have previously suggested. God is not in control of the whole of history, able to move anything around like pieces on a chessboard, Vardy argues, and it is wrong to suggest that everything which happens is because of the will of God.

Vardy suggests that God created the universe in such a way that his ability to act is necessarily limited. The whole of the universe is finely tuned in such a way that if God acted in any different way, everything would not be able to exist in the way that it does. He argues that the universe is perfectly suited for the existence of free, rational human beings, and that in order for it to remain this way, God's omnipotence has to be very much limited. However, this limitation is self-imposed. God chose to create the universe in this way, knowing what it would mean, and therefore it is still right to call God omnipotent because nothing limits his power except when he chooses.

Vardy concludes:

To call God Almighty, therefore, is to recognise the ultimate dependence of the universe and all things within it on God. It is to recognise God's creative and sustaining power. However, it specifically does not mean that God has total power to do anything he wishes. God is limited by the universe he has chosen to create. … This limitation does not, however, lessen God in any significant way. It is rather a recognition of God's wish to create a universe in which human beings can be brought into a loving relationship with him. (The Puzzle of Evil, Fount, 1999)

John Macquarrie, in *Principles of Christian Theology* (SCM Press, 1966) makes a similar point. He also emphasises the need for believers to remember that when they speak of the power of God, they are using analogy, and should understand that God's power is very different from our own; following Aquinas, he argues that there will always be aspects of God's nature that remain unknowable to us. Even if we can understand them partially, and express them partially with the use of analogy, we should nevertheless bear in mind that God's omnipotence is something we have difficulty comp-rehending, which is only to be expected, given that we have small fallible human minds whereas God is God.

Like Vardy and Aquinas before him, Macquarrie also emphasises that any limitations on God's omnipotence are self-imposed. God is not constrained by logic, nor by the physical world, nor by the actions of human beings, but is constrained in his omnipotence merely because he chooses to limit his own power out of love for humanity. This is an idea which has been explored by Christian theologians, particularly in the context of Christology (understanding the nature of Christ). In answer to the puzzle of how Jesus could have been the Son of God, given that Jesus did not always display God's attribute of omnipotence, theologians have developed a doctrine known as kenosis. The doctrine is based on a passage from the letter to the Philippians, where the writer encourages his readers to imitate Christ's humility:

Your attitude should be the same as that of Christ Jesus:

Who, being in very nature God,
did not consider equality with God something to be grasped,
but made himself nothing,
aking the very nature of a servant,
being made in human likeness.
And being found in appearance as a man,
he humbled himself

Key terms

atemporal – eternal, outside the constraints of time.

sempiternal – everlasting, moving along the same timeline that we do.

and became obedient to death —
even death on a cross! (Philippians 2:5–8)

According to the doctrine of kenosis, God 'emptied himself' of his own omnipotence in order to come to earth as a man. It was a deliberate choice made by God for the benefit of humanity, to put limitations on his own powers so the people could make a free choice.

Most scholars, therefore, have qualified the idea of God's omnipotence, and have concluded that God's omnipotence means being able to do that which is logically possible and within the nature of God. In this understanding of omnipotence, God could not do evil, because it is not in his nature. He could not give us free will without the existence of evil, because it is not logically possible.

Practice exam question

'If God is omnipotent, then he must be able to do absolutely anything.' Discuss.

This is a straightforward question. You need to be able to discuss the nature of omnipotence, and what it might mean when applied to God. A good answer would probably include the views of Descartes, and also of other thinkers who have rejected Descartes' view in favour of a more modified understanding of omnipotence. Aim for a structured argument with a clear distinction between different points of view.

The eternity of God

What does it mean to say that God is eternal? There are two main views:

1 One view, which is the one most commonly adopted by classical theologians, is that God is timeless. In other words, God is outside time, and is not bound by time; God is the creator of time. God is described as atemporal.

2 The other view is that God is everlasting. In other words, it is the belief that God moves along the same timeline that we do but never begins or ends. The past is past for God as well as for us, and past events are fixed for God just as they are for us – the future is unknown to us and is also, to some extent at least, unknown to God because it has not happened yet. In this view of God, he is described as sempiternal.

Is God outside time, or does he move along the same timeline that we do?

Our understanding of what it means for God to be eternal is important, because it affects many other ideas about the attributes of God. It affects ideas such as:

• omniscience (can God know with certainty the details of events which have not yet happened?)
• the problem of evil (can God see the whole picture from the beginning, in which case can he be at least partly blamed for things being the way that they are?)
• omnipotence (can God change the past, and undo events which have already happened, or is that beyond his power?).

Questions of the relationship between God and time also raise questions connected with prayer. If God is unchanging, and knows with perfect certainty what will happen in the future, is there any point in praying except for the psychological benefit to the worshipper? However, if prayer can change God's mind, so that he ends up acting differently from the way he might have acted without the prayers, then is God really a perfect being 'than which nothing greater can be conceived'? Perhaps we could conceive of a more perfect being, one who knew from all time the wisest course of action to take, and who is unchanging.

If God exists eternally, outside time, is there any point in praying about worldly events?

Key term

immutable – incapable of change.

The view that God is timeless (atemporal)

This is the view that has been the more popular among Christian thinkers, and has been held by, for example, Anselm, Augustine, Boethius, Aquinas, and Schleiermacher. It is the idea that God exists outside time, and can see the past, the present and the future, all with perfect knowledge. Time, it is argued, is an aspect of the created world, like space, and God is in control of it. God is not bound by space, in the Christian view; he can be and is everywhere at once. In the same kind of way, he is not bound by time but exists in every part of history and in every part of the future while being present in the world today.

The view is popular because it shows that God is not limited. As an aspect of the created world, time is something introduced by God rather than something to which God is subject. God's omnipotence is not threatened if God is not bound by the constraints of time – perhaps a God who could not know the future would be less powerful than one who could. It is a view which also allows that God is immutable (unchangeable), which is argued by some thinkers to be necessary if God is also perfect.

People who do not like the idea of God being everlasting rather than eternal argue that if God were bound by time, then he would be much more limited. He would not know what the outcomes of actions might be; he would have to wait and see how events turned out, before he decided what to do next. There might be times when God's plans were thwarted because of unforeseen difficulties, and then God would have to resort to a different plan. His omnipotence and omniscience are reduced to a point where God can hardly be called *all*-powerful and *all*-knowing. A God who was sempiternal rather than atemporal would not meet Anselm's definition of 'that than which nothing greater can be conceived', because we would be able to conceive of a greater being than one who was constrained by having to exist within time.

> ## To think about
>
> Do you agree that a God who exists outside time would be a greater being than one who exists within time?

Those who defend the view that God is outside time argue that other concepts of God's relationship with time do not recognise the uniqueness of God. God can bring things about in time, and cause changes in people without being changed himself, because God is not a person in the same way that we are. There are things which are possible for God, because of the unique nature of his existence, even if we may not be able to see how they could be possible from within our limited understanding.

The view that God is everlasting

Other people have raised objections to the view that God is timeless, saying that it creates more problems than it resolves. It has been argued that if God is timeless, and therefore immutable, then God cannot be a person, or be said to have a 'life' – this view has been expressed by, for example, Nelson Pike and Richard Swinburne. A person with a life has to be changeable, it is argued, in order to have relationships and respond to people according to what they do. A timeless God would not be able to love, because a timeless God is immutable and therefore is not affected by anything. This view that God can be affected is associated with 'process theologians' such as Charles Hartshorne and Jürgen Moltmann.

To think about

Would it be possible to have a relationship with someone who was always exactly the same, no matter what you did or how you were feeling?

Their argument is that love (even unconditional love which is not because of our deserving but because of the nature of God) cannot be compatible with immutability. A loving being responds to the object of his or her love. If the loved one is feeling happy, the one who loves shares in that happiness; if the loved one suffers, then the one who loves feels pain too. But these changes – sometimes happy, sometimes sad – happen within time, as a process and a sequence of events. Therefore God has to exist within time, so that God is able to respond to us with love. If there is a living God, who has relationships with people as individuals, then God cannot also be timeless, it is argued.

Richard Swinburne writes that the view of a timeless God contradicts the Bible:

> If God had thus fixed his intentions 'from all eternity' he would be a very lifeless thing; not a person who reacts to men with sympathy or anger, pardon or chastening because he chooses to there and then. Yet ... the God of the Old Testament, in which Judaism, Islam and Christianity have their roots, is a God in continual interaction with men, moved by men as they speak to him, his action being more often in no way decided in advance. We should note, further, that if God did not change at all, he would not think now of this, now of that. His thoughts would be one thought which lasted for ever. (The Coherence of Theism, Oxford University Press, 1977)

Swinburne argues that the view of a God outside time is one which is not biblical, but which has permeated Christian thought first through the influence of the ancient

Greeks, and then promoted by Thomas Aquinas. Swinburne does not see why a perfect being should have to be changeless; it was Plato who planted the idea in Western minds that a world of unchanging and unchangeable concepts was inevitably more perfect than the changing world, but we do not have to accept Plato's ideas.

In the Bible, Swinburne argues, God does not have fixed purposes for all eternity. He does not intend for all time that something should happen on a particular day and then remain unchanged. In contrast, God interacts with people, and God's decisions about what will happen may change, because of the ongoing process of his relationship with individuals. A biblical example which might support Swinburne's view is the story in Isaiah of King Hezekiah's illness:

> *In those days Hezekiah became ill and was at the point of death. The prophet Isaiah son of Amoz went to him and said, 'This is what the Lord says: Put your house in order, because you are going to die; you will not recover'. Hezekiah turned his face to the wall and prayed to the Lord, 'Remember, O Lord, how I have walked before you faithfully and with wholehearted devotion and have done what is good in your eyes'. And Hezekiah wept bitterly.*
>
> *Then the word of the Lord came to Isaiah: 'Go and tell Hezekiah, "This is what the Lord, the God of your father David, says: I have heard your prayer and seen your tears; I will add fifteen years to your life".'* (Isaiah 38:1–5)

Perhaps, then, Swinburne is right; God had been planning to end Hezekiah's life, but was persuaded to change his mind in response to the King's prayer. However, there are also passages where the changelessness of God is emphasised:

> *God is not a man, that he should lie,*
> *nor a son of man, that he should change his mind.*
> *Does he speak and then not act?*
> *Does he promise and not fulfil?* (Numbers 23:19)

In this passage, at least, God does seem to have fixed intentions, which do not change. Unlike humanity, God knows with perfect knowledge what he will do, and has no need to alter his views or intentions.

Augustine considered the question of whether the Bible supports the idea of a God who is atemporal, or a God who is sempiternal, and reached the opposite conclusion from Swinburne. For Augustine, the problem was that God had made the world at a particular point in time, which raised the issue of what God had been doing all the while beforehand, if God moves along the same timeline as we do. Augustine wondered why, if God is everlasting, he picked that particular moment to create the universe, and how God might have been spending his time (because God would have had time, just as we understand it) in the eternity before the universe existed. For Augustine, the biblical account of creation points towards a timeless God, who chooses to create day and night, and chooses to create the seasons, just as described in Genesis, but who transcends notions of 'before' and 'after'.

God as impassible

One attribute that the early founders of Christianity ascribed to God is the view that God is impassible, which means that he is unaffected by anything. In the Roman Catholic tradition, following the ideas expressed by Thomas Aquinas, God cannot be changed by anything outside himself. Just like Aristotle's Prime Mover, which sets things in motion but is itself unaffected by any cause, God cannot be acted upon.

To think about

Why might impassibility be understood as a 'perfection'?

The view that God is impassible has some subtly different understandings. To Origen, one of the early Christian fathers, it meant lacking all emotion, being unperturbed, incapable of being emotionally affected by others and incapable of feeling emotion towards others; and therefore, at one point in his career, Origen concluded that God could not suffer.

Clement of Alexandria, another early Christian teacher, suggested it meant that God could not be distracted from his essential nature: God is single-minded in his purposes. It does not mean that God is uninterested, but that God's will comes entirely from within God and is not affected by any outside influences.

R. S. Franks, in the entry on 'Passibility and impassibility' in the *Encyclopaedia of Religion and Ethics* (T&T Clark, 1999), suggested that impassibility refers to whether God is capable of being acted upon from outside, but need not rule out that God could cause feelings and emotions within himself; so God could still have feelings of love and compassion and forgiveness, but these would be feelings that arose as part of God's own nature, rather than feelings into which God was, in effect, forced by the deeds of his creation.

This classical view of the immutability of God has its origin in Plato's and Aristotle's views of the Ultimate, the Perfect, the Unmoved. For Plato, the 'Form of the Good' was a concept, incapable of being affected by the goodness or otherwise of everything else because it had no personality. For Aristotle, the 'Prime Mover' is first in the chain of cause and effect precisely because it is uncaused – nothing acts upon it, it is unchanged by anything.

Key term

impassible – incapable of suffering pain or harm; unfeeling.

Augustine and Aquinas took up this idea, and have influenced much of Christian thought. According to Augustine, in his book *The City of God*, God is absolutely immutable, completely unchangeable, and cannot be other than he is. This is firmly bound to the idea that God is timeless. Aquinas followed Augustine's view, adding the important point that when we speak of God, we need to recognise that the language we use is analogical and not univocal. This means that any words which we use to describe God cannot be applied directly, because God is not like us. We have to use words from our own experience of the world when we speak, because those are the only words which our language has; words come from a need to express common experience. But God is not like anything else in the world, and so when we use language, according to Aquinas, we have to use analogy, mentally putting the characteristics which we ascribe to God into inverted commas. We might say that God 'moves' in mysterious ways – and when we do, we are using the word 'moves' analogically; we are not saying that God goes from one place to another so that he is not in the former place any more. We might say that God is a 'loving father'; we are not saying that God's love is limited to the kind of love a human is capable of feeling and expressing, nor that God can only do as much for us as a human father could do. Aquinas, then, wanted to point out that some of the philosophical difficulties which people have when trying to understand the attributes of God, arise because we are taking our own language too literally, and failing to take account of the unknowability of God.

The idea that God is outside time, combined with the idea that God does not change, has presented Christian believers with problems. It is suggested that God cannot answer prayer, or be the source of miracles, or interact with people in a personal way at all, if he is changeless and outside time. The immutable, impassible God of classical theism might be seen to be indifferent to creation; whatever happens, however marvellous or tragic, God remains completely unmoved.

When there is a disaster which causes great human suffering, does God feel exactly the same way before, during and after the tragedy?

One of the most influential critics of the idea that God is impassible is Charles Hartshorne. Hartshorne not only makes a reasoned criticism of the idea of God's impassibility, but gives a coherent alternative view of a God who is capable of acting in the world. Hartshorne argues that God cannot be loving if he is at the same time impassible:

> *Love involves sensitivity to the joys and sorrows of others, participation in them – but we cannot infect God with our sufferings (since he is cause of everything and effect of nothing), and our joys can add nothing to the immutable perfection of God's happiness … one can do nothing for God, and our worst sins harm God as little as the finest acts of sainthood can advance him.* (Man's Vision of God and the Logic of Theism, *Shoe String Press, 1983*)

Hartshorne argues that, according to the classical view of the impassibility of God, God cannot enter into any give and take with the world. God is seen to be pure activity, or actuality; he can give, but not take, and remains uninfluenced by the world. Hartshorne concludes that the world could suffer the most enormous tragedies and, in this classical view, God would be completely unaffected, in just the same way that a glass of water remains unaffected by the reading of an eloquent poem. In his books *Divine Relativity* and *The Logic of Perfection*, Hartshorne concludes that if God is impassible, he cannot know us, interact with us, sympathise with us, or hear or respond to our prayers. Hartshorne also argues that an immutable God could not have a purpose which related to a changing world. God is no more of a person than someone dead. Richard Creel, in his summary of the view of Hartshorne, says:

> *If God is impassible, then he is beyond our reach; for all practical purposes, he is dead – and surely one cannot have a personal relationship with a dead person. Just as clearly, such a picture of God is the opposite of the biblical picture of a living, dynamic, responding God.'* (Divine Impassibility, *Cambridge University Press, 1986*)

Nelson Pike argues that where there are relationships, there must be response to the feelings and needs of each other.

Nelson Pike is another modern scholar who has rejected the view that God is impassible. In his book *God and Timelessness* (Wipf & Stock, 2002), in which he considers the philosophical implications of the idea that God exists outside time, Pike argues that the impassibility of God is bound up with the idea that God is timeless, saying:

> *a timeless being could not be affected or prompted by another ... Responses are located in time after that to which they are responses. .... I doubt if one could be emotionally involved with such a person. I don't think one could take him as a friend – or as an enemy. Further, I don't think that a timeless person could be emotionally involved with another. To be emotionally involved, one must be able to respond in some way to the actions or inactions of others. A timeless individual could not respond.*

Pike, Hartshorne, and other scholars such as Moltmann, have been part of the movement in Christian philosophy called process theology (see pages 166–71). This system of thought uses the idea that God is not outside time at all, but present in the world with us, acting and responding, loving, rejoicing and suffering as we do. God does not know the future, but only knows what possibilities there are, and people have real free will.

Defending the view that God is immutable

Aquinas' defence against the criticism of these twentieth-century thinkers would be that God can be both loving and immutable, just because he is God. People cannot be loving and at the same time unchanging; but God is different from us, and things which are not possible for us can still be possible for God. Aquinas drew a distinction between God's nature combined with God's will, which are immutable, and God's activity – God's making a change in other things. Aquinas argued that God's nature, because it is perfect, is unchanging, always love, always perfect goodness. God's will, then, is always the same in that God does not change his mind. He knows perfectly what the good is because he is goodness itself, and he does not change his will because of circumstances which he did not expect. However, God is still capable of having loving relationships, because other things change in relation to God.

Creel, in his book *Divine Impassibility*, also argues that God can be loving as well as immutable. God can know what his own will is, in response to any of an infinite number of possibilities. He does not have to wait until people exercise their free will, then see how they act, and then decide how he will respond to them. Although people have a genuine free will, according to Creel, God can still know what all the possibilities are, and can know in advance what his will is in response to each of those possibilities.

For example, we can decide in advance what we will do tomorrow, depending on the weather. If it is sunny, I will take the children out for a picnic, but if it rains, we will go to the cinema. The weather is still 'free' to 'make up its mind', and the way I act as a result, in response, depends on the weather, but I do not *change my mind*; I know in advance the possibilities, and act according to what I have decided. Creel's argument is that God works in the same kind of way, and therefore can be seen to be immutable while at the same time responding to us, as we live and make decisions according to our free will.

God's will, then, remains immutable, unchanging because of his unchanging nature. God does not have to be changeable in order to love, because God's essence is love; God's love is not caused by anything, God does not love because of our merit but just because God is love, and therefore God can be loving and immutable at the same time. It is only our imperfect version of love which involves change.

Omniscience

What does it mean to say that God is omniscient? Most people understand the omniscience of God to mean that God knows everything; there is nothing that he cannot know. Also, it means that God has no false beliefs, and cannot be mistaken. If God knows something, then that thing is true. So if God is omniscient, God's knowledge includes things which are unavailable to the human mind. God knows, for example, long-forgotten details of history; he knows whether there is life on other planets, in other galaxies; he knows whether there are other universes besides this one. He knows people's secret thoughts even when they are never expressed. He knows how many grains of sand there are in the Sahara.

If God is omniscient, then he knows everything.

However, attributing omniscience to God raises questions. If God knows everything, does this include events in the future as well as those in the past? Does God know, for example, the numbers that will be drawn in next week's national lottery, and does he also know who will buy the winning ticket? Perhaps God does not just know who will win, but has decided who will win, and predetermined which numbers people will choose and which will be drawn.

More significantly for theology is the question of whether God knows in advance all the moral decisions that people will make in their lives. If he does know this (and his knowledge is always true) then it raises the issue of whether people have any real freedom of choice. If God knew yesterday, and a hundred years ago, and in fact from the beginning of time, that I would make a donation of £10 to Oxfam this afternoon – and if God's knowledge is always true, so that he could never be mistaken – then am I really free to do anything other than make that donation? Or, perhaps, does the very fact of God's knowing I will do it prevent me from changing my mind? If I have no other choice than to give the money, then there is no 'moral value' in my donation. I cannot be admired for giving it, as I had no choice but to give it. Similarly, I cannot be blamed for giving a mere £10, as there was no way that I could have had second thoughts and made it £20, if the figure is fixed in God's knowledge at £10.

In Christianity, Judaism and Islam, alongside belief that God is omniscient is the belief that humans are morally responsible for at least some of the actions they perform. It is believed that people have a genuinely free choice about what to do when faced with a moral dilemma. God does not compel them to choose one way rather than another, but leaves it to individuals to decide, independently, what to do in different situations as they arise, which means that they can then be held responsible for their choices. Islam, in particular, stresses that this earthly life is a testing place, where people make choices between right and wrong. Their responses to these choices are judged by Allah, and their place in heaven depends on whether they make the right decisions. There is, then, a firm belief that moral choice is genuinely free, alongside belief in an omniscient God.

Friedrich Schleiermacher argued that there is a possible solution to the problem of whether God's omniscience restricts our freedom. He drew the analogy of the knowledge that close friends have of each other's behaviour, to conclude that God could be omniscient while still allowing people to act freely:

In the same way, we estimate the intimacy between two persons by the foreknowledge one has of the actions of the other, without supposing that in either case, the one or the other's freedom is thereby endangered. So even the divine foreknowledge cannot endanger freedom. (Schleiermacher, The Christian Faith, *trans. W. R. Matthew, 1928)*

His analogy, then, claims that God's knowledge of our actions is rather like the knowledge very close friends have of each other's future behaviour. Perhaps

Schleiermacher is right. If you tell my friend that you plan to travel from A to B, she will immediately start giving you advice about the best route to take and the best time of day to travel. I know that, if I ever mention to her that I am planning to make a journey, she will do this. But does this mean that, by telling her I plan to visit Oxford next week, I am somehow limiting her choice so that she is not free to say anything else but 'If I were you I'd avoid Milton Keynes'?

Schleiermacher would say that the answer was no; because although I 'know' what she will say, I am only making a *reliable guess*. There is the possibility that I could be wrong; something might fall on her head while I'm speaking to her, for example, and she might say 'ouch', or other words to express surprise, instead. She is quite free to do this. There is nothing in my knowledge of what she always says that compels her to say it.

The problem with Schleiermacher's idea is that, unlike the knowledge friends have of each other, God's knowledge is said to be infallible. I could be wrong in guessing what my friend will say, but God cannot be wrong; he never makes mistakes. There is nothing that God knows that could turn out to be untrue. So, if God knows that my friend will give travel advice, does this not make it inevitable that she will do it, so that she could not do anything else? Is her freedom to choose only apparent?

To think about

How would an omniscient God's knowledge of us differ from the knowledge that our close friends have of us?

If our freedom to act morally were only apparent, then there would be serious implications. We would not be able to be held morally responsible for our actions, because we would not have been able to behave in any other way. A genuine freedom of choice is considered by ethicists to be essential as a basis for morality. Kant, for example, argued that without freedom, there can be no moral choices. So, if God's omniscience determines our choices, then God cannot justifiably punish us when we do wrong, nor reward us when we do good.

 Develop your knowledge

Bernhard Schlink's novel *The Reader* (Weidenfeld & Nicholson, 1997) raises the issue of freedom and morality. In it he explores questions of whether people can be condemned for actions they perform in wartime, when they are under threat of death.

The problem for our moral freedom becomes even more acute when belief in God's omniscience is coupled with belief that God intends and creates every individual life, fashioning each person in accordance with his plans. If, for example, you made a robot, and then programmed it to smash a vase with a hammer, you could not then blame the robot for the broken vase – it would be your own fault, because you had done the programming and knew, when you made the robot, what it was going to do. You could have chosen to programme it differently, or not make it at all. So if God not only knows the future with certainty, but knew when he made us exactly what we would choose at every point of our lives, perhaps God can be held responsible for all kinds of evil, including so-called moral evil. There is the added difficulty that God might know, in advance, each person's religious choices. Perhaps God knows from the beginning of time which of us will have faith and which will doubt or disbelieve; perhaps God knows, even before we are born, whether we will end up in heaven or hell, so that there is nothing we can do about it.

If, however, God does not have a clue what we will do, and wondered when he made Pol Pot or Martin Luther King how they would turn out, and was taken aback by the choices they made, then this seems to imply a less than all-powerful God. It suggests that God can be surprised, or can make choices which turn out to have been unwise. God's capabilities seem to be limited.

Did God know, from the beginning of time, exactly what choices Nelson Mandela would make with his life? If so, were any of them real choices?

Some of the answers to the problem of omniscience and freedom depend on our understanding of eternity. If God is timeless, and can see the whole picture, then his omniscience is eternal. He knows the present, the past and the future because he is not confined by these temporal limits.

If, however, God is everlasting, and moves on the same timeline that we do, then he knows the past and the present but cannot know the future, *except that* he understands us so perfectly and knows our conditioning so well, and knows all the contributory factors to our decision making, so that *he will know what we will choose to do as far as this is logically possible.* But our choice remains free, in the same way that my friend can choose what to say next when we talk about travel plans. This is a view taken by Richard Swinburne.

Boethius and *The Consolation of Philosophy*

The sixth-century Christian philosopher Boethius took up the problem of God's omniscience and the effect it might have on our moral freedom. When he wrote his book *The Consolation of Philosophy* he was a prisoner awaiting execution. He had led a life of great ups and downs. He was born in Greece into a renowned family with excellent connections and received a very good education; in his middle years, he held positions of great power in the government, and he had many academic interests. However, it all went wrong when political rivalries led to an accusation of treason, and Boethius was sentenced to death. While in prison, he completed *The Consolation of Philosophy*, and he was executed in 524.

Boethius was worried about the problem of God's omniscience, because it seemed on the surface that if God knows the future, then he is wrong to reward us or punish us for our behaviour; and yet the Bible does teach about divine reward and punishment very clearly.

Boethius' 'consolation of philosophy' discusses questions of God's omniscience.

Thinking 'aloud' in Book V of *The Consolation of Philosophy*, Boethius considers the different possibilities. He asks himself 'How can God foreknow that these things will happen, if they are uncertain?' If God knows that something will happen, when in fact it is uncertain, then God's knowledge is mistaken, and that cannot possibly be. However, if God knows that something might happen, and then again it might not, then it can hardly be called 'knowledge' at all, and it puts God in the position of being no wiser than we are. But if God firmly knows things, then they become inevitable. Things which at the moment seem fair – the reward of the good, and the punishment of the bad – become unfair:

That which is now judged most equitable, the punishment of the wicked and the reward of the good, will be seen to be the most unjust of all; for men are driven to good or evil not by their own will but by the fixed necessity of what is to be.

Boethius reaches the conclusion that he has made a mistake – he is forgetting that God can see things in a different way from the way in which we see them. Humans exist within time. They have pasts which are fixed once they have happened, they have a present which is gone in an instant, and futures which are uncertain. Because the future is uncertain, humans have genuine free will.

However, when God is knowing, he does not have the same constraints in time that we have. God, therefore, does not have a past, present and future, and so 'his knowledge, too, transcends all temporal change and abides in the immediacy of his presence'. God can look down on us, moving along our timelines, 'as though from a lofty peak above them'. God can see us in the present, and also can see us in our pasts, and in our futures, so that he has perfect knowledge of what we will freely choose to do. He does not know what moral choices we will make in advance of our making them because there is no such thing as 'in advance' for God. All events occur simultaneously for God, in his eternal presence.

As God does not know things in advance of them happening, it makes no sense to talk of what God should have known in the past or what God will know in the future. God cannot be accused of a lack of wisdom in not realising that Adam and Eve would disobey him, nor of a lack of morality in allowing evil dictators to be born. God does not know what we will do in the future, because there is no future for God, so we have a genuine free choice and can therefore be rewarded or punished with justice.

To think about

Do you think that Boethius has successfully solved the problem of God's foreknowledge and human freedom?

 ## Develop your knowledge

The Consolation of Philosophy, Book V, by Boethius (trans. V. Watts, Penguin Classics, 1999)
Teach Yourself Philosophy of Religion by Mel Thompson (Teach Yourself, 2003)
An Introduction to the Philosophy of Religion by Brian Davies (Oxford University Press, 1982)

Practice exam question

'If God knows all our moral choices in advance, then we cannot be justly blamed or rewarded for what we do.' Discuss.

This was the issue that preoccupied Boethius, so you should make sure that you mention him in your answer. The question requires an exploration of the idea of God's omniscience and the implications for human moral freedom; there is also the linked issue of whether God is eternal or everlasting, which you should explore. As usual, you should aim to make reference to scholarly work and give evidence of your reading, as well as using specialist vocabulary where appropriate.

God as omnibenevolent

The Christian understanding of God holds unequivocally that God's nature is love. This idea is not just a New Testament concept, but can be seen in the Old Testament too. The Old Testament speaks mainly of God's love for Israel, rather than for particular individuals. The Hebrew word used is *hesed*. God's love is not caused by any special worth in its object. God did not choose to love Israel because Israel had especially loveable qualities; Israel has special worth because of God's love: 'The Lord did not set his affection on you and choose you because you were more numerous than other peoples, for you were the fewest of all peoples' (Deuteronomy 7:7). God's love, like God's existence, has no cause. It is not brought into being by something else but is part of the nature of God from the start.

Love as an attribute of God is closely connected to ideas about God's goodness and righteousness.

In the Bible, God's love is compared with the love of a human parent, full of tenderness for the child and profoundly hurt when the child rejects the love shown:

> *When Israel was a child, I loved him,*
> *and out of Egypt I called my son.*
> *But the more I called Israel,*
> *the further they went from me.*
> *They sacrificed to the Baals*
> *and they burned incense to images.*
> *It was I who taught Ephraim to walk,*
> *taking them by the arms;*
> *but they did not realize*
> *it was I who healed them.* (Hosea 11:1–3)

The prophet Hosea, living in the eighth century BCE, was given the unenviable task of forming a marriage which was to work as a symbol of God's love for Israel. Hosea was told to marry Gomer, a woman known to be adulterous, and this marriage became a kind of visual aid for Hosea as he taught the people about their behaviour and its consequences. Gomer was repeatedly unfaithful to Hosea, just as Israel was repeatedly unfaithful to God – but Hosea loved her, and took her back even though he knew she would probably repeat her behaviour. In the same way, Israel is tempted away from God by the attractions of other religions and by a secular lifestyle, and God, because of his love for Israel, is hurt and angry, determined to punish the people even though he wants to be able to restore their loving relationship:

Woe to them, because they have strayed from me!
Destruction to them, because they have rebelled against me!
I long to redeem them
but they speak lies against me. (Hosea 7:13)

This understanding of the love of God has created some philosophical problems for Christians. Does God's love come and go, or does it stay the same? Can God be affected, and be hurt, and suffer, or does this imply a limitation to his omnipotence? Does God remain unchanging? If God loves his people unconditionally, and is also omnipotent, then why does he not stop them from doing the things which hurt him?

Although the love of God illustrated by Hosea appears to be part of a stormy relationship, in the Psalms, the emphasis is on the reliability of the love of God:

… steadfast love belongs to you, O Lord. (Psalm 62:12)

Because your steadfast love is better than life, my lips will praise you. (Psalm 63:3)

O give thanks to the Lord, for he is good; his steadfast love endures forever! (Psalm 118:1)

In the Old Testament there is a strong theme of the love which the people should have for God, and for each other as a result of loving God. It is taken for granted that God should be obeyed and that his laws are right. Showing loving concern for each other's welfare is the proper response to the love that God has shown for them. When the Hebrew people have been rescued from slavery in Egypt, have been led to Mount Sinai and are about to be given the ten commandments, they are reminded that they have this special role because of the love that God has shown for them:

You yourselves have seen what I did to Egypt, and how I carried you on eagles' wings and brought you to myself. Now if you obey me fully and keep my covenant, then out of all nations you will be my treasured possession. Although the whole earth is mine, you will be for me a kingdom of priests and a holy nation. (Exodus 19:4–6)

The love shown to them by God results in heavy responsibilities. They are to become a kingdom of priests, setting an example for the rest of the world: a holy nation, set apart because of their relationship with God. God's love seeks moral fellowship with Israel. The love of God cannot be separated from righteousness. It is not sentimental love, and it goes with a demand that the people should keep the commandments.

God's love is expressed through judgement and forgiveness; his punishment of sin is precisely because of his love. The best known example comes from the book of the prophet Amos. The people were expecting to hear that although God would punish their neighbours, they would be protected because they were God's holy nation. But no. God's special love for Israel meant that they were to be singled out for punishment: 'For you alone have I cared among all the nations of the world; therefore will I punish you for all your iniquities' (Amos 3:2).

Some Jewish post-Holocaust theologians have built on this idea, claiming that the Jews were singled out for God's punishment during the twentieth century precisely because they are his chosen people. However, this view has not been attractive to everyone, as it implies that the atrocities of the Holocaust were God's own doing, and that God wanted them to happen.

In the New Testament, the word used for love is *agape*, which contrasts with other Greek words for love. Agape has the connotations of showing love through action, rather than love being just a feeling or emotion. In the first letter of John, the writer summarises Christian understanding of the love of God. He equates love with God. God is the source of love, and demonstrated his love by becoming incarnate in Jesus, giving people the opportunity to see God through seeing his love for the world. The source of all human love is God, and the love of God requires that people reciprocate by showing love for each other:

Dear friends, let us love one another, for love comes from God. Everyone who loves has been born of God and knows God. Whoever does not love does not know God, because God is love. This is how God showed his love among us: He sent his one and only Son into the world that we might live through him. (1 John 4: 7–9)

In the New Testament, the theme of God's love is strongly linked with concepts of salvation, reconciliation and redemption. The life and especially the suffering and death of Christ is seen as proof of the love of God.

In the Christian view, then, God is equated with love; any love shown by humans for each other is a reflection of God. God is not only love in the Platonic sense of being the 'Ideal' love; God's love involves activity, shown supremely in the sacrifice and death of Christ. This is taken as evidence of the love of God.

The Christian understanding of the love of God is that it is perfect love. It is unconditional (*agape*); it is everlasting; and it is personal to each individual, as well as to humanity as a whole: '… even the hairs of your head are all counted. So do not be afraid; you are of more value than many sparrows' (Matthew 10:30). Paul, in his letter to the Corinthians, counts love as the greatest of the three things that last for ever. He explains the importance of love underpinning everything else that Christians do, and he explains how the love of God will be revealed in the way that people treat each other:

> *If I speak in the tongues of men and of angels, but have not love, I am only a resounding gong or a clanging cymbal. If I have the gift of prophecy and can fathom all mysteries and all knowledge, and if I have a faith that can move mountains, but have not love, I am nothing. If I give all I possess to the poor and surrender my body to the flames, but have not love, I gain nothing.*
> *Love is patient, love is kind. It does not envy, it does not boast, it is not proud. It is not rude, it is not self-seeking, it is not easily angered, it keeps no record of wrongs. Love does not delight in evil but rejoices with the truth. It always protects, always trusts, always hopes, always perseveres.*
> *Love never fails.* (1 Corinthians 13:1–8)

The existence of evil and suffering in the world appear to some people (such as Hume and J. S. Mill) to contradict the idea that there is an all-loving, all-powerful God.

Aquinas argued that we need to remember that when we speak of the love of God, we are using analogy; we are talking of a love which is like ours in some respects, but we have to bear in mind that God is infinitely greater than us and that we can only understand a tiny proportion of divine love (see page 215).

The usual Christian view is that people cannot fully understand the love of God. We experience it whenever we experience love, because all love comes from God, but we do not know why God acts in the ways he does. However, for many Christians, the key is that God does not leave us to suffer on our own. Christians believe that in Christ, God came to earth in human form and suffered with us. He is with us in our pain, even if we do not understand the reasons for it. This is the theme of Jürgen Moltmann's book *The Crucified God*, arguing (along with other process theologians) that Christianity shows that God does not just sit outside time being perfect and immutable; he gets involved with us and shares the pains of human existence to the extent of suffering death by torture. In the Christian understanding, we may not understand the love of God or the reasons why people suffer, but we can still be confident of God's love and confident of a life after death when all will be made plain:

For now we see in a mirror, dimly, but then we will see face to face. Now I know only in part; then I will know fully, even as I have been fully known. And now faith, hope and love abide, these three; and the greatest of these is love. (1 Corinthians 13:12–13)

Life after death

The world is like a picture with a golden background, and we the figures in the picture. Until you step off the plane of the picture into the large dimensions of death you cannot see the gold. (C. S. Lewis, The Problem of Pain, *Geoffrey Bles, 1940)*

One of the central teachings of Christianity, and of many other religions, is that we will in some sense survive death – that death is not the end of life, but merely a stage through which we shall pass. Paul, in his letter to the Corinthians, speaks with absolute certainty of life after death, persuading the first Christians that their struggle against persecution was worth fighting because, even if they were killed, they would continue in the next life:

For the perishable must clothe itself with the imperishable, and the mortal with immortality. When the perishable has been clothed with the imperishable, and the mortal with immortality, then the saying that is written will come true: 'Death has been swallowed up in victory. Where, O death, is your victory? Where, O death, is your sting?' (1 Corinthians 15:53–5)

The resurrection of Jesus is at the core of traditional Christian doctrine. Christians believe that after Jesus was crucified, he rose again back to life and could be seen walking around and heard talking to people – he could even be touched. They believe that the resurrection of Jesus shows that life after death is not only possible but certain.

For Muslims, too, life after death is a certainty, because it is promised in the Qur'an. This life is understood to be a preparation for the afterlife, when people will be judged. Their bodies will be resurrected from the graves, and there will be reward for believers and punishment for unbelievers.

In Hinduism, Buddhism and Sikhism, life after death is seen in a different way.

Muslims believe that this earthly life is a time of preparation and testing for the afterlife.

These religions teach that people do not have just one life on this earth, but many. When they die, they are reborn into the world as another human being (or in some beliefs, as an animal), and they have many opportunities to develop spiritually, to rid themselves of greed and eventually to escape the cycle of birth and death.

To think about

What do you think happens after people die? Do they simply stop existing, or do they live on after death in some way? How would you justify your beliefs about the existence or absence of life after death?

Yet the concept of life after death is immediately problematic. Life and death are usually considered to be mutually exclusive states. Living things, according to biologists, exhibit certain characteristics: they feed, move, respire, grow, excrete, reproduce and are sensitive. Non-living things lack these characteristics, and when something which was alive no longer has the ability to do these things, it is dead, there is no more life in it. There does not seem to be the possibility of being dead but also being alive.

Antony Flew, for example, in his book *Merely Mortal: Can You Survive Your Own Death?* (Prometheus, 2001) argued:

In the ordinary, everyday understanding of the words involved, to say that some-one survived death is to contradict yourself; while to assert that all of us live forever is to assert a manifest falsehood, the flat contrary of a universal truth: namely, the truth that all human beings are mortal. For when, after some disaster, the 'dead' and the 'survivors' have both been listed, what logical space remains for a third category?

Flew and others argue that the whole idea of life after death, whether it is reincarnation or resurrection, is unfalsifiable and therefore devoid of any real content. Logical positivists (see pages 227–31) in general hold this view – life after death is impossible to test empirically (using the senses), it can neither be verified nor falsified, and is therefore not a suitable subject for scientific investigation. Not only is survival of death incapable of being tested, it is a totally incoherent concept. Religious believers, then, when faced with philosophical questions about life after death, have to be able to show that it makes coherent sense as a concept, as well as showing that it is not unreasonable for people to believe that it happens.

There are various different ways in which we might be believed to 'live on' after our deaths. We could be said to live on through other people's memories of us, and through work we have produced and left behind, for example. Not many people would disagree that this happens, although few would want to go as far as to call it 'life after death'. We could also be said to live on through our descendants, by passing on our genes as a contribution to the world 'gene pool'; but this too is not the kind of living after death that religious believers mean us to understand. 'Life after death' as a religious belief involves the survival of the individual as a person, able to do at least some of the things that a person does, and in a conscious way.

Kant and life after death

Immanuel Kant (1724–1804) believed that life after death is necessary for moral reasons. According to Kant, we all have an innate sense that we should behave morally – not because doing good will bring us benefits and rewards, but simply because doing good is the right thing to do. He argued that we share a sense that we should strive to achieve 'the highest good', or the *summum bonum*. The *summum bonum* is not just a state of virtue, but is a state where goodness is rewarded with happiness – we all feel, according to Kant, that this is the ideal and something which we ought to work towards.

From these premises, Kant went on to argue that if we feel we ought to strive to achieve the *summum bonum*, then it must also be possible. 'Ought' implies 'can' – we only feel we ought to do those things which are actually within our power. So we might feel that we ought to save water by not leaving taps running unnecessarily and by taking showers instead of baths, and we feel we ought to do this because these are things we can do. We do not, however, feel that we ought to provide clean, safe, plentiful water for the planet, because this is beyond our reach as individuals. If, then, we feel that we ought to aim for the *summum bonum*, where goodness is rewarded with happiness (although the reward must never be the motivation for the good acts), then this in Kant's view must mean that we can achieve it.

Key term

postulate – to assume the existence of something, for the purposes of reasoning.

Kant argued that our sense of justice requires that there should be life after death.

However, clearly, in this life goodness is not always rewarded with happiness. Some people lead morally good lives, devote themselves to the service of others and try to deal fairly and honestly with everyone they meet and yet they never make very much money, or they suffer tragedies. Others are selfish, greedy and prosperous. Kant came to the conclusion that we therefore have to postulate the existence of God, and the existence of an afterlife, in order to achieve justice. Without God, and without an afterlife, our sense that we ought to be good would be futile.

Critics of Kant's argument point out, of course, that there is no reason to assume there is any justice. We might have a strong sense that life should be fair, the good should be rewarded and the wicked should be punished, but our sense that it ought to be so is not evidence that it is so. Our sense that we ought to be good might very well be futile. It might also be argued that, whatever life after death is like, it cannot compensate for the unfairness of this life.

To think about

Do you think that life after death could solve the problem of life's unfairness? What sort of afterlife would the parents of a murdered child need to have, to compensate for their suffering?

What is the soul?

Belief in life after death suggests a particular understanding of the relation between the 'person', or the 'essential self', and the body. The body is seen as a kind of vehicle which the person lives in, and which the person needs in order to be able to continue. Not all thinkers, however, have agreed about this relationship between the 'person' and the body, and nor have they agreed on what it is that identifies a person. The concept of the 'soul' has been understood in a variety of different ways throughout history, and even today there is no definite agreement on the nature of the soul and the ways in which it relates to other aspects of the human person.

Do people have souls? The answer to this, of course, is dependent on our understanding of what the soul is. Thinkers in all cultural contexts have struggled with this question, asking themselves exactly what it is that defines a 'person'. What makes me *this* individual, rather than another? Am I no more than a mixture of chemical elements, as the materialist would claim, or do I have some kind of extra 'essential nature'?

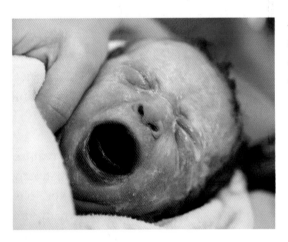

Is it possible to explain humanity, and all other life forms, purely in terms of physical elements? Or does each individual have an essential 'self' or 'soul'?

John Locke (1632–1704) raised the problem of what it is that makes us individuals. He presented a story of a prince and a cobbler, to illustrate his point. The story says that once a cobbler and a prince woke up to find themselves in each other's bodies. The cobbler was anxious to explain that he had not broken into the palace, but that he had no idea how he got there – but because he had the appearance of the prince, no one understood what his problem was. The prince, waking up in the cobbler's body, was angry with the cobbler's wife in bed beside him, thinking that she had kidnapped him, and demanded to be returned to the palace. Locke raised the question: which person was which? Is it the mind that makes the individual, or the body? What makes us what we are? Is it our appearance, our memories, our individual personality traits, or is it something else?

The problems raised by Locke have implications for theories of resurrection and of reincarnation. For many, saying that one person who has died is identical with another person in a different body is incoherent.

Discussion of the relation between the mind and the soul is also unresolved. We talk about someone having, or being, 'a good soul' but we mean something very different from what we mean when we say someone has 'a good mind'. Most theists believe that people have souls, even when their minds have been almost completely destroyed through accident or old age; yet the soul is described as the part of a person which develops a relationship with God, the part which is conscious and which makes moral decisions. It can be difficult to see how this could be possible for someone with very little mental awareness. When people talk about life after death, they almost invariably refer to mental abilities such as memory as well as moral capabilities, suggesting that the mind and the soul are inextricably linked.

In some religions, such as Christianity and Judaism, the soul and the body are not separate, but are different aspects of a single entity. In other religions, such as Hinduism, the soul is 'more real' than the body – the person is, essentially, the soul, and the body is simply the physical vehicle which the soul inhabits. Buddhism, in contrast, teaches that there is no such thing as a soul, and that people's sense of themselves as having a unique immortal essence is based on illusion.

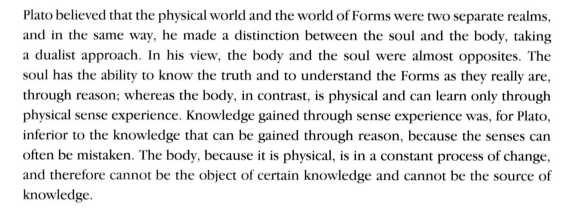

Plato's understanding of the soul

Plato believed that the physical world and the world of Forms were two separate realms, and in the same way, he made a distinction between the soul and the body, taking a dualist approach. In his view, the body and the soul were almost opposites. The soul has the ability to know the truth and to understand the Forms as they really are, through reason; whereas the body, in contrast, is physical and can learn only through physical sense experience. Knowledge gained through sense experience was, for Plato, inferior to the knowledge that can be gained through reason, because the senses can often be mistaken. The body, because it is physical, is in a constant process of change, and therefore cannot be the object of certain knowledge and cannot be the source of knowledge.

The soul, however, is capable of certain knowledge. Plato deduced that this must mean that the soul is unchanging – and therefore, it must be immortal, not only existing after death but also pre-existing before birth.

Plato's views about the soul developed during the course of his life, so that for the modern reader, it can be difficult to pin down exactly what he meant.

Plato thought that people's inner, mental life was the most important thing about them. This inner life included their hopes, their motives, their opinions and emotions. He gave the name psyche to this inner life, making a distinction between it and the physical body, which was imperfect because it was always changing, like the rest of the physical world. The psyche, or soul, was the 'real' part of the person, somehow temporarily attached to a physical body but immortal and destined to live on after death.

The soul was seen as a kind of guiding force, helping the mind and the body to work together in the same direction for the benefit of the individual. According to Plato, the soul was made up of three distinct elements:

• reason
• emotion
• appetite.

These, in Plato's view, are the three basic instincts which animate us and inspire us into action. Reason is the highest, most superior of the three elements, followed by emotion, with appetite as the most inferior. Reason allows us to gain knowledge, to distinguish right from wrong, and to understand the Forms. Emotion allows us to love, and inspires us to acts of courage, but if it is left unchecked, we can become reckless and conceited. Appetites are necessary to encourage us to look after the physical needs of our bodies, but again, if left unchecked, can cause us to drift into lives of hedonism and become little better than animals.

Each of the three elements of the soul plays a part in the balance of the individual. Plato gave the analogy of a charioteer guiding two horses to show how he thought the three different strands worked together. Reason is the charioteer, the guiding force with the sense of purpose. It keeps the other two 'horses', emotion and appetite, in check, making sure that they are heading in the same direction and are not distracted. Plato thought a person should always allow reason and logic to take the lead, rather than letting the demands of emotion or appetites obscure wisdom.

To think about

Do you think there are any times when decisions should be based largely on emotion or appetite, rather than reason?

Plato thought that the soul worked as a charioteer, allowing reason to keep the emotions and the appetites in check.

Plato believed that the soul survived the death of the body; he also believed that the soul lived before physical birth too, so that when we learn things, we are actually remembering them rather than encountering them for the first time. What we understand as intuition was, for Plato, memory. In the soul's life before birth, it lives in the world of Forms and gains true knowledge of ideals and of how things really are, so that when in this life we feel we intuitively know what is good or just or beautiful, it is really because we have already encountered these qualities in their ideal form before birth.

In his work *Phaedo*, Plato puts into the mouth of Socrates his beliefs about the immortality of the soul. Plato wanted to show that Socrates had not failed in his mission to educate people, even though he had been executed, because his soul would continue to immortality after death. It would be released from the body and able to renew its contemplation of the Form of the Good. Socrates argues that the soul continues to live on in a state where it still has thought and intelligence, and after death, it is undisturbed by the distractions of constant bodily demands so that it can reach its highest state. Socrates also argues that the soul necessarily must continue in living, because life is the essence of what a soul is. The soul animates the person by giving it life; so if a soul is a life-giving essence, then it was obvious (to Socrates and Plato) that it must always have life.

Cebes, the character in dialogue with Socrates in the *Phaedo*, is not entirely convinced and asks for an explanation to support belief in the immortality of the soul. Cebes suggests that perhaps, at the point of death, the soul simply dissolves and disperses 'like breath or smoke'. In response, Plato (through the mouthpiece of Socrates) presents arguments to justify the view that the soul is immortal. He argues that every quality comes into being from its own opposite, or at least depends on its opposite to have any existence at all. Something is 'big' because there are smaller things; something else is 'bright' because there are duller things; something else again is 'hot' because there are colder things. Qualities, then, depend on their status relative to each other. Plato uses this notion to draw the conclusion that therefore life comes from death, and death comes from life, in an endless chain of birth, death and rebirth.

Plato also uses an argument from knowledge to support his belief in the immortality of the soul. In the dialogue *Meno*, a slave-boy with no education is given a geometry puzzle to solve. Through questioning, the boy is able to work out the answer to the problem, which (to Plato) illustrated that the boy must have been using knowledge he already had, from before birth. Plato thought that our intuitions were evidence of knowledge attained before birth. This, to Plato, was evidence that our souls had once lived in the world of perfect Forms.

To think about

How might we explain sudden flashes of intuition, if they are not evidence of having lived before in the world of Forms?

The Myth of Er

At the end of Plato's *Republic*, Plato introduces a story known as the Myth of Er, in which he raises some ideas about life after death. In the story, told by Socrates of course, a soldier called Er died on the battlefield. At least, he appeared to die, but ten days later, when it was safe for the bodies to be recovered for funerals, there was no sign that Er's body had decomposed at all. On the twelfth day, when Er's body had been placed on the funeral pyre, he suddenly came back to life, and was able to tell everyone all that he had experienced of the afterlife.

He told them that, once he had died, he set out on a journey in which he encountered judges who rewarded and punished the souls of those who had died. Those who had lived morally good lives went upward into a place where they were rewarded for all their good deeds; those who had been immoral were punished with pain equal to ten times the amount of pain they had inflicted on earth. Some had committed crimes so bad that they could never be released from underground punishment. Er also witnessed the way in which souls choose for themselves a new life on earth, either animal or human, before being reborn. Sometimes, those who had been rewarded chose new lives of great power and dictatorship, without considering the sorts of deeds they might have to commit in order to achieve such power. Those who had been punished sometimes chose more wisely, having learned from their experiences. Only the philosophical, who understood the importance of choosing a new life of peace and justice, benefited from the cycle of life and death. The others simply ricocheted between happiness and misery, reward and punishment.

According to many scholars, the Myth of Er is meant to demonstrate the necessity of seeking wisdom through philosophy in order for the soul to benefit. People come to understand what makes a good life and leads to reward, and what to avoid. Each person has a conscious choice to make about his or her next life, and therefore carries all the responsibility for it.

Once the souls had chosen their destinies, they were given some water to drink from the River of Forgetfulness, which made them forget all of their previous life and their afterlife experiences; except for Er, who was freed to return to his funeral pyre and educate his friends.

Criticisms of Plato's view of the soul

One criticism that has been made of Plato's understanding of the soul is that it does not seem to match our experience of ourselves as unified wholes. The theory does not do justice to the way we perceive ourselves as having a single, unified mind and personality.

Another criticism is that Plato's ideas about the immortality of the soul depend on our accepting the rest of his beliefs about the world of Forms and the nature of knowledge. We may not agree with him that there is an eternal world of unchanging Forms from which we get our knowledge, in which case the belief that we will one day return to the world of Forms has no basis.

Plato's 'argument from the cycle of opposites' has been criticised on the grounds that it is not supported by experience. We can think of plenty of things which are not 'brought about' by their opposite. Black does not bring about white, and hunger does not bring about satisfaction. We might recognise things for what they are, because of their opposites, so that for example we know when something is warm because we understand coolness, but this does not necessitate any kind of cycle. Life can be the opposite of death, without it meaning that life must be brought about by death.

Aristotle and the soul

Aristotle, in contrast to Plato, thought that the soul and body were inseparable. He gave the example of a wax tablet with a stamp impressed on it – the shape made by the stamp is inseparable from the wax, just as the soul is inseparable from the person. In Aristotle's view, the soul is a 'substance', which was a term he used in his own way to mean the 'essence' or 'real thing'. Aristotle saw a problem: how could we say that the newborn baby, the toddler, the child, the adolescent, the adult, and the elderly man are all the 'same person'? The physical body is in a continual state of change, but the 'substance' remains the same, in terms of the continuing identity. This was what Aristotle understood to be the soul.

Aristotle considered the soul to include the matter and structure of the body with its functions and capabilities. Unlike Plato, he thought that the soul could be explained in purely natural terms, rather than by making reference to any supernatural realm. In his treatise *De Anima* (*On the Soul*) he began by saying that 'the soul is in some sense the principle of animal life'. Aristotle thought that there were various kinds of soul. Plants have a vegetative or 'nutritive' soul, in that they have the capability to get nourishment for themselves and to ensure the reproduction of the species, but they have no ability to reason or to make plans. Animals have 'perceptive' souls, because they have senses with which to experience the world around them, and they react to different stimuli. They have enough intelligence to distinguish between pleasure and pain. Humans have a higher degree of soul because they have the ability to reason, and they can tell right from wrong. For Aristotle, then, the soul was not some separate entity, distinct from the body, but was completely dependent on the body. The soul is the capacity that the body has to do whatever it is meant to do.

If an axe, for example, had a soul, then that soul would involve chopping, because that is the function of an axe and the reason why it is structured the way that it is. The 'soul' of a human person is the potential for rational thought and activity.

Because Aristotle believed that the soul and the body could not be separated, his view did not allow for the idea that the soul could survive the death of the body in any way. However, as his thought developed, Aristotle began to wonder if perhaps the reason might be able to survive even when the body had died; but his thoughts on the nature of human reason and the extent to which the reason requires a physical body are among the most difficult and obscure of his writings. He did not seem to think that the reason could continue in the sense of it still being an individual personality, and it is not likely that Aristotle believed people could live after death in any personal sense. 'To attain any assured knowledge of the soul is one of the most difficult things in the world' (Aristotle, *De Anima*, Book 1).

Richard Dawkins' materialist view

Modern materialist views, such as those held by Richard Dawkins, assume that there is no part of a person that is non-physical. Following the traditions of Aristotle, materialists believe that the consciousness cannot be separated from the brain, because for the materialist, nothing exists except matter. The materialist view, then, rules out the possibilities of any form of conscious life after death, since consciousness is caused by purely physical phenomena. Once the brain has died, the consciousness must end.

Richard Dawkins, in his book *The Selfish Gene* (1976), proposes that humans are nothing more than 'survival machines', and he completely discounts the idea that humans have any kind of soul to distinguish them from other species. Humans, like other living creatures, are the vehicles of genes, which are only interested in replicating themselves in order to survive into the next generation. Of course, Dawkins understood that genes do not have the capacity to think and to have intentions in any literal way, so that to speak of what they are 'interested in' or of their 'selfishness' is to use metaphor and analogy. His point was that human beings do not have immortal souls and instead are simply a mixture of chemicals: 'survival machines – robot vehicles blindly programmed to preserve the selfish molecules known as genes'.

In his book *River out of Eden*, Dawkins asserts: 'there is no spirit-driven life force, no throbbing, heaving, pullulating, protoplasmic, mystic jelly. Life is just bytes and bytes and bytes of digital information.' This does not, for Dawkins, mean that life has nothing awe-inspiring about it. He finds the whole evolutionary process awe-inspiring, and also the achievements of great men and women. However, he does not believe that we need any additional supernatural 'soul' to explain this.

In Dawkins' view, human self-awareness is not due to any kind of soul but has developed because self-awareness has evolutionary advantages. Genes replicate themselves more effectively if they 'work together' in 'colonies' (and again, it should be understood that Dawkins uses these words metaphorically rather than literally). The individual person is really a 'colony' of genes working together in an animal that has become so complex that it is aware of itself. It can make plans, envisage the world with itself as an active part of that world, and imagine different futures, because this consciousness has the evolutionary advantage of allowing deliberate choices to be made.

Whatever philosophical problems with consciousness, for the purposes of this story it can be thought of as the culmination of an evolutionary trend towards the emancipation of survival machines as executive decision takers from their ultimate masters, the genes. Not only are brains in charge of the day to day running of survival machine affairs, they have also acquired the ability to predict the future and act accordingly, they even have the power to rebel against the dictates of the genes, for instance in refusing to have as many children as they are able to. In this respect man is a very special case. (Dawkins, The Selfish Gene*)*

Dawkins argues, as did Bertrand Russell, that religious belief in ideas such as the immortality of the soul have no sound basis. They are beliefs based on wish-fulfilment for those who lack courage, who fear death and who cannot cope with the idea of their own mortality.

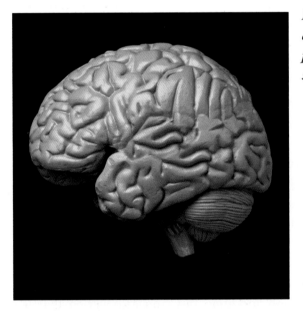

In the materialist view, consciousness and self-awareness are explicable in physical terms. There is no need to suppose the existence of a soul.

For the materialist, consciousness is no more than electro-chemical events within the brain, and therefore the individual person is incapable of surviving brain death. Consciousness is not some extra-special 'magic ingredient' that gives humanity special status as the 'image of God', but is simply a rather wonderful aspect of evolution. However, the relation between consciousness and the brain is something which remains a mystery to science. Some believe that one day, neuroscientists will understand precisely how the chemicals in our bodies lead us to self-awareness and personality, while others believe that this will always be beyond our comprehension. We might one day know the neural processes which underpin consciousness, but we will never know for certain whether consciousness is no more than physical chemical changes.

Christian understanding of the soul

In the Christian tradition, as well as in many other religions, the whole concept of personhood is closely associated with the belief that people have souls, which sets them apart from other created life forms. It is believed that God gives people their souls as a kind of 'divine spark', so that they are made in God's image. In the Bible, when the animals are made, they are just living creatures, but when humanity is made, God puts something of himself into the man: 'The Lord God formed man from the dust of the ground and breathed into his nostrils the breath of life, and man became a living being' (Genesis 2:7).

Many Christians believe that the soul will be judged by God after death. Those who have repented of their sins and turned to Jesus will be saved, while those who never repent will be separated from God for ever.

Traditional Christian thinking explains that the soul is the 'subject of' mental and spiritual states, the 'essential person'. The soul is seen to encompass the mind and the spirit (although this, of course, begs the question of what we mean by 'spirit' and whether it is different from the soul). The soul goes beyond mental intelligence and reason, while also including it, so that it is possible for the religious believer to put reason and argument to one side in the search for spiritual enlightenment, and experience God in a 'cloud of unknowing'. For the Christian, a machine with artificial intelligence could have the powers of reason and logic, but it could never have a soul because it would lack the spiritual capacity to develop a relationship with God.

In Christian history, there have been many discussions about the origins and nature of the soul and its relation to other aspects of the human person. Thinkers have considered where the soul originates from, and have produced various different theories.

- One view is called *creationism*, which can be rather confusing as in this context it has nothing to do with belief in the literal truth of Genesis. In the context of the soul, creationism is the belief that God creates each individual soul every time a new baby is born. The point at which the body receives the soul has also been debated, particularly because it has a bearing on the ethical issue of abortion. If, perhaps, the soul is given to the body at the point of birth, then abortion might not count as 'murder' because the foetus would not yet be a full human being. However, if the soul becomes part of the person at the moment of conception, as the Roman Catholic Church teaches, then to end the life of a foetus is to end the life of a human soul and therefore much more serious. Creationism remains the most popular Christian view of the origin of the soul.

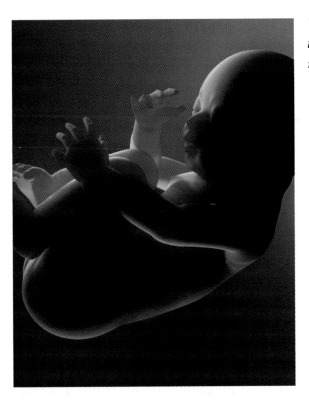

What are the implications of the belief that humans have souls from the moment of conception?

- *Traducianism* is the name given to the belief that the soul is inherited from the parents, in the same way that eye colour is inherited. This is not a mainstream view today, but early Christian leaders considered it as a possibility because they were grappling with the problem of original sin. How could a person be born sinful, and deserve punishment for something Adam and Eve had done? It had to be because their souls were already tainted through inheritance.

- Another possibility considered was the Platonic idea that the soul pre-existed the body, and lived with God before each baby was born. This idea had its followers, as it seemed to solve the problem of how a soul could be eternal – in order to be eternal, perhaps it had to have no beginning. However, this belief has not become part of mainstream Christian teaching.

John Hick on the soul

John Hick's view of the soul is an essential part of his theology. Hick argues that the whole of this earthly life is a 'vale of soul-making', a testing-ground for people in which they develop their moral characters and are given a free choice about whether or not they should have a relationship with God (see pages 346–9). This is a somewhat Platonic view of the soul, in which the soul and the body are seen as distinct, but Hick gives it a more traditional Christian perspective by claiming that the soul needs a body in order to continue with its journey in the afterlife. Although Hick understands the soul to be capable of everlasting life with God, it is not unchanging in the Platonic sense. The soul has to grow and develop, just as the body does in earthly life. There is an evolutionary process in which people continue to learn and to make conscious choices of their own free will, until they reach a stage when they are able to live in a full relationship with God. For some, this takes much longer than for others.

In Hick's view, the most coherent understanding of life after death is a physical rebirth, in which the body is replicated by God (see pages 347–9). Hick, in his book *Death and Eternal Life* (1976) accepts that the immortality of the soul is not something that can be proved in this life, but nevertheless he argues that it is something that is not unreasonable, and something that a rational person could accept.

Richard Swinburne and Keith Ward: defending the soul

Both Richard Swinburne and Keith Ward defend, from within the Christian tradition, the idea that human beings have souls which are distinct from physical bodies and which are capable of survival after death. Swinburne, in his book *The Evolution of the Soul*, explains his beliefs that the soul and the body are distinct from each other, so that the soul is capable of surviving even when the body is destroyed. He argues that there are fundamental truths about us as individuals which cannot be explained in purely physical terms, and also that the most important and significant aspects of us which give us our identity are not to be found in our physical bodies. In Swinburne's view, the human soul is unique in that it is capable of logical, ordered and complex thought. The soul is aware of its own freedom to make choices, and also aware of moral obligation. It is because we have souls that we recognise goodness when we see it in other people, and because of our souls that we have consciences, letting us know when we are right or wrong.

Keith Ward's book *Defending the Soul* is written as a response to scientists who claim that humans are, in the end, just physical beings:

Richard Dawkins, Jacques Monod, Desmond Morris and many others have all written popular and influential books, proclaiming that science has now entered the secret citadel of the human soul, and found it empty. Human persons, they say, are not free spiritual agents with a special dignity. They are physical organisms for reproducing genes; and as such, they have no more intrinsic dignity than walking bags of chemical compounds.

In the book, Ward focuses on the problems he foresees for humanity if belief in the soul is abandoned. He argues that without belief in the soul, morality becomes simply a matter of personal choice and taste, whereas we need the moral claims that the soul recognises as coming from God in order to progress and to achieve that special dignity of being human rather than simply animal. Without the soul, humanity lacks any sense of final purpose.

Keith Ward argues that it is the soul which gives humanity its special dignity and sense of progress.

Ward attacks the materialist position of those who claim that we are nothing more than physical organisms, by returning to the Genesis account of the creation of humankind. He writes:

The Bible puts it supremely well when it says, 'The Lord God took some soil from the ground and formed a man out of it; he breathed life-giving breath into his nostrils, and the man began to live.' Man is made of dust; but he is filled with the spirit of God. He emerges from the simplest material forms, but finds his true kinship in the goal and fulfilment of his existence, the supreme Goodness.

Practice exam question

Critically assess the view that human beings have immortal souls.

For this question, you are asked to give a critical assessment, so although you will probably want to include a lot of information about thinkers who have supported either side of the debate, you should make sure that the information is used as part of a line of argument. Try to decide for yourself whether you believe people have immortal souls, and think how you would justify that point of view. Then explain it, supported by scholars who also hold the same opinion. In the course of your argument, introduce the ideas of those with whom you disagree, and say why you think their views are weaker, so that by the time you reach your conclusion, you have given a critical assessment.

Develop your knowledge

The Selfish Gene by Richard Dawkins (Oxford University Press, 1976)
The Evolution of the Soul by Richard Swinburne (Clarendon Press, 1997)
Defending the Soul by Keith Ward (OneWorld, 1992)

Key terms

reincarnation
– being reborn into this world after death into a new physical body.

atman –
the 'essential Self' in Hindu thought.

anatta –
the Buddhist belief that there is no self and that the sense of self is an illusion.

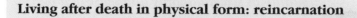

Living after death in physical form: reincarnation

Usually, when religious believers talk about life after death, they are referring either to rebirth (reincarnation) or to resurrection. In both of these understandings of life after death, the individual continues to live after death in bodily form – the soul is not separated from the body in some kind of spirit world, but has a physical existence. Obviously people cannot continue to live in the same body that has died, because the body begins to corrupt once death has taken place; therefore there is some kind of new body for the person to inhabit.

Hindu beliefs in reincarnation

Reincarnation, or rebirth, is a key feature of Hindu beliefs. According to Hindu teaching, each person has an essential 'self' known as *atman*, which is eternal and which seeks unity with God. In the Hindu sacred texts known as the Upanishads, one of the key messages is that spiritual wisdom comes when people recognise the ultimate identity of the atman with the divine. God manifests himself in the atman of each individual, and through the succession of births, deaths and rebirths, the person comes to an understanding and a union of the atman with God. Once this union has been realised, there is no need for the atman to continue in the cycle of rebirth; it has attained release, known as *moksha*. For the Hindu, the physical body is nothing more than a vehicle for the atman. The atman holds a person's true nature. It leaves a body at the time of death, and enters another at birth, so two apparently different people can in reality be identical.

> *As a caterpillar, having come to the end of one blade of grass, draws itself together and reaches out for the next, so the Self, having come together at the end of one life and shed all ignorance, gathers in its faculties and reaches out from the old body to a new.*
> (Brihadaranyaka Upanishad III. 4.3, The Upanishads, *trans. Eknad Easwaran, Arkana, 1988*)

Hindus believe that the process of rebirth is controlled by the law of karma. Each deliberate action that a person performs is believed to have 'fruits', or consequences. If the action is a good action, then it will bring good consequences for the individual, and conversely, if the action is bad, then the consequences will also be bad. Those who lead morally good lives, who care about the welfare of others and who are not greedy for personal gain, will benefit from their actions because they will have good fortune and others will be kind to them. Those who are selfish or violent or careless will suffer the consequences in the form of bad fortune. Of course, when we look at the lives of people around us, we can see that often someone who is apparently good and kind

suffers an illness, is the victim of crime, is made redundant or is disappointed in an endeavour – but this is because of the karmic fruits of their behaviour in previous lives. If they cope with their suffering bravely and without complaint, and try to turn it in some way to the good of others, then they will become closer to achieving moksha.

The karmic 'fruits' attach themselves to the atman and keep it in the cycle of birth, death and rebirth. This is not seen in terms of the judgement of God, rewarding or punishing people, but is seen as a natural law, in just the same way as Newton saw the laws of motion, where action and reaction are equal. People are reborn entirely because of their own behaviour, and everything that happens to them is something they deserve. The balance of good and evil karmic fruits attached to each atman will determine quality of life of the individual in future rebirths – those who have accumulated good karma will be born healthy and strong into affluent families, while those with bad karma might be poor or disabled.

According to the Hindu doctrine of karma, if someone is poor or disabled, this is because of his or her own deeds in past lives.

In some ways, this can seem to make Hinduism a religion which lacks compassion for the poor and the weak. They are only poor or weak because of their own behaviour, after all; they have brought it on themselves and it serves them right. However, this is not how Hindus understand it. Concern for the well-being of others is important, not only because those who care for the poor will reap the karmic benefits of their compassion, but because of the belief that everyone has an atman and so everyone is connected as part of the divine essence. Also, because everyone is born and reborn time and again, the beggar at your gate or the refugee you see on a news broadcast might be your own parent or child in the past or in future lives.

> ## Key point
>
> • Hindus believe that each person has an essential atman which is reborn many times into the world.

Buddhist beliefs in reincarnation

One of the ways in which Buddhism differs from Hinduism is that Buddhists have no belief in the soul. Buddhists teach a doctrine of *anatta*, or soullessness; they believe that there is no God and no essential individual self. Belief in the self is based on an illusion, they argue, and encourages egotism.

According to Buddhism, a person is made up of five *skandhas*, ('aggregates' or 'strands'), beyond which there is no essential self. These skandhas are matter, sensation, perception, volition (acts of will) and consciousness. All of these five strands are interdependent and woven together to make a person who attracts karma; but there is nothing more beyond this. The wise person is the one who realises that any sense of atman is an illusion.

However, despite the conviction that there is no soul, Buddhism nevertheless shares with Hinduism a belief in the workings of karma and the cycle of rebirth. Like Hinduism, Buddhism teaches that actions have fruits which lead to rebirth in future lives, even if there is no essential self to which the karma can attach itself. This raises questions for the Buddhist – what is it that is reborn, if there is no essential person? How can it be said that one person is the reincarnation of another, if there is nothing which stays the same from one life to the next?

Buddhist teaching answers this question by saying that the person is neither the same nor different. The analogy is given with a lighted candle, which in turn lights another candle – the two flames are neither the same nor different, but the energy from one candle begins the flame of the next.

Buddhists use the analogy of a lighted candle to explain how one person is reborn as another even though there is no essential soul.

The Buddhist sacred text 'The Questions of King Milinda' deals with issues of personal identity and questions about how rebirth might operate in the absences of any 'essential self'. Nagasena, a wise monk, visits the king, and through dialogues the monk helps the king to understand essential Buddhist teaching. The king is puzzled about the workings of karma when there is no self to which the karmic fruits can attach themselves:

The king asked: 'Is there, Venerable Nagasena, any being which passes on from this body to another body?'

'No, Your Majesty!'

'If there were no passing on from this body to another, would not one then in one's next life be freed from the evil deeds committed in the past?'

'Yes, that would be so if one were not linked once again with a new organism. But since, Your Majesty, one is linked once again with a new organism, therefore one is not freed from one's evil deeds.'

'Give me a simile!'

'If a man should steal another man's mangoes, would he deserve a thrashing for that?'

'Yes, of course!'

'But he would not have stolen the very same mangoes as the other one had planted. Why should he deserve a thrashing?'

'For the reason that the stolen mangoes had grown because of those that were planted.'

'Just so, Your Majesty, it is because of the deeds one does, whether pure or impure, by means of this psycho-physical organism, that one is once again linked with another psycho-physical organism, and is not freed from one's evil deeds.'

Key point

- Unlike Hindus, Buddhists believe that people have no 'essential self' or soul.

Western belief in reincarnation

Many famous figures from Western history have been convinced by the idea of reincarnation. Pythagoras, for example, claimed to have memories of past lives, and believed that as the individual passed through each successive life, he or she gained in wisdom and in virtue. Benjamin Franklin, Thomas Huxley, Mark Twain, Gustav Mahler, Robert Graves and David Lloyd George are among those who have, at some point, expressed the conviction that they have lived before and will return to the world to live another life – although, of course, the mere fact that a lot of people believe something to be the case does not actually prove it to be true.

To think about

Have you ever had an experience in which you have had a strong sense that you have visited a place before, or met someone before, even though it is impossible that you could have done so? Do you think that such experiences provide evidence of past lives?

Is there any evidence for reincarnation?

Twenty Cases Suggestive of Reincarnation (University Press of Virginia, 1974) was written by Ian Stevenson, an American professor of Psychiatry, and primarily intended for scientists when it was first published as part of a psychical research programme in 1966. In this book, as the title suggests, the author explores twenty different cases in which there is apparent evidence that an individual is the reincarnation of someone else who lived in the past but has died. Stevenson took examples mainly from India, Ceylon and Brazil, of children who had 'memories' of past lives, and whose memories bore an unusual resemblance to the lives of deceased people they had never met. He interviewed the children and their families himself. Stevenson chose to confine his study to children rather than adults, because he thought they were less likely to be motivated by attention-seeking desires, and were less likely to be able to fabricate the evidence and sustain a hoax for any length of time. Stevenson described the 20 cases in detail, and then provided a discussion of the issues arising.

One of the cases, for example, was of Swarnlata, a child in India, who was taken at the age of three to a town called Katni 170 miles away from the place where she had lived all her life. When she arrived in Katni, she pointed out the road where 'my house' was. She described how she had lived there as a member of a family called Pathak, and she commented on the ways in which the place had changed. Over the next few years, Swarnlata performed songs and dances for her brothers and sisters that she claimed she had learned when she was a member of the Pathak family. Later investigation showed that the language of these songs was Bengali, although Swarnlata had grown up knowing only Hindi. Her statements, and her description of the house with its trees and balconies in an inner courtyard which could not be seen from the road, corresponded closely with the building, and with the life events of the Pathak family who had lived there. The Pathaks' daughter Biya had lived to adulthood, learned Bengali songs and dances, married and then died. Swarnlata recognised Biya's brothers and sisters and when she was introduced to them, she greeted them 'with warm affection'.

Another example Stevenson explored was the case of Imad, who lived in the Lebanon and was a member of the Druse faith. Druses believe that reincarnation happens immediately at the moment of death, so there was nothing in his culture to discourage Imad from talking about his experiences with his family. Imad was only a little over five years old when Stevenson met him, and he was of particular interest because he was so young and because there had not, at the time of interview, been any contact between Imad and the family that he claimed to remember belonging to. Stevenson was able to go with Imad and his family on their first visit to the village that he claimed to remember, and was able to see for himself Imad's reactions to the buildings and to the people he met.

As soon as he had begun to talk, between the ages of 18 months and two, Imad had been making references to a previous life. He gave the name of the village (Khriby) where he said he had lived, and the name of his family there (Bouhamzy); he talked about people he had known there, events he remembered and property he had owned. The first words he ever spoke were 'Jamileh' and 'Mahmoud', and as his speech developed he compared Jamileh with his mother, saying that Jamileh was more beautiful. He also spoke of an accident where a truck drove over a man and broke both of his legs, and where the injuries eventually led to the man's death. As Imad learned to walk, he expressed an unusual happiness about being able to do this, and often said how pleased he was that he could now walk. Imad's family concluded that in a previous life, the boy was Mahmoud Bouhamzy, who had a wife called Jamileh, and who had been fatally injured in a truck accident.

When Stevenson went with Imad to the village of Khriby, about 15 miles away from his home on the map but about 25 miles by the winding road, Stevenson was just as interested in the inaccuracies in Imad's description as he was in the parts which matched the facts. A man called Mahmoud Bouhamzy had indeed lived in the village – but he still did. A relative, called Said Bouhamzy, had been killed by a truck which had broken both his legs. Said's life did not match details given by Imad, but when the researchers looked back at the notes they had made when Imad was talking to them, it became clear that Imad had never claimed that the accident had happened to him, although he had described it in detail. Another family member, Ibrahim Bouhamzy, however, had died of tuberculosis at the age of 25, and the disease had affected his spine and made it impossible for him to walk. He had also had a mistress called Jamileh, who was renowned for her beauty. Stevenson thought that the original confusion added to the authenticity of Imad's identity with Ibrahim, because if Imad's parents or the Bouhamzy family had concocted the story, they would have been careful not to have made these mistakes.

Imad was taken to the house where Ibrahim had lived. He had been able to point in the general direction of the house, but incorrectly identified it. However, once inside the house, Imad pointed out the cupboard where Ibrahim had secretly kept a gun; he showed which bed was Ibrahim's, and correctly said that the bed had since been moved to a different position in the room; he showed the place outside where the dog was kept, and was able to name a brother of Ibrahim's and Ibrahim himself when he was shown photographs. Ibrahim had not died immediately before Imad's birth – Ibrahim died in 1949, and Imad was not born until 1958. The explanation of this was that there must have been an intermediate life, which would also account for people Imad claimed to remember but who could not be traced in Khriby.

In discussion of these 20 different cases, Stevenson looked at a number of possible ways in which they could be explained. He considered the possibility of fraud, and thought this unlikely, as the children had little to gain from sharing these experiences. There was no money or favourable publicity for them, for example, and many found the media attention (if any) to be a nuisance. Swarnlata's family was, unusually, offered money for her education from the more wealthy Pathak family, but her father refused it. In other cases, there were reasons why sharing the experiences would have a negative effect. For example, if a young girl talked about having previously had a husband, it would not be advantageous to her when it was time for her to marry. Stevenson argued that there was little motivation for such elaborate fraud, which would have to have involved careful research and coaching.

He also considered cryptomnesia, which he thought was far more probable. This is where a person thinks they remember something, but in fact has heard about it from another source such as parents or relatives (for example, when children think they remember events that their older siblings often mention, even though the events actually took place before they were born). However, in these cases, there was little to suggest that this could have been possible. There was rarely any written or broadcast evidence of the life of the person who had died, and the deceased was usually completely unknown to the family of the child. Perhaps a very brief or casual acquaintance could have been sufficient to implant false memories, but Stevenson argues that the richness of minutely remembered detail counted against this, and also the casual passing of information would not account for such things as Swarnlata recognising Biya's relations.

Another idea that Stevenson considered was genetic memory, of the sort that enables birds to 'remember' how to build nests even when they are very young. However, there was very rarely a genetic link between the remembering child and the deceased. In cases where there was a long gap in time between the 'rememberer' and the deceased (for example, if someone claimed to remember a life lived three hundred years ago), the possibilities of genetic link became slightly stronger, but the questions raised about being able to remember such vivid detail through genetic transference seems to raise more questions than it answers.

Stevenson also looked at some length at the possibility of extra-sensory perception. Because this involves the paranormal and telepathic links, this theory is unlikely to receive much enthusiasm from sceptics. Perhaps the children did have paranormal skills. However, they claimed that they were remembering past lives, not that they were in touch in some way with another person who had once lived. Their own understanding of what was going on could be taken seriously as an interpretation of events.

Stevenson concluded that reincarnation was the most likely explanation, based on the evidence. However, he did think that people should go on looking for other possible explanations of these and other cases.

Key point

• Stevenson's detailed case studies of children with claims to have lived former lives led him to the conclusion that there is evidence to support belief in reincarnation.

Criticisms of belief in rebirth

Many people argue against reincarnation for religious reasons. If they are members of other faiths which have different teachings about life after death – a Christian or a Jew or a Muslim, for example – they would object to theories of reincarnation on the grounds that they contradict the teachings of the Bible or the Qur'an. They might argue that Christianity or Islam or Judaism teaches that each individual is given one life which is of prime importance as the determinant of our future salvation or condemnation; teaching about reincarnation is incompatible with teaching about the resurrection of the body. Conversely, there are those who argue the opposite, and support belief in reincarnation because it is what their religion teaches, for example Hindus, Buddhists, Jains and Sikhs.

Some argue that reincarnation is made less plausible by the fact that many of the cases suggestive of reincarnation come from countries where reincarnation is already an accepted belief. John Hick considers the cases presented by Ian Stevenson's *Twenty Cases Suggestive of Reincarnation*, and points out (in his book *Death and Eternal Life*) that the vast majority of such cases come from cultures where reincarnation is already a widely held and accepted belief. Hick suggests that the cases in Stevenson's book might be explained by some kind of extra-sensory perception, where the dead person leaves behind some kind of psychic traces or 'husks', and that the individual might have some kind of telepathic extra-sensitivity to these psychic traces, enabling a 'memory' of a previous individual or of a life. Hick does not go so far as to say that this alternative explanation is the right one, but he does say that it is another possibility, so that reincarnation is not the only conclusion that can be drawn from the cases. Stevenson, in contrast, argued that the weight of evidence that he has seen makes reincarnation a plausible possibility.

Some argue that the issue of personal identity is unresolved with doctrines of reincarnation (and the same applies to resurrection). They say that there is no reason to identify the person who is living now with someone who has died. Similarities, however close, are not the same as identity. Shared memory is also not the same as identity. It is argued that it is simply impossible for two different individuals to be in any way 'the same person' – it is a contradiction in terms.

Although the doctrine of karma and rebirth might appear to solve problems about the apparent unfairness of life, it could be argued that the solution is not as coherent as it first appears. Perhaps it is unjust for someone to suffer bad consequences as a result of crimes or faults they cannot remember committing. Even in the space of one lifetime, it might be argued that it is unjust to punish people for wrongs that were committed long in their past, when they are 'different people' now and have learned a lot since then – some try to use their personal transformation when they become born-again Christians as reasons why they should be released from Death Row, with varying degrees of success. How much more unfair is it, then, if someone suffers for something unremembered, done in a previous life and in a different body?

To think about

Do you think that it is fair to punish someone for a crime committed a long time ago? Should people today be punished for war crimes committed during the 1940s, or can they be considered to be different people now? Do you think that suffering for faults committed in a previous life would be fair?

For the Hindu or the Buddhist, however, karma works with perfect justice. It is seen as a natural law, rather than as a reward or punishment decided upon by any god. Whether or not someone can remember the deed that caused the reward or punishment, it will always be just – and memory of past lives is considered to be a skill which is perfected by those with the greatest wisdom, so suffering for an unremembered sin would simply be indicative of the ignorance of the person suffering.

Living after death in physical form: resurrection

Resurrection in Judaism

Judaism does not give any single firm teaching about life after death, but there are Jews who believe that there will be resurrection from the dead at a time of God's choosing.

In the early days of Judaism, there was no real notion of life after death, because to have a soul meant to be animated with life, as illustrated in the creation stories where God breathes into Adam with the breath of life. Therefore it seemed obvious that a dead person no longer had a soul, because death was when the animating breath of God left the body:

> It is not the dead who praise the Lord,
> those who go down to silence. (Psalm 115:17)

There are stories where the prophets Elijah and Elisha raise young boys from the dead back to life. However, in both cases, the traditions of the rabbis taught that the boys went on to live out their days and then died again – the stories tell of a healing from death to normal earthly life, rather than a resurrection to a new immortal spiritual body.

> The Lord heard Elijah's cry, and the boy's life returned to him, and he lived. Elijah picked up the child and carried him down from the room into the house. He gave him to his mother and said, 'Look, your son is alive!' Then the woman said to Elijah, 'Now I know that you are a man of God and that the word of the Lord from your mouth is the truth.' (I Kings 17:22–24)

Life after death is by no means a prominent theme in the Jewish scriptures, but there are passages about future hope and the 'Last Days', in which there is clear reference to resurrection. For example, in the apocalyptic Book of Daniel, there is a prophecy about the end of time where the writer says 'Multitudes who sleep in the dust of the earth will awake: some to everlasting life, others to shame and everlasting contempt' (Daniel 12:2).

The book of Daniel is one of the latest books of Jewish scriptures, probably written in about 165 BCE as a way of encouraging Jews who were being persecuted for their faith. It may have been the case that the Jews began to change their ideas about life after death as a way of coping with their circumstances. During religious persecution, those who remained the most faithful and obedient to God's commands seemed to be the ones who came off worst, whereas those who wanted to survive at all costs and abandoned Judaism for pragmatic reasons sometimes escaped. Life after death may have seemed to the Jews, as it did to Kant, the obvious solution to the problem of God's apparent injustice in this earthly life.

At the time of Jesus, in first-century Palestine, debates about life after death divided opinion amongst the Jews. The Pharisees were distinctive in their belief in resurrection while the Sadducees taught that there was no life after death.

Moses Maimonides, a Jewish philosopher and rabbi of the twelfth century, lived under Muslim rule in Spain until he was exiled for refusing to convert to Islam. He was influenced by Muslim thinking, as well as by the newly rediscovered thinking of Aristotle, and was a supporter of the *via negativa* (see pages 210–14) for conveying an understanding of God. Maimonides set down thirteen main principles of the Jewish faith, and resurrection is the thirteenth of them, and is printed in all rabbinic prayer books even today. It states:

> *I believe with perfect faith, that there will be resurrection of the dead, at the time which pleases the Creator. Blessed be His name, and may His remembrance arise, forever and ever.*

Many Jews believe that when the Messiah comes, there will be a 'Messianic age', when the dead will be raised. Some rabbis taught that this would be a spiritual resurrection, when bodies would not be needed any more; others argued that this was heresy, and that dead bodies would be lifted from the graves to live again on the earth in a perfected form.

Resurrection in Islam

Belief in life after death (*al-akhirah*) is essential in Islam, to the extent that someone who doubts it is considered to be an unbeliever; the Qur'an contains more teaching about the Day of Judgement than about any other topic. Muslims believe that a person's earthly life is merely a preparation for the afterlife. The Qur'an teaches that there will be life after death, and for Muslims this is the authoritative word of Allah, giving support for a belief which would be impossible to support or discredit using experiment or rational argument. Muslims argue that a God of perfect justice, who is interested in his creation, would obviously give people life after death, because otherwise justice would not be done and lives would be pointless. This life is viewed as a test for people, who are faced with difficulties and struggles which they must tackle in accordance with Muslim teaching. This tackling of difficulties is known as *jihad*.

Muslims believe that people will be resurrected from the dead on a day of Allah's choosing, in accordance with his plans. During their lives, people shape their souls with the deeds that they do, whether good or bad, and when the body dies, the soul continues on to be judged by Allah. At the Day of Judgement (*Qiyamma*), an angel will blow his trumpet. The earth will be destroyed, and people will be resurrected and called to account, starting with the prophet Muhammad. Those who have led morally good lives and have been faithful to the teachings of Islam will go to heaven, which is described as a garden of paradise, while those who have rejected God will go to hell.

Allah has decreed: 'It is I and My messengers who must prevail': For Allah is One full of strength, able to enforce His Will. Thou will not find any people who believe in Allah and the Last Day, loving those who resist Allah and His Messenger, even though they were their fathers or their sons, or their brothers or their kindred. For such He has written Faith in their hearts, and strengthened them with a Spirit from Himself. And he will admit them to Gardens, beneath which Rivers flow, to dwell therein (for ever). Allah will be well pleased with them, and they with Him. They are the Party of Allah. Truly it is the Party of Allah that will achieve Felicity. (Surah 58:21)

Resurrection in Christianity

In Christianity, the belief is that people have just one life here on earth, and after death they will be resurrected. Christians believe that after Jesus died on the cross he was resurrected, and this is evidence that the same will happen to the rest of us.

According to the Bible, after Jesus died, his body was placed in a tomb – but on the third day after the death, when some of his female followers went to the grave to anoint the body, they discovered that the grave was empty, even though the entrance had been guarded and covered with a heavy stone. Jesus was seen as a physical person, walking around. He could be heard and touched, although even the people who had been Jesus' closest friends did not always recognise him immediately, suggesting that his appearance had changed in some way. After Jesus had spent some time on earth in physical form, he 'ascended into heaven'; it is not clear whether he discarded the resurrected physical body at this point and lived on in some kind of spiritual form, or whether he continued in the resurrected body for eternity.

Christians believe Jesus was resurrected from the dead.

Christians believe that life after death will involve some kind of judgement. The parable of the sheep and the goats in Matthew's Gospel describes how there will be a separation between those who have treated other people well and those who have selfishly ignored the needs of others: 'Then they will go away to eternal punishment, but the righteous to eternal life' (Matthew 25:46). The story of the rich man and Lazarus gives a similar message, where the rich man who has been too interested in material possessions and has ignored the poor man at his gate is sent into eternal punishment, while Lazarus is united with Abraham in heaven. In this story, the inhabitants of heaven and hell are aware of each other, but are unable to do anything about their position:

The time came when the beggar died and the angels carried him to Abraham's side. The rich man also died and was buried. In hell, where he was in torment, he looked up and saw Abraham far away, with Lazarus by his side. So he called to him, 'Father Abraham, have pity on me and send Lazarus to dip the tip of his finger in water and cool my tongue, because I am in agony in this fire.'

But Abraham replied,

'Son, remember that in your lifetime you received your good things, while Lazarus received bad things, but now he is comforted here and you are in agony. And besides all this, between us and you a great chasm has been fixed, so that those who want to go from here to you cannot, nor can anyone cross over from there to us.' (Luke 16:22–26)

To think about

Would heaven be heavenly if the people there could see what was going on in hell?

Questions raised by resurrection

The idea of eternal resurrected bodies creates philosophical difficulties. It suggests that life after death must happen in some kind of space, since bodies take up room. Peter Cole, in his book *Philosophy of Religion* (Hodder Murray, 1999) asks: 'If Christians are in a physical, resurrected state and physical environment, will they have to queue to see Jesus? Where will this physical existence be? And what will they be doing all the time?'

The idea that our post-death existence involves having a body implies that heaven must be a physical place. Would it have a climate? Would we need some kind of clothing, housing and food, just as we do now? If our resurrected bodies are like the bodies we have now, then we would assumedly have the same physical needs, but it is difficult to conceive of a heaven where people still had to eat meals and have haircuts. It also raises questions of whether our heavenly bodies will age – if so, would they ever stop, or would we just keep on getting older and older? If someone dies at the age of 103, will their resurrected body be that of an old person? What about babies who die – will their resurrected bodies be forever in infancy, or will they be resurrected into a body that they never actually had in this earthly life? Can a resurrected body grow, put on or lose weight, get a tan, hurt itself?

Perhaps the concept of physical resurrection causes problems for people who have bodily imperfections in this life – which is almost all of us. In their resurrected bodies, will they still have those imperfections or disabilities, or would they have disappeared? Will people who are not so good-looking become more beautiful, and if so, how will we recognise each other?

Christians usually respond to questions like these by saying that we will all be perfected versions of ourselves, and that we will all be given the ability by God to recognise each other despite a change in appearance.

But someone may ask, 'How are the dead raised? With what kind of body will they come?' How foolish! What you sow does not come to life unless it dies. When you sow, you do not plant the body that will be, but just a seed, perhaps of wheat or of something else. But God gives it a body as he has determined, and to each kind of seed he gives its own body. All flesh is not the same: Men have one kind of flesh, animals have another, birds another and fish another. There are also heavenly bodies and there are earthly bodies; but the splendour of the heavenly bodies is one kind, and the splendour of the earthly bodies is another. The sun has one kind of splendour, the moon another and the stars another; and star differs from star in splendour.

So will it be with the resurrection of the dead. The body that is sown is perishable, it is raised imperishable; it is sown in dishonour, it is raised in glory; it is sown in weakness, it is raised in power; it is sown a natural body, it is raised a spiritual body. (1 Corinthians 15:35–44)

Practice exam question

'Reincarnation is a more coherent concept than resurrection.' Discuss.

This question asks whether these concepts are coherent; in other words, you are being asked if they make sense or not. You might think that neither concept makes sense, because both involve the idea of bodily life after death; if you reject this as a coherent concept, you are not going to accept either reincarnation or resurrection. You might, however, prefer one over the other. In your essay, you should explain the different concepts and give reasons why people might believe they are true. Remember, you are presenting an argument, so information should be used to support it rather than for its own sake.

Heaven and hell

Belief in heaven and hell is characteristic of Christianity and Islam, and to some extent Judaism. For some people, both of these ideas raise difficult philosophical questions, although others are content to accept that we cannot have a clear idea of the afterlife until we actually get there.

The moral philosopher Bernard Williams, for example, wondered whether an eternity in heaven would really be desirable – surely however pleasurable heaven was at the beginning when we first arrived, it would become boring after a while? We would have literally all the time in the world, and so we would be able to do and achieve everything we wanted, especially if we had perfected bodies so that we were not hindered by physical limitations. Every target that we set for ourselves would be achievable, even if it took a long time to get there. If we wanted to learn to play an instrument, we would have forever to master it; in fact we would have time to master them all and to invent new ones – and then what? Whatever we wanted to do, we would be able to do it, and perhaps the excitement of anticipation would disappear. Williams argued that part of the pleasure of living is making choices about what we will do with our limited life-spans, and setting ourselves challenging objectives which we might or might not be able to achieve, so that if and when we do achieve them, we feel a sense of pride. However, if we have time to choose absolutely everything, and have infinite time so that eventually everything is achieved, the pleasure is gone.

Some respond to these objections by saying that in heaven, God would make sure that this did not happen; perhaps we might miraculously never be bored, just as we would never be sad and never suffer. However, if our minds and emotions are going to be controlled and programmed like this, we would lose our free will, and it also raises the question of why God did not make us like this in the first place, so that we were never bored or sad or suffering in this life either.

To think about

Can you think of any kind of food that you would want to eat endlessly, if miraculously you never became over-full? Or any kind of music that you would want to hear endlessly? Is Bernard Williams right in his view that heaven would be boring, or is he interpreting the idea too literally?

The concept of hell also raises a difficult issue. Can the existence of hell, with eternal punishment that can never be escaped, be compatible with the existence of a perfectly loving and perfectly just God? It might be hard to think of any sin that we could commit where eternal pain with no chance of parole would be a fair punishment. David Hume raised this problem, suggesting that the whole idea of hell calls God's justice into question because a finite sin can never deserve an infinite punishment.

Some argue that whenever we do wrong, we wrong God, and that every kind of wrong deserves eternal punishment because wronging God is eternally bad; but this would mean that pain for all eternity would be a fair punishment for relatively minor offences, such as pretending that your friend looks great in the jeans she is trying on, just because you are bored with shopping and want to go home. It is hard to imagine a perfectly loving God allowing his creatures to suffer for all eternity. When a loving parent punishes a child, even if severely, the punishment does not go on for ever, but for just long enough to teach the child a lesson – so surely a loving God would not allow eternal punishment in hell?

Eternal punishment might be, in the end, as boring as eternal pleasure. We might become immune to pain and suffering and stop feeling it any more. And what would eternal punishment achieve, if there were no possibility of redemption and if the good were too far away to need protection from the bad?

To think about

What, if anything, could be a crime or sin so bad that it deserved eternal punishment in hell?

John Hick's views about life after death

John Hick argues that religious belief carries a 'cosmic optimism' that one day we will have the chance to improve ourselves, to become more perfect, to overcome our own failings and to reach the potential that we could have achieved on earth if only we were not so flawed. Within Eastern traditions, this optimism is understood in terms of a succession of rebirths into this physical world, where people have the opportunity for further growth and development. In Western traditions, the optimism is translated into belief in eternal life in heaven, or in hell for some.

Hick argues that if, in our future life after death when we have improved significantly, we could look back at ourselves living in the present, we would be able to see much more clearly the importance of the challenges and sufferings we face. We will, in the future, be able to understand how our pain was justified by its outcome, and will understand what it was all for and where it was leading us. Hick uses the imagery of John Bunyan's *Pilgrim's Progress* in the hero's journey towards the Celestial City. Although we might fall into periods of doubt, just as the Pilgrim fell into the Slough of Despond, we will be able to look back at the end of the journey and see the progress that we have made. He accepts that the existence of life after death is not provable, but argues that it is not an unreasonable belief, and that if we do continue our spiritual journeys after death, this provides a coherent explanation for the problem of evil in the world.

Hick rejects the traditional doctrine of an eternal hell, because in his view, it is incompatible with belief in a God of love. He argues that this belief was developed as a form of social control, encouraging people to be fearful of disobeying the teachings of those in religious authority, but that it is not conceivable that a God of infinite love and mercy would consign his creatures to a punishment from which they had no hope of escaping.

According to Hick, religious belief is largely determined and shaped by a person's culture. Someone brought up in central India is likely to find his or her religious feelings and needs met by Hinduism, whereas someone in France is likely to seek God through the Roman Catholic tradition. Hick advocates a **pluralist** understanding of the truth of religion, where people can find truth each within their own faith. His belief in the love of God leads him to the conclusion that God would not prevent people from the possibilities of eternal life just because they were members of one religious group rather than another. He sees as equally valid the attempts of different religious faiths to understand what he terms 'the Real'. Everyone has the opportunity to continue with their development in the next life, regardless of the place in the world that luck provided for them in their earthly lives.

Key point

- In Hick's view, life after death is necessary to give everyone the opportunity to develop further, and to provide an explanation for the existence of evil and suffering in the world.

Hick's view is that the body and soul are inseparable. Therefore, if there is to be life after death for the soul, the body has to be resurrected. He holds that when an individual dies, God creates a replica of the individual in another world. God is the only entity that could achieve such a feat because God is the only entity with omnipotence. This replica is exactly the same person as the original, holding the same thoughts, memories, appearance and personality – except that it is a replica of the person, made in his or her idealised state, as many people die injured, or disabled, or at a very young age. Hick argues that it is 'logically possible' for people to exist in different worlds with the same identity (as they could be 'replicated' on to the new world by God), but maybe in a different form. This world of the resurrected is not spatially related to our world, but objects within it are spatially related to each other.

In his book *Death and Eternal Life* (1976), Hick argues that it is conceivable that a person could die in one body, but could continue to live on in a new and different one, while still being the same person. In order to illustrate this, he gives examples to illustrate what he means by a 'replica'. When he uses the word 'replica', he puts it into inverted commas to show that he is not using the word in exactly the same way that it is used in normal conversation.

Hick asks us to imagine someone suddenly disappearing from place A, and reappearing in place B – he chooses London and New York for his example. The man who appears in New York is 'exactly similar' to the man who disappeared in London. He has the same physical characteristics, even the same stomach contents; he has the same memories, the same beliefs, the same mental abilities … 'in fact there is everything that would lead us to identify the one who appeared with the one who disappeared, except continuous occupancy of space'. Everyone who knew the man would be baffled – but nevertheless they would all admit that it was the same person.

Hick then asks us to imagine the same scenario but with an important change. This time, the man has died, and then a 'replica' of him at the moment before death appears in New York. According to Hick, this is not inconceivable – we can imagine it happening, he says, and therefore it is not totally illogical to suppose that when we die, a 'replica' of ourselves survives death and lives on in a new form of life.

Brian Davies, however, rejects this idea of a 'replica' being the same person as the one who had just died. Davies writes:

Suppose you give me a lethal dose of poison. This, of course, does not make me very happy. You say: 'Don't worry. I've arranged for a replica of you to appear. The replica will seem to have all your memories. He will be convinced that he is you. And he will look exactly like you. He will even have your fingerprints.' How relieved should I be?

Speaking for myself, I should not be in the slightest bit relieved. Knowing that a replica of myself will be wining and dining somewhere is not at all the same as knowing that I will be wining and dining somewhere. For the continued existence of a person, more is required than replication. (Brian Davies, An Introduction to the Philosophy of Religion, *Oxford University Press, 1982)*

To think about

If an exact replica of a famous work of art could be recreated, so that there was no physical difference at all between the two paintings or sculptures, would they be worth equal amounts of money? If you owned the original, would you be happy to exchange it for the replica? Why, or why not?

As a follower of the Irenaean kind of theodicy, Hick holds the view that the afterlife is a continuation of the 'soul-making' that went on in this world. In this life, we cannot attain our true potential, and so we continue to develop after death, moving from self-centredness to 'reality-centredness' until the process is completed. His concept of life after death is in many ways similar to the Catholic doctrine of Purgatory, with the belief that souls need to be prepared to enter the presence of God.

Hick's understanding of life after death is unusual in that he believes that it is not conditional on accepting the doctrines of any particular religion. In Hick's view, belief in a God of love is incompatible with beliefs about eternal damnation, and incompatible with claims that heaven is exclusively for members of one religion.

Criticisms of Hick's view

- It is often said that Hick's view is inconsistent with mainstream Christian teaching that Jesus' death on the cross saves those who believe in him. If people can get to heaven whether they accept Jesus or not, because there are so many other routes as well, then this seems to make Jesus' death pointless.

- Other religious believers, too, would argue that Hick's view is inconsistent with their teaching. Perhaps it has most in common with the Hindu view of tolerance to other faiths and endless rebirths in which to improve – but Hindus believe in rebirth into this world, rather than in resurrection.

- Another argument is that Hick's view removes any incentive for people to struggle to fulfil their potential and to become better people in the present world. If we are all going to get there in the end, in the afterlife, then why bother to struggle now? We might as well lead debauched lives while we can, secure in the knowledge that an eternity of opportunity awaits for us to catch up on virtue.

- Some argue that Hick's belief that all earthly suffering will be worthwhile and will make sense in the afterlife is overly optimistic. They might argue, along with Dostoevsky's Ivan Karamazov, that nothing makes innocent suffering worthwhile, and that God would have been better not to have made the world at all.

- Others criticise Hick because his view of universal salvation suggests a lack of free will. If, ultimately, we are all saved, even if it takes some of us a good deal longer than others, then do we have any real choice? Hick's view seems to undermine the argument that God desires people to make a free choice about whether or not to believe, even though free will is argued to be so important that it is worth paying the price of suffering.

- Hick's 'replica theory' has also been criticised, for example by Brian Davies, who argues that a replica is not identical with the original, however similar it might appear to be.

Disembodied existence after death

One of the issues raised in discussion of life after death is that of whether people have to have physical bodies in order to exist. Doctrines of reincarnation and resurrection involve living in a new body – but might it be possible for us to survive without bodies?

Some thinkers, such as Richard Swinburne, argue that this is completely possible and coherent as a view. We can imagine a situation where we could exist without a body, he believes; and if we can imagine it, then it is a coherent concept. Others who agree that disembodied existence is coherent point out that we have an intuitive sense of being not the same as our bodies: we say (in the English language, at least) that we 'have' bodies, not that we 'are' bodies, which suggests that we feel ourselves to be separate and distinct from the purely physical. People who believe in a distinction between the consciousness and the body argue that we can have mental processes and

Key term

disembodied existence – living without physical form.

events which are not translated into anything physical at all – we might be thinking all kinds of things without any evidence of them appearing on our faces or in our body language. Scientific research has not reached the point where it is possible to tell what someone is thinking from looking at physical evidence such as activity in the brain, and perhaps it never will reach this point. Perhaps there is something about ourselves and our mental 'inner' lives that goes beyond the physical. To some, then, it seems as if the consciousness and the body, although linked, are distinct from one another, and therefore it could make sense to suggest that the consciousness might be able to exist on its own, without the body, once the body has died.

For others, the idea of disembodied existence is incoherent. Writers such as Brian Davies argue that just because we can conceive of ourselves as being disembodied, this does not make it an actual possibility. We can conceive of all sorts of things – we might imagine ourselves invisible, or able to fly or to travel back in time, but being able to imagine such things does not make them actually possible. Davies argues that those things which make us into human persons are linked with having a body, and that survival as disembodied entities seems impossible.

H. H. Price and life after death

The British philosopher H. H. Price (1889–1984) was concerned with the issue of the intelligibility of ideas about survival after death. In his paper 'Survival and the Idea of Another World', he argued that before we can have meaningful discussions about whether different beliefs about the afterlife are true, we have to establish that these beliefs are coherent. If the whole idea of survival after death is something we cannot possibly imagine, then there is no point in taking discussion of evidence for or against it any further. Price asks:

> *Can we form any idea, even a rough and provisional one, of what a disembodied human life might be like? Suppose we cannot, it will follow that what is called the Survival Hypothesis is a mere set of words and not a hypothesis at all ... There cannot be evidence for something which is completely unintelligible to us.*

He goes on to suggest that survival after death is not inconceivable, and in order to show this, he gives a picture of what an afterlife might be like. Price takes the view that the afterlife could involve disembodied, or discarnate, existence.

In order to explain his ideas, Price draws a comparison with dreaming. In dreams, we 'live' in a 'world' which is made up of mental images. We feel as if these images are real – we can 'see' and 'hear' things, we have the sense that we have bodies. We have experiences, but we are not bound by physical time and space; in a dream, we might be at home one moment, and the next moment we might be by the sea or in an aeroplane or falling off a building. Price suggests that the afterlife might be like dreaming. It might be made up of mental images, and they might be so vivid that people might not understand that they had died. Although we would not have bodies with which to have sensory perceptions, the mental images would seem like real perceptions.

Price argues that disembodied existence need not mean the end of personal identity, because the mental images which survived death would be made from the individual's own memories, desires and ways of looking at the world. As long as people had mental images after death that resembled physical sensation, and felt as though they had identities, this would be enough. Although the image-world would not be 'real' in the sense of having the physical characteristics that this world has, it would be real in that it would seem real to those who experienced it. Price draws an analogy between a 'real' piece of silver and a piece of brass that has been plated to look like silver. The plated brass is not 'real' silver, but it is still a real object – it is only 'unreal' in the sense of it giving the impression of being something that it is not.

To think about

Do you think that a world of images, such as Price suggests, can be described as 'real'? Would you describe the 'worlds' created in online role-playing games, where individuals make identities for themselves and interact with others, as 'real'?

In answer to questions about where this 'other world' might be, Price suggests that it is another world in the sense of a different kind of consciousness, rather than in a different location. As in a dream, the 'other world' would be perceived as having space – in a dream, he argues, we can perceive a large tiger, with black stripes in spatial relationship to the yellow and so on, but the tiger does not have a location in the sense that we could measure how far it was from the foot of the bed. In the afterlife, as in a dream, it would be possible to move from one 'location' to another without these 'places' actually occupying space.

The afterlife, in Price's suggestion, would be composed of the mental images of the individual, so in a sense, the person would make his or her own future life. The places and people with which the person was familiar in this world would reappear in the next, in more or less detail depending on the degree of the person's familiarity with them. The content of the afterlife would be drawn from memories and from desires, so people might find themselves encountering some unpleasant experiences – perhaps revisiting in the afterlife a traumatic experience in this world, or acting out feelings that were repressed in the physical world. Each person's inner conflicts would manifest themselves. Price gives the analogy of a nightmare from which the person cannot wake. Perhaps, once the desire and memories have reached the end of their life-span, they will be replaced by others, just as our dreams about the nasty midday

Price's suggestion of the afterlife is that it might be in many ways similar to a dream-world.

supervisor when we were small are replaced by dreams about the intriguing shop assistant when we are in our early teens, and later on dreams about our children.

This implies a strong degree of subjectivity in the afterlife, without any connection between different individuals; my afterlife, for example, might contain people from my favourite television programmes and films, but the afterlives of these actors are unlikely to contain me. Price, however, argues that this is not necessarily going to be the case, because telepathy might work much more easily in an afterlife which is unconstrained by physical laws. There could be, he argues, shared 'other worlds' of like-minded people; but there would nevertheless be many of these other worlds, rather than a single 'heaven' for example, and people might be able to move from one to another.

Price was not aiming to prove the existence of such an afterlife, but to show that the concept of disembodied existence is not a contradiction in terms. However, he did think that there was some evidence which might support his suggestions – for example, in the claims of mediums to have telepathic contact with those who have died. Mediums often give reports of the afterlife which suggest that it is very similar to this world, and the people who 'live' there often seem to have the same interests and concerns that they had in their earthly lives. Perhaps the dreams that we have in this world are evidence of this 'other world' of consciousness – maybe we already slip into these other worlds when we are asleep.

Key point

• Price argued that the concept of disembodied existence is coherent, as we can imagine an afterlife made of mental images.

Criticisms of H. H. Price's 'afterlife'

Probably the most common criticism of Price's view is that his suggestions are not consistent with traditional Christian teaching (nor the teaching of other world religions). There is a big difference between coming up with a theory which is plausible, and that theory actually being true, as Price himself admits. The idea of mental worlds in which people live after death, worlds which are created by each individual, is in direct contradiction to beliefs about the resurrection of the body. Christians might argue that the life after death demonstrated by Jesus in the Gospel stories is a physical resurrection – he foreshadows his resurrection by raising others from the dead (for example Lazarus and Jairus' daughter) – and once he is resurrected, he can be seen and touched and he can eat. Christians and Muslims might argue that if life after death really is as Price suggests, then God would have said so in his revelation.

Religious believers might also object to Price's suggestions on the grounds that if the individual survives in a kind of dream-world, then there appears to be no contact with ultimate reality or God. The hopes of an eternal life in which the individual comes face to face with God, is judged and is able to enjoy being in God's presence, are disappointed. The afterlife is, according to religious believers, a time when we see things as they really are, where (in Platonic terms) the distractions and delusions of the physical world are removed. Paul writes: 'Now we see through a glass darkly; but then we shall see face to face' (1 Corinthians 13:12). Price's view makes the afterlife an illusory world.

Price's suggestion does not seem to account for people whose mental processes are insufficient for them to be able to have memories and desires. What of babies who live only for a few hours? Or those who are born with severe brain damage, so that they never have the opportunity to have the same kind of mental processes that other people have? It is difficult to image how they could have any kind of mental image-world at all to carry on into the next life. If someone had been blind from birth, would the afterlife also be missing any kind of visual imagery, or any enjoyment of colour or form? What about those with severe mental illnesses, whose memories might not bear much relation to anything that has actually happened, or who are constantly tortured by self-hatred and depression? The mental image-worlds which they create for themselves are not likely to be very pleasant, yet through no fault of their own. It does not fit with our sense of justice that those who suffer in these ways in their earthly life should have to continue to suffer.

His ideas also imply that to get the best kind of afterlife, we should in this life surround ourselves with comforts and pleasure, avoiding unpleasant images. We would need to turn off news programmes about the suffering of others, and turn our faces away from those in difficulty to avoid revisiting them after death.

However, Price was never suggesting that his model of the afterlife was going to be good, or that it was going to be fair. He does not suggest that the afterlife is determined by a good God, or that it is compensation for our earthly sufferings or reward for good moral behaviour in this life (although, perhaps, a virtuous character would have assembled a more pleasant set of images and memories than someone who had led a life in the criminal underworld).

Someone arguing against Price from a Freudian perspective, using the ideas of Feuerbach, might point out the elements of wish-fulfilment in his view. They might say that he is imagining that our wishes will come true in the afterlife (or at least 'true' in an illusory sense) because of a childish inability to cope with reality, and that such a belief might be damaging. We take what we would like to be the case, and make for ourselves a world in which this is the case, and pin our hopes on it, rather than facing ourselves in the world and coming to terms with life as it really is.

In *Death and Eternal Life,* Hick argues against the view Price puts forward, saying that if we all live after death in our own mental self-created worlds, then we have little genuine contact with each other. Hick questions the quality of this sort of life, and asks whether it really meets the definition 'living'. He writes:

> *… he would not have ceased to exist: for he would certainly exist from his own point of view! He would be conscious and would be undergoing experiences, but he would not be interacting with realities external to his own mind. This amounts only to a very truncated sense of being alive, in comparison with normal waking life. … Man is essentially a social creature, existing and developing as a person in interaction with other persons; and yet in the post-mortem world that we are now imagining his social environment would be unreal and his commerce with other people delusory. This consideration must, surely, count to some extent at least against a theory of this kind.*

Price argued that in the afterlife, we might come to realise that our desires, although on the face of it very pleasant, are not actually good for us at all. We might grow and learn and form new desires or modify the ones that we already had, so that we become more highly developed spiritually. Hick approves of Price's suggestion that during life after death, the individual might continue to grow and to learn, because this fits in with his own belief in a 'vale of soul-making'. Hick's own views of life after death involve a continuation of the human process of drawing closer to God – the point of death does not 'stop the clock' for a person so that they are judged on what they have managed to achieve by this point (unlike a written exam), but moral development continues until everyone is saved.

To think about

Do you think that the sort of afterlife described by Price can be called 'living'?

What sort of life do you think a person would have to lead in this world, in order to have the most pleasant kind of afterlife, if Price is correct in his suggestions?

If a person was intensely religious in this world, what kind of afterlife might he or she experience, in Price's view?

Are 'near-death experiences' evidence of life after death?

The term 'near-death experience', or NDE, refers to the wide range of experiences people have had (or claim to have had) at a point when they nearly died. People report having 'out-of-body experiences' for example, when they felt as if they were high above the room looking down on their own bodies as medical staff worked hard to resuscitate them. Some report a sensation of peace or of an overwhelming presence; many talk about having 'seen' a bright light, often at the end of a tunnel. It is sometimes argued that such experiences, because they share many similar features, can be taken as evidence that there is life after death. It might seem unlikely that these reported experiences would have so many features in common, unless they related to an objective reality. If they were simply hallucinations or tricks played by the brain when the body is in a state of crisis, it is difficult to understand why people might all have the same (or very similar) hallucinations.

Medical studies suggest that NDE is reported by between eight and twelve per cent of patients who have been resuscitated after suffering cardiac arrest. Serious study of it began with a doctor and researcher called Raymond Moody, who recorded the descriptions of patients who claimed to have had NDEs and found several common features. Experiences differed, but Moody isolated several key features that recurred in many different accounts:

- the subjective sense of being aware of one's own death
- a pleasant feeling of peace and painlessness – this seemed to be unrelated to the circumstances of the death, even if the person had been horribly injured
- a sense of being outside the body, and in particular, being able to look down on one's own body as if from above
- a sense of going into somewhere dark and tunnel-like
- encountering a presence or hearing a voice

- feeling an intense sense of being surrounded with love
- meeting people who 'glow with light' – often, these are relatives or friends who have died
- looking back over one's whole life and thinking about what had been achieved and what was regretted
- seeing or being surrounded by light
- seeing beautiful colours.

Many people who report near-death experiences claim to have had the sensation of being in a dark tunnel with a bright light glowing at the end of it.

Kenneth Ring, another researcher, was impressed by Moody's findings and followed it with studies of his own, including studies of blind people, who reported experiences where they were able to see in the NDE and during 'out-of-body experiences'. Ring's research suggested that NDEs were not related to a person's religious inclinations. Regardless of whether they had been devoutly religious or strongly atheistic, the sense of being surrounded by a loving presence was the same. Ring also followed up the patients after they had recovered, and found that the NDEs had a lasting effect. People reported that they were no longer afraid of death, and that their lives had been transformed; they had a new appreciation of the world and the people in it, were less concerned with material possessions and were more patient and forgiving. Ring believed his research led to the conclusion that life after death is a genuine reality, and that these experiences offered the potential to be of great comfort to those approaching the ends of their lives.

When William James wrote his *Varieties of Religious Experience*, he suggested that a religious experience could be validated by its lasting effects. If the experience had made the person more caring and more moral, for James this validated the religious experience. It has been suggested that this test could be applied to NDEs, as many of those who experienced them claimed that afterwards their outlook on life changed completely. They became more appreciative of their families and of the natural world; they became more patient and compassionate, and were inclined to lose their tempers less often.

Key point

- Some people argue that near-death experiences share many common features and that this suggests evidence of an afterlife. Others are more sceptical.

Scepticism about NDEs

1. NDEs only happen (or at least are only reported) in a small proportion of those who become clinically dead for a while, and this could be taken to show that the balance of evidence indicates that there is no afterlife. However, it could be the case that many people do not remember their experiences once they recover, or perhaps they were not close enough to death, or perhaps not everyone has an afterlife.

2. One argument against using NDEs as evidence of life after death is that the feelings and sensations typical of NDEs can also be experienced by people who are not near death at all. Similar sensations can be caused by psychoses, or by hallucinogenic drugs, without the person being anywhere near death. Attempts to recreate these experiences artificially have been at least in part successful; for example a build-up of carbon dioxide in the brain and the release of endorphins can lead to the same perceptions of being in a 'tunnel' with a light at the end. All people who are in the physical state of being near to death are in a similar physiological condition, which could account for the similarities of their sensations.

3. Experiments have been conducted to test whether anything really does leave the body during 'out-of-body experiences'. The researcher Susan Blackmore describes sophisticated studies involving infra-red detectors and magnetometers, none of which have detected anything at all. However, others would argue that this is hardly surprising if the soul does not have physical properties.

4. Other experiments have been conducted to see if the sensations of looking down on one's own body have any objective basis. Madelaine Lawrence in Connecticut designed an experiment where an electronic screen in a cardiac rehabilitation ward

displayed a sentence, which changed randomly, and could only be seen from a 'bird's eye view' of the ward and was not within range of the patients' beds or the staff. The idea was that if a patient had an out-of-body experience during an NDE, he or she might be able to report correctly what the sentence said. The experiment did not show any evidence of patients who reported NDEs being able to read the sentence correctly.

5. It could be argued that people have been so fascinated by NDEs that there are expectations of what 'ought' to be experienced, and this might be influencing people's ideas and memories, making NDEs seem much more common and consistent than they actually are.

6. Another argument in support of the evidential force of NDEs is that they feel very real to the people experiencing them, but this does not constitute evidence that NDEs reflect an external reality. Nightmares, hallucinations and psychoses feel real but this does not mean that they are veridical. Some researchers claim that information has been obtained in NDEs by means other than sensory perception, but there is no experimental evidence to support these claims.

7. Finally, the fact that people experience positive personality transformations after NDEs does not necessarily indicate that they have encountered the afterlife. Sometimes, a 'near-death experience' might not involve any physical illness at all, but might be a danger narrowly avoided. The novelist Naomi Alderman, for example, talked in a BBC Radio 4 interview about her decision to become a writer. Sitting at her desk in her New York office one sunny September day, she witnessed the planes hitting the Twin Towers, and realised that she could have died. This realisation led her to give up her office job and begin the writing career she had always wanted, because she suddenly understood that life does not last forever. Kenneth Ring's study suggests that it is the whole experience of coming close to death, rather than the specific NDE, that is the cause of the transformation of lives, and therefore a change in outlook might not be any evidence at all for the existence of an afterlife.

 Develop your knowledge

Death and Eternal Life by John Hick (Collins, 1976) is a huge book, but very thorough and useful for reference.
An Introduction to the Philosophy of Religion by Brian Davies (Oxford University Press, 1982)
Philosophy of Religion by Peter Cole (Hodder Murray, 2004)
Religious Experience by Peter Cole (Hodder Murray, 2005) gives a good overview of issues related to near-death experiences.

Glossary

analogy – when similar things are compared as a way of clarifying or supporting a point.

anatta – the Buddhist belief that there is no self and that the sense of self is an illusion.

anthropic principle – the argument that the natural laws of the universe have been 'fine tuned' to allow human life to exist.

atemporal – eternal, outside the constraints of time.

atman – the 'essential Self' in Hindu thought.

Cartesian – relating to Descartes and his thought.

contingent – depending on something else.

deductive arguments – depend only on logic and not on experience. If the premises are true, then the conclusion is proved.

disembodied existence – living without physical form.

dualism – belief in two distinct principles; they are often opposites, but this depends on the context in which the word 'dualism' is used.

empiricism – this is the belief that knowledge is gained through the senses, through evidence which can be tested. This is the view of the Logical Positivists, for example. All real knowledge of the world, for the empiricist, is based on sensation. We can add to our knowledge through testing, using the senses, to discover whether something is true or false. Empiricists follow in the tradition of Aristotle.

empirical – to do with evidence that is available to the five senses.

epistemic distance – a distance in knowledge or awareness.

forms – a name Plato gave to ideal concepts.

grace – grace is defined by the Oxford Dictionary of the Christian Church (Oxford University Press, 3rd edn, 1997) as: 'the supernatural assistance of God bestowed upon a rational being with a view to his sanctification.' In other words, it is the help given to us by God to enable us to become holy. This view has been particularly influential for Catholics, because it was taken up by Thomas Aquinas, one of the key thinkers who influenced Roman Catholic doctrine.

immutable – incapable of change.

impassible – incapable of suffering pain or harm; unfeeling.

inductive arguments – cannot prove, but they try to persuade by providing evidence from human experience in support of the conclusion.

infinite regress – a chain going infinitely back in time with no beginning, rather like the chicken and the egg idea.

karma – the doctrine that all deliberate actions have fruits, or consequences, which will work themselves out either in this lifetime or in a future life.

monist – the belief that everything has an essential unity.
moral evil – the evil and suffering caused by humanity's own deliberate fault.

natural evil – the evil and suffering caused by the structure of the natural world.
natural selection – the process by which evolution is said to take place, through the survival of the fittest who pass on their genes to the next generation.
necessary – in this context, the word necessary is used to mean the opposite of contingent. A necessary being has no cause and depends on nothing else for its continued existence.
numinous – a word used by Rudolph Otto to mean the 'wholly other'.

objectivist view – the view that if a religious experience truly happens, it demonstrates the existence of a God 'out there'.

omniscience – all-knowing.
omniscient – all, or infinitely, knowing.
omnipotent – all, or infinitely, powerful.
omnipresent – present everywhere, not confined by space.
ontological – to do with existence.

postulate – to assume the existence of something, for the purposes of reasoning.
pragmatism – a way of thinking which says that the truth or meaning of something depends, at least in part, on its practical consequences.
process theology – a theology which proposes that God moves along the same timeline that we do, does not know the future and cannot force people to behave in a way which compromises their free will.

rationalism – the belief that the mind is the source of knowledge, and truth can be induced using the powers of reason. Sense experience is secondary, and what really counts is the way in which we interpret our experiences of the world. A rationalist would hold that all data which can be gained through the senses is fallible; the only certainties come through the mind. The senses can be mistaken; for example, we can see someone in the street and mistake them for someone we know, and then realise that it is a complete stranger. Rationalists follow in the tradition of Plato.
reincarnation – being reborn into this world after death into a new physical body.

sceptic – someone who is inclined to doubt what he or she is told or wishes to suspend judgement unless there is certainty; someone who is keen to point out the limitations of knowledge.

sempiternal – everlasting, moving along the same timeline that we do.
subjectivist view – the view that religious experience can be true for the believer.

teleological – looking at the 'tail end', or end result, in order to draw conclusions.
theodicy – an attempt to justify God in spite of the existence of evil and suffering.
transcendent – going beyond human limits; surpassing.

veridical – if an experience is described as veridical, it means that it is a genuine experience of something that is actually there.
verifiable – capable of being shown to be true, through the use of evidence.

Index

Acknowledgements

The author and publishers wish to thank the following for permission to use copyright material: p.98 – *Free Inquiry* for an extract from Peter Atkins, 'Awesome vs. Adipose: Who Really Works Hardest to Banish Ignorance?' *Free Inquiry* (Spring 1998) 18:2. Copyright (c) 1998 Council for Secular Humanism.

Front Cover: Death Valley dunes © iStock
Graphic elements used on each page (clouds etc.) © Photodisc

AS: p.7 © Getty; p.10; © iStock; p.13 © iStock; p.14 © iStock; p.16 © iStock; p.18 © iStock; p.19 iStock; p.22 © iStock; p.23 © iStock; p.27 © iStock; p.31 © Bridgeman; p.34 © iStock; p.36 © iStock; p.39 © Getty Images; p.41 iStock; p.42 © iStock; p.44 © iStock; p.45 © iStock; p.47 © Bridgeman; p.52 © Bridgeman; p.55 © Bridgeman; p.56 © iStock; p.59 © iStock; p.61 © Photodisc (Health and Medicine Series; p.67 © iStock; p.72 © Alexey Klementiev/Fotolia; p.74 © iStock; p.78 iStock; p.80 © Lucidio Studio Inc./ Corbis; p.84 © iStock; p.86 © iStock; p.88 © iStock; p.92 © iStock; p.95 © Society of Jesus; p.96 © Hulton Archive/Getty; p. 100 © Fotolia; p.102 © Fotolia; p.104 © iStock; p.107 © iStock; p.108 © iStock; p.109 © iStock; p.111 © Time Life Pictures/Getty; p.113 © iStock; p.118 © iStock; p.119 © iStock; p.134 © iStock; p.136 ©Rob Howard/Corbis; p.138 © iStock; p.139 © iStock; p.141 And my servant Job shall pray for you (pen and ink with w/c on paper), Blake, William (1757–1827) © Leeds Museums and Galleries (City Art Gallery) U.K./The Bridgeman Art Library; p.143 © iStock; p.146 © iStock; p.148 Malaysia, Kuala Lumpar, the word Allah inscribed in Arabic calligraphy in windows of the Masjid Ne © Steve Raymer/Getty.

A2: p.150 © iStock; p.151 © iStock; p.153 © iStock; p.156 © Photodisc; p.158 © iStock; p.161 © iStock; p.165 © Getty; p.169 © iStock; p.170 © iStock; p.173 © iStock; p.177 Rene Descartes, French Philosopher. Etching by Joannes Tangena. Photography, around 1650. (Photo by Imagno/Getty Images) [Rene Descartes, Franzoesischer Philosoph. Kupferstich von Joannes Tangena. Photographie, um 1650.] © Getty Images; p.180 © iStock; p.183 © Christie's Images/CORBIS; p.186 © iStock; p.187 © Private Collection/The Bridgeman Art Library; p.189 © Getty Images; p.189 English naturalist Charles Robert Darwin (1809–1882), the originator, with Alfred Russel Wallace, of the theory of evolution by natural selection. Original artwork: Engraving by T H Maguire 'Darwin Aged 40' after a painting by T H Maguire. One of a set of British Museum Portraits of 1851. (Photo by Hulton Archive/ Getty Images) © Getty Images; p.192 Jury in the Scopes trial also known as the 'Monkey Trial' when Professor John Scopes was tried for teaching Darwinian evolution theory in Dayton, Tennessee. (Photo by Hulton Archive/Getty Images) © 2007 Getty Images; p.193 © iStock; p.195 © iStock; p.196 Father Pierre Teilhard de Chardin (1881–1955) on a bridge of the imperial road at Shiensien, China, c. 1924 (b/w photo), French Photographer (20th century)/Fondation Teilhard de Chardin, Paris, France, Archives Charmet/The Bridgeman Art Library; p.199 © iStock; p.201 © Bridgeman; p.202 © Polkinghorne.net.org; p.207 ©